THE IDEA OF
COMEDY

PRENTICE-HALL INTERNATIONAL, INC., *London*
PRENTICE-HALL OF AUSTRALIA, PTY. LTD., *Sydney*
PRENTICE-HALL OF CANADA, LTD., *Toronto*
PRENTICE-HALL OF INDIA PRIVATE LTD., *New Delhi*
PRENTICE-HALL OF JAPAN, INC., *Tokyo*

THE IDEA OF
COMEDY

Essays in Prose and Verse

Ben Jonson to George Meredith

Edited by

W. K. WIMSATT
Yale University

PRENTICE-HALL, INC., Englewood Cliffs, New Jersey

For
M. E.
and
J. C.
in memory of
Alex

PR
631
W47

PREFACE

This book of essays on the comic has two special features which I believe deserve a few words of explanation and advertisement: a fairly rigorous degree of selectivity and a correspondingly close kind of coherence or unification. The theme of the book, or its plot line, is English critical thought about comedy, from the approximate beginning of the classical tradition, with Ben Jonson, to its approximate end about two and a half centuries later, with George Meredith. The essays that constitute the main text are all English originals of established reputation; all, as it seems to me, are in fact interesting and significant; and all are presented in entirety. More specifically, I have chosen the twenty-six essays in prose and verse, the work of thirteen authors, according to a criterion of weight or pregnancy in proportion to length. Thus a few well-known essays—for example, George Farquhar's *Discourse upon Comedy,* Samuel Johnson's *Rambler* Number 125, and William Hazlitt's lecture *On Wit and Humor*—are not included as texts, because they seemed to me to suffer by reason of length, miscellaneity, or extreme topicality. These and some other such staples, however, are among the considerable number of texts represented by excerpts at various places in the editorial discussion. Wider horizons are sketched in the general Introduction, touching on ancient, Medieval, and Renaissance ideas of the comic; in a later excursus on Molière; and in three Postscripts to the book, narrating the rise of the modern psychology of laughter and the metaphysics of the laughable, and of recent comic moods of the grotesque, the violent, and the absurd.

Texts of the main essays are taken from the original editions or the authors' last corrected editions, and are identified. But they have been normalized in a few respects, mainly in the spelling of authors' names and in spelling and italicization of titles. Footnote references to English comedies follow recent editorial practice in scene divisions.

Among senior friends who have given me various kinds of advice and comfort in connection with this work, I make grateful acknowledgement to Sheridan Baker, Edward Bowden, Imbrie Buffum, Wallace Fowlie, Alvin B. Kernan, Jeffry L. Sammons, Warren H. Smith, and Eugene Waith. Maynard Mack read the copy for the whole.

A collection of critical essays is related very directly to the *study* of literature, and hence to students of literature. And so I look upon this book as indebted in a special way to some of my students of the past few years who have written instructive papers for me concerning the history of comic theory. It gives me pleasure to name Marillene Anderson, Pauline Clarke, Susan Fox, Elizabeth Ahlgren Francis, Joseph Graham, Margaret Cardwell Hale, John Hodgson, Dale Iwataki, Janet Adelman, Jack Klein, Judith Kroll Zaidi, Joaquin Kuhn, Sylvia Bank Manning, Frank D. McConnell, Helen McNeill, Stephen J. Miko, Diane Lee Pelkus, Gail N. Simon Reed, Thomas Scheye, and Roger Swearingen.

Comedy, as several of the authorities present in this volume instruct us, is a sociable art; there is no laughing except in concert with other persons. Even comic theory, I could argue at some length if it were necessary, moves better in company. And so I have the further pleasure of acknowledging five sociable and keen-minded students who undertook jobs for me during recent summers: in the order of something like seniority, Janet Adelman, Patricia Clarke Smith, Laurence Sandberg, Ronald Macdonald, and William Keach. Ronald Macdonald typed one version of most of the book.

I owe a special acknowledgement also to Randall Q. Au, Yale College, 1970, my helper on a Bursary Appointment. Without his nimble Olivetti and firm grasp of purposes, the date below would not have been inscribed.

Jonathan Sisson was the copyeditor. Mary Price made the index.

W. K. Wimsatt
Silliman College
Yale University
8 December 1968

BIBLIOGRAPHICAL AIDS

I. LIST OF PLAYS

L iterary criticism and theory form a humanistic discipline which has
its own kind of interest and even a kind of autonomy—given, on the
part of the reader, a certain measure of preoccupation with literature
and of acquaintance with literary masterpieces. The present anthology
supposes a student who either is familiar with or is in the course of
becoming familiar with some selection of plays in the classical tradition.
The following list is representative of the kind of comedy with which
the essays in this volume are concerned.

Aristophanes, *The Frogs*, 405 B.C. Translated by John Hookham Frere,
1839; by Dudley Fitts, New York: Harcourt, Brace & World, Inc. 1955;
by Richmond Lattimore, in *The Complete Greek Comedy*, ed. William
Arrowsmith, Ann Arbor: The University of Michigan Press, 1962.

Menander, *The Arbitration* (fragmentary), before 292 B.C. Translated by
Francis G. Allinson, *Menander*, Loeb Library, 1921; "translated and
completed" by Gilbert Murry, London: George Allen & Unwin Ltd.,
1945.

Plautus, *The Braggart Soldier*, c. 206 B.C. Translated by Paul Nixon, Loeb
Library, *Plautus*, Vol. III, 1924; by E. F. Watling, *The Pot of Gold
and Other Plays*, Baltimore: Penguin Books, 1965.

Terence, *The Woman of Andros*, 166 B.C. Translated by John Sargeaunt,
Terence, Loeb Library, Vol. I, 1912; by Betty Radice, *Phormio and
Other Plays*, Baltimore: Penguin Books, 1967.

William Shakespeare, *A Comedy of Errors*, 1593.
King Henry the Fourth, First Part, 1598.

Ben Jonson, *Every Man in his Humour*, 1598.
Volpone, 1606.
Epicoene, or the Silent Woman, 1609.

Molière, *L'Ecole des Femmes*, 1662; *La Critique de L'Ecole des Femmes*,
1663. Both translated by Morris Bishop, *Eight Plays by Molière*,
New York: Random House, Inc., The Modern Library, 1957; and
by Donald M. Frame, *Tartuffe and Other Plays by Molière*, New
York: The New American Library, 1967.
Le Misanthrope, 1666; translated by Richard Wilbur, New York:
Harcourt, Brace & World, Inc., 1955; by Morris Bishop, *Eight*

Plays (see above); by Donald M. Frame, *Tartuffe* (see above).

John Dryden, *Marriage à la Mode*, 1673.

William Wycherley, *The Plain-Dealer*, 1674.

George Etherege, *The Man of Mode, or Sir Fopling Flutter*, 1676.

Colley Cibber, *Love's Last Shift*, 1696.

John Vanbrugh, *The Relapse, or Virtue in Danger*, 1697.

William Congreve, *The Way of the World*, 1700.

George Farquhar, *The Beaux' Stratagem*, 1707.

Richard Steele, *The Conscious Lovers*, 1722.

John Gay, *The Beggar's Opera*, 1728.

David Garrick and George Colman, *The Clandestine Marriage*, 1766.

Hugh Kelly, *False Delicacy*, 1768.

Oliver Goldsmith, *She Stoops to Conquer*, 1773.

Richard Brinsley Sheridan, *The School for Scandal*, 1777.

Oscar Wilde, *The Importance of Being Earnest*, 1895.

II. Books about Phases of the Classical Tradition in Comedy

A few substantial articles are added. The list inclines toward recent and readily available publications, and especially paperbacks. (General histories and anthologies of classical and neoclassical theater and criticism are for the most part not included.) Other titles appear in footnotes throughout the volume.

A. Classical Greek and Latin

Francis Macdonald Cornford, *The Origin of Attic Comedy* (1914), ed. Theodore H. Gaster, Garden City, N.Y., Doubleday & Company, Inc., 1961 (paperback).

Lane Cooper, *An Aristotelian Theory of Comedy*, New York: Harcourt, Brace, & World, Inc., 1922.

Mary A. Grant, *The Ancient Rhetorical Theories of the Laughable*, Madison: The University of Wisconsin Press, 1924.

Gilbert Norwood, *Greek Comedy* (1931), New York: Hill and Wang, 1963 (paperback).

————, *Plautus and Terence*, New York: Longmans, Green & Co., 1932.

Philip Whaley Harsh, *A Handbook of Classical Drama*, Stanford: Stanford University Press, 1944.

George E. Duckworth, *The Nature of Roman Comedy*, Princeton: Princeton University Press, 1952.

Katherine Lever, *The Art of Greek Comedy*, London: Methuen & Co., Ltd., 1956.

Peter D. Arnott, *An Introduction to the Greek Theatre,* Bloomington: Indiana University Press, 1959; paperback ed., 1963.

Erich Segal, *Roman Laughter, the Comedy of Plautus,* Cambridge: Harvard University Press, 1968. A richly informed account of Plautine comedy as the expression of a spirit of slave-holiday Saturnalian misrule.

B. The Renaissance, Italy and France

H. W. Lawton, ed. *Handbook of French Renaissance Dramatic Theory: A Selection of Texts,* Manchester: Manchester University Press, 1949. Includes useful excerpts, in Latin and English translation, from the late classical grammarians Donatus and Diomedes.

Marvin T. Herrick, *The Fusion of Horatian and Aristotelian Literary Criticism, 1531–1555,* Urbana: University of Illinois Press, 1946.

———, *Tragicomedy, Its Origin and Development in Italy, France and England,* Urbana: University of Illinois Press, 1955; paperback ed., 1962.

———, *Italian Comedy in the Renaissance,* Urbana: University of Illinois Press, 1960; paperback ed., 1966.

C. Shakespeare and Jonson

John Russell Brown, *Shakespeare and his Comedies,* London: Methuen & Co., Ltd., 1957.

C. L. Barber, *Shakespeare's Festive Comedy,* Princeton: Princeton University Press, 1959.

Bertrand Evans, *Shakespeare's Comedies,* Oxford: At the Clarendon Press, 1960.

Northrop Frye, *A Natural Perspective: The Development of Shakespearean Comedy and Romance,* New York: Columbia University Press, 1965.

Peter G. Phialas, *Shakespeare's Romantic Comedies, The Development of Their Form and Meaning,* Chapel Hill: The University of North Carolina Press, 1966.

L. C. Knights, *Drama and Society in the Age of Jonson,* London: Chatto and Windus, 1937.

John J. Enck, *Jonson and the Comic Truth,* Madison: The University of Wisconsin Press, 1957.

Jonas A. Barish, *Ben Jonson and the Language of Prose Comedy,* Cambridge: Harvard University Press, 1960.

———, ed. *Ben Jonson: A Collection of Critical Essays,* Englewood Cliffs, N.J.: Prentice-Hall Inc., 1963 (paperback).

D. The Restoration

Joseph Wood Krutch, *Comedy and Conscience after the Restoration,* New York: Columbia University Press, 1924; paperback ed., 1961.

Bonamy Dobrée, *Restoration Comedy: 1660–1720,* Oxford: At the Clarendon Press, 1924.

Katheleen M. Lynch, *The Social Mode of Restoration Comedy*, New York: The Macmillan Company, 1926.

Leslie Hoston, *The Commonwealth and Restoration Stage*, Cambridge: Harvard University Press, 1928.

John Harold Wilson, *The Court Wits of the Restoration*, Princeton: Princeton University Press, 1952.

Thomas H. Fujimura, *The Restoration Comedy of Wit*, Princeton: Princeton University Press, 1952.

Dale Underwood, *Etherege and the Seventeenth-Century Comedy of Manners*, New Haven: Yale University Press, 1957.

John Loftis, *Comedy and Society from Congreve to Fielding*, Stanford: Stanford University Press, 1959.

Leo Hughes, *A Century of English Farce*, Princeton: Princeton University Press, 1956.

Norman H. Holland, *The First Modern Comedies: The Significance of Etherege, Wycherley, and Congreve*, Cambridge: Harvard University Press, 1959.

Wallace Fowlie, ed. and trans., *Classical French Drama*, New York: Bantam Books, Inc., 1962. Original translations of Molière, *Les Femmes Savantes;* Marivaux, *Le Jeu de l'Amour et du Hasard;* Beaumarchais, *Le Barbier de Séville;* with an introduction to each.

Frank Harper Moore, *The Nobler Pleasure: Dryden's Comedy in Theory and Practice*, Chapel Hill: The University of North Carolina Press, 1963.

Rose A. Zimbardo, *Wycherley's Drama: A Link in the Development of English Satire*, New Haven: Yale University Press, 1965.

John Harold Wilson, *A Preface to Restoration Drama*, Boston: Houghton Mifflin Company, Riverside Studies in Literature, 1965 (paperback).

Earl Miner, ed., *Restoration Dramatists: A Collection of Critical Essays*, Englewood Cliffs, N.J.: Prentice-Hall, Inc., 1966 (paperback).

John Loftis, ed., *Restoration Drama: Modern Essays in Criticism*, New York: Oxford University Press, 1966 (paperback).

Eugene Waith, ed., *Restoration Drama:* New York: Bantam Books, Inc., 1968. Texts of Wycherley, *The Country Wife;* Etherege, *The Man of Mode;* Vanbrugh, *The Relapse;* Congreve, *The Way of the World;* with an introduction to each.

E. The Eighteenth Century

Ernest Bernbaum, *The Drama of Sensibility*, Boston: Ginn & Co., 1915.

F. W. Bateson, *English Comic Drama, 1700–1750*, Oxford: At the Clarendon Press, 1929.

John W. Draper, "The Theory of the Comic in Eighteenth-Century England," *Journal of English and Germanic Philology*, XXXVII (1938), 207–23.

E. N. Hooker, "Humour in the Age of Pope," *The Huntington Library Quarterly*, XI (August 1948), 361–85.

John Loftis, *Steele at Drury Lane*, Berkeley: University of California Press, 1952.

Arthur Sherbo, *English Sentimental Drama*, East Lansing: Michigan State University Press, 1957.

Stuart M. Tave, *The Amiable Humorist: A Study in the Comic Theory and Criticism of the Eighteenth and Early Nineteenth Centuries*, Chicago: The University of Chicago Press, 1960.

Mary E. Knapp, *Prologues and Epilogues of the Eighteenth Century*, New Haven: Yale University Press, 1961.

John Loftis, *The Politics of Drama in Augustan England*, Oxford: At the Clarendon Press, 1963. Chapters V and VI deal with Fielding's plays; cf. Chapter V of Loftis, 1959, listed above.

F. The Recent French Theater

Wallace Fowlie, *Dionysus in Paris: A Guide to Contemporary French Theatre*, New York: Meridian Books, 1959.

L. C. Pronko, *Avant-garde: The Experimental Theatre in France*, Berkeley: University of California Press, 1960.

Toby Cole, *Playwrights on Playwriting*, New York: Hill and Wang, 1961.

Martin Esslin, *The Theatre of the Absurd*, Garden City,, N.Y., Doubleday & Company, Inc., 1961 (paperback).

Jacques Guicharnaud and June Beckelman, *Modern French Theatre from Giraudoux to Beckett*, New Haven: Yale University Press, 1961; 2nd ed., revised, 1967 (paperback).

Eugene Ionesco, *Notes and Counter Notes*, trans. Donald Watson, New York: Grove Press, 1964.

G. Recent General Surveys, Collections

L. J. Potts, *Comedy*, London: Hutchinson's University Library, 1948.

Albert Cook, *The Dark Voyage and the Golden Mean, A Philosophy of Comedy*, Cambridge: Harvard University Press, 1949.

Louis Kronenberger, *The Thread of Laughter: Chapters on English Stage Comedy from Jonson to Maugham*, New York: Alfred A. Knopf, Inc., 1952.

Susanne K. Langer, *Feeling and Form*, New York: Charles Scribner's Sons, 1953. Chapter 18, esp. pp. 330–33, expounds the deep human difference between tragedy as the rhythm of man's individual death-bound adventure and comedy as the rhythm of the springtime festival of fertility and perpetual rebirth.

Northrop Frye, *Anatomy of Criticism: Four Essays*, Princeton: Princeton University Press, 1957; esp. pp. 163–86, "The Mythos of Spring: Comedy."

John J. Enck, Elizabeth T. Forter, and Alvin Whitley, eds. *The Comic in Theory & Practice,* New York: Appleton-Century-Crofts, Inc., 1960 (paperback). Excerpts from theoretical works; humorous essays, narratives, verse.

Marvin Felheim, ed. *Comedy, Plays, Theory, and Criticism,* New York: Harcourt, Brace & World, Inc., 1962.

Paul Lauter, ed. *Theories of Comedy,* Garden City, N.Y., Doubleday & Company, Inc., 1964 (paperback). A wide assortment of short pieces and excerpts (some are original translations): Ancient, Medieval, Renaissance Italian and English, Neoclassic French and Italian, English of the seventeenth, eighteenth, and early nineteenth centuries, German romantic, modern.

Robert W. Corrigan, ed., *Comedy: Meaning and Forms,* San Francisco: Chandler Publishing Company, 1965. A selection of progressive modern essays on the "spirit," "form," "characteristics," "nature," "psychology," "criticism" of comedy, and on farce and satire.

CONTENTS

THE IDEA OF
COMEDY

C'est une étrange entreprise que celle de faire rire les honnêtes gens.

—*Molière*
La Critique de L'Ecole des Femmes, *vi*

INTRODUCTION

For reasons which have perhaps never been satisfactorily expounded, literary works for the stage in the Western tradition have tended to divide more clearly than other kinds (epic poems, lyrics, or prose stories) into those which are sad and painful (tragedies) and those which are funny and pleasant (comedies). A further sort of unevenness in the literary categories appears in the fact that, whereas tragedies, at least in the modern era, are not expected to be so sad and painful that the audience will either weep or groan aloud, comedies are surely expected to raise a laugh. They do. And most likely they always have. A stage comedy at which nobody laughed would be an odd sort of success. One outcome of this situation is that critical theory about the tragic has succeeded fairly well in keeping its attention focused on literary works thought to be tragedies, and, except for one classical question, about *catharsis,* has not characteristically, even in modern times, moved into less manageable questions àbout what in general is painful or sad, harmful or destructive,[1] or into the general psychology or physiology of sighs, groans, and tears. Theory of comedy, on the other hand, has in modern times, taking up some hints from antiquity and the Renaissance (Plato, Hobbes, Shaftesbury), moved over on a very wide front into speculations about what kind of "incongruity" in general is ludicrous or laughable (ponderous examples in elucidation of difficult logic in Kant or Schopenhauer, a sprightlier management in Baudelaire or Bergson, will come to mind), and these speculations extend readily, or convert readily, into pronouncements about the ticklish physiology or bravado psychology of laughter itself.[2] (Freud, with equally ponderous equipment, is the master figure here.) Nevertheless, these two kinds of theorizing, about what in general is funny and what in general it is to laugh, can still be distinguished from the earlier sort of theory which was the starting point—critical theory

---

[1] A few masterpieces in the psychological or metaphysical mode, such as Miguel de Unamuno's *Tragic Sense of Life* (Spanish, Madrid, 1913; English, London, 1921) and Karl Jaspers' *Von der Wahrheit* (1947—a part of it translated into English as *Tragedy Is Not Enough,* Boston, 1952), are manifest exceptions, which have proved little adaptable to the idiom of the literary critic.

[2] See these themes pursued a little further in a Postscript to this volume, pp. 284–88.

1

about a recognizable and at least partially describable, if not strictly
definable, sort of stage drama—namely, comedy.

II

Comedy and tragedy, if we can believe what were thirty or forty
years ago the most advanced speculations upon the subject, were once
the same thing. Or at least they were like two complementary segments
in the same big round thing. They were phases in the same big cycle,
which was the enactment and the image, the ritual and the drama, of
the whole of primitive man's fearful, wishful, and magical proto-
religious and proto-aesthetic way of responding to the not altogether
smooth, friendly, or adequately humanized world in which he found
himself. Not nomadic hunting societies, but agricultural and stationary
societies, such as clustered around the eastern end of the Mediterranean,
gave birth to those things. There were crops and there were seasons,
spring warmth and rainfall and flood time, and rebirth and autumn
fullness and harvest, and cold and death. There was a Year God
(*Eniautos Daimōn*) who represented or generated these things. And
there were rituals to celebrate or help to bring about appropriate
phases of his cyclically repeated career, his joyous and laughing birth
in the spring and his fruitful marriage, and in the autumn his necessary
decline and sacrificial murder at the hands of an invading god of the
new year—or last year's god reborn. Thus apparently a kind of alternation between two phases of the same *Daimōn*.
  Out of such rituals evolved folk dramas, acted in villages or about
the countryside by traveling troupes of mummers, sometimes presumably sad and slaughterous, sometimes funny and bawdy. All that is
prehistory, happening at a time about which nobody now knows anything at all, except what can be extrapolated or projected back from
what is known or guessed about primitive societies in the modern
world or from the earliest vestiges of knowledge that we have about
religious festivals and Dionysiac rituals in the Grecian world. These
dramas were either dithyrambic choruses (in their full development
"circular" or stationary about an altar) or vinous, rustic, riotous, and
laughing revels (*komoi*), mélanges of procession (*parabasis*), singing,
dancing, acting, lampooning, phallic costumes, and animal masks,
presented along the village streets. This kind of fun presumably was
still prevalent in the Greek world during the sixth century B.C., and
in some shape persisted down to much later eras, even, it is said, into
very recent times.
  Behind the brilliant Apollonian actuality of the Athenian theater

which was to flourish during the fifth and fourth centuries, we may
well believe there had been an extended and variegated prehistory of
primitive folk mummery; and behind that, even further in the shadows
of an unknown past, we can picture, if we will, the ur-period of magic
and ritual. In this way we can get a sense of what lay behind the
cryptic record of dramatic history as it has come down to us, and we
can put in its place what is in some ways a more satisfying primordial
mystery. "Great things in literature, Greek plays for example," wrote
the Cambridge anthropologist Jane Ellen Harrison, "I most enjoy
when behind their bright splendour I see moving darker and older
shapes."[3] In such quasi-religious substitutes for the actual dramatic
fictions which we know, we may well find a special further aesthetic
value, as in a richly endowed world, a hinterland prehistory, called into
being in great measure by our own volition. We may enjoy a sort of
second fiction, which we may even take for a reality[4] and for something better than the immediate perspective from which we have
departed. We may, if we are of a certain temperament. But at the

---

[3] Quoted in W. K. C. Guthrie, *The Greeks and Their Gods* (London, 1954), p. xi.
"Someone pours some hydrochloric acid...on some loaf sugar, and in a moment
the quiet white sugar is a seething black volcano. Things are never the same to you
again. You know they are not what they seem; you picture hidden terrific forces"
(Jane Ellen Harrison, *Reminiscences of a Student's Life,* London, 1925, p. 37).
I have been following the main line of the ritual-myth hypothesis as it is still
received by literary theorists so inclined. One should consult Harrison's *Pro-
legomena to the Study of Greek Religion* (Cambridge, 1922), and her *Themis*
(Cambridge, 1912), especially Chapter II. Gilbert Murray's famous thesis that the
structural conventions of Attic tragedy derive from the Dionysiac ritual was first
published as an excursus in *Themis,* at the end of Chapter VIII. F. M. Cornford,
in *The Origin of Attic Comedy* (Cambridge, 1914), argued a similar development
of Attic Old Comedy. As a corrective to the exuberance of Harrison, Cornford,
and Murray, one should note the reservations voiced by A. W. Pickard-Cambridge
in *Dithyramb, Tragedy, and Comedy* (Oxford, 1927), pp. 16, 185 ff., 329 ff. Some
of these passages ("long refutations of details") are eliminated or reduced by
T. B. L. Webster in his new edition (Oxford, 1962—see p. vii). Theodor H. Gaster,
a Near-Eastern scholar specializing in Judaica, has brought out a revision of Cornford's *Origin* (New York, 1963). In a Foreword he warns the reader against
"Cornford's enthusiasm" and his not infrequent tendency to overshoot the mark
(p. xxiii), and he notices Pickard-Cambridge's objections. At the same time, he
believes that recent Near-Eastern study (e.g., in his own book *Thespis,* New York,
1950, on the seasonal pattern in Hittite and Babylonian ritual and poetry) "tips
the scales of probability in Murray's and Cornford's favor."
Another recent entrant into the debate, Gerald F. Else, *The Origin and Early
Form of Greek Tragedy* (Cambridge, 1965), argues, to my mind very persuasively,
for a peculiarly Athenian and abruptly dramatic development of tragedy, in two
jumps, by Thespis and Aeschylus.
[4] C. S. Lewis, "The Anthropological Approach," in *English and Medieval
Studies Presented to J. R. R. Tolkien,* ed. Norman Davis and C. L. Wrenn (London,
1962), p. 229.

same time there are the better-known features of a theatrical history to be noticed.

III

The first clearly ascertainable events of that history occurred in the late sixth and early fifth centuries at Athens. A poet named Thespis introduced speeches by an actor (*hupocrites*) into a kind of performance hitherto choral, and he won a victory at the festival of the Greater Dionysia (c. 534 B.C.).[5] Two generations later we have the plays of Aeschylus. In the *Poetics* of Aristotle we read that Aeschylus admitted a second actor to the stage, thus, one might think, making possible what it is difficult to conceive as happening in tragedy before, a debate or dispute between *personae*.[6] Meanwhile, the archon had granted the first chorus to a comic play at Athens about the year 486, and, with the help of Aristotle again and of anthropological conjectures, we are to suppose for this period a comedy proceeding on the vestiges of a broken-down ritual plot, with *parabasis* (or village processional song), *agōn* (or dispute), iambic lampoon, actors, animal costumes, and scenes of Megaric Dorian farce. And then the fully developed "Old Comedy," apparently a confluence of mingling forces, emerging from the Periclean age (460–429). Cratinus (a poet whose proneness to tippling is mocked by Aristophanes in *The Knights* and is celebrated and defended in his own play *The Bottle* [*Putinē*] in 423), was an advanced lampooner. But Crates, we read in the *Poetics* of Aristotle, was the first comic writer (c. 450) to abandon the old iambic lampooning way and construct his plays along the lines of the mime and generalized plot introduced a century earlier by Epicharmus and other Dorians of Syracuse. Eupolis, a collaborator with Aristophanes and then a rival, was another lampooner.[7] As Horace would later tell us, "Eupolis and Cratinus and Aristophanes and other good and true poets of the Old Comedy set their mark" on the rogues and scallywags of their day "with great freedom."[8] We have by far the best and most exciting evidence of what that older tradition was like

---

[5] A. W. Pickard-Cambridge, *Dithyramb, Tragedy and Comedy,* pp. 97–98, 107, 109, 120–21; ed. Webster, 1962, pp. 69–76, 76–78, 88–89.

[6] Else, *The Origin and Early Form of Greek Tragedy,* p. 96, argues, again to my mind convincingly, that Aeschylus introduced also the third actor, and it was only the third that made possible the *agōn* or debate. "The second actor was irrevocably cast as Messenger, Herald, and the like."

[7] The main explicit evidence is Aristotle, *Poetics* IV and V, and Aristophanes, *The Knights* and *The Archarnians.*

[8] *Satires,* I.iv.1–5.

in the uproarious kind of musical revue which survives for us in nine of the eleven extant plays of Aristophanes—those galaxies of Birds, Wasps, Frogs, Clouds, politically vigilant choral Knights, and female dismissers of armies, Lysistrata and her cohorts.

Near the end of the long career of Aristophanes (444–386) and after the defeat of Athens by Sparta (404) and the loss of both wealth and independence, the comedy of the city too declined; it lost both its expensive chorus (the descendants of the opinionated and satiric village revel) and the gaiety and freedom of political and personal criticism which had been the wild life of the Old Comedy. A kind of "Middle Comedy," taking a cue from Euripidean tragedy, was inclined to philosophy and parody of myth and was melodramatic, romantic, and plotty, as in a few of the last plays by Aristophanes and especially his *Plutus,* acted in 388. (A twist of discovered identity in the *Plutus* may remind us of that in the *Ion* of Euripides.[9])

In the course of about two generations, and after the second Athenian defeat, by the Macedonians (at Chaeronea, 338), there was "New Comedy" (a comedy of manners), as we can consult it today (after many centuries of entombment) in a few large fragments and one virtually complete play of Menander (343–292). Here we encounter the fully established classical pattern of funny, romantic story, bold boy and sweet girl winning gaily against churlish elders with the help of a crafty slave or two, amulets and birthmarks, surprising discoveries. This was a far less socially significant kind of comedy.

* * *

At Rome, after primitive phases of Etrurian mimetic dance, "Fescennine" harvest or vintage flytings, farce, and satire,[10] Livius Andronicus (c. 284–204), probably a manumitted Greek slave, translated the *Odyssey* into native accentual verses (Saturnians) and was the first to write tragedies and comedies in the Greek manner,[11] beginning in 240 at the *ludi Romani,* which were celebrated that year with special pomp to mark the close of the First Punic War. Gnaeus Naevius (c. 270–c. 199), in his old age the epic poet of the War and of the legendary origins of Rome, also wrote tragedies on Trojan themes and comedies in the vein of the old-style political lampoons.[12] The distinctively Roman genre of conversational satire (*sermo, satura*) was, as

---

[9] Aristophanes' *Ecclesiasuzae* (*Women at the Assembly*) is also counted for Middle Comedy but shows fewer of the romantic features. Two other Aristophanic Middle Comedies, *Cocalus* and *Aeolosicon,* are lost.

[10] Primary sources are Horace, *Epistle to Augustus* (*Epistles* II.i.), and Livy, *History,* VII.ii.

[11] The titles of nine tragedies and small fragments of three comedies survive.

[12] The titles of thirty-four survive.

Horace tells us, first inspired (in the rough hexameters of Lucilius, c. 180–102) from the same Athenian source.[13] But the two best-known or most largely surviving comic poets of the brief Roman theatrical history, Plautus (254–184) and Terence (c. 195–159), were both professed "adapters" of Attic New Comedy. The numerous Plautine comedies,[14] partly rendered in song and musically accompanied declamation by actors wearing masks,[15] made romance funnier than ever, specializing in a medley of slaves, rogues, and tricksters, courtesans, pimps, crusty old fellows, gullible fathers, churls, and bullies. The characteristic braggart soldier in the Plautine play of that title (*Miles Gloriosus*), from a Hellenistic *Alazōn,* merged with a Thraso in the *Eunuchus* of Terence to become archetypal for later ages. Feminism and romance, taken mostly from Menander, prevail in the six polished plays of Terence, especially in the tenderly lachrymose *Woman of Andros* and in *The Mother-in-Law.*

IV

The earliest surviving Greek literary theory is concerned with poetic inspiration (the Muse) and with the *uses* of poetry, pleasurable or didactic. This theory shares the serious tone of the high poems in which it is embedded, the *Odyssey* of Homer, the *Theogony* of Hesiod, the *Odes* of Pindar. Later, the comic drama of Aristophanes supplies us with one extended and even rather technical passage of criticism, an *agōn* or debate in *The Frogs.* But comedy is not the critical topic; rather, the rival merits of the tragedians Aeschylus and Euripides, weighed against each other, comically, in a pair of actually present, physical scales. Ironic inquisitions and critical misgivings about the nature and function of laughter and the comic appear first during the period of "Middle Comedy," in several dialogues of Plato.

> ...there remained only Socrates, Aristophanes, and Agathon, who were drinking out of a large goblet which they passed round, and Socrates was discoursing to them. Aristodemus was only half awake, and he did not hear the beginning of the discourse; the chief thing which he remembered was Socrates compelling the other two to acknowledge that the genius of comedy was the same with that of tragedy, and that the true artist in tragedy was an artist in comedy also. To this they were constrained to assent, being drowsy, and not quite following the argument.[16]

---

13 *Satires* I.iv.6; x.3–4, 48.
14 Of 130, twenty survive.
15 Pollux, a writer of the second century A.D., describes forty-five types.
16 Concluding passage of Plato's *Symposium,* trans. Benjamin Jowett.

Interpreters of Plato have differed about this passage. Those who in a Shelleyan mood read Plato as a literal celebrator of genius and poetry want to read Socrates as meaning just what he says: genius is genius, poetry is poetry, they transcend differences. Other readers, however, may remember Socrates in the *Ion* arguing that if poetry were an art guided by reason, a writer of one kind of poetry *should* be able to write another kind (as a carpenter can make either a bench or a table), but that as a matter of fact, poets do not show such ability. In the light of that argument, from fact to destructive theoretical conclusion, the passage at the end of the *Symposium* may sound more like an oblique contrivance, starting with high theory and, for fun, urging it against the well-known contrary fact. Agathon and Aristophanes, seated we may suppose on either side of Socrates, were the tragic and comic champions.

In any event, these passages in Plato, like certain equally well-known staccato assertions about comedy which we are about to consult in Aristotle's *Poetics*, testify to something which Greek dramatic history of the preceding century also writes for us in large letters: that tragedy and comedy, at the start of our recognizable Western tradition, were parts of one poetic whole; both were arts of verbal, visual, and musical mimesis. Yet they were different, too, in that both the objects and the mood of their mimesis were conspicuously different.

Plato also had ideas about laughter in general, and hence some further ideas about comedy, which was apparently a chief public or organized occasion for laughter in the city-state which he knew. These were moral and psychological ideas, not very directly imaging the dramatic art work, but important because they were the start of much which could be developed in the thought of later ages. In Books III and X of the *Republic* and in Books VII and XI of the later and drier *Laws*, he says that the actions performed in comedy are a frivolous and giddy experience, demoralizing to the spirit of serious citizenship. (Let us "command slaves and hired strangers" to act our comedies for us.[17]) Freedom from restraint is license. A longer passage of a very mature dialogue, *Philebus*, Plato's *Examination of Pleasure*, working still within an orientation of unfriendliness to dramatic art, makes his shrewdest contribution to the psychology of laughter. The *Philebus* urges a difference between the purity of certain more rational (e.g., geometric) pleasures and the mixture of suffering inherent in the emotive kinds. These latter are pleasures by contrast to or relief from something painful.

And you remember how spectators at a tragedy sometimes smile through their tears?

---

17 *Laws* VII.816.

Certainly I do.

And you are aware that even at a comedy the mind experiences a mixed feeling of pain and pleasure?

The discussion of laughter is a good deal longer than this; it is somewhat repetitious and even circuitously wandering. The argument seems to be that there is a painful passion called "envy," or perhaps "malice," which we experience in the presence of those who either are or think they are wealthier, wiser, or more handsome than we. If they are actually strong and can avenge themselves if laughed at, then we feel only pain. If they are both vainly conceited and weak, then they are ridiculous, and we enjoy it.

> Then the argument shows that when we laugh at what is ridiculous in our friends, we mix pleasure with envy, that is, our pleasure with pain; for envy has been acknowledged by us to be mental pain, and laughter is pleasant, and we envy and laugh at the same instant.
> True.
> And the argument makes clear that this combination of pleasures and pains exists not only in laments, or in tragedy and comedy, but also off the stage in the entire tragi-comedy of human life on countless occasions.[18]

The text does not quite say—perhaps we wish it did—that bullies and braggarts who in real life may be dangerous are safely *reduced* to comic self-delusion on the stage.

Aristotle's courteous retort to Plato on poetry, so far as it survives in the twenty-six chapters of the Aristotelian lecture notes called *Poetics*, is directed mostly to the problem of tragedy. For Aristotle tragedy is not a mimetic falsification of some higher, or Platonized, reality, but an image of human character, passion, and action, which in some way carries a very serious and more universalized, or idealized, meaning than the facts of any real history (Chap. IX). Aristotle's *Poetics*, though sketchy, gives a richly suggestive account of the imperfect and suffering character of the princely protagonist of tragedy and his downfall. The more slender remarks on comedy are mostly part of an introductory historical survey and point to a further development (Part II of the *Poetics*, after tragedy and epic), which, if it was actually written, is now missing. But read within the general frame of reference of the Aristotelian mimetic view of poetry and alongside the apparently close, if antithetic, parallel of tragedy, the account of comedy is not jejune. Three ideas seem central:

1. That comedy is more realistic than tragedy; it deals with ordinary, humble, or low characters—perhaps making them even lower than they are in real life (Chap. II). The lowly character of comedy sorts

---

18 *Philebus*, 48–50, trans. Jowett.

with its obscure history, as a despised genre confined to the rural circuits (Chap. V).

2. That in keeping with this lowness and ordinariness, comic characters, as opposed to the mythic personages of tragedy, are stereotypes, and they show this, among other ways, in having label names (Chap. IX). (Through the whole Platonic and Aristotelian way of thinking there runs the paradox, appearing here and there in different ways, that what is ideal or more fully realized than ordinary experience is in one sense also more real, though what is inferior to the ideal, or what is ordinarily experienced, is also in a very good sense more real.)

3. That the object of laughter (*to geloion*) is a species of fault or deficiency—a kind of ugliness (*to aischron*)—but not of the most offensive or dangerous kind (not painful and not destructive, *anōdunon kai ou phthartikon*—Chap. V). A good symbol of this degree of offense (and of the appropriate response to it) may be seen in the grimace of the comic mask (*to geloion prosōpon*).

This essentially normative view of the laughable is flanked in another passage with the historical note that the old-fashioned comedy, of the village revel variety, did aim to inflict pain by name-calling lampoon and personal abuse. The fifth-century poet Crates (to whom we have alluded) first broke away from that harsh tradition and introduced at Athens an earlier Syracusan refinement of generalized comic meaning (Chap. V). Such a conception of comedy would seem to imply, or at least to be very friendly to, the further idea of a comic happy ending. And a later passage in the *Poetics,* about distributive justice in comic plays (punishment for evildoers, rewards for the virtuous—Chap. XIII) glances at and approves what was indeed mainly the fact in Middle and New Comedy—that the outcome of the comic action was happy for the young lovers and their allies.

Aristotle's *Ethics* tells us much about human character types as conceived according to a certain distinction: between the virtuous, who achieve a kind of wise moderation with regard to some human interest or energy, and the vicious, who veer off to either side, driven by either too much or not enough of that energy (*Nicomachean Ethics* II.6). Thus, for instance, a certain norm of truth and restraint should operate in the good opinion which we have or express of our own powers (IV.7). Outside this, there is the exaggeration or excess which makes a man a boaster or braggart (*alazōn*), and perhaps a bully. There is also the complementary fault, or deficiency, of either real or pretended depreciation of our own powers. This we see either in a trifling, mock-modest bore (*baukopanourgos*) or in a subtle ironic dialectician (*eirōn*), like Socrates. Again, there is the virtue of showing just the right degree of self-assertion and liveliness in conversation, and being thus the gentlemanly wit (*eutrapelos*) (IV. 8). And on either side of the gentleman appear the excessive wit, the loud-mouthed funny man or buffoon (*bōmolochos*), and the surly, defective, or unsociable boor (*agroikos*).

These characters, like some named also in the *Ethical Characters* of Aristotle's pupil and successor Theophrastus (the schoolmaster of Menander), have a close resemblance to characters in the Greek and Roman New Comedy and in a few instances even have names identical with titles of plays.[19] In distinguishing the buffoon from the witty conversationalist, Aristotle actually alludes (IV.7) to the "Old Comedy" (which specialized in abusive language, *aischrologia*—he means even Aristophanes, one must suppose) and the "New Comedy" (i.e., what we call "Middle Comedy"), which had developed the innuendo, *huponoia*. How did Aristotle reconcile the ordinariness—even worse, the ordinary lowness—which he saw as the comic subject matter, with the refinement of dialogue, perhaps even the kindliness, which he seems also to have observed in comedy and to have approved? The paradox may be more closely specified if we observe that the ironist, while he suffers from a defect in the virtue of true self-estimate, yet is a relatively agreeable and forgivable instance of this kind of vice. *Eirōnia,* in fact (as we see more plainly in Aristotle's *Rhetoric*[20]), is very close to *eutrapelia,* the virtue of the witty gentleman talker. Some sort of incipiently realized division of comic characters into butts and wits, the element of earthy fault and the force of witty criticism, may be adumbrated here.

In any case, the problem of reconciling low subject matter with sophisticated treatment of it was not a superficial one. It may be said to persist and to remanifest itself in every age. A certain energetic theoretical effort to grapple with it, in reference not just to stage comedy but to the whole issue of the satiric and ironic in poetry, has produced in our own time the conception of a poetic "fallacy of imitative form."[21] How, we might generalize, can creative intelligence lend itself, not simply to the criticism, but to the *mimesis* of the unintelligent or the unintelligible, when *mimesis* is a kind of partici-pation?

Some of the features of Aristotle's theory of the comic are slightly developed and few notions are added (largely by deduction or extra-polation, it would seem, from Aristotle's poetics of tragedy) in a late

---

[19] The names of six of the thirty Theophrastan *Characters* are the same as titles of the lost plays of Menander (*Menander,* ed. F. G. Allison, Cambridge, Mass., 1951, p. xiii, n. 4).

[20] In *Rhetoric* III.18 the buffoon (*bōmolochos*) is contrasted to the gentleman (*eleutheros*), whose technique in joking is irony (*eirōnia*). *Rhetoric* II.12 defines wit (*eutrapelia*) as "cultured insolence" (*pepaideumenē hubris*).

[21] Yvor Winters, *Primitivism and Decadence* (New York, 1937), pp. 49, 51.

Peripatetic *Tractate,* or outline of comic theory, which, after a long period of oblivion, has come to light in recent times.[22] Certain clear echoes from Aristotle concern the low characters of comedy and the difference between Old Comedy and New; other ideas seem derived from brief remarks on verbal jokes to be found in Aristotle's logical works, in his *Rhetoric,* and in a passage of the *Poetics* referring to inappropriate metaphors (Chap. XXII). The most interesting effort of the compiler appears, however, in the introduction of a comic "catharsis." Let us recollect that tragedy, according to what still seems the most plausible interpretation of the earthy-minded and pragmatic Aristotle, induced a healthy working off of potentially destructive emotions, pity and fear and "such like."

Comedy, then, we might think, could be a complementary occasion for blowing off the impulse to laughter—which Plato indeed had marked as frivolous and weakening, and which Aristotle himself in a passage of the *Politics* (VII.17) seems to view with a degree of misgiving. ("The legislator should not allow youth to be spectators of iambi or of comedy until they are of an age to sit at the public tables or to drink strong wine."[23]) Tragedy and comedy, we may conjecture, Aristotle looked upon as alike therapeutic, not inflammatory or debilitating, as they were for Plato. There is nothing improbable about ascribing this clinical view to Aristotle—though for either tragedy or comedy we may well wish to develop our own critical ideas less affectively and rather along the lines of his descriptive hints at what a stage tragedy or a stage comedy itself was like (as an object of knowledge) and what it *ought* to be like according to its nature or kind.

v

Many poems and plays and many works of criticism and literary history, even encyclopedic works, were produced, especially at Alexan-

---

[22] The *Tractatus Coislinianus,* as it was named after a French nobleman who had owned it, survives in a manuscript of the tenth century A.D., and is attributed to the first century B.C. It was found in the National Library at Paris and published in 1839. See J. A. Cramer, *Anecdota Graeca* (Oxford, 1839), I, 403–6; Lane Cooper. *An Aristotelian Theory of Comedy* (New York, 1922), p. 10.

[23] Cf. J. C. Ransom, *The World's Body* (New York, 1938), pp. 188–89, "The Cathartic Principle." Lane Cooper, in a later work, *Fifteen Greek Plays* (New York, 1954), p. 787, changed his translation of *tēn tōn toioutōn pathematōn katharsin* (used in the *Tractatus,* echoing Aristotle's *Poetics,* Chap. VI) from *purgation of the like emotions* (i.e., "pleasure and laughter"—*hedonē kai gelōs*— in the *Tractatus*) to *catharsis of disturbing emotions,* thus making the comic catharsis an allopathic one—a notion which he had indeed expounded in his earlier *Aristotelian Theory of Comedy,* pp. 66–70, but for which there would seem to be not much support.

dria, between the time of Aristotle and the era of Augustan Rome. But most of these works have disappeared, so that our next lively critic of comedy is encountered in a context not very immediately connected with fourth-century Greek ideas. Neither comic nor tragic drama was in an ascendant phase at Rome. Terence and Plautus had come and gone and were now classics of Roman drama. Satire, too, as we have seen, had arrived a century earlier with Lucilius, and now the poet Horace (65–8 B.C.) was the most accomplished practitioner of this living genre. Oratory, another flourishing contemporary genre, had recently had its most eminent theorist in the Republican statesman-philosopher Cicero, and he had given his opinion about the use of jokes in conversation and speeches.[24] But Cicero tells us little to our purpose—except perhaps that (as in Aristotle's *Poetics* implicitly) we ought to be careful about going too far: don't make either obscene jokes or jokes about things that are really painful or sad.

Horace says several things about stage comedy in his critical master-piece, the lengthy poetic *Epistle to the Pisos,* his *Ars Poetica,* as it soon came to be known. He says more about it in several of his other verse *Epistles* and in his *Satires* (or satiric conversations, *Sermones*). The balance of his real interest, as we might expect of a master satirist, is toward the socially critical or satiric side of comedy. At the same time, certain miscellaneous finely polished fossils of the Greek classical tradition are embedded in the *Ars Poetica.* We can infer, for instance, that the norm of well-defined literary genres and of corre-sponding character types has now achieved the status of a well-estab-lished truism (For every sort and phase of human life, a correct description—*Mobilibusque decor naturis dandus et annis,* 158). It is sound advice. One doesn't speculate much about it. One can recite the formulas very neatly and smoothly, with a knowing smile.[25] Even tragic and epic protagonists have their definitions and descriptions. Achilles, for instance, *impiger, iracundus, inexorabilis, acer.* In like

---

[24] *De Oratore* II.lviii–lxxi. He sums up the doctrine in his *Orator,* 88. In *De Officiis* I.103–4, he says that telling jokes (jesting) is like sleep and other kinds of relaxation: we may indulge in it, but only after we have earned the right to it by a hard day's work. Even then, it ought to be refined and witty (*elegans, urbanum, ingeniosum, facetum*), not gross or immoral (*illiberale, petulans, flagi-tiosum, obscenum*). The former kind may be illustrated in Plautus, in Old Comedy[!], and in "the books of the Socratic philosophy."

[25] A competent poet will not have country characters, Fauns, acting like gallants of the Forum, speaking mawkish verses or bawdy jokes (244 ff.). Opposite instances, however, may be adduced—as when the poet for good reasons allows a lowly comic character to rise to ranting and raging (*tumido delitigat ore,* 94). The phrase *operis lex* (135), often quoted as a serious Horatian formula for the rule of decorum, is actually used by Horace to describe the kind of law that acts as a hobble to a poet of the plodding sort.

capsules, *Medea ferox...flebilis Ino, perfidus Ixion, Io vaga, tristis Orestes* (121–24). And likewise, of course, the everyday (comic) types —the beardless and prodigal youth, the crotchety old man, full of difficulties and complaints, the encomiast of days gone by—*difficilis, querulus, laudator temporis acti* (161–76). Tragic and comic, epic, lyric, each kind has even its proper meters. Certain mingled snatches of dramatic history—about plays acted on wagons, actors' faces smeared with lees of wine, satyr plays, and the music of lutes—are more quaint and picturesque than clearly informative or of compelling interest. These are passages in Horace which the grammarian Donatus in the fourth century, in a compendium of remarks *De Comoedia,* would remember and quote. Such repetition is a sort of contrasting testimony to the apparently casual originality of Horace in other passages and his superiority to the now partly mysterious antiquarian articles which he no doubt felt constrained to recite.

One of Horace's most memorable concerns in the *Ars Poetica* is language. He was helping to usher out a period of Alexandrian affectation (macaronics or exotic vocabulary) and of a contrary Patrician nationalism and archaism. So he devoted some of his best wit to asserting and exemplifying both the energy and reality of living Roman speech (the tyrannical law of usage—*usus...jus et norma loquendi*), and with that the need for the cunning turn of words (*series juncturaque, callida junctura,* 47, 242) which is the special token and force of the poet's art. In the *Satires* devoted to defending the art (especially I.iv and I.x), observations about a verse language that sounds like daily speech and about a plodding inspiration (*musa pedestris,* II.vi.17) merge with humble-sounding assertions about the realism and lowness of both satiric and comic writing. Take it out of verse, he says, and you wouldn't have the obviously poetic fragments (*disjecta membra poetae*) of something still essentially noble, as you would, for instance, if you broke up an archaic epic poet like Ennius. You would have just snatches of ordinary conversation—*sermoni propiora.* But it is difficult to believe that a sleek poet like Horace, professing a high regard for the fine-filed phrase and confident that he had surpassed the rough pioneering of Lucilius, could really believe that. ("Some other time we'll see whether this kind of writing is true poetry or not"—I.iv. 63–65.)

He knew of course that he was a better poet than old Ennius— even when, or especially when, he talked about real life, in its own accents. ("I'll give a twist to the familiar that will make anybody think he could do the same, but he will waste his perspiration if he tries"—*sudet multum frustraque laboret.*[26]) No doubt he considered

---

[26] *Ars Poetica,* 241.

stage comedy, when it was polished, like that of Menander and Terence
(though scarcely that of Plautus[27]), to be real poetry. In another of
his smart conversational defenses of poetry, the *Epistle to Augustus,*
Horace framed a somewhat different, but again memorable, testimony
to the Roman conviction about comic realism. The argument has
been repeated, both consciously and unconsciously, many times in the
course of Western literary criticism.[28] Tragedy may be loftier, but
there is a sense in which comedy is a more difficult achievement. For
no free fantasy, no cheating, is possible. The Roman audience always
has the daily facts of life as a yardstick. It will know whether a comedy
is good *mimesis* or not.

> creditur, ex medio quia res accersit, habere
> sudoris minimum, sed habet comoedia tanto
> plus oneris, quanto veniae minus.[29]

Another Roman writer who left a few neatly trimmed formulae of
the realistic doctrine was Cicero, not in his rhetorical theory, but in
some lost work, from which they were quoted in the fourth century by
Donatus. Cicero said that comedy was *imitatio vitae, speculum con-
suetudinis, imago veritatis.*[30]

It might be thought, on the evidence just presented, that this phase
of classical theory not only gives a low view of the comic stage, repeating an Aristotelian disparagement, but an overly sober and prosy view,
like certain journalistic art criticism during the mid-nineteenth century, the era of the first Daguerreotype studios. We shall be more fair
to this Roman criticism if we look on its slogans about realism as a
thoughtful effort to complement or offset a different kind of assumption
which was so deeply established as scarcely to invite frequent repetition—namely, that stage comedy was tricky, lively, exciting, bawdy,
funny, and a lot of fun. A passage in an anonymous rhetorical treatise

---

[27] *Ars Poetica,* 270; *Epistle to Augustus,* 57 ff., 168. Cicero, Caesar, and Quintilian praise the polish and purity of Terence (H. R. Fairclough, *American Journal
of Philology,* XXXIV, 1913, 188–89).

[28] Molière, or his spokesman, in *La Critique de l'Ecole des Femmes,* Scene vi
(See below p. 61), observes that we can portray our heroes according to desire;
nobody expects them to look real. But ordinary characters have to be painted to
the life; they must seem contemporary.

[29] "Some think that comedy is easy to write, because it is just a report on
everyday life. That in fact makes it all the harder. The slightest inaccuracy is
inexcusable"—*Epistle to Augustus,* 168–70.

[30] "An imitation of life, a mirror of the ordinary, an image of the truth"—
Donatus, *De Comoedia,* in *Commentum Terenti,* ed. Paul Wessner (Leipzig,
1902), I.22. In his oration *Pro Sexto Roscio Amerino,* XVI.47, Cicero says that
the fictions of dramatic poetry give an image of daily life (*imaginem nostrae vitae
cotidianae*). In a passage of the fragmentary fourth book of his *De Re Publica,*
he uses the expression *consuetudo vitae* in conjunction with *comoedia* (IV.13).
Quintilian, *Institute* X.i.69, says of Menander: *omnem vitae imaginem expressit.*

contemporary with Cicero and for centuries attributed to him, the *Rhetorica ad Herennium,* is perhaps an admissible if indirect kind of evidence. The author is giving instructions, not for playwriting, but for a kind of dramatic "narration" in forensic speech-writing. The passage sounds very much like a description of Plautine comedy, and the technique described seems closely associated with a mode of "realistic" and "factual" narration which the author likens explicitly to "comedy."

> The kind of narrative which is based on the persons ought to be marked by gaiety of dialogue, diversity of character, seriousness, gentleness, hope, fear, suspicion, desire, deceit, pity, variety of events, changes of fortune, unexpected disaster, sudden joy, and a happy ending.[31]

VI

We may imagine formal criticism of drama, either tragedy or comedy, as lapsing into a kind of suspension for about ten centuries. This is not, however, to say that we suppose an utter cessation either of literary learning or of the comic stage. Aelius Donatus, the writer of the fourth century whom we have cited above, was a grammarian and the tutor of St. Jerome, the translator of the Latin Vulgate Bible. The Latin *Grammar* of Donatus was so standard a text throughout the "Dark" and the Middle Ages that in English the name "Donat" acquired the generic meaning of "elementary textbook." His commentary on five of the six Terentian plays, with his two prefixed synopses (one from another grammarian, Evanthius) on tragedy and comedy, was "rediscovered" at Mainz by Giovanni Aurispa, an Italian traveler to the Council of Basel, in 1433.[32] Still it seems likely that this commentary, coming down with other scholia in the manuscripts of the plays, had been *known*—to somebody, somewhere, at almost any moment of the long era which we are considering. We discover, for instance, that in the middle of the ninth century a learned abbot of Ferrières, Servatus Lupus, wrote to Pope Benedict III asking if he could borrow a copy.[33] And the numerous manuscripts now known to the world of scholarship are an ample enough testimony to the activity

---

[31] *Rhetorica ad Herennium* I.viii.13. See the edition of Harry Caplan (Cambridge, Mass., 1954), p. 24; also IV.i.63, pp. 387 ff., an example of comic character delineation (*notatio*). In the English Augustan age, Sir Richard Steele would prefix the Latin text as a title-page epigraph to the first edition of his comedy *The Conscious Lovers,* 1723. One of his editors would later translate *in personis positum* as "presented on the stage" and thus complete the association with comedy.

[32] J. E. Sandys, *A History of Classical Scholarship* (Cambridge, 1924), II, 34.

[33] Sandys, I, 487, Letter 103 of Lupus, dated 855–858. Cf. M. L. W. Laistner, *Thought and Letters in Western Europe A.D. 500 to 900* (London, 1931), pp. 205–12.

of copying Donatus on Terence during the early Middle Ages.[34] During
the tenth century, the Benedictine abbess Hrotswitha, at Gandesheim
in Saxony, adapted comedies of Terence for conventual use.

It is, to say the least, probable, however, that a greater volume of
laughter occurred during the early Middle Ages in response to popular
dramatic forms—monologues or mimes, let us say, performed in market-
places or baronial halls. The surviving evidence is scrappy. In the
thirteenth century, one notices, for instance, the performance at Arras
of Adam de la Halle, a *trouvère* who composed a sort of satirical
revue (or *Jeu*) in which he himself, his wife, and various fellow citizens
stepped forth in a sequence of gay scenes, and also a sort of comic
pastourelle opera, both dialogue and song, in which a shepherd and
shepherdess outwitted a philandering knight.[35] But Adam seems to
have had no rivals and to have left no descendants. The historian of
French literature is compelled to record that "the records of comedy
in the fourteenth century are virtually blank."[36]

If we would inquire more broadly, beyond the stage, into the
Medieval sense of mirth, we can learn from the poetry of one great
English author alone, Chaucer in his *Canterbury Tales*, c. 1387, that
this sense was at moments robust, obscene, and satirical (as in tales
by such Medieval types as Miller, Reeve, Friar, or Summoner), or
sly and subtle (as in the author's self-portrait), or delicate and sympathetic (as in his portrait of a Prioress), or grimly macabre and
grotesque (as in an exemplary tale told by a preaching Pardoner), or
allegorical and humorous (as in a fable of a Cock and a Fox). Behind
Chaucer we may recollect a wealth of folk humor and satire, sources
and analogues of his tales, bawdy French short stories (*fabliaux*) and
beast fables. Or, we can look around more widely at a somewhat
different kind of example: Dante's hookwinged black demons in the
Inferno, or the gargoyles (*Chimères*) of Notre Dame Cathedral, in the
High Middle Ages, and then, two centuries later (at the last waning of
those Middle Ages), the immense pleasantries of Pantagruel and
Gargantua (1532–1534), Holbein's woodcut series *The Dance of Death*,
the crowded town squares, sports, and peasant feasts of the elder
Breughel, the wilder grotesqueries of Breughel and Hieronymus Bosch.
We encounter a line of images suggesting a peculiarly Medieval strong
stomach in laughter, a kind of broad-bottomed sturdiness and athletic

---

34 Paul Wessner, ed. *Aeli Donati quod fertur Commentum Terenti* (Leipzig,
1902), I, Introduction.

35 *Le Jeu de la Feuillée* and *Le Jeu de Robin et de Marion*. See the next note.

36 Geoffrey Brereton, *A Short History of French Literature* (Baltimore, 1954–
1956), p. 49. The chapter on "The Medieval Drama" is a pleasantly intelligible
summation of episodes that can be found at much greater length in the bigger
histories.

vigor. This spirit could appear in certain homely and folksy forms of drama too—for example, in a splatter of satiric *sotties,* clowning *moralités,* and knock-about farces,[37] the specialty of the numerous societies of Fools (*Sots*) which flourished all over France from about 1400 for a century and a half—wild, irreverent, and ragging clubs of students, momentary lords of misrule—at Paris, for instance, the *Enfants sans souci* and the young lawyers and law-clerks, *Basochiens.* We can sample a similar spirit in the rough episodes and elements of humor prominent in the cycles of Biblical "mystery" plays which reached their heyday in the town squares of both France and England during the fifteenth century. "Now to helle the wey I take," says Lucifer in the play about his fall in the Coventry cycle.

For fere of fyre a fart I crake.

Drama, we know, evolved primordially from ritual—the fertility ritual came before the story about the king.[38] So that it ought to seem normal enough to us that Medieval liturgy, though itself derived from the Bible story, should evolve its own dramatic forms, or "tropes," and that they in turn should move out of the Church to the square.[39] In these "collective displays" of both "piety and merriment,"[40] not only were scolding wives and contending husbands funny (Noah and his wife in the York cycle) and thieving and double-talking peasants like Mak (the sheep-stealer in the Second Shepherd's Christmas play in the Towneley cycle), but also all the more hugely wicked characters who crowded the same stage—Lucifer and his devils and the human potentates who pushed the devils' business, Pharaoh, Herod, Octavian, Pilate. Ugly, pompous, arrogant, and vile-tempered, these princes of evil ranted, raged, despaired, huffed and puffed, and snorted fire—all in a context of revealed providence and corresponding dramaturgic convention which made their pretensions the more ludicrous. "The Middle Ages found it good for man's soul to be taken down a peg whenever it started to soar."[41]

This kind of drama was part of a much greater Medieval vision of

---

37 Gringore's *Jeu du Prince des Sots,* 1512, satirizes the Pope. The master-piece of the farces, *La Farce de Maître Pathelin,* an anonymous satire of "legal cunning and commercial stupidity," is a distant analogue of Racine's *Les Plaideurs.* See Brereton, pp. 49–50. The farces in general were in the tradition of the *fabliaux,* and they looked forward two centuries to the dazzling frolics of Molière.

38 See above p. 2.

39 At about the tenth century.

40 Brereton, pp. 43–47.

41 Willard Farnham, "The Medieval Comic Spirit in the English Renaissance," *Joseph Quincy Adams Memorial Studies,* ed. James G. McManaway *et al.* (Washington, D.C., 1948), p. 434, quoted in Douglas Cole, *Suffering and Evil in the Plays of Christopher Marlowe* (Princeton, N. J., 1967), p. 14.

evil as a kind of grotesque dilapidation, deformity, or deficiency of good sense and virtue which, in the long run, was *always* destined not only for defeat but to make its own special kind of contribution to the harmony of the *Divine Comedy*. (The most conspicuous appearance of the term "comedy" in the whole Middle Ages, or perhaps in the whole Western tradition, is that in the title of Dante's epic. In his dedicatory letter to the Lord of Verona, Can Grande della Scala, prefixed to the third and happy part of the poem—the *Paradiso,* after the *Inferno* and the *Purgatorio*—Dante explains that he calls his poem a "comedy" because comedy begins in adversity but ends in happiness—"as doth appear in the comedies of Terence. . . . If we consider the style of language," he adds, it is "careless and humble, because it is the vulgar tongue, in which even housewives hold converse.")

The Medieval sense of the grotesque and the strong Medieval laugh may be further adduced as evidence for a certain hearty wholeness of world view or a resilient and full awareness of both the heavenly and the earthly. The Medieval world view may be looked on as in a special way represented in the comic vision of life. Comedy, says a modern theologian (and he might be thinking especially of the Medieval and earlier Renaissance comic) is "an art that is dedicated to telling the Whole Truth." The comic catharsis involves a "restoration of our confidence in the realm of finitude." It enables us to see the "daily occasions of our earth-bound career as being not irrelevant inconveniences but. . .possible roads into what is ultimately significant life." The "mud in man" is "nothing to be ashamed of. It can produce. . . the face of God. . . . To recall this, to recall this incredible relation between mud and God, is, in its own distant, adumbrating way, the function of comedy."[42]

VII

But if we look for theoretical discussion of comedy, or of laughter, that is something else. As we rang the curtain down on late classical criticism with a grammarian who wrote a commentary on Terence, it will not surprise us to find the renascence of the classical spirit of critical comment on comedy, late in the fifteenth and early in the sixteenth century, again closely connected with the plays of Terence and the "rediscovered" commentary of Donatus. Not long after the

---

[42] Nathan A. Scott, Jr., "The Bias of Comedy and the Narrow Escape into Faith," *The Christian Scholar,* XLIV (Spring 1961), 21, 32, 39. In the third sentence, Scott quotes William F. Lynch, S. J., *Christ and Apollo* (New York, 1960), p. 109. The title phrase "Narrow Escape into Faith" is taken from Christopher Fry, "Comedy," *The Tulane Drama Review,* IV (March 1960), 77.

advent of printing, new editors and commentators on Terence were legion—in Italy, in France, in Germany, in the Netherlands. The number includes such eminent humanists as Erasmus and Melanchthon. If we consult the now all-but-forgotten history of this subject, we find the Latinized names of such scholars as Joannes Calphurnius, who in 1477 published at Treviso an original commentary on the *Self-Tormentor*, the only one of the six plays of Terence which Donatus had omitted; and Guido Juvenalis, who was the first person ever to write a commentary on all six of the plays, published at Lyons in 1498; and Iodocus Willichius, who in his edition published at Zurich in 1550 analyzed the rhetoric of every scene in every play, "pointing out how Terence invented his arguments, how he put them together, and how he clothed them in the proper sentiments and figures"; and Matthias Bergius, who, objecting to the bias of Willichius, in his edition of 1574 favored the use of Terence as an object of grammatical and metrical study.[43] Terence monopolized Renaissance critical thought about comedy—in part because he was a classically safe ground for schoolmasters. Aristophanes was too coarse, Plautus both coarse and highly "irregular." One is reminded of the fact that Aristophanes had been preserved by Byzantine grammarians not for his supreme comic genius, but for the purity of his Attic Greek.

About the middle of the fifteenth century, Aristotle's *Poetics* (in the Greek and Latin texts of Alessandro de' Pazzi, 1536, and the learned editions of Francesco Robortello, 1548, and Vincenzo Maggi, 1550) became so far ascendant that ideas expounded by Aristotle largely in connection with tragedy, but plainly enough available for comedy, merged with details of Terentian commentary to produce a discussion in which nowadays anybody moderately familiar with the ancient documents will find few surprises: *plot*, complicated, with introduction, rise, and catastrophe, five acts, and a degree of concern about unity of action—and also of time and place; *characters*, low, or at least humble; *sentiments* (i.e., thoughts), humble too, conversable, commonplace; *diction*, low, humble, everyday, but interesting, not dull—and in Terence, of course, pure and terse and proper. At moments, as Horace had said, diction might be elevated and ranting. One finds these ideas in a vast body of Latin and vernacular writings: notably, to name but a few, in the treatise on comedy (*Explicatio eorum omnium quae ad Comediae artificium pertinent*) included in the *Poetics* edited by Robortello, 1548[44]; in the novelist and defender of "romance"

---

[43] I have been following Marvin T. Herrick, *Comic Theory in the Sixteenth Century* (Urbana, Ill., 1950). H. W. Lawton's *Handbook of French Renaissance Dramatic Theory: A Selection of Texts* (Manchester, 1949) includes generous extracts from Donatus, with a translation.

[44] Herrick, pp. 227–39, gives us a very readable translation.

Giraldi Cinthio's *Discorsi,* 1554; in the immense hyper-classical Latin treatise by the French scholar Julius Caesar Scaliger, *Poetices Libri Septem,* 1561; and in the Italian commentary which is such an important part of Lodovico Castelvetro's edition of the *Poetics* (*Poetica D'Aristotele Vulgarizzata et Sposta*), 1570.[45]

We must understand too a flourishing neoclassic or humanistic theater, both tragic and comic, in parallel Italian and French phases, though at not quite the same dates. Fifteenth-century Italian humanists at several centers of learning (Bologna, Pavia, Padua, Ferrara) not only put on productions of Terence and Plautus but wrote Latin comedies of a more or less Plautine or Terentian cast. And these led rather quickly to five-act Terentian intrigue plays in the vernacular, the not inconsiderable achievements of the poet Ariosto at Ferrara from 1508 on, those of the now less-well-remembered Bernardo da Bibbiena beginning at Urbino in 1513, or Niccolò Machiavelli's immoral prose work *La Mandragola* (*The Mandrake*), written before 1520.[46] Tragic drama began later and was less impressive. The careful humanist and Aristotelian critic Giovanni Giorgio Trissino's *Sofonisba,* 1515, was the first regular tragedy, scrupulous in observation of the rules. The approximate climax came with the heroic poet Torquato Tasso's *Torrismondo,* 1587, remarkable for the Grecian ring of its choruses. In France both regular tragedy and regular comedy begin at the mid-century with the Pléiade poet Jodelle's *Cléopatre Captive* and *Eugène,* played in the winter of 1552–1553 at the court of Henri II.[47] And this drama matures slowly, toward the reign of the *Grand Monarque* and the masterpieces of Dryden's contemporaries, Corneille, Racine, and Molière.

In Italy during the sixteenth century the comic theater shows a peculiar and very important development when the Terentian *commedia erudita,* weakening in the middle decades, gives way before a vulgar rival, the *commedia dell'arte* of traveling troupes. These were professionals in the fullest sense: their staples were improvised dialogue, clowning pantomime, and stock character types (Pantaloon, Doctor,

---

45 Translated excerpts from the major Italian critics may be read in Allan H. Gilbert's *Literary Criticism: Plato to Dryden* (New York, 1940), and extended digests in Bernard Weinberg's *History of Literary Criticism in the Italian Renaissance,* Vols. I–II (Chicago, 1961). Brief statements by French writers, in prefaces and verse epistles, may be consulted in H. W. Lawton, *Handbook of French Renaissance Dramatic Theory,* and Bernard Weinberg, *Critical Prefaces of the French Renaissance* (Evanston, Ill., 1950). J. E. Spingarn's *A History of Literary Criticism in the Renaissance* (New York, 1899; Italian translation by Antonio Fusco, 1905, with additions and corrections by Spingarn) remains the ablest effort to organize the Renaissance materials into a history.

46 Marvin T. Herrick, *Italian Comedy in the Renaissance* (Urbana, Ill., 1960), pp. 71 ff.

47 Brereton, pp. 131, 155.

Pedant, Capitano or Braggart Soldier, valet Scaramouche, the servant maid Columbine, and later her sweetheart Harlequin). *Commedia dell'arte* migrated to France by the middle of the century, established itself as a feature of French life during the reign of Henri III (1574–1589), and during the next century continued to flourish in the southern French provinces and at Paris, where the actors became a permanent troupe. There was no kind of theater to which the French public was more steadily exposed. It must have become in imagination almost indistinguishable from life. The *commedia dell'arte* actors were to be the instructors of Molière during his years on the road, and during his Parisian heyday at his own theater, the *Palais Royal,* they were his rivals at the *Hôtel de Bourgogne.*[48]

In England developments were at first slower, but by the end of the sixteenth century the drama seems more spontaneous and vigorously native and less inhibited by the classical models than that on the Continent. One marks with special interest the Westminster head-master Nicholas Udall's doggerel Plautine scamper *Ralph Roister Doister,* the first English comedy, perhaps played by Westminster boys about 1553; a first regular or Senecan English tragedy, *Gorboduc, or Ferrex and Porrex,* by Sackville and Norton, acted at the Inner Temple in 1561; a second English verse comedy, with close unity of time and place, *Gammer Gurton's Needle,* acted at Christ's College, Cambridge, in 1566; in the same year, *Supposes,* by George Gascoigne, at Gray's Inn, adapted from Ariosto, the first English comedy in prose; and the "university wit" John Lyly's "quaint and vulgar" Plautine extravagance *Mother Bombie,* 1594. And then Shakespeare, who breaks all bounds, whether in a Plautine *Comedy of Errors,* in a farcical taming of a shrew, or in a Forest of Arden romance where all ends well. George Meredith, the Victorian novelist whose celebration of Terentian and Molièresque comedy is the last text in the present volume, was content to pay incidental homage to a few transcendent "spirits"—Aristophanes, Rabelais, Shakespeare, Cervantes—without serious attempt to assimilate their greatness to his argument. The deeply imaginative blends of "festive,"[49] and no doubt in some sense primordial, ritual, and mythic[50] strains of laughter which enter into Shakespeare's transmuted braggart soldier Falstaff, his "high" comedies of young love, his "dark" comedies of lechery, and his twilight romances of reconciliation, make a vaster theme than the present.

---

48 Brereton, pp. 155–56.

49 C. L. Barber, *Shakespeare's Festive Comedy* (Princeton, N. J., 1955).

50 Northrop Frye, *A Natural Perspective: The Development of Shakespearean Comedy and Romance* (New York, 1965); Susanne K. Langer, *Feeling and Form* (New York, 1953). Cf. Bibliographical Aids II.G.

BEN JONSON

[1572–1637]

In his exuberant, Italianate *Defence of Poesie,* written perhaps during the early 1580's, and published posthumously in 1595, the Elizabethan gentleman and poet Sir Philip Sidney had mustered enough classical rigor to look around him on the scene of English dramatic beginnings and to notice with much distaste a prevalent wild disregard of nature, the unities, decorum, and verisimilitude, a love of gross spectacle, and in comedy a coarse enough idea of purposes. "Our tragedies and comedies [are] not without cause cried out against, observing rules neither of honest civility nor of skilful poetry... faulty both in place and time...neither right tragedies nor right comedies." They mingle

> kings and clowns, not because the matter so carrieth it, but thrust in the clown by head and shoulders to play a part in majestical matters, with neither decency nor discretion; so as neither the admiration and commiseration, nor the right sportfulness, is by their mongrel tragicomedy obtained.... Our comedians think there is no delight without laughter, which is very wrong.

Rather, delight and laughter in themselves "have, as it were, a kind of contrariety":

> I speak to this purpose, that all the end of the comical part be not upon such scornful matters as stir laughter only, but mixed with it that delightful teaching which is the end of poesy. And the great fault, even in that point of laughter, and forbidden plainly by Aristotle, is that they stir laughter in sinful things, which are rather execrable than ridiculous; or miserable, which are rather to be pitied than scorned.[1]

Sidney's younger contemporary Ben Jonson, classically educated bricklayer, soldier, player, and duellist, both a grittier and a more methodical personality than the Arcadian courtier, produced his first comedy, *Every Man in His Humour,* in 1598, with his friend and

---

[1] *The Defense of Poesy, Otherwise Known as An Apology for Poetry,* ed. Albert S. Cook (Boston, 1890), pp. 47–51.

colleague Shakespeare in the cast. Jonson was later the author of the earliest and one of the few best formal encomiums of Shakespeare (his poem "To the memory of my beloved, the Author," in the 1623 folio of Shakespeare's plays), but also, in a commonplace book, he penned one of the boldest criticisms:

> I *remember,* the Players have often mentioned it as an honour to *Shakespeare,* that in his writing, (whatsoever he penn'd) hee never blotted out line. My answer hath beene, would he had blotted a thousand.[2]

One way, not of disparaging Jonson's neoclassic art, but of describing its peculiar success within peculiar limits, might be to venture the opinion that in comparison to the tumultuous prose of Sidney or to the native woodnotes wild of Shakespeare, Jonson's verse, and even his dramatic verse, has both the accuracy and the pointed stiffness of a meticulous sort of bricklaying. Jonson is the first English poet of a square enough and hard enough character to produce a comedy carefully and reasonably constructed on what might then be conceived as classical, and hence natural, lines. "A scholar's excogitation of the comic," George Meredith was to call it. Jonson's *Every Man in His Humour,* a gayer and more lighthearted satire than most of his other comedies, displays Plautine or Theophrastan character types intricately involved in a New Comedy intrigue. The play at first had an Italian scene and Italian character names, but sometime after the quarto of 1601 and before the folio collection of 1616, these were changed to English, to match the deep contemporary grain of the play's materials. We behold London versions of the deceived old gentleman, his sporty son, and a sweetheart, their ally the crafty servant (Brainworm), and —even more indigenous—the "plain squire," "merry magistrate," and "water-bearer" (Cob), the booby types, "town gull" and "country gull," and, most prominent as a "humour," Captain Bobadill, a simpler and grosser version than Shakespeare's of the braggart soldier. The Prologue (appearing in 1616), one of Johnson's more relaxed and smiling expressions of his artistic norms, has some close echoes of Sidney and seems to glance at some of the admired Mr. Shakespeare's history plays (*King Henry VI, King Henry V*) and perhaps even at so late a Shakespearean comedy as *The Tempest* (1611), with its storm and its monster.

---

[2] *Timber,* paragraph [64], *De Shakespeare nostrati.*

PROLOGUE

TO

Every Man in His Humour

[*1616*]

Though neede make many *Poets,* and some such
As art, and nature have not betterd much;
Yet ours, for want, hath not so lov'd the stage,
As he dare serve th'ill customes of the age:
Or purchase your delight at such a rate,
As, for it, he himselfe must justly hate.
To make a child, now swadled, to proceede
Man, and then shoote up, in one beard, and weede,
Past threescore yeeres: or, with three rustie swords,
And helpe of some few foot-and-half-foote words,
Fight over *Yorke,* and *Lancasters* long jarres:
And in the tyring-house bring wounds, to scarres.
He rather prayes, you will be pleas'd to see
One such, to day, as other playes should be.
Where neither *Chorus* wafts you ore the seas;
Nor creaking throne comes downe, the boyes to please;
Nor nimble squibbe is seene, to make afear'd
The gentlewomen; nor roul'd bullet heard
To say, it thunders; nor tempestuous drumme
Rumbles, to tell you when the storme doth come;
But deedes, and language, such as men doe use:
And persons, such as *Comoedie* would chuse,
When she would shew an Image of the times,
And sport with humane follies, not with crimes.
Except, we make 'hem such by loving still

From *The Workes of Beniamin Jonson*...London. Printed by William Stansby. An⁰ D. 1616, folio, pp. 3–4 (Yale University, Beinecke Rare Book and Manuscript Library). The play was first acted at the Curtain Theater in 1598. It was published in quarto in 1601 and not again until the 1616 folio *Works.*

Our popular errors, when we know th'are ill.
I meane such errors, as you'll all confesse
By laughing at them, they deserve no lesse:
Which when you heartily doe, there's hope left, then,
You, that have so grac'd monsters, may like men.

In 1599, one year after his first "humor" play, Jonson produced
its companion, *Every Man Out of His Humour,* and illustrated the
principle that poets write their best criticism not always as an
annex to their best creations. Fastidious Brisk, Fungoso, and
Sordido, well-enough known figures in English literary history,
engage in a less shapely drama than the austere dialogue of Asper
(the conscience of the master satirist) and his friends Cordatus
(Prudent) and Mitis (Meek, of "no character" at all) in the justly
celebrated *Induction* to the play. Today the best-known idea of this
Induction is the definition of "humor" derived, in Elizabethan
psychological terms, from Medieval and ancient Galenic physiology:

> ...in every human body,
> The choler, melancholy, phlegm, and blood,
> By reason that they flow continually
> In some one part, and are not continent,
> Receive the name of humours. Now thus far
> It may, by metaphor, apply itself
> Unto the general disposition....

A recent commentator has argued, persuasively if perhaps not quite
irresistibly, that Jonson is trying to say that, not this natural sort
of "humor," but rather the foppish or conceited affectation of it,
which he alludes to briefly, is the true object of comic imitation.
Neither notion of "humor" seems actually the most important thing
in the *Induction.* This is rather the persistent, dry, and earnest
rasping of Asper on the theme of good sense, restraint, nature,
serious meaning, ugly truth in comedy.

INDUCTION

TO

Every Man Out of His Humour

[*1600–1616*]

After the second Sounding
GREX[1]
CORDATUS, ASPER, MITIS

MITIS.[2] Nay, my deare Asper, Stay your mind:
ASPER.   Away.
Who is so patient of this impious world,
That he can checke his spirit, or reine his tongue?
Or who hath such a dead unfeeling sense,
That heavens horrid thunders cannot wake?
To see the earth, crackt with the weight of sinne,
Hell gaping under us, and o're our heads
Blacke rav'nous ruine, with her saile-stretcht wings,
Ready to sinke us downe, and cover us.
Who can behold such prodigies as these,
And have his lips seal'd up? not I: my soule
Was never ground into such oyly colours,
To flatter vice and daube iniquitie:
But (with an armed, and resolved hand)
Ile strip the ragged follies of the time,
Naked, as at their birth:
CORDATUS.   (Be not too bold.
  You trouble me)
    ASPER.   and with a whip of steele,

From the 1616 folio, pp. 81–87. The text differs in minor ways from three quarto editions which appeared in 1600. The play was first acted in 1599 at the Globe Theater.

[1] Chorus.

[2] Names of speakers are abbreviated throughout the folio text but are here expanded.

26

Print wounding lashes in their yron ribs.
I feare no mood stampt in a private brow,
When I am pleas'd t'unmaske a publicke vice.
I feare no strumpets drugs, nor ruffians stab,
Should I detect their hatefull luxuries;
No brokers, usureres, or lawyers gripe,
Were I dispos'd to say, they're all corrupt.
I feare no courtiers frowne, should I applaud
The easie flexure of his supple hammes.
Tut, these are so innate, and popular,
That drunken custome would not shame to laugh
(In scorne) at him, that should but dare to taxe 'hem.
And yet, not one of these but knowes his workes,
Knowes what damnation is, the devill, and hell,
Yet, howerly they persist, grow ranke in sinne,
Puffing their soules away in perj'rous aire,
To cherish their extortion, pride, or lusts.

MITIS. Forbeare, good Asper, be not like your name.

ASPER. O, but to such, whose faces are all zeale,
And (with the words of Hercules) invade
Such crimes as these! that will not smell of sinne,
But seeme as they were made of Sanctitie!
Religion in their garments, and their haire
Cut shorter than their eye-browes![3] when the conscience
Is vaster than the Ocean, and devoures
More wretches than the Counters.[4]

MITIS.   Gentle Asper,
Containe your spirit in more stricter bounds,
And be not thus transported with the violence
Of your strong thoughts.

CORDATUS. Unlesse your breath had power
To melt the world, and mould it new againe,
It is in vaine, to spend it in these moods.

Here hee makes adresse to the People.

ASPER. I not observ'd this thronged round till now.
Gracious, and kind spectators, you are welcome,
Apollo, and the Muses feast your eyes

---

[3] Puritans, Roundheads. Cf. the description of false Stoics in Juvenal's *Satire* XIII.121.

[4] Debtor's prisons. The spelling was later "Compter."

With gracefull objects, and may our Minerva
Answere your hopes, unto their largest straine.
Yet here, mistake me not, judicious friends.
I doe not this, to begge your patience,
Or servilely to fawne on your applause,
Like some drie braine, despairing in his merit:
Let me be censur'd, by th'austerest brow,
Where I want arte, or judgement, taxe me freely:
Let envious Censors with their broadest eyes
Looke through and through me; I pursue no favour.
Onely vouchsafe me your attentions,
And I will give you musicke worth your eares.
O, how I hate the monstrousnesse of time,
Where every servile imitating spirit,
(Plagu'd with an itching leprosie of wit)
In a meere halting fury, strives to fling
His ulc'rous body in the *Thespian* spring,
And streight leap's forth a Poet! But as lame
As Vulcan, or the founder of Cripple-gate.[5]

MITIS. In faith, this Humour will come ill to some,
You will be thought to be too peremptory.

ASPER. This Humour? good; and why this Humour, Mitis?
Nay doe not turne, but answere.

MITIS.   Answere? what?

ASPER. I will not stirre your patience, pardon me,
I urg'd it for some reasons, and the rather
To give these ignorant well-spoken dayes,
Some taste of their abuse of this word Humour.

CORDATUS. O doe not let your purpose fall, good Asper,
It cannot but arrive most acceptable,
Chiefly to such, as have the happinesse,
Daily to see how the poore innocent word
Is rackt, and tortur'd.

MITIS.   I; I pray you proceede.

ASPER. Ha? what? what is't?

CORDATUS.   For the abuse of Humour.

ASPER. O, I crave pardon, I had lost my thoughts.
Why Humour (as 'tis *ens*[6]) we thus define it

---

[5] One of the gates of the city of London, in Jonson's time thought to have been
so named from the number of cripples that had once gathered there.
[6] A term of Medieval philosophy, meaning "entity," "thing," "substance."

To be a quality of aire or water,
And in it selfe holds these two properties,
Moisture and fluxure: As, for demonstration,
Powre water on this floore, 'twill wet and runne:
Likewise the aire (forc't through a horne or trumpet)
Flowes instantly away, and leaves behind
A kind of dew; and hence we doe conclude,
That whatsoe're hath fluxure, and humiditie,
As wanting power to containe it selfe,
Is Humour: so in every humane body
The choller, melancholy, flegme, and bloud,
By reason that they flow continually
In some one part, and are not continent,
Receive the name of Humours. Now thus farre
It may, by *Metaphore,* apply it selfe
Unto the generall disposition:
As when some one peculiar quality
Doth so possesse a man, that it doth draw
All his affects, his spirits, and his powers,
In their confluctions, all to runne one way,
This may be truly said to be a Humour.
But that a Rooke,[7] in wearing a pyed feather,
The cable hat-band, or the three-pild ruffe,
A yard of shoe-tie, or the *Switzers* knot
On his *French* garters, should affect a Humour!
O, 'tis more then most ridiculous.
CORDATUS. He speakes pure truth: now if an Idiot
  Have but an apish, or phantasticke straine,
  It is his Humour.
ASPER.   Well I will scourge those Apes;
  And to these courteous eyes oppose a mirrour,
  As large as is the stage, whereon we act:
  Where they shall see the times deformity
  Anatomiz'd in every nerve, and sinnew,
  With constant courage, and contempt of feare.
MITIS. Asper (I urge it as your friend) take heed,
  The dayes are dangerous, full of exception,
  And men are growne impatient of reproofe.

---

7 A gull, a simpleton. See *Every Man in His Humour,* I.v: "Hang him, rooke,
he! why, he has no more judgement than a malt-horse!"

ASPER. Ha, ha:
  You might as well have told me, yond' is heaven,
  This earth, these men; and all had mov'd alike.
  Doe not I know the times condition?
  Yes Mitis, and their soules, and who they be
  That either will, or can except against me.
  None, but a sort of fooles, so sicke in taste,
  That they contemne all phisicke of the mind,
  And like gald camels kicke at every touch.
  Good men, and vertuous spirits, that lothe their vices,
  Will cherish my free labours, love my lines,
  And with the fervour of their shining grace,
  Make my braine fruitfull to bring forth more objects,
  Worthy their serious, and intentive eyes.
  But why enforce I this? as fainting? no.
  If any here chance to behold himselfe,
  Let him not dare to challenge me of wrong,
  For, if he shame to have his follies knowne,
  First he should shame to act 'hem: my strict hand
  Was made to ceaze on vice, and with a gripe
  Squeeze out the humour of such spongie soules,
  As licke up every idle vanitie.
CORDATUS. Why this is right *Furor Poeticus!*
  Kind gentlemen, we hope your patience
  Will yet conceive the best, or entertaine
  This supposition, that a mad-man speakes.
ASPER. What? are you ready there? Mitis sit downe:
  And my Cordatus. Sound hough, and begin.
  I leave you two, as censors, to sit here:
  Observe what I present, and liberally
  Speake your opinions, upon every *Scene,*
  As it shall passe the view of these spectators.
  Nay, now, y'are tedious Sirs, for shame begin.
  And Mitis, note me, if in all this front,
  You can espy a gallant of this marke,
  Who (to be thought one of the judicious)
  Sits with his armes thus wreath'd, his hat pull'd here,
  Cryes meaw, and nods, then shakes his empty head,
  Will shew more several motions in his face,

Then the new *London, Rome,* or *Niniveh,*[8]
And (now and then) breakes a drie bisquet jest,
Which that it may more easily be chew'd,
He steeps in his owne laughter.
CORDATUS.   Why? will that
Make it be sooner swallow'd?
ASPER.   O, assure you.
Or if it did not, yet as Horace sings,
Ieiunus raro stomachus vulgaria temnit,[9]
"Meane cates are welcome still to hungry guests."
CORDATUS. 'Tis true, but why should we observe 'hem, Asper?
ASPER. O I would know 'hem, for in such assemblies,
Th'are more infectious then the pestilence:
And therefore I would give them pills to purge,
And make 'hem fit for faire societies.
How monstrous, and detested is't to see
A fellow, that has neither arte, nor braine,
Sit like an Aristarchus,[10] or starke-asse,
Taking mens lines, with a tabacco face,
In snuffe, still spitting, using his wryed lookes
(In nature of a vice) to wrest, and turne
The good aspect of those that shall sit neere him,
From what they doe behold! O, 'tis most vile.
MITIS. Nay, Asper.
ASPER.   Peace, Mitis, I doe know your thought.
You'le say, your guests here will except at this:
Pish, you are too timorous, and full of doubt.
Then, he, a patient, shall reject all physicke,
'Cause the physicion tels him, you are sicke:
Or, if I say, That he is vicious,
You will not heare of vertue. Come, y'are fond.
Shall I be so extravagant to thinke,
That happy judgements, and composed spirits,
Will challenge me for taxing such as these?
I am asham'd.

---

8 Puppet shows, or, as they were styled then, "motions," were in great vogue.
9 *Satires,* II.ii.38.
10 Aristarchus of Samothrace, head of the Alexandrian Library from c. 180 to
c. 145 B.C., and "the founder of scientific scholarship."

CORDATUS.   Nay, but good pardon us:
We must not beare this peremptorie saile,
But use our best endevours how to please.
ASPER. Why, therein I commend your carefull thoughts,
And I will mixe with you in industrie
To please, but whom? attentive auditors,
Such as will joyne their profit with their pleasure,
And come to feed their understanding parts:
For these, Ile prodigally spend my selfe,
And speake away my spirit into ayre;
For these, Ile melt my braine into invention,
Coine new conceits, and hang my richest words
As polisht jewels in their bounteous eares.
But stay, I loose my selfe, and wrong their patience;
If I dwell here, they'le not begin, I see:
Friends sit you still, and entertaine this troupe
With some familiar, and by-conference.
Ile haste them sound. Now gentlemen, I goe
To turne an actor, and a Humorist,
Where (ere I doe resume my present person)
We hope to make the circles of your eyes
Flow with distilled laughter: if we faile,
We must impute it to this onely chance,
"Arte hath an enemy cal'd *Ignorance."*
CORDATUS. How doe you like his spirit, Mitis?
MITIS. I should like it much better, if he were lesse confident.
CORDATUS. Why, doe you suspect his merit?
MITIS. No, but I feare this will procure him much envie.
CORDATUS. O, that sets the stronger seale on his desert, if he had no
enemies, I should esteeme his fortunes most wretched at this instant.
MITIS. You have seene his play, Cordatus? pray you, how is't?
CORDATUS. Faith sir, I must refraine to judge; only this I can say
of it, 'tis strange, and of a particular kind by it selfe, somewhat
like *Vetus Comoedia*[11]*:* a worke that hath bounteously pleased me,
how it will answere the generall expectation, I know not.
MITIS. Does he observe all the lawes of *Comedie* in it?
CORDATUS. What lawes meane you?
MITIS. Why, the equall division of it into *Acts,* and *Scenes,* according
to the *Terentian* manner, his true number of Actors; the furnishing

---

[11] Old Comedy. See Introduction. pp. 4, 10.

of the *Scene* with Grex, or Chorus, and that the whole Argument
fall within compasse of a dayes businesse.

CORDATUS. O no, these are too nice observations.

MITIS. They are such as must be received, by your favour, or it cannot
be authentique.

CORDATUS. Troth, I can discerne no such necessity.

MITIS. No?

CORDATUS. No, I assure you, Signior. If those lawes you speake of,
had beene delivered us, *ab initio,* and in their present vertue and
perfection, there had beene some reason of obeying their powers:
but 'tis extant, that that which we call *Comoedia,* was at first
nothing but a simple, and continued *Song,* sung by one only person,
till Susario invented a second, after him Epicharmus a third;
Phormus, and Chionides devised to have foure Actors, with a
Prologue and *Chorus;* to which Cratinus (long after) added a fift,
and sixt; Eupolis more; Aristophanes more then they[12]: every man
in the dignitie of his spirit and judgement, supplyed some-thing.
And (though that in him this kinde of *Poeme* appeared absolute,
and fully perfected) yet how is the face of it chang'd since, in
Menander, Philemon, Cecilius, Plautus,[13] and the rest; who have
utterly excluded the *Chorus,* altered the property of the persons,
their names, and natures, and augmented it with all liberty, according to the elegancie and disposition of those times, wherein they
wrote? I see not then, but we should enjoy the same licence, or

---

12 Susarion, fl. 581–560 B.C., perhaps a mythical figure, said to be the inventor
of the comic chorus and thus the founder of Attic comedy. Epicharmus, fl. 490–
470, at Syracuse. Aristotle (*Poetics,* III, V) credits him with having invented
comedy or comic plot. Surviving fragments of his work indicate that he used a
third character. Phormus of Syracuse, named by an annotator of Aristotle (*Poetics,*
V), with Epicharmus, as an inventor of plot. Chionides, fl. 486; Aristotle implies
that (along with Magnes) he was the earliest to compose comedy at Athens.
Cratinus and Eupolis were early contemporaries of Aristophanes. (See Introduction, p. 4.) Jonson echoes Renaissance constructions of the history of Greek
comedy which go beyond the evidence. See A. W. Pickard-Cambridge, *Dithyramb,
Tragedy, and Comedy,* 2d ed., revised by T. L. Webster (Oxford, 1962); Gerald
Else, *Aristotle's Poetics: The Argument* (Cambridge, Mass., 1957), pp. 110–13, 183,
197–98; Katherine Lever, *The Art of Greek Comedy* (London, 1956), pp. 52–53,
71; Gilbert Norwood, *Greek Comedy* (London, 1931), pp. 5, 15, 178–79. The
slender documents concerning Susarion, Chionides, Cratinus, and Eupolis are
assembled by John Maxwell Edmonds, *The Fragments of Attic Comedy* (Leiden,
1957–1961), I, 2–5, 15–23, 310–17.

13 For Menander and Plautus, see Introduction, pp. 5–6. Philemon, c. 361–
263 B.C., a prolific Athenian writer of New Comedy. Caecilius Statius, c. 219–c. 166,
Roman comic writer, between Plautus and Terence. A number of his titles are
identical with those of works by Menander.

free power, to illustrate and heighten our invention as they did; and not bee tyed to those strict and regular formes, which the nicenesse of a few (who are nothing but forme) would thrust upon us.

MITIS. Well, we will not dispute of this now: but what's his *Scene?*

CORDATUS. Marry, *Insula Fortunata*, Sir.

MITIS. O, the fortunate Iland? masse, he has bound himselfe to a strict law there.

CORDATUS. Why so?

MITIS. He cannot lightly alter the *Scene,* without crossing the seas.

CORDATUS. He needs not, having a whole Iland to run through, I thinke.

MITIS. No? how comes it then, that in some one Play we see so many seas, countries, and kingdomes, past over with such admirable dexteritie?

CORDATUS. O, that but shewes how well the Authors can travaile in their vocation, and out-run the apprehension of their auditorie. But leaving this, I would they would begin once: this protraction is able to sowre the best-settled patience in the Theatre.

MITIS. They have answered your wish Sir: they sound.

CORDATUS. O, here comes the *Prologue*: Now sir! if you had staid a little longer, I meant to have spoke your prologue for you, I faith.

Jonson's major comedies in demonstration of the theme of his trenchant *Induction* followed at intervals: *Volpone, or the Fox* (1606), *Epicoene, or the Silent Woman* (1609), *The Alchemist* (1610), *Bartholomew Fair* (1614). At some period of his middle years, perhaps about 1623, when he may have been a surrogate professor of rhetoric at the College newly founded by Sir Thomas Gresham, he translated from various ancient and Renaissance Latin sources certain passages of rhetorical and poetic theory which form a large part of his major prose work, the commonplace book entitled *Timber or Discoveries Made Upon Men and Matter,* published in Volume II of the posthumous folio edition of Jonson's *Works,* 1640–1641.[1] A passage on comedy (or on comic *poetry*), derived in part from a Dutch Latinist Daniel Heinsius—and as a result

---

[1] Our quotation follows the Bodley Head Quartos reprint from a British Museum copy of the folio *Workes,* edited by G. B. Harrison (London, 1923–1930): *Ben Jonson, Discoveries, 1641. Conversations with William Drummond of Hawthornden, 1619,* pp. 99–101.

embodying a peculiar misinterpretation of Aristotle's *Poetics*—must seem to a modern student a curious extreme of ethical asperity and anticomic severity. It makes an instructive backdrop for a number of more gentlemanly statements against laughter that were to be made during the age of refinement that was ahead—by Swift, for instance, by Pope, by Lord Chesterfield.[2]

Horace did so highly esteeme *Terence* his Comedies, as he ascribes the Art in Comedie to him alone, among the *Latines*, and joynes him with *Menander*.[3]

Now, let us see what may be said for either, to defend *Horace* his judgement to posterity; and not wholly to condemne *Plautus*.[4]

The parts of a Comedie are the same with a *Tragedie*, and the end is partly the same. For, they both delight, and teach; the *Comicks* are call'd διδάσκαλοι,[5] of the *Greekes*; no lesse then the *Tragicks*.

Nor, is the moving of laughter alwaies the end of *Comedy*, that is rather a fowling for the peoples delight, or their fooling. For, as *Aristotle* saies rightly, the moving of laughter is a fault in Comedie, a kind of turpitude, that depraves some part of a mans nature without a disease.[6] As a wry face without paine moves laughter, or a deformed vizard, or a rude Clowne, drest in a Ladies habit, and using her actions, wee dislike, and scorne such representations; which made the ancient Philosophers ever thinke laughter unfitting in a wise man. And this induc'd *Plato* to esteeme of *Homer*, as a sacrilegious Person; because he[7] presented the *Gods* sometimes laughing.[8] As, also it is divinely said of *Aristotle*, that to seeme ridiculous is a part of dishonesty, and foolish.[9]

So that, what either in the words, or Sense of an Author, or in the language, or Actions of men, is awry, or depraved, doth strangely stirre meane affections, and provoke for the most part to laughter. And therfore it was cleare that all insolent, and obscene speaches, jest upon the best men; injuries to particular persons; perverse, and sinister Sayings (and the rather unexpected) in the old Comedy did move laughter;

---

2 See below pp. 149–50.

3 *Epistles* II.i (*To Augustus*), 56–59.

4 Horace considered Plautus coarse in wit and metrically incorrect (*Ars Poetica*, 270–74). Cf. Introduction, p. 14. In a previous paragraph (p. 98) Jonson has noted that the Dutch scholar Daniel Heinsius, in his *De Satyra Horatiana* (appended to his edition of Horace, 1612) defends the opinion of Horace against many who object. Jonson's interest in the moral efficacy of lively drama seems to counsel him, though he feels some uneasiness about dissenting from Horace, to prefer the "Oeconomy" of Plautus to Terence's "sticking in of sentences" (p. 70).

5 *Teachers*, or *teaching*.

6 *Poetics* V. See Introduction, p. 9.

7 Corrected by Harrison from a misprint, "the," in the folio.

8 *Republic* III.388E–389A. Cf. X.606C–607A.

9 *Politics* VII.17. Jonson seems to have this passage in mind, though interpreting freely.

especially, where it did imitate any dishonesty; and scurrility came
forth in the place of wit: which who understands the nature and
Genius of laughter, cannot but perfectly know.

Of which *Aristophanes* affords an ample harvest, having not only
out, gone[10] *Plautus*, or any other in that kinde; but express'd all the
moods, and figures, of what is ridiculous, oddly. In short, as Vinegar is
not accounted good, untill the wine be corrupted: so jests that are
true and naturall, seldome raise laughter, with the beast, the multitude.
They love nothing, that is right, and proper. The farther it runs from
reason, or possibility with them, the better it is.

What could have made them laugh, like to see *Socrates* presented,
that Example of all good life, honesty, and vertue, to have him hoisted
up with a Pullie, and there play the Philosopher, in a basquet. Measure,
how many foote a Flea could skip *Geometrically*, by a just Scale, and
edifie the people from the ingine.[11] This was *Theatricall* wit, right
Stage-jesting, and relishing a Play-house, invented for scorne, and
laughter; whereas, if it had favour'd of equity, truth, perspicuity, and
Candor, to have tasten[12] a wise, or a learned Palate, spit it out
presantly; this is bitter and profitable, this instructs, and would informe
us: what neede wee know any thing, that are nobly borne, more then
a Horse-race, or a hunting-match, our day to breake with Citizens, and
such innate mysteries.

This is truly leaping from the Stage, to the Tumbrell againe, reduc-
ing all witt to the Originall Dungcart.

Did Jonson wish the audience to laugh at his own plays?[13] Most
likely he did. Some of them, and notably *Every Man in His Humour,
Volpone*, and *The Alchemist*, have been great plays of the London
stage, active until well toward the end of the eighteenth century.
It is difficult to conceive a competent comedy at which people do
not laugh. If we will study Jonson's topicalities, the jargon and
cant spoken by his London characters, closely enough, his plays
can still seem vastly and explosively funny. In that light the dour
assertion of the passage in *Timber* takes on a special lustre and
interest.

> All gall and copperas from his ink he draineth,
> Only a little salt remaineth,
> Wherewith he'll rub your cheeks, till red with laughter,

---

10 *Outgone*, i.e., *outdone*.
11 In *The Clouds* of Aristophanes.
12 *Pleased*.
13 Alvin B. Kernan, *The Plot of Satire* (New Haven, 1965), pp. 121–42, studies
Jonson's *Volpone*, as a satire of Renaissance materialism, in terms that suggest at
least that it is irrelevant for a critic to worry about whether we are expected to
laugh.

They shall look fresh a week after.[14]

We hope to make the circles of your eyes
Flow with distilled laughter.[15]

---

[14] Last lines of the Prologue to *Volpone*. The first edition of *Volpone* (1607) carries Jonson's curiously turgid prose Dedicatory Epistle to the "most reverenced" sister universities of Oxford and Cambridge, deploring the bawdy, blasphemous, and slanderous character of comic "stage poetry" in that day, indignantly asserting his own innocence and pure didactic aim, and defending the punishment of vice at the end of the play.

[15] Induction to *Every Man Out of His Humour* (1599); reprinted in this volume, pp. 26–34.

JOHN DRYDEN

[1631–1700]

Moving along easily in the spirit of courtly conversation that in 1661 succeeded the dour Protectorate, the still youthful celebrator of Justice Restored[1] (1660) and a Marvelous Year of fire and battle[2] (1667) announced himself a theorist of drama before he had done very much to prove himself an important dramatist. To the end of his long career, his conversationally adept theoretical prefaces, dedications, and defenses have a degree of distinction which he approached or achieved as a playwright perhaps only in one moment of classically poised tragedy, *All for Love* (1678), which he extracted and purified from the global and dolphin-like delights of Shakespeare's *Antony and Cleopatra*. His earliest measured statement about comedy appears not in the *Preface* and *Epilogue* (both of 1671), which we present below, but in one section of his dialogue *Essay of Dramatic Poesy*, written during his rural retirement from the plague in 1665 or 1666 and published at London in the spring of 1668, just as he assumed the title of Poet Laureate. The critical themes of this leisurely and ample essay are all the important ones arising in the late phases of the Renaissance transition from classic to native drama: Ancients vs. Moderns, the "Last Age" in England (before the Puritan Flood) and the "Present"; wit, conceits, versification, "verisimility," nature, passions, humors, the "just," and the "lively"—all these qualities managed by the poet for the "instruction and delight" of mankind.

Dryden's anagrammatic representative, Neander (the New Man),[3] shows a discreet respect for the prevalent French classical rules, especially as these appear in a version formulated with some freedom by

---

[1] Dryden's poem *Astraea Redux* greeted the Restoration of the Stuart monarch Charles II.

[2] Dryden's heroic poem in rhymed quatrains, *Annus Mirabilis*, narrates three naval battles fought against the Dutch, August 1665–July 1666, and the Great Fire of London, September 2–7, 1666.

[3] He debates with three interlocutors: Crites (critic loyal to the Greek and Roman models), Eugenius (modernist, yet oriented still by classical rules), and Lisideius (representative of the new French classicism).

the master tragedian Pierre Corneille in a recent collected edition of his works.[4] At the same time, and more significantly, Neander makes himself a thoughtful spokesman for the irregular gusto and the boyish physical energies of the English native drama. At the right moment, he is speaking out as an Englishman. ("Whether custom has so insinuated itself into our countrymen, or nature has so formed them to fierceness, I know not; but they will scarcely suffer combats and other objects of horror to be taken from them."[5]) Frenchmen are more frivolous and airy and need to be sobered by the declamatory speeches of their theater. The English, more sullen, need their own livelier kinds of entertainment.

Neander, after a crescendo series of dicta upon the great English writers of the last age (Beaumont and Fletcher, gentlemen and wits in repartee; Jonson, "learned and judicious"; Shakespeare, "the largest and most comprehensive soul"[6]—"I admire [Jonson], but I love Shakespeare"), proceeds to demonstrate a special concern for comedy as he settles into a considered *Examen* of what is probably the most classically regular of all the comedies of Ben Jonson, *Epicoene or the Silent Woman*. The comic action of this play takes place in only two London houses (actually four houses and a lane), all within a few hours (between the late rising of gallants and an afternoon dinner party), and, climactically, on a "signal and long-expected day." The main character, or "humour," Morose, a rich old uncle who cannot tolerate people or noise, is both delightful and plausible (and besides, Jonson had *actually* known such a man—here the classic universal wobbles). But the "intrigue" (the marrying of the Morose uncle to a Silent Woman who at the uproariously managed wedding party turns out to be a chatterbox who, after due torture of Morose, is next discovered to be a boy—whereby the witty Sir Dauphine releases his uncle and is rewarded with a fortune), the "intrigue!" says Neander, is "the greatest and most noble of any pure unmixt comedy in any language."[7] Echoes of Jonson and Sidney, and perhaps of Plato, are heard in Neander's dicta that the humorous comic object (a specimen of "nature" displayed) begets in the audience "malicious pleasure," which is "essential," but that the laughter which testifies to this pleasure is itself "accidental," and presumably dispensable.

Dryden himself had already tried his hand at a few somewhat less

---

4 The three volumes of Corneille's *Oeuvres* appearing in 1660 are equipped with three introductory essays on the drama and with an *Examen* or critical defense of each play.

5 *Essays of John Dryden,* ed. W. P. Ker (Oxford, 1926), I, 74.

6 Ker, I, 79. "Undoubtedly a larger soul of poesy than ever any of our nation" (*Dedication* of *The Rival Ladies, 1664,* Ker, I, 6).

7 Ker, I, 86.

than "noble" comic intrigues.[8] Within a few months of publishing his
appreciation of Jonson in the *Essay of Dramatic Poesy,* he had on the
stage at the King's Theater a medley of "humour," repartee, and
farcical intrigue, derived from a Spanish source, through the French of
Thomas Corneille, and entitled *An Evening's Love or the Mock Astrologer.* When he published this play in 1671, he prefaced it with an
essay in defense of comedy and of what he conceived as his own
characteristic style of inventive or "witty" writing, something which
he now wished to distinguish from the mere "judgment" or observant
realism of the Jonsonian humor comedy—and at the same time, of
course, from the unintelligent slapstick of French farce. He professed
to "approve most" a "mixed way of Comedy," both "wit and humour."
At the same time he was willing to yield the palm for humor to
Jonson. "I pretend not that I can write humour."[9] When he published
this essay, he may have been already at work on his highly successful
fusion of romance and high comedy, *Marriage à la Mode,* acted in
1672, published in 1673—a play which is perhaps a better illustration
of his theories. George Etherege's *Comical Revenge or Love in a
Tub* (acted in 1664), usually seen as the beginning of Restoration
Comedy of Manners, has, like Dryden's *Marriage à la Mode,* serious
parts in heroic couplets, with the comic and realistic parts in prose.

The new style of witty comedy had something to do with a new
breed of audience and authors centering in the gentlemanly and refined
life—the "conversation"—of the Restored Royal Court. This kind of
life and cultural milieu had close affinities also for another part of
the late Renaissance imagination—the stage spectacle of the "heroic"
—which was also the exotic and the romantic, as in Sir William
D'Avenant's *Siege of Rhodes,* an opera produced even during the dreary
days of the Protectorate. Dryden was deeply smitten with this mode
at about the same time that he was experimenting with his comedies.
Thus the verse *Epilogue* which he wrote for his two-part rhymed
heroic play *The Conquest of Granada* (acted in 1670, published 1671)
sounds much as if it had been written in defense also of the new kind
of comedy. This *Epilogue,* as an argument, needed bolstering. When
the play was published, Dryden appended a further essay in prose, a
Defence of the Epilogue, in which his public learned, no doubt
immensely to their satisfaction, that "Gentlemen" would now be
"entertained with the follies of each other."[10]

---

[8] His first play, *The Wild Gallant,* acted in 1663, was published in 1669. His
Rival Ladies, a Tragi-Comedy was acted and published in 1664. His *Sir Martin
Mar-all, or the Feign'd Innocence; a Comedy,* was published in 1668.

[9] Ker, I, 137, 139.

[10] Ker, I, 176–77. With an accent less on gentlemanliness, more on folly, Molière
wrote in his *Impromptu de Versailles* (1663; see below, p. 58): "A marquis now-

Both the older and the newer kinds of comedy professed to ridicule the weaker parts of the human makeup. Yet these were indeed conceived as parts of a makeup or *nature*—perhaps near its center—rather than merely accidents or appendages. The most laughable figures of the older or Jonsonian comedy of "humors" were all eccentrics and isolationists engaged in a kind of free-lance war with society.[11] Yet they did show a kind of universality of character in their very isolation; otherwise they would hardly have satisfied the classic norm— would hardly in fact have been intelligible or interesting. Dryden noticed twice, once in the *Essay of Dramatic Poesy*[12] and once later in a "Grounds of Criticism in Tragedy" prefixed to his improved version of Shakespeare's *Troilus and Criseyde* (1679),[13] the difficulty of explaining how such a "miscellany of humours" as Falstaff can be reconciled to the classical canon of consistency in character. In the *Essay of Dramatic Poesy* he had taken a rather arbitrary stance in asserting the superior *naturalness* of the simple "humor," that happily "ridiculous extravagance of conversation, wherein one man differs from all others."[14] Still he did apparently conceive the English "humor" as a kind of "concrete universal," a form of dramatic characterization that had both particularity and universal nature and was hence much more satisfactory than either the unnatural and obscene *geloion* of the Old Comedy or the mere stereotyped *ēthos* of the New Comedy. The kind of wit comedy now at the moment of taking possession of the London stage—otherwise called comedy of "manners" (*Comédie des Moeurs*)—of course had to show the same classic quality of universality and intelligibility. And for this effect it had one advantage over the comedy of humors. Wit comedy exploited another, and in one way more obvious, kind of universal—precisely in such foibles as were epidemic, or universal, in society itself or the social set. Comedy of wit or manners ridiculed these foibles precisely as they were social foibles. Braggadocio and stinginess are characteristically individualist or "humors" faults. Scandal and adultery are social vices *par excellence*. They cannot be committed in surly retirement or isolated vainglory.

Another important thing to be noticed is that the social set is high

a-days is the funny man of a play; just as in all the old comedies there was always a clownish valet to make the audience laugh, so in all our plays now, there must always be a ridiculous marquis. . . ."

[11] Jonson had achieved bizarre, nightmarish effects by marshaling his humors in squads or thematic groups—such as Voltore, Corbaccio, and Corvino in *Volpone*.

[12] Ker, I, 85.

[13] Ker, I, 215.

[14] Ker, I, 84; cf. I, 86: "Some extravagant habit, passion, or affection, particular . . .to some one person, by the oddness of which, he is immediately distinguished from the rest of men. . . ."

and sophisticated; its weaknesses may be graver than the "humors" of the humbler classes, yet are not so grossly and publicly inept. And hence for Dryden, both in his own comedy and in his prefaces, arises a complication concerning folly and the critique of folly which is a counterpart, on a higher social plane, of Aristotle's complication concerning low targets and critical wit. The low humorist, like Jonson, may be said to criticize his objects, in a sense, just by portraying them—even though close portrayal may run the risk of participation. Jonson's humorous portrayal, the vigorous and salty rubbing which he gave the city, was itself a kind of wit, rising superior to his objects. (Dryden goes so far as to say that even "folly itself, well represented, is wit in a larger signification.") But how if the objects of criticism themselves are not simply foolish but are elegant and witty gentlemen? ("Gentlemen will now be entertained with the follies of each other.") Wit, says Dryden, ought to be appropriate to the character who utters it.[15] And hence a second paradox—a counterpart of the first—wit itself becomes a kind of humor. To this we might add the further reflection: One witty character may be able to see the "humor" fault (or folly) of another, but not his own, which, however, the other can see. Wits tend to show each other up. A confrontation of reciprocally humorous wits seems to be a requirement of the new kind of comedy.

Perhaps the most satisfactory, mordant, and somberly funny of all the versions of that comedy (and an international model for much that followed) was achieved not in England but in France, in 1666, when Molière produced his *Misanthrope*—in which the morose, misanthropic, solitary and retiring protagonist is the legitimate target of the giddy feminine society laughter but is also its most true and telling critic.

---

[15] *Defence of the Epilogue* (Ker, I, 172). "I knew a poet...who, being too witty himself, could draw nothing but wits in a comedy of his; even his fools were infected with the disease of their author. They overflowed with smart reparties, and were only distinguished from the intended wits by being called coxcombs, though they deserved not so scandalous a name" (Dryden, *A Parallel of Poetry and Painting*, 1695, in Ker, II, 142).

PREFACE

TO

An Evening's Love

or

The Mock-Astrologer

[*1671*]

I had thought, Reader, in this Preface to have written somewhat concerning the difference betwixt the Plays of our age, and those of our Predecessors, on the *English* Stage: to have shown in what parts of Dramatique Poesie we were excell'd by *Ben. Jonson,* I mean, Humour, and Contrivance of Comedy; and in what we may justly claim precedence of *Shakespeare* and *Fletcher,* namely in Heroic Plays: but this design I have wav'd on second considerations; at least deferr'd it till I publish the Conquest of *Granada,* where the Discourse will be more proper.[1] I had also prepar'd to Treat of the improvement of our Language since *Fletcher's* and *Jonson's* days,[2] and consequently of our refining the Courtship, Raillery, and Conversation of Plays: but as I am willing to decline that envy which I shou'd draw on my self from some old opiniatre[3] Judges of the Stage; so likewise I am prest

---

From the first edition: *An Evening's Love, Or The Mock-Astrologer*...[London] In the Savoy, Printed by T. N. for Henry Herringman...1671. First acted in 1668. Help with the annotation has been found in W. P. Ker, ed., *Essays of John Dryden* (Oxford, 1926), I, 307–8; and George Watson, ed., *Of Dramatic Poesy and Other Critical Essays* (London, 1962), I, 144–55.

[1] Dryden's *Of Heroic Plays, An Essay,* prefixed to his two-part heroic play *The Conquest of Granada,* 1672, may be consulted in W. P. Ker's edition of the *Essays,* I, 148–59.

[2] Dryden's *Epilogue To the Second Part of "The Conquest of Granada"* is reprinted in this volume. His prose *Defence of the Epilogue,* an Appendix to *The Conquest of Granada,* 1672, carries out his plan of expounding the improvement of the English language since the days of Jonson and Fletcher—and Shakespeare. See Ker, I, 164–72.

[3] A Gallicism, meaning *stubborn.*

in time so much that I have not leisure, at present, to go thorough with it. Neither, indeed, do I value a reputation gain'd from Comedy, so far as to concern my self about it any more than I needs must in my own defence: for I think it, in its own nature, inferior to all sorts of Dramatic writing. Low Comedy especially requires, on the Writers part, much of conversation with the vulgar, and much of ill nature in the observation of their Follies. But let all Men please themselves according to their several tastes: that which is not pleasant to me, may be to others who judge better. And, to prevent an accusation from my Enemies, I am sometimes ready to imagine that my disgust of Low Comedy proceeds not so much from my judgement as from my temper; which is the reason why I so seldom write it; and that when I succeed in it, (I mean so far as to please the Audience) yet I am nothing satisfy'd with what I have done; but am often vex'd to hear the people laugh, and clap, as they perpetually do, where I intended 'em no jest; while they let pass the better things without taking notice of them. Yet, even this confirms me in my opinion of slighting popular applause, and of contemning that approbation which those very people give, equally with me, to the Zany of a Mountebank; or to the appearance of an Antic on the Theatre, without wit on the Poets part, or any occasion of laughter from the Actor, besides the ridiculousness of his Habit and his Grimaces.

But I have descended before I was aware, from Comedy to Farce; which consists principally of Grimaces. That I admire not any Comedy equally with Tragedy, is, perhaps, from the sullenness of my humour: but that I detest those Farces, which are now the most frequent Entertainments of the Stage, I am sure I have reason on my side. Comedy consists, though of low persons, yet of natural actions, and characters; I mean such humours, adventures, and designs, as are to be found and met with in the World. Farce, on the other side, consists of forc'd humours, and unnatural events: Comedy presents us with the imperfections of humane nature. Farce entertains us with what is monstrous and chimerical: the one causes laughter in those who can judge of Men and Manners; by the lively representation of their folly or corruption; the other produces the same effect in those who can judge of neither, and that only by its extravagances. The first works on the judgement and fancy; the latter on the fancy only: There is more of satisfaction in the former kind of laughter, and in the latter more of scorn. But, how it happens, that an impossible adventure should cause our mirth, I cannot so easily imagine. Something there may be in the oddness of it, because on the Stage it is the common

effect of things unexpected to surprize us into a delight: and that is
to be ascrib'd to the strange appetite, as I may call it, of the fancy;
which, like that of a longing Woman, often runs out into the most
extravagant desires; and is better satisfy'd sometimes with Loam, or
with the Rinds of Trees, than with the wholesome nourishments of
life.[4] In short, there is the same difference betwixt Farce and Comedy,
as betwixt an Empirique[5] and a true Physitian: both of them may
attain their ends; but what the one performs by hazard, the other
does by skill. And as the Artist is often unsuccessful, while the Mountebank succeeds; so Farces more commonly take the people than
Comedies. For to write unnatural things, is the most probable way
of pleasing them, who understand not Nature. And a true Poet often
misses of applause, because he cannot debase himself to write so ill
as to please his Audience.

After all, it is to be acknowledg'd, that most of those Comedies,
which have been lately written, have been ally'd too much to Farce:
and this must of necessity fall out till we forbear the translation of
French Plays:[6] for their Poets wanting judgement to make, or to
maintain true characters, strive to cover their defects with ridiculous
Figures and Grimaces. While I say this, I accuse myself as well as
others: and this very Play would rise up in judgement against me, if
I would defend all things I have written to be natural: but I confess
I have given too much to the people in it, and am asham'd for them
as well as for my self, that I have pleas'd them at so cheap a rate:
not that there is any thing here which I would not defend to an ill-
natur'd judge: (for I despise their censures, who I am sure wou'd
write worse on the same subject:) but because I love to deal clearly
and plainly, and to speak of my own faults with more criticism, than
I would of another Poets; Yet I think it no vanity to say that this
Comedy has as much of entertainment in it as many others which
have been lately written: and, if I find my own errors in it, I am
able at the same time, to arraign all my Contemporaries for greater.
As I pretend not that I can write Humour, so none of them can
reasonably pretend to have written it as they ought. *Jonson* was the
only man of all Ages and Nations, who has perform'd it well; and
that but in three or four of his Comedies: the rest are but a *Crambe*

---

4 Folklore has it that pregnant women "long" to eat such substances.

5 An untrained practitioner in physic or surgery; a quack.

6 See Leo Hughes, "Attitudes of Some Restoration Dramatists toward Farce,"
Philological Quarterly, XIX (July 1940), 268–87; *A Century of English Farce*
(Princeton, N. J., 1956).

bis cocta;[7] the same humours a little vary'd and written worse: neither was it more allowable in him, than it is in our present Poets, to represent the follies of particular persons; of which many have accus'd him. *Parcere personis, dicere de vitiis,*[8] is the rule of Plays. And *Horace* tells you, that the old Comedy amongst the *Grecians* was silenc'd for the too great liberties of the Poets.

> *In vitium libertas excidit et vim*
> *Dignam lege regi: lex est accepta chorusque*
> *Turpiter obticuit, sublato jure nocendi.*[9]

Of which he gives you the reason in another place: where having given the precept.

> *Neve immunda crepent; ignominiosaque dicta:*

He immediately subjoyns,

> *Offenduntur enim, quibus est equus, et pater, et res.*[10]

But *Ben. Jonson* is to be admir'd for many excellencies; and can be tax'd with fewer failings than any *English* Poet. I know I have been accus'd as an enemy of his writings; but without any other reason than that I do not admire him blindly, and without looking into his imperfections. For why should he only be exempted from those frailties from which *Homer* and *Virgil* are not free? Or why should there be any *ipse dixit* in our Poetry, any more than there is in our Philosophy? I admire and applaud him where I ought: those who do more do but value themselves in their admiration of him: and by telling you they extoll *Ben. Jonson's* way, would insinuate to you that they can practice it. For my part I declare that I want judgement to imitate him: and should think it a great impudence in my self to attempt it. To make men appear pleasantly ridiculous on the Stage was, as I have said, his talent: and in this he needed not the acumen of Wit, but that of Judgement. For the Characters and Representations of folly are only the effects of observation; and observation is an effect of judgement. Some ingenious Men, for whom I have a particular esteem, have thought I have much injur'd *Ben. Jonson,* when I have not allow'd his Wit

---

7 *Cabbage twice cooked.* Juvenal, *Satires,* VII.154, has *crambe repetita.*

8 *To spare persons, speak of vices*—a Latin tag.

9 Horace, *Ars Poetica,* 282–84: "Freedom of speech reached a vicious excess, calling for legal restraint. A law was passed, and the chorus, deprived of its privilege of abuse, fell silent, in disgrace."

10 *Ars Poetica,* 247–48: "Nor let them get off anything indecent or scurrilous—at which gentlemen of birth and fortune will only take offence."

to be extraordinary: but they confound the notion of what is witty, with what is pleasant. That *Ben. Jonson's* Plays were pleasant, he must want reason who denies: But that pleasantness was not properly Wit, or the sharpness of Conceit; but the natural imitation of folly: which I confess to be excellent in its kind, but not to be of that kind which they pretend. Yet if we will believe *Quintilian* in his Chapter *de Movendo risu*, he gives his opinion of both in these following words, *Stulta reprehendere facillimum est; nam per se sunt ridicula: et a derisu non procul abest risus: sed rem urbanam facit aliqua ex nobis adjectio.*[11]

And some perhaps, wou'd be apt to say of *Jonson*, as it was said of *Demosthenes; Non displicuisse illi jocos, sed non contigisse,*[12] I will not deny but that I approve most the mixt way of Comedy; that which is neither all Wit, nor all Humour, but the result of both. Neither so little of Humour as *Fletcher*[13] shews, nor so little of Love and Wit, as *Jonson*. Neither all cheat, with which the best Plays of the one are fill'd, nor all adventure, which is the common practice of the other. I would have the characters well chosen, and kept distant from interfering with each other; which is more than *Fletcher* or *Shakespeare* did: but I would have more of the *Urbana, venusta, salsa, faceta* and the rest which *Quintilian* reckons up as the ornaments of Wit;[14] and these are extremely wanting in *Ben. Jonson*. As for repartie in particular, as it is the very soul of conversation, so it is the greatest grace of Comedy, where it is proper to the Characters: there may be much of acuteness in a thing well said; but there is more in a quick reply: *sunt, enim, longe venustiora omnia in respondendo quam in provocando.*[15] Of one thing I am sure, that no man ever will decry

11 *Institutio Oratoria*, VI.iii.71 ("On Making People Laugh"): "It is easy enough to lampoon folly, for folly is in itself ridiculous, and our feeling about it always verges on laughter. But to make a graceful joke requires some contribution from our own wit."

12 *Institutio Oratoria*, VI.iii.2: "Not that he disliked jokes, but none ever occurred to him."

13 John Fletcher (1579–1625), author of numerous comedies of romance and adventure (e.g. *The Humorous Lieutenant*, 1619, and *The Island Princess*, 1621) and collaborator with Francis Beaumont in such masterpieces of romantic drama as *Philaster or Love Lies a-Bleeding* and *A King and No King,* both acted in 1611. In his *Essay of Dramatic Poesy* (see above, p. 39) Dryden saw Beaumont and Fletcher as eminently the gentlemen and wits among the dramatists of the last age.

14 *Institutio Oratoria*, VI.iii.17–20: "wit" is something urbane, graceful, salty, elegant.

15 *Institutio Oratoria*, VI.iii.13: Dryden's phrase immediately preceding the Latin gives the gist of it.

Wit, but he who despairs of it himself; and who has no other quarrel
to it but that which the Fox had to the Grapes. Yet, as Mr. *Cowley,*
(who had a greater portion of it than any man I know) tells us in his
Character of Wit, rather than all Wit let there be none;[16] I think
there's no folly so great in any Poet of our Age as the superfluity and
waste of wit was in some of our Predecessors: particularly we may
say of *Fletcher* and *Shakespeare,* what was said of *Ovid, In omni ejus
ingenio, facilius quod rejici, quam quod adjici potest, invenies.*[17] The
contrary of which was true in *Virgil* and our incomparable *Jonson.*

Some enemies of Repartie have observ'd to us, that there is a great
latitude in their Characters, which are made to speak it: And that
it is easier to write wit than Humour; because in the characters of
Humour, the Poet is confin'd to make the Person speak what is only
proper to it. Whereas all kind of wit is proper in the Character of a
witty person. But by their favour, there are as different characters in
Wit as in Folly. Neither is all kind of wit proper in the mouth of
every ingenious person. A witty Coward, and a witty Brave must speak
differently. *Falstaff* and the *Liar,* speak not like *Don John* in the
Chances, and *Valentine* in *Wit without Money.*[18] And *Jonson's Truewit*
in the *Silent Woman,* is a Character different from all of them. Yet
it appears that this one character of Wit was more difficult to the
Author, than all his images of Humour in the Play: For those he could
describe and manage from his observations of Men; this he has taken,
at least a part of it, from Books: witness the Speeches in the First
Act, translated *verbatim* out of *Ovid de Arte Amandi.* To omit what
afterwards he borrowed from the sixth Satyre of *Juvenal* against
Women.

However, if I should grant, that there were a greater latitude in
Characters of Wit, than in those of Humour; yet that latitude would be
of small advantage to such Poets who have too narrow an imagination
to write it. And to entertain an Audience perpetually with Humour,
is to carry them from the conversation of Gentlemen, and treat them
with the follies and extravagances of *Bedlam.*

---

[16] The injunction is found in Abraham Cowley's *Ode: Of Wit,* 35–36:
> Jewels at nose, and lips but ill appear;
> Rather than all things, Wit, let none be there.

[17] *Institutio Oratoria,* VI.iii.5: "It is easier to find parts of his wit that need
pruning than any that need expansion."

[18] The Liar is Dorante in Corneille's *Le Menteur. Wit without Money* is a
comedy by Fletcher, printed in 1639, and *The Chances* is another of his comedies,
printed in 1647. Don John is a Spanish gallant in *The Chances* who comes to the
aid of an eloping duke and his sweetheart.

I find I have launch'd out farther than I intended in the beginning of this Preface. And that in the heat of Writing, I have touch'd at something, which I thought to have avoided. 'Tis time now to draw homeward: and to think rather of defending my self, than assaulting others. I have already acknowledg'd that this Play is far from perfect: but I do not think my self oblig'd to discover the imperfections of it to my Adversaries, any more than a guilty person is bound to accuse himself before his Judges. 'Tis charg'd upon me that I make debauch'd persons (such as they say my Astrologer and Gamester are) my Protagonists, or the chief persons of the *Drama;* and that I make them happy in the conclusion of my Play; against the Law of Comedy, which is to reward Virtue, and punish Vice. I answer first, that I know no such Law to have been constantly observ'd in Comedy, either by the antient or Modern Poets. *Chaerea* is made happy in the *Eunuch,* after having deflour'd a Virgin: and *Terence* generally does the same through all his Plays, where you perpetually see, not only debauch'd young men enjoy their Mistresses, but even the Courtezans themselves rewarded and honour'd in the Catastrophe. The same may be observ'd in *Plautus* almost every where. *Ben. Jonson* himself, after whom I may be proud to erre, has given me more than once the example of it. That in the *Alchemist* is notorious, where *Face,* after having contriv'd & carried on the great cozenage of the Play, and continued in it, without repentance, to the last, is not only forgiven by his Master, but inrich'd by his consent, with the spoils of those whom he had cheated. And, which is more, his Master himself, a grave man, and a Widower, is introduc'd taking his Man's counsel, debauching the Widow first, in hope to marry her afterward. In the *Silent Woman, Dauphine,* (who with the other two Gentlemen, is of the same Character with my *Celadon* in the *Maiden Queen,*[19] and with *Wildblood* in this) professes himself in love with all the Collegiate Ladies: and they likewise are all of the same character with each other, excepting only Madam *Otter,* who has something singular: yet this naughty *Dauphine,* is crown'd in the end with the possession of his Uncles Estate, and with the hopes of enjoying all his Mistresses. And his friend Mr. *Truewit* (the best Character of a Gentleman which *Ben. Jonson* ever made) is not asham'd to pimp for him. As for *Beaumont* and *Fletcher,* I need not alledge examples out of them; for that were to quote almost all their Comedies. But now it will be objected that I patronize Vice by the Authority of former Poets, and extenuate my own faults by recrimi-

---

[19] I.e., *Secret Love, or the Maiden Queen,* 1668.

nation. I answer, that as I defend my self by their example; so that example I defend by reason, and by the end of all Dramatique Poesie. In the first place therefore give me leave to shew you their mistake who have accus'd me. They have not distinguish'd as they ought, betwixt the rules of Tragedy and Comedy. In Tragedy, where the Actions and Persons are great, and the Crimes horrid, the Laws of Justice are more strictly to be observ'd: and examples of punishment to be made to deterre Mankind from the pursuit of Vice. Faults of this kind have been rare amongst the antient Poets: for they have punish'd in *Oedipus,* and in his posterity, the sin which he knew not he had committed. *Medea* is the only example I remember, at present, who escapes from punishment after murder.[20] Thus Tragedy fulfills one great part of its institution; which is by example to instruct. But in Comedy it is not so; for the chief end of it is divertisement and delight: and that so much, that it is disputed, I think, by *Heinsius,* before *Horace* his Art of Poetry, whether instruction be any part of its employment.[21] At least I am sure it can be but its secondary end: for the business of the Poet is to make you laugh: when he writes Humour, he makes Folly ridiculous; when Wit, he moves you, if not always to Laughter, yet to a pleasure that is more noble.[22] And if he works a cure on folly, and the small imperfections in mankind, by exposing them to public view, that cure is not perform'd by an immediate operation. For it works first on the ill nature of the Audience; they are mov'd to laugh by the representation of deformity; and the shame of that laughter, teaches us to amend what is ridiculous in our manners. This being then establish'd, that the first end of Comedy is delight, and instruction only the second; it may reasonably be inferr'd, that Comedy is not so much oblig'd to the punishment of the faults which it represents, as Tragedy. For the persons in Comedy are of a lower quality, the action is little, and the faults and vices are but the sallies of Youth, and the frailties of humane nature, and not premeditated

---

[20] The barbarian princess and enchantress Medea in the tragedy *Medea* by Euripides, enraged on being deserted by her husband Jason, murders his new bride and his father-in-law the King of Corinth, and then her own two children, and, taunting Jason, escapes to Athens in a chariot pulled by dragons. The later *Medea* by the Roman philosopher Seneca follows the same lines.

[21] The Dutch scholar Daniel Heinsius, in his commentary on Horace (see above, p. 34), annotates *Ars Poetica* 270: *Delectare enim ac docere est Comediae*—the end of comedy is both to teach and to delight.

[22] For a book-length examination of Dryden's comic theory in relation to his plays, with special attention to his emergent preference for "high comedy" and wit, see Frank Harper Moore, *The Nobler Pleasure* (Chapel Hill, N. C., 1963).

crimes: such to which all men are obnoxious, not such as are attempted only by few, and those abandon'd to all sense of virtue: such as move pity and commiseration; not detestation and horror; such, in short, as may be forgiven, not such as must of necessity be punish'd. But, lest any man should think that I write this to make libertinism amiable; or that I car'd not to debase the end and institution of Comedy, so I might thereby maintain my own errors, and those of better Poets; I must farther declare, both for them and for myself, that we make not vicious persons happy, but only as Heaven makes sinners so: that is by reclaiming them first from Vice; for so 'tis to be suppos'd they are, when they resolve to marry; for then enjoying what they desire in one, they cease to pursue the love of many. So *Chaerea* is made happy by *Terence,* in marrying her whom he had deflour'd: and So are *Wildblood,* and the *Astrologer* in this Play.

There is another crime with which I am charg'd, at which I am yet much less concern'd, because it does not relate to my manners, as the former did, but only to my reputation as a Poet: A name of which I assure the Reader I am nothing proud; and therefore cannot be very sollicitous to defend it. I am tax'd with stealing all my Plays, and that by some who should be the last men from whom I would steal any part of 'em. There is one answer which I will not make; but it has been made for me by him to whose Grace and Patronage I owe all things,

Et spes et ratio studiorum, in Caesare *tantum.*[23]

And without whose command they shou'd no longer be troubl'd with any thing of mine; that he only desir'd that they who accus'd me of Theft, would always steal him Plays like mine. But though I have reason to be proud of this defence, yet I should wave it, because I have a worse opinion of my own Comedies than any of my Enemies can have. 'Tis true, that where ever I have lik'd any story in a Romance, Novel, or forreign Play, I have made no difficulty, nor ever shall, to take the foundation of it, to build it up, and to make it proper for the *English* Stage. And I will be so vain to say it has lost nothing in my hands: But it always cost me so much trouble to heighten it, for our Theatre (which is incomparably more curious in all the ornaments of Dramatic Poesie, than the *French,* or *Spanish*) that when I

---

23 Juvenal, *Satires* VII.i: "On Caesar alone depend all hope and plan of studies." *An Evening's Love* is dedicated to the Duke of Newcastle, himself the author of several comedies.

had finish'd my Play, it was like the Hulk of Sir *Francis Drake,* so strangely alter'd, that there scarce remain'd any Plank of the Timber which first built it.[24] To witness this I need go no farther than this Play: It was first *Spanish,* and call'd *El Astrologo Fingido;* then made *French* by the younger *Corneille:* and is now translated into *English,* and in Print, under the name of the *Feign'd Astrologer.* What I have perform'd in this, will best appear, by comparing it with those: you will see that I have rejected some adventures which I judg'd were not divertising: that I have heightened those which I have chosen, and that I have added others which were neither in the *French* nor *Spanish.* And besides you will easily discover that the Walk of the *Astrologer* is the least considerable in my Play: for the design of it turns more on the parts of *Wildblood* and *Jacinta,* who are the chief persons in it. I have farther to add, that I seldom use the wit and language of any Romance, or Play which I undertake to alter; because my own invention (as bad as it is) can furnish me with nothing so dull as what is there. Those who have call'd *Virgil, Terence,* and *Tasso Plagiaries* (though they much injur'd them) had yet a better colour for their accusation; For *Virgil* has evidently translated *Theocritus, Hesiod,* and *Homer,* in many places; besides what he has taken from *Ennius* in his own language. *Terence* was not only known to translate *Menander,* (which he avows also in his Prologues) but was said also to be help't in those Translations by *Scipio* the *African,* and *Laelius.*[25] And *Tasso,* the most excellent of modern Poets, and whom I reverence next to *Virgil,* has taken both from *Homer* many admirable things which were left untouch'd by *Virgil,* and from *Virgil* himself where *Homer* cou'd not furnish him.[26] Yet the bodies of *Virgil's* and *Tasso's* Poems were their own: and so are all the Ornaments of Language and Elocution in them. The same (if there were any thing commendable

---

[24] After his circumnavigation of the globe, Francis Drake was knighted, 1581, by Queen Elizabeth at a banquet on board his ship the *Golden Hind* at Deptford on the Thames below London. The ship (or "hulk"—as an old vessel laid by is called) was, by royal decree, kept thereafter in dock under cover as a museum; she was visited by several generations of sightseers, until by the middle of the next century she had fallen apart and was carried away piecemeal for souvenirs.

[25] Scipio Africanus Minor, who ended the Third Punic War by destroying Carthage in 146 B.C., was a patron of letters and the center of a circle that included the soldier Gaius Laelius, consul in 140, and also Terence, who is said to have received help with his plays from his friends.

[26] Torquato Tasso's *Gerusalemme Liberata,* 1581, is a Homeric, Virgilian, and romance epic, narrating the capture of Jerusalem in the eleventh century by crusaders under the French leader Godfrey of Bouillon.

in this Play) I could say for it. But I will come nearer to our own Countrymen. Most of *Shakespeare*'s Plays, I mean the stories of them, are to be found in the *Hecatommuthi,* or hundred Novels of *Cinthio.*[27] I have, my self, read in his *Italian,* that of *Romeo* and *Juliet,* the *Moor of Venice,* and many others of them. *Beaumont* and *Fletcher* had most of theirs from *Spanish* Novels: witness the *Chances,* the *Spanish Curate, Rule a Wife, and Have a Wife;* the *Little French Lawyer,* and so many others of them, as compose the greatest part of their Volume in folio.[28] *Ben. Jonson,* indeed, has design'd his Plots himself; but no man has borrow'd so much from the Ancients as he has done: And he did well in it, for he has thereby beautify'd our Language.

But these little Critics do not well consider what is the work of a Poet, and what the Graces of a Poem: The Story is the least part of either: I mean the foundation of it, before it is modell'd by the Art of him who writes it; who forms it with more care, by exposing only the beautiful parts of it to view, than a skillful Lapidary sets a Jewel. On this foundation of the Story the Characters are rais'd: and, since no Story can afford Characters enough for the variety of the *English* Stage, it follows that it is to be alter'd and inlarg'd, with new persons, accidents, and designs, which will almost make it new. When this is done, the forming it into Acts and Scenes, disposing of actions and passions into their proper places, and beautifying both with descriptions, similitudes, and propriety of Language, is the principal employment of the Poet; as being the largest field of fancy, which is the principal quality requir'd in him: For so much the word ποιητής implies. Judgement, indeed, is necessary in him; but 'tis fancy that gives the life-touches, and the secret graces to it; especially in serious Plays, which depend not much on observation. For to write Humour in Comedy (which is the theft of Poets from mankind) little of fancy is requir'd; the Poet observes only what is ridiculous, and pleasant folly,

27 The poet and critic Giraldi Cinthio's collection of tales, *Hecatommithi,* 1565, was a source for *Othello* and a few other Shakespearian plays, but not for *Romeo and Juliet.*

28 The four plays named appear in Beaumont and Fletcher's folio volume *Fifty Comedies and Tragedies,* 1679, but two of them, *The Chances,* 1620, and *Rule a Wife,* 1624, are mainly or entirely by Fletcher, and the other two are by Fletcher either certainly or probably in collaboraiton with Philip Massinger. Fletcher based his two plays on stories in the *Novelas Exemplares* (x and xi) by Cervantes. Fletcher and Massinger are said to have borrowed *The Little French Lawyer,* 1619–1622, from Mateo Aleman's picaresque romance *Guzman de Alfarache* (translated into English as *The Rogue* in 1622), and *The Spanish Curate,* 1622, from Gonzalo de Céspedes' *Gerardo, the Unfortunate Spaniard* (English, 1622).

and by judging exactly what is so, he pleases in the representation of it.

But in general, the employment of a Poet, is like that of a curious Gunsmith or Watchmaker: the Iron or Silver is not his own; but they are the least part of that which gives the value: the price lies wholly in the workmanship. And he who works dully on a story, without moving laughter in a Comedy, or raising concernments in a serious Play, is no more to be accounted a good Poet, than a Gunsmith of the *Minories*[29] is to be compar'd with the best workman of the Town.

But I have said more of this than I intended; and more, perhaps, than I needed to have done: I shall but laugh at them hereafter, who accuse me with so little reason; and withall, contemn their dulness, who, if they could ruin that little reputation I have got, and which I value not, yet would want both Wit and Learning to establish their own, or to be remembered in after ages for any thing, but only that which makes them ridiculous in this.

---

[29] A street near the Tower of London noted for shops of gunsmiths and the like.

EPILOGUE

TO

The Second Part of
The Conquest of Granada

[*1672*]

They, who have best succeeded on the Stage,
Have still conform'd their Genius to their Age.
Thus *Jonson* did Mechanic humour show,
When men were dull, and conversation low.
Then, Comedy was faultless, but 'twas coarse:
Cobb's Tankard was a jest, and *Otter's* horse.[1]
And as their Comedy, their love was mean:
Except, by chance, in some one labour'd Scene,
Which must atone for an ill-written Play.
They rose; but at their height could seldom stay.
Fame then was cheap, and the first comer sped;
And they have kept it since, by being dead.
But were they now to write, when Critics weigh
Each Line, and ev'ry word, throughout a Play,
None of 'em, no not *Jonson*, in his height,
Could pass, without allowing grains for weight.
Think it not envy that these truths are told;
Our Poet's not malicious, though he's bold.
'Tis not to brand 'em that their faults are shown,
But, by their errours, to excuse his own.
If Love and Honour now are higher rais'd,

Our text follows the first edition of the play, *The Conquest of Granada By the Spaniards: In Two Parts*...Printed by T. N. for Henry Herringman...1672. The play was first acted in 1670–1671.

[1] Cobb is a poor water-carrier in Jonson's *Every Man in his Humour;* Otter is a braggart but henpecked captain in Jonson's *Epicoene;* he has a favorite tankard called "Horse."

'Tis not the Poet, but the Age is prais'd.
Wit's now ariv'd to a more high degree;
Our native Language more refin'd and free.
Our Ladies and our men now speak more wit
In conversation, than those Poets writ.
Then, one of these is, consequently, true;
That what this Poet writes comes short of you,
And imitates you ill (which most he fears),
Or else his writing is not worse than theirs.
Yet, though you judge (as sure the Critics will),
That some before him writ with greater skill,
In this one praise he has their fame surpast,
To please an Age[2] more Gallant than the last.

---

[2] Cf. Molière, *La Critique de L'Ecole des Femmes* (1663), Scene vi, quoted below p. 61.

INTERNOTE
MOLIÈRE

Scholars dispute the extent to which Molière (Jean Baptiste Poquelin, 1622–1673) contributed to the birth and randy juvenile career of manners comedy in England.[1] Without subscribing to the extreme view that everything in English comedy for two centuries pays the compliment of travesty to Molière, we may sketch a few relations.

He began his theatrical career early, as an actor and then as manager of a traveling company calling themselves *L'Illustre Théâtre*. They put on plays in an Italian tradition of farce and impromptu *(commedia dell'arte)*, involving also the use of masks to designate stock characters. (To show the conscious or unconscious mask in the moment of slipping would be one of Molière's mature specialities.[2]) After about thirteen years of such valuable experience, Molière and his troupe made their first great impression at Paris with his comedy-farce of highfalutin female talk and romance expectations *Les Précieuses Ridicules*, 1659. Molière was theatrical, in a practical way, to the flicker of an eyelash. His plays are, supremely, managers' and actors' plays. And when we recollect both how his early experience on the road must have made the miming or stage business, the postures and acting tricks, the core of every scene he conceived, and how a study of his plays bears this expectation out, the marvelously poetic verbal texts which he leaves us are all the more astonishing. He took a major role in nearly all of his own plays. He was, for instance, Mascarille (Little Mask—the disguised valet in *Les Précieuses*), Sganarelle (the *cocu imaginaire* in the play of that title), Arnolphe (the middle-aged guardian who would be the bridegroom in *L'Ecole des Femmes*); Orgon (the duped patron of the *faux dévot*, Tartuffe), Sganarelle (valet to the dark hero of *Dom Juan*), Alceste (the *atrabilaire amoureux*, the Misanthrope), Sganarelle (the physician in spite

---

[1] Contrast the chauvinistic view of André de Mandach, *Molière et la Comédie des Moeurs en Angleterre, 1660–1668* (Neuchatel, 1946), with the reserve of John Wilcox, *The Relation of Molière to Restoration Comedy* (New York, 1938).

[2] See W. G. Moore, *Molière: A New Criticism* (Garden City, N. Y., 1962), Chap. III, "Mask."

of himself[3]); he was George Dandin, Harpagon, Pourceaugnac, Jourdain, Scapin, Chrysale, Argan. He could personate *himself,* or play a role (in *L'Impromptu de Versailles*) where he slid back and forth between being himself straight, *le sieur de Molière,* actor-manager, and a foppish Marquis named Molière, who denies that he has been a target of Molière's criticism.

Often he planned, composed, rehearsed, and presented comedies in great haste, at the command of the young king (who was his good patron).[4] The ease and seemingly natural funniness of his dialogue in verse and prose constantly suggest the energetic luck of the impromptu. (Where the great tragic verse of Racine may remind an English reader of Pope's carefully processed pentameter couplets in Homeric declamations, the verses of Molière fall together in complete prose phrases, even conversational tags, with fun in the twist of them, much as in the antisublime English tetrameters of Jonathan Swift.) "...In the simplest language," says George Meredith, "the simplest of French verse." And Molière's wit, he says, is not, like Congreve's, the Toledo blade of the dueling satirist, but "like a running brook, with innumerable fresh lights in it at every turn of the wood through which its business is to find a way."[5] Molière's constant preoccupation with the puncturing of the inflated or the overstuffed finds perhaps an apt emblem in the fact that his father was a court upholsterer (*tapissier du roi*), and that Molière himself had fled to the stage after a brief application to the same kind of job. Despite monitory ideas expressed or soon to be expressed in his own plays (*L'Ecole des Maris,* June 1661; *L'Ecole des Femmes,* December 1662), he married Armande Béjard (February 1662), an actress of his troupe, in age a few months less than half his own. For himself and her he wrote such brilliantly successful October-and-May roles as those of Arnolphe and Agnès in *L'Ecole des Femmes,* Orgon and Elmire in *Le Tartuffe,* Alceste and Célimène in *Le Misanthrope.* Toward the end of his life, they were separated, but only for a while (1667–1670). He wrote in all more than thirty farces, comedies, and comedy-ballets. He died, an early death, in February 1673, being stricken on the stage, on the fourth day of his acting the title role of his last comedy, *Le Malade Imaginaire.*

English playwrights had not been slow in showing an appreciation of the new French model. Somewhat rude or slight examples during the first decade, 1660–1670, are of interest at least as showing a trend: adaptations, from Molière's earlier works, by the veteran of the

---

[3] And two other Sganarelles also.

[4] The record seems to have been five days for *L'Amour Médecin,* at Versailles, in September 1665. *Les Fâcheux,* 1661, was accomplished in fifteen.

[5] In the lecture *On the Uses of Comedy and of the Idea of the Comic Spirit,* 1877, the last of the texts presented in this volume.

last age Sir William D'Avenant; by Dryden's figure of paternal Dullness, Richard Flecknoe; by his heir Thomas Shadwell (Mac Flecknoe); and by Dryden's witty friend Sir Charles Sedley, likely original of the spokesman for the French drama in the *Essay of Dramatic Poesy*.[6] Dryden himself would speak of the "frippery" and "farce" of French comedy (1664, 1671),[7] but he put a polishing hand to a raw translation of *L'Etourdi* (1653) by the Duke of Newcastle (*Sir Martin Mar-All*, 1667). Molièresque ideas no doubt account in part for the sketches of *précieuses* females in Dryden's *Marriage à la Mode* and *An Evening's Love*.

After about 1670,[8] it is difficult to narrate the full presence of Molière on the English stage. In the spirit of nineteenth-century evolutionary refinement, George Meredith would stress the grossness of the transformation. Wycherley's *Plain Dealer* (1676) is "a coarse prose adaptation of the *Misanthrope*, stuffed with lumps of realism."[9] Scene v, Act II, the classic scene of gossip (*scène des portraits*), in *Le Misanthrope*, "is repeated in succession by Wycherley, Congreve, and Sheridan, and as it is at second hand, we have it done cynically...in the manner of 'below stairs.' "[10] Certain it is that in *Le Misanthrope* (which we shall see to be the center of Meredith's dithyrambic discourse) Molière had given crystal definition to three major motifs of high comedy: the scene of coterie gossip ("at every word a reputation dies"); the figure of the morose, or atrabilious, antagonist of the social scene, the self-ostracizing misanthrope; and blended delicately, both sweetly and bitterly, with these, the complications of coquetry and the salon battle between the sexes.[11]

---

6 D'Avenant's *Play House to be Let,* from *Sganarelle,* 1660, was acted, without his name, about 1663, and published, after his death, in his *Works,* 1673. Flecknoe's *Damoiselles à la Mode,* 1667, follows *Les Précieuses* and *L'Ecole des Maris,* 1661. Shadwell's *Sullen Lovers,* 1668, is from *Les Fâcheux,* 1661. Sedley's *Mulberry Garden,* 1668, incorporates parts of *L'Ecole des Maris.*

7 Epistle Dedicatory of *The Rival Ladies,* 1664 (W. P. Ker, ed., *Essays of John Dryden,* Oxford, 1926, I, 6); Preface to *An Evening's Love,* 1671 (reprinted in this volume).

8 *Le Tartuffe,* 1664–1669, came over without disguise in Matthew Medburne's *Tartuffe, or the French Puritan,* 1670. For the early phase of Molière's influence, see André de Mandach, *Molière et la Comédie de Moeurs en Angleterre,* Appendix, pp. 92–113.

9 See below, p. 248. Wycherley's *Country Wife,* 1675, had followed scenes in *L'Ecole des Maris,* 1661, and *L'Ecole des Femmes,* 1662. *Les Fourberies de Scapin,* 1671, was adapted by Otway in 1677.

10 See below, p. 249. Cf. Bonamy Dobrée, *Restoration Comedy 1660–1720* (Oxford, 1924), p. 48.

11 See Moore, *Molière,* pp. 77–81, 144; Martin Turnell, *The Classic Moment* (New York, 1946), p. 101. R. Jasinski, *Molière et le Misanthrope* (Paris, 1951), returns to biography, psychology, morality.

All three of these themes enter into the pinnacle of English manners comedy, Congreve's *Way of the World*, 1700. Poor Mirabell (I.1), hoping for an opportunity to make a declaration of love, has stumbled into "one of their cabal nights...where they come together like the coroner's inquest, to sit upon the murdered reputations of the week." "A man," says he (II.ii), "may as soon make a friend by his wit, or a fortune by his honesty, as win a woman by plain dealing and sincerity." In one of the great scenes of English comedy (IV.i), he arrives at the triumph of eliciting from the tantalizing Millamant this surrender: "And lastly, wherever I am, you shall always knock at the door before you come in. These articles subscribed, if I continue to endure you a little longer, I may by degrees dwindle into a wife."

So successful a playwright, so accurate and telling a satirist as Molière could not escape embroilment over his plays. As early as *Les Précieuses*, he was in hot water. Thenceforth he enjoyed a career of more or less constant embattlement with several classes of persons: with various objects of his satire—foppish *marquis*, *précieuses*, *coquettes*, cuckolds; with government officials and churchmen; with rival artists, especially the Italian comedians of the *Hôtel de Bourgogne*, the established theater against which his *Palais Royal* competed. He was, as we have said, theatrical and dramatic to an eyelash, but by force of circumstance, perhaps even *malgré lui*, he became also a literary critic and theorist. *Le Tartuffe*, 1664–1669, about hypocritical piety, came under especially heavy fire and elicited, in a *Préface* to its first edition and in three vindicatory statements, or *Placets*, addressed to the King and printed in a second edition, some professions of the satirist's moral aim which we quote on a later page. During his four-year strife to get *Tartuffe* before the public, he either inspired or himself wrote a *Lettre sur l'Imposteur*, 1667, which contains some interesting formulations concerning comedy as external portraiture of whatever is a scandal to the intelligence. "Nous estimons ridicule ce qui manque extrêmement de raison...il s'ensuit que tout mensonge, déguisement, fourberie, dissimulation, toute apparence différente du fond, enfin toute contrariété entre actions qui procèdent du même principe, est essentiellement ridicule."[12]

He had a few years earlier defended himself against certain other bodies of critics, his society targets, and his rivals, in a short play or dramatic dialogue, with seven actually alive and amusing characters (a comic *Essay of Comic Dramatic Poesy*). This was a counter-attack

---

[12] Quoted in W. G. Moore, *Molière*, pp. 148–49: "We consider comic anything extremely unreasonable.... Thus any lie, disguise, trick, pretense, any disparity between appearance and fact, any inconsistency in actions proceeding from the same motive—all these are essentially comic."

in what is described by the French scholars as a kind of *guerre comique* that was being waged against his popular success *L'Ecole des Femmes* (1662). It was entitled *La Critique de L'Ecole des Femmes* and was both acted at the *Palais Royal* and published in 1663. An intelligent chevalier named Dorante, abetted by a fun-loving young lady, Uranie, comes to the defense of his friend Mr. Molière and answers the objections of a circle of carpers led by a rival dramatic poet named Lysidas. The conversation, though brief, is in effect ambitious and manages to touch effectively on several of the main issues of the neoclassic debate about comedy: whether we should see *ourselves* in the comic mirror; whether it is more difficult (as Horace too had wondered) to write serious heroic poetry or comic realism; whether the *beau monde* does not judge better of plays than the rusty pedants; whether we *ought* to enjoy a play that breaks the rules. In a concluding demonstration, Lysidas invokes a series of perspectives (rules) for finding this and that fault in Mr. Molière's play, and Dorante invokes counter-perspectives (other rules) for showing they are not in fact faults. This scene would be a capital text for an anthology of French essays on comedy.

> URANIE. Pour moi, je me garderai bien de m'en offenser et de prendre rien sur mon compte de tout ce qui s'y dit.... Toutes les peintures ridicules qu'on expose sur les théâtres...sont miroirs publics, où il ne faut jamais témoigner qu'on se voie.

> CLIMÈNE. Pour moi, je vous avoue que je suis dans une colère épouvantable, de voir que cet auteur impertinent nous appelle *des animaux.*

> URANIE. Ne voyez-vous pas que c'est un ridicule qu'il fait parler?

> DORANTE. Lorsque vous peignez des héros, vous faites ce que vous voulez. Ce sont des portraits à plaisir, où l'on ne cherche point de ressemblance.... Mais lorsque vous peignez les hommes, il faut peindre d'après nature. On veut que ces portraits ressemblent; et vous n'avez rien fait, si vous n'y faites reconnaître les gens de votre siècle...il y faut plaisanter; et c'est une étrange entreprise que celle de faire rire les honnêtes gens.

> DORANTE. Sachez...que la grande épreuve de toutes vos comédies, c'est le jugement de la cour; que c'est son goût qu'il faut étudier pour trouver l'art de réussir; qu'il n'y a point de lieu où les décisions soient si justes;...que, du simple bon sens naturel et du commerce de tout le beau monde, on s'y fait une manière d'esprit, qui sans comparaison juge plus finement des choses que tout le savoir enrouillé des pédants.

> URANIE. J'ai remarqué une chose de ces Messieurs-là: c'est que ceux qui parlent le plus des règles, et qui les savent mieux que les autres, font des comédies que personne ne trouve belles.

DORANTE. Et c'est ce qui marque, Madame, comme on doit s'arrêter peu à leurs disputes embarrassées. Car enfin, si les pièces qui sont selon les règles ne plaisent pas et que celles qui plaisent ne soient pas selon les règles, il faudrait de nécessité que les règles eussent été mal faites.[13]

---

[13] URANIE. So far as I am concerned—I'll take pains not to be hurt by anything it says; I'll find nothing in it that refers to me.... These comic galleries on the stage...are public mirrors. Never admit that you see yourself in them....CLIMÈNE. I say that it burns me up to hear that scribbling nincompoop refer to women as 'animals.' URANIE. Can't you see he puts that in the mouth of a clown?... DORANTE. You can draw your heroes according to desire, make fancy portraits. Nobody expects them to look real.... But ordinary men have to be copied to the life; the likeness must be good, the portrait of the age, or it is no good at all...it must be amusing. And what a tricky job that is, to get a laugh from a smart audience.... DORANTE. Understand...that the real criterion for all your comic writing is the judgment of the court. The taste of the court is your formula for success. Their pronouncements are above all others correct.... The simple, natural good sense and daily intercourse of high society generate a mode of intelligence and judgment which is beyond comparison superior to all the rusty thinking of the pedants....URANIE. I have noticed one thing about these gentlemen: the ones who talk the most about the rules and who know the most about them are the ones who write comedies nobody can endure. DORANTE. And that shows, my lady, how little attention we need pay to their clumsy arguments. For, in a word, if plays which observe the rules are not entertaining, and if those which *are* entertaining do not observe the rules, it must be that the rules have not been well conceived. —Molière, *La Critique de l'Ecole des Femmes* (*The School for Wives Criticized*), Scene vi.

THOMAS SHADWELL

[1642?–1692]

It sometimes happens that a man of at least respectable talents comes down to posterity in the image of a dunce—through the misfortune of his having been the adversary of a satiric genius. Such in the next age was Pope's victim, the Shakespeare scholar Lewis Theobald, and such the memorialist of the theater Colley Cibber, a conscious coxcomb whose energies won him the attention of both Pope and Fielding. Such too was Dryden's political and literary opposite Thomas Shadwell. As a poet (a nasty satirist without wit) he certainly did not deserve the Laureateship which he was awarded when Dryden was stripped of it after the Glorious Revolution of 1688. As a dramatist, however, he was the creator of some not contemptible scenes of local manners in his *Epsom Wells* (1673), praised by St. Evremond, his *Squire of Alsatia* (1688), and his *Bury Fair* (1689).[1] He lives today most vividly in Dryden's two portraits of him, as Og the seditious Whig, and as Mac Flecknoe, the sovereign inheritor of poetic nonsense. These satires became public during the paper warfare of 1681–1682 relating to Shaftesbury's part in promoting the aspirations of the Duke of Monmouth.[2]

> Shadwell alone my perfect image bears,
> Mature in dullness from his tender years:
> Shadwell alone, of all my sons, is he
> Who stands confirm'd in full stupidity.
> The rest to some faint meaning make pretense,
> But Shadwell never deviates into sense.[3]

---

[1] "Alsatia" was a district in London. See below p. 216. Rochester, *An Allusion to Horace,* 41–43, coupled Shadwell and Wycherley as the only "true" comic writers of the time, one prolific, the other not ("...hasty Shadwell and slow Wycherley"), and, 120–24, he included Shadwell in his Horatian jury of the competent few (*pauci lectores*).

[2] *Absalom and Achitophel* (1681), *The Medal* (1681), *The Medal of John Bayes* (by Shadwell, 1682), *The Second Part of Absalom and Achitophel* (by Nahum Tate and Dryden, 1682), and *Mac Flecknoe* (published in 1682).

[3] *Mac Flecknoe,* 15–20. Dryden, in his masterly practice of this art so closely neighboring comedy, elegantly violates a rule of "not-calling-blockhead" which, with equal aplomb, he would later announce in a long essay prefixed to his edition of Juvenal's *Satires* in translation, 1693.

The 1682 publication of *Mac Flecknoe* was piratical. It was precipitated, appropriately enough, by the political climate prevailing, but the poem had very likely been written and well circulated in manuscript as early as 1678, and probably relates to an even earlier literary irritation.[4] Shadwell had first appeared on the scene during a polemical crisis of 1668 at which we have already glanced.[5] He had undertaken to score, in a play and a preface, upon both Dryden and Dryden's brother-in-law Sir Robert Howard—at a time when they themselves were engaged in a public argument about rhyme in dramatic poetry and the classic unities. Shadwell had come forward as a defender of "humor" writing and a custodian of the reputation of Ben Jonson. Even before Dryden's most pointed pronouncements upon "humor," in his critical essays attached to *An Evening's Love* (1671) and *The Conquest of Granada* (1672),[6] or only about three months after his balanced appreciation of Jonson in the *Essay of Dramatic Poesy* (published in May or June of 1668), Shadwell had taken the field in a Preface to his own first play, *The Sullen Lovers*.[7]

---

[4] See Mark Van Doren, *John Dryden: A Study of His Poetry* (New York, 1946), pp. 266–78, esp. pp. 274–75. On Shadwell's satiric portrait of Dryden in *The Medal of John Bayes,* see James M. Osborn, *John Dryden: Some Biographical Facts and Problems* (Gainesville, Florida, 1965), pp. 171–83.

[5] Cf. above, pp. 38–39.

[6] Cf. above, pp. 40–42.

[7] From Molière's *Les Fâcheux.* Acted in May 1668, at the Duke's Theater, Lincoln's Inn Fields, published by early September. Shadwell's thrust against Dryden appears in his Preface, that against Sir Robert Howard in the play itself. The diarist Samuel Pepys recorded on May 4, 1668, that Sir Positive At-all in *The Sullen Lovers* was Howard.

PREFACE

TO

The Sullen Lovers

[*1668*]

Reader,

The success of this Play, as it was much more than it deserv'd, so was much more than I expected: Especially in this very Critical Age, when every man pretends to be a Judge, and some, that never read Three Plays in their lives, and never understood one, are as Positive in their Judgment of Plays, as if they were all *Jonsons*. But had I been us'd with all the severity imaginable, I should patiently have submitted to my Fate; not like the rejected Authors of our Time, who, when their Plays are damn'd, will strut, and huff it out, and laugh at the Ignorance of the Age: Or, like some other of our Modern Fopps, that declare they are resolv'd to Justifie their Plays with their Swords (though perhaps their Courage is as little as their Wit) such as peep through their loop-holes in the Theatre, to see who looks grum upon their Plays: And if they spy a Gentle Squire making Faces, he poor soul must be *Hector'd* till he likes 'em, while the more stubborn *Bully-Rock* damn's, and is safe: Such is their discretion in the Choice of their men. Such Gentlemen as these I must confess had need pretend they cannot Err. These will huff, and look big upon the success of an ill Play stuffed full of Songs and Dances, (which have that constraint upon 'em too, that they seldom seem to come in willingly;) when in such Plays the composer and the Danceing Master are the best Poets, and yet the unmerciful Scribler would rob them of all the Honour.

I am so far from valuing my self (as the Phrase is) upon this Play, that perhaps no man is a severer Judge of it than my self; yet if any thing could have made me proud of it, it would have been the great

From *The Works of Tho. Shadwell, Esq.* . . . . London, Printed for F. Saunders . . . 1693.

Favour and Countenance it receiv'd from His Majesty and their Royal Highnesses.

But *I* could not perswade my self that they were so favourable to the Play for the Merit of it, but out of a Princely Generosity, to encourage a young beginner, that did what he could to please them, and that otherwise might have been baulk'd for ever: 'Tis to this *I* owe the success of the Play, and am as far from presumption of my own merits in it, as one ought to be who receives an Alms.

The first hint I receiv'd was from the report of a Play of *Molière's* of three Acts, called *Les Fâcheux,* upon which I wrote a great part of this before *I* read that[1]; and after it came to my hands, *I* found so little for my use (having before upon that hint design'd the fittest Characters I could for my purpose) that I have made use of but two short Scenes which I inserted afterwards (*viz.*) the first Scene in the Second Act between *Stanford* and *Roger,*[2] and *Molière's* story of Piquette, which I have translated into Back-gammon,[3] both of them being so vary'd you would not know them. But I freely confess my Theft, and am asham'd on't, though I have the example of some that never yet wrote Play without stealing most of it; and (like men that lye so long, till they believe themselves) at length, by continual Thieving, reckon their stoln goods their own too: Which is so ignoble a thing, that I cannot but believe that he that makes a common practise of stealing other Mens Wit, would, if he could with the same safety, steal any thing else.

I have in this Play, as near as I could, observ'd the three Unities, of Time, Place, and Action; The time of the Drama does not exceed six hours, the place is in a very narrow Compass, and the Main Action

---

[1] Molière's *Les Fâcheux* was acted in 1661, and printed in 1662. The two lovers of Molière's play, Eraste and Orphise, are pestered by a set of courtly bores (Les Fâcheux). In Shadwell's play the lovers, Stanford and Emilia, are similarly beset by troublesome "impertinents." However, the irritation of Stanford and Emilia is partly due to their own sullen, morose humors, which are contrasted to the airy, carefree natures of another pair of lovers, Lovel and Carolina, who are only amused by the loquacity of their "impertinent" friends.

[2] In Shadwell's scene (II.ii) Stanford is exasperated by the teasing digressions of his man Roger, who brings some eagerly awaited news from Lovel. The idea and many of the devices of this scene are borrowed from Act II, Scene iii of Molière's play, in which La Montagne, Eraste's valet, angers his master by delaying his report of some important news from Orphise.

[3] After ridding himself of a series of pestiferous talkers, Eraste anxiously awaits news of Orphise, only to be found by yet another acquaintance, who relates every detail of a narrowly lost game of Piquet (II.ii). In *The Sullen Lovers* (III.i) the first private conversation between Stanford and Emilia is interrupted by a sponging friend who describes a game of backgammon in which he has unfortunately "lost every penny."

of the Play, upon which all the rest depend, is the Sullen Love betwixt *Stanford* and *Emilia*, which kind of Love is only proper to their Characters: I have here, as often as I could naturally, kept the Scenes unbroken,[4] which (though it be not so much practised, or so well understood, by the *English*) yet among the French Poets is accounted a great Beauty; but after these frivolous excuses the want of Design in the Play has been objected against me: which fault (though I may endeavour a little to extenuate) I dare not absolutely deny: I conceive, with all submission to better Judgments, that no man ought to expect such Intrigues in the little actions of Comedy, as are requir'd in Plays of a higher Nature: But in Plays of Humour, where there are so many Characters as there are in this, there is yet less Design to be expected: For, if after I had form'd three or four forward prating Fopps in the Play, I made it full of Plot, and Business; at the latter end, where the turns ought to be many, and suddenly following one another, I must have let fall the Humour, which I thought wou'd be pleasanter than Intrigues could have been without it; and it would have been easier to me to have made a Plot than to hold up the Humour.

Another Objection, that has been made by some, is, that there is the same thing over and over: Which I do not apprehend, unless they blame the unity of the Action; yet *Horace de Arte Poetica,* says,

Sit quod vis, simplex duntaxat, et unum.[5]

---

[4] In the Prologue to *Secret Love, or The Maiden Queen* (1668), Dryden wrote (11. 1-6):

> He who writ this, not without pains and thought,
> From *French* and *English* theatres has brought
> Th' exactest rules, by which a play is wrought.
>
> The Unities of Action, Place, and Time;
> The scenes unbroken; and a mingled chime
> Of *Jonson's* humour, with *Corneille's* rhyme.

The French *liaison des scènes* meant that each new scene, within one act, began with a character on stage who had been part of the preceding scene. In his *Discours des Trois Unités,* one of the three general essays on drama included in his collected *Oeuvres* of 1660, Corneille had written: "La liaison des scènes, qui unit toutes les actions particulières de chaque acte l'une avec l'autre, est un grand ornement dans un poème, et qui sert beaucoup à former une continuité d'action par la continuité de la représentation; mais enfin ce n'est qu'on ornement et non pas une règle." ("The liaison of scenes, which links together all the actions of a given act, is a great ornament in a dramatic poem, and does much to shape the continuity of action in a continuous representation. But it is after all an ornament, not a requirement.")

[5] Horace, *Ars Poetica,* 23: "Make it anything you like, so long as it's one simple thing."

Or whether it be the carrying on of the Humours to the last, which the same Author directs me to do,

> *Si quid inexpertum Scenae committis, et audes*
> *Personam formare novam, Servetur ad Imum*
> *Qualis ab incepto processerit, et sibi constet.*[6]

I have endeavour'd to represent variety of Humours (most of the persons of the Play differing in their Characters from one another) which was the practise of *Ben. Jonson,* whom I think all Dramatic Poets ought to imitate, though none are like to come near; he being the only person that appears to me to have made perfect Representations of Humane Life. Most other Authors that *I* ever read, either have wild Romantic Tales wherein they strain Love and Honour to that Ridiculous height, that it becomes Burlesque; or in their lower Comedies content themselves with one or two Humours at most, and those not near so perfect Characters as the admirable *Jonson* always made, who never wrote Comedy without seven or eight excellent Humours. I never saw one, except that of *Falstaff,* that was in my Judgment comparable to any of *Jonson's* considerable Humours: You will pardon this digression when I tell you he is the man, of the World, *I* most passionately admire for his Excellency in Dramatic Poetry.

Though I have known some of late so Insolent to say, that *Ben. Jonson* wrote his best Plays without Wit; imagining, that all the Wit in Plays consisted in bringing two persons upon the Stage to break Jests, and to bob one another, which they call Repartie, not considering that there is more Wit and Invention requir'd in the finding out good Humour, and Matter proper for it, than in all their smart Reparties.[7]

---

6 Horace, *Ars Poetica,* 125–27: "If you try some new scene or character, stick with it to the end, a consistent conclusion."

7 "One cannot say he [Ben Jonson] wanted wit, but rather that he was frugal of it." "They [Beaumont and Fletcher] understood and imitated the conversation of gentlemen much better; whose wild debaucheries, and quickness of wit... no poet can ever paint as they have done." Dryden, *An Essay of Dramatic Poesy,* 1668 (*Essays,* ed. W. P. Ker, I, 81). Dryden would answer Shadwell in the Preface to *An Evening's Love,* 1671 (reprinted in this volume). In an essay written in 1677 and first published in 1685, the French gentleman critic Charles de Saint-Evremond, long resident in England, expressed a Shadwellian preference for humors over wit, and thus for English comedy over the French. "Il n'y a point de Comédie qui se conforme plus à celle des Anciens, que l'*Angloise,* pour ce qui regarde les Moeurs. Ce n'est point une pure Galanterie pleine d'Avantures & de discours amoureux, comme en *Espagne* & en *France;* c'est la Représentation de la vie ordinaire, selon la diversité des humeurs, & les differens caractères des hommes." —*De la Comédie Angloise,* in *Oeuvres Meslées,* ed. Pierre Des Maiseaux (London, 1705), II, 98. ("There is no comedy which in regard to manners is closer to

For in the Writing of a Humour, a Man is confin'd not to swerve from the Character, and oblig'd to say nothing but what is proper to it: But in the Plays which have been wrote of late, there is no such thing as perfect Character, but the two chief persons are most commonly a Swearing, Drinking, Whoring, Ruffian for a Lover, and an impudent ill-bred *Tomrig* for a Mistress, and these are the fine People of the Play; and there is that Latitude in this, that almost any thing is proper for them to say; but their chief Subject is bawdy, and profaneness, which they call *Brisk Writing,* when the most dissolute of Men, that rellish those things well enough in private, are *shock'd* at 'em in public: And methinks, if there were nothing but the ill Manners of it, it should make Poets avoid that Indecent way of Writing.

But perhaps you may think me as impertinent as any one I represent; that, having so many faults of my own, shou'd take the liberty to judge of others, to impeach my fellow Criminals: I must confess it is very ungenerous to accuse those that modestly confess their own Errours; but Positive Men, that justifie all their faults, are Common Enemies, that no man ought to spare, prejudicial to all Societies they live in, destructive to all Communication, always endeavouring Magisterially to impose upon our Understandings, against the Freedom of Mankind: These ought no more to be suffer'd amongst us than wild beasts: For no correction that can be laid upon 'em are of power to reform 'em; and certainly it was a positive Fool that *Solomon* spoke of, when he said, *Bray him in a Mortar, and yet he will retain his folly.*[8]

But I have troubled you too long with this Discourse, and am to ask your pardon for it, and the many faults you will find in the Play; and beg you will believe, that whatever I have said of it, was intended not in Justification, but Excuse of it: Look upon it, as it really was, wrote in haste, by a Young Writer, and you will easily pardon it; especially when you know that the best of our Dramatic Writers have wrote several before they could get one to be Acted; and their best Plays were made with great expense of labour and time. Nor can you expect a very Correct Play, under a Years pains

---

the ancient model than the English. English comedy is not a simple affair of gallantry, full of adventures and lovers' talk, like the Spanish and the French. It is a representation of ordinary life, according to the diversity of humors and various characters of men.")

[8] Proverbs xxvii.22: "Though thou shouldest bray a fool in a mortar among wheat with a pestle, yet will not his foolishness depart from him."

at the least, from the Wittiest Man of the Nation; It is so difficult a thing to write well in this kind. Men of Quality, that write for their pleasure, will not trouble themselves with exactness in their Plays; and those that write for profit would find too little encouragement for so much pains as a Correct Play would require,

Vale.

Shadwell's second comedy, *The Humorists,* was acted and published in 1671. His Preface to the play continues his debate with his "particular friend" Dryden, who had meanwhile, as we have seen, formulated further patronizing statements about Jonson's humors and had advertised his own "mixed way" of both wit and humor. ("I will not say," ventures Shadwell, "his is the best way of writing, yet I am sure his manner of writing it is much the best that ever was.") Shadwell's new Preface wanders somewhat among polemic topicalities but displays moments, paragraphs, of very good critical sense—reminiscences and anticipations of some of the most serious questions about comedy that have been raised in the classical tradition.

It were ill nature, and below a man, to fall upon the natural imperfections of man, as of Lunaticks, Ideots, or men born monstrous.... These can never be made the proper subjects of a Satire; but the affected vanities and artificial fopperies of men, which (sometimes even contrary to their natures) they take pains to acquire, are the proper subject of Satire.

If a man should bring such a humor upon the Stage (if there be such a humor in the world) as onely belongs to one or two persons, it would not be understood by the Audience, but would be thought, for the singularity of it, wholly unnatural, and would be no jest to them neither.

If this argument that the enemies of humor use be meant in this sense, that a Poet, in the writing of a Fools Character, needs but have a man sit to him, and have his words and actions taken, in this case there is no need of wit. But 'tis most certain that if we should do so, no one fool, though the best about the Town, could appear pleasantly upon the Stage: he would be there too dull a Fool, and must be helped out with a great deal of wit in the Author.[1]

---

[1] *Critical Essays of the Seventeenth Century,* ed. J. E. Spingarn (Oxford, 1908), II, 154, 157, 160. Dryden's *An Evening's Love* was licensed for publication on February 13, 1671, and Shadwell's *The Humourists* on May 30.

WILLIAM CONGREVE

[1670–1729]

William Congreve, son of an English garrison commander, grew up in Ireland. He was a fellow student with Swift at Kilkenny School and at Trinity College, Dublin. He came to London to study law but gave it up. A Middle Temple dropout, he cultivated fashionable society and arrived at sudden prominence[1] in the theater with his first comedy, *The Old Bachelor*, in 1693. He followed this with a further small, sparkling cluster: *The Double Dealer*, 1694, *Love for Love* (with which he and the actor Thomas Betterton opened the new theater in *Lincoln's Inn Fields*, 1695), and his coolly received comic masterpiece *The Way of the World*, 1700. Dryden welcomed the new genius in a commendatory verse epistle for *The Double Dealer*, reading in him all the wit, judgment, courtliness, and purity of Jonson, Fletcher, Etherege, and Southerne, "The satire, wit, and strength of manly Wycherley."

> Oh, that your brows my laurel had sustain'd,
> Well had I been depos'd, if you had reign'd![2]

Congreve was one of the targets of the nonjuring clergyman Jeremy

---

[1] In a lecture of 1851 (see below p. 229), the novelist W. M. Thackeray gives us a vivid Victorian retrospect of the young Congreve. He was "the most eminent literary 'swell' of his age." He "splendidly frequented the coffee-houses and theatres, and appeared in the side-box, the tavern, the Piazza, and the Mall, brilliant, beautiful, and victorious from the first. Everybody acknowledged the young chieftain.... He loved, and conquered, and jilted the beautiful Bracegirdle, the heroine of all his plays, the favorite of all the town of her day." The facts are recited by Samuel Johnson, *Lives of the English Poets*, ed. G. B. Hill (Oxford, 1905), II, 212–34; and in more depth by John C. Hodges, *William Congreve the Man: A Biography from New Sources* (New York, 1941). "Surprisingly little is known of Congreve's life. He remains a man of mystery...." (Kathleen M. Lynch, *A Congreve Gallery*, Cambridge, Mass., 1951, p. vii).

[2] After the Revolution in 1688 Thomas Shadwell (see above, p. 63) had succeeded Dryden both as Poet Laureate and as Historiographer Royal. In 1692, when Shadwell died, Nahum Tate became Poet Laureate, and Thomas Rymer Historiographer Royal. Dryden's poem addressed to Congreve continues: "But now, not I, but poetry is curs'd;/For Tom the Second reigns like Tom the First."

Collier's *Short View of the Immorality and Profaneness of the English Stage*, 1698, and he responded in the same year with *Amendments of Mr. Collier's False and Imperfect Citations*.[3] His comedies were of the sharp, scintillating kind, the brief zenith of the English Molièresque comedy of wit and manners—acid researches into the mores of the contemporary artificial and narrow world of high fashion, gallantry, and adultery. Critical appreciation of Congreve always stresses the conversational wit, refinement, and polish both of the author (the wittiest man who ever wrote for the English stage) and of the superior personages who inhabit his plays. His characters tend to be defined either by a talent in lively repartee (Millamant and Mirabell, hero and heroine of *The Way of the World*), or by some opposite energy, malignant or stupid (Witwoud and Petulant in the same play), or by some kind of feigned, affected, or false wit (their friend Fainall). In his short biography of the playwright, Samuel Johnson writes that he supposed comedy to "consist in gay remarks and unexpected answers.... His scenes exhibit not much of humour, imagery, or passion; his persons are a kind of intellectual gladiators; every sentence is to ward or strike."

Congreve's casually turned letter *Concerning Humour in Comedy*, published by the recipient, the critic John Dennis, in 1695, attempts to treat the English tradition of humor in a broader and more nearly Jonsonian sense than actually appears in his own comedies, and is hence not a close commentary on his own inspiration or practice. He takes up the already established issues, of wit versus humor, of true or natural humor versus scatterbrained and shallow farce, but scarcely succeeds in reasoning about them with as much clarity or logic as Dryden, or even perhaps Shadwell, had done more than twenty years earlier. The sequence of paragraphs (the fourth through the seventh) on the interplay of wit and humor in character suffer not a little from at least the appearance of self-contradiction. Sentence by sentence, however, the prose proceeds with the same immediate and pungent comprehensibility as the talk of one of the insouciant gentlemen in his plays—in both instances, of course, the effect is one of art and not strictly of actual life, though Congreve did fancy himself in the role of fine gentleman. A memorable *obiter dictum* of this letter, though it is only that and not a main part of the argument, is the sentence in which Congreve takes the commonsensical and skeptical side of the quarrel we have witnessed in Dryden's mind about the adequacy of real conversation to stand as a model for the stage.

A further theme, which is not arrived at until late in the letter, and almost as an afterthought (in the last paragraph), illustrates the

---

[3] Cf. below, p. 109.

pleasure and self-gratulation which the English were now experiencing
in the contemplation of the variety and strength of the national
"humours." Congreve's postscript is one early (though not the earliest)
testimony to a shift which was now taking the English humor a long
way beyond the gritty, coarse, smelly, obscene, shameful, unlovable
object of censure which it had been in such a world as that of Jonson's
Volpone or *Epicoene.* Even Jonson, as we have seen, was happy in the
opportunities for stage comedy afforded by the richness and ripeness
of the English character.

> No clime breeds better matter for your whore,
> Bawd, squire, imposter, many persons more,
> Whose manners now call'd humours, feed the stage.[4]

By the 1690's, however, the "humour" was becoming a cultural asset
of a far wider and a more benign sort, a symptom and eruptive
manifestation of admirable qualities that were thought to lie deep in
the national grain.[5] As the revolutionary atmosphere of the seventeenth
century cooled off into the peace of the Augustans, it became much
easier to tolerate and even to love all but the most jagged forms of
personal independence and eccentricity. Swift's patron, the diplomatist
Sir William Temple, in his masterly long essay *Of Poetry* (1690), had,
in spite of a general preference for ancient poetry, confessed a strong
partiality for a certain native English vein:

> ...which with us is called Humour, a Word peculiar to our Language
> too, and hard to be expressed in any other; nor is it, that I know of,
> found in any Foreign Writers, unless it be *Molière,* and yet his itself
> has too much of the Farce to pass for the same with ours. *Shakespeare*
> was the first that opened this Vein upon our Stage, which has run so
> freely and so pleasantly ever since, that I have often wondered to find
> it appear so little upon any others. . . .
>
>   It may seem a Defect in the ancient Stage that the Characters intro-
> duced were so few, and those so common, as a Covetous Old Man, an
> Amorous Young, a Witty Wench, a Crafty Slave, a Bragging Soldier.
> The Spectators met nothing upon the Stage, but what they met in the
> Streets and at every Turn.

How came it that the English people were so favored by this
plenitude of natural humors, a variety in life that so happily supported
a variety upon the stage? Three kinds of causes could be defined
(chthonic, meteorological, and political): "the Native Plenty of our
Soyl, the unequalness of our Clymat, as well as the Ease of our
Government, and the Liberty of Professing Opinions and Factions."

---

[4] Prologue to *The Alchemist,* 1610.
[5] See Edward N. Hooker, "Humour in the Age of Pope," *The Huntington
Library Quarterly, XI,*No. 4 (August 1948), 361–85; cf. below, pp. 148–51, 234–35.

Thus we come to have more Originals. . . . We are not only more unlike
one another than any Nation I know, but we are more unlike our selves
too at several times. . . .

There are no where so many Disputers upon Religion, so many
Reasoners upon Government, so many Refiners in Politics, so many
Curious Inquisitives, so many Pretenders to Business and State-Imploy-
ments, *greater* Porers upon Books, nor Plodders after wealth. And yet
no where more Abandoned Libertines, more refined Luxurists, Extravagant Debauchers, Conceited Gallants, more Dabblers in Poetry as
well as Politics, in Philosophy, and in Chemistry. I have had several
Servants far gone in Divinity, others in Poetry; have known, in the
Families of some Friends, a Keeper deep in *Rosicrucian* Principles, and
a Laundress firm in those of *Epicurus.*[6]

Temple's eloquent testimony looks not a little like an immediate
source for the paragraph we shall find at the end of Congreve's *Letter*
(below, p. 84).

In two letters to the witty Mr. Congreve the aspiring young litterateur John Dennis had criticized the *Fox* (*Volpone*) of Ben Jonson
and then Jonson's comic achievement more generally. The following
passage from the second letter possibly did most to elicit Congreve's
valued reply.

The Plots of the *Fox,* the *Silent Woman,* the *Alchemist,* are all of them
very Artful. But the Intrigues of the *Fox,* and the *Alchemist,* seem to
me to be more dexterously perplexed, than to be happily disentangled.
But the Gordian knot in the *Silent Woman* is untyed with so much
Felicity, that that alone, may Suffice to show *Ben Jonson* no ordinary
Heroe. But, then perhaps, the *Silent Woman* may want the very
Foundation of a good Comedy, which the other two cannot be said to
want. For it seems to me, to be without a Moral. Upon which
Absurdity, *Ben Jonson* was driven by the Singularity of *Morose's*
Character, which is too extravagant for Instruction, and fit, in my
opinion, only for Farce. For this seems to me, to Constitute the most
Essential Difference, betwixt Farce and Comedy, that the Follies which
are expos'd in Farce are Singular; and those are particular, which are
expos'd in Comedy. These last are those, with which some part of an
Audience may be suppos'd Infected, and to which all may be suppos'd
Obnoxious.[7] But the first are so very odd, that by Reason of their
Monstrous Extravagance, they cannot be thought to concern an Audience; and cannot be supposed to instruct them. For the rest of the

[6] *Miscellanea, the Second Part, in Four Essays,* The Third Edition, London,
1692; the text quoted here is taken from J. E. Spingarn, *Critical Essays of the
Seventeenth Century,* III (Oxford, 1909), 103–6.

[7] Liable to be infected by. By "Singular" Dennis seems to mean utterly unique,
or freakish; by "particular," what is abnormal in some recurrent and classifiable
form.

Characters in these Plays, they are for the most part true, and Most of the Humorous Characters Master-pieces. For *Ben Jonson's* Fools, seem to shew his Wit a great deal more than his Men of Sense. I Admire his Fops, and but barely Esteem his Gentlemen. *Ben* seems to draw Deformity more to the Life than Beauty. He is often so eager to pursue Folly, that he forgets to take Wit along with him. For the Dialogue, it seems to want very often that Spirit, that Grace, and that Noble Railery, which are to be found in more Modern Plays, and which are Virtues that ought to be Inseparable from a finish'd Comedy. But there seems to be one thing more wanting than all the rest, and that is Passion,[8] I mean that fine and that delicate Passion, by which the Soul shows its Politeness, ev'n in the midst of its trouble. Now to touch a Passion is the surest way to Delight. For nothing agitates like it. Agitation is the Health and Joy of the Soul, of which it is so entirely fond, that even then, when we imagine we seek Repose, we only seek Agitation. You know what a Famous Modern Critic has said of Comedy.

> Il faut que ses acteurs badinent noblement,
> Que son Noeud bien formé se dénoue aisément;
> Que l'action Marchant où la raison la guide,
> Ne se perde Jamais dans une Scène vuide,
> Que son Stile humble et doux se relève à propos,
> Que ses discours par tout fertiles en bons mots,
> Soient pleins de passions finement maniées,
> Et les Scènes toujours l'une à l'autre liées.[9]

I leave you to make the Application to *Jonson*—Whatever I have said my self of his Comedies, I submit to your better Judgment. For you who, after Mr. *Wycherley,* are incomparably the best Writer of it living; ought to be allowed to be the best judge too.[10]

---

[8] In his later critical writings (see below p. 123) Dennis was to make "Passion" the distinguishing feature of all true poetry.

[9] Boileau, *L'Art Poétique* (1674), III. 405–12: "Requirements for comedy: elegant repartee and a neatly contrived intrigue sliding easily to a denouement, events proceeding in a reasonable way and not getting lost in vacuities; a gracefully low style, yet rising somewhat at the right moments, many good jokes, refined feelings, and all the scenes closely linked together."

[10] John Dennis, *Letters upon Several Occasions* (London, 1696), pp. 76–79.

A Letter to Mr. Dennis

Concerning Humour in Comedy

[July 10, 1695]

Dear Sir,

You write to me, that you have Entertained yourself two or three
Days, with reading several Comedies, of several Authors; and your
Observation is, that there is more of *Humour* in our English Writers,
than in any of the other Comic Poets, Ancient or Modern. You desire
to know my Opinion, and at the same time my Thought, of that
which is generally call'd *Humour* in Comedy.

I agree with you, in an Impartial Preference of our English Writers,
in that Particular. But if I tell you my Thoughts of *Humour,* I must
at the same Time confess, that what I take for true *Humour,* has not
been so often written, even by them, as is generally believed: And
some who have valued themselves, and have been esteem'd by others,
for that kind of Writing, have seldom touch'd upon it. To make this
appear to the World, would require a long and labour'd Discourse,
and such as I neither am able nor ·villing to undertake. But such
little Remarks, as may be continued[1] within the Compass of a Letter,
and such unpremeditated Thoughts, as may be Communicated between
Friend and Friend, without incurring the Censure of the World, or
setting up for a *Dictator,* you shall have from me, since you have
enjoyn'd it.

To define *Humour,* perhaps, were as difficult, as to Define *Wit;* for
like that, it is of infinite variety. To Enumerate the several *Humours*
of Men, were a Work as endless, as to sum up their several Opinions.
And in my Mind the *Quot homines tot Sententiae,*[2] might have been

---

From Dennis's volume *Letters upon Several Occasions: Written by and between
Mr. Dryden, Mr. Wycherley, Mr.＿＿＿＿, Mr. Congreve and Mr. Dennis* (London, 1696), pp. 80–96.

[1] The text of 1696 has *continued.* J. E. Spingarn, *Critical Essays of the Seventeenth Century* (Oxford, 1908–1909), III, 242, 335, plausibly emends to *contained.*

[2] "So many men, so many opinions."—Terence, *Phormio,* II.iv.14.

more properly interpreted of *Humour;* since there are many Men, of the same Opinion in many things, who are yet quite different in Humours. But though we cannot certainly tell what *Wit* is, or, what *Humour* is, yet we may go near to show something, which is not *Wit* or not *Humour;* and yet often mistaken for both. And since I have mentioned *Wit* and *Humour* together, let me make the first Distinction between them, and observe to you that *Wit is often mistaken for Humour.*

I have observed, that when a few things have been Wittily and Pleasantly spoken by any Character in a Comedy; it has been very usual for those, who make their Remarks on a Play, while it is acting, to say, *Such a thing is very Humorously spoken: There is a great Deal of Humour in that Part.* Thus the Character of the Person speaking, may be, Surprizingly and Pleasantly, is mistaken for a Character of *Humour;* which indeed is a Character of *Wit.* But there is a great Difference between a Comedy, wherein there are many things *Humorously,* as they call it, which is *Pleasantly* spoken; and one, where there are several Characters of *Humour,* distinguish'd by the Particular and Different Humours, appropriated to the several Persons represented, and which naturally arise, from the different Constitutions, Complexions, and Dispositions of Men. The saying of Humorous Things, does not distinguish Characters; For every Person in a Comedy may be allow'd to speak them. From a Witty Man they are expected; and even a *Fool* may be permitted to stumble on 'em by chance. Though I make a Difference betwixt *Wit* and *Humour;* yet I do not think that Humorous Characters exclude Wit: No, but the Manner of *Wit* should be adapted to the *Humour.* As for Instance, a Character of a Splenetic and Peevish *Humour,* should have a Satirical Wit: A Jolly and Sanguine *Humour,* should have a Facetious Wit. The Former should speak Positively; the Latter, Carelessly: For the former Observes, and shews things as they are; the latter, rather overlooks Nature, and speaks things as he would have them; and his *Wit* and *Humour* have both of them a less Alloy of Judgment than the others.

As *Wit,* so, its opposite, *Folly, is sometimes mistaken for Humour.*

When a Poet brings a *Character* on the Stage, committing a thousand Absurdities, and talking Impertinencies, roaring Aloud, and Laughing immoderately, on every, or rather upon no occasion; this is a Character of Humour.

Is any thing more common, than to have a pretended Comedy,

stuff'd with such Grotesques, Figures, and Farce Fools? Things, that either are not in Nature, or if they are, are Monsters, and Births of Mischance; and consequently as such, should be stifled, and huddled out of the way, like *Sooterkins;*[3] that Mankind may not be shock'd with an appearing Possibility of the Degeneration of a God-like *Species.* For my part, I am as willing to laugh as any body, and as easily diverted with an Object truly ridiculous: but at the same time, I can never care for seeing things that force me to entertain low thoughts of my Nature. I dont know how it is with others, but I confess freely to you, I could never look long upon a Monkey, without very Mortifying Reflections; though I never heard any thing to the Contrary, why that Creature is not originally of a Distinct *Species.* As I dont think *Humour* exclusive of *Wit,* neither do I think it inconsistent with *Folly;* but I think the Follies should be only such, as Mens Humours may incline 'em to; and not Follies intirely abstracted from both Humour and Nature.

Sometimes, *Personal Defects are misrepresented for Humours.*

I mean, sometimes Characters are barbarously exposed on the Stage, ridiculing Natural Deformities, Casual Defects in the Senses, and Infirmities of Age. Sure the Poet must both be very Ill-natur'd himself, and think his Audience so, when he proposes by shewing a Man Deform'd, or Deaf, or Blind, to give them an agreeable Entertainment; and hopes to raise their Mirth, by what is truly an object of Compassion. But much need not be said upon this Head to any body, especially to you, who in one of your Letters to me concerning *Jonson*'s *Fox* have justly excepted against this Immoral part of *Ridicule* in *Corbaccio*'s Character;[4] and there I must agree with you to blame him, whom otherwise I cannot enough admire, for his great Mastery of true Humour in Comedy.

External Habit of Body is often mistaken for Humour.

By *External Habit,* I do not mean the Ridiculous Dress or Cloathing of a Character, though that goes a good Way in some received Characters. (But undoubtedly a Man's Humour may incline him to

---

3 An imperfect or deformed offspring. Dutch women were supposed to be delivered, along with their children, of a "Sooterkin," a small, ratlike afterbirth.

4 Dennis had written: *"Corbaccio* the Father of *Bonario* is expos'd for his Deafness, a Personal defect; which is contrary to the end of Comedy, Instruction. For Personal Defects cannot be amended; and the exposing such, can never Divert any but half-witted Men. It cannot fail to bring a thinking Man to reflect upon the Misery of Human Nature; and into what he may fall himself without any fault of his own." Cf. above, pp. 74–75.

dress differently from other People.) But I mean a Singularity of Manners, Speech, and Behaviour, peculiar to all, or most of the same Country, Trade, Profession, or Education. I cannot think, that a *Humour*, which is only a Habit, or Disposition contracted by Use or Custom; for by a Disuse, or Compliance with other Customs, it may be worn off, or diversify'd.

Affectation is generally mistaken for Humour.

These are indeed so much alike, that at a Distance, they may be mistaken one for the other. For what is *Humour* in one, may be *Affectation* in another; and nothing is more common, than for some to affect particular ways of saying, and doing things, peculiar to others, whom they admire and would imitate. *Humour* is the Life, *Affectation* the Picture. He that draws a Character of *Affectation*, shews *Humour* at the Second Hand; he at best but publishes a Translation, and his Pictures are but Copies.

But as these two last distinctions are the Nicest, so it may be most proper to Explain them, by Particular Instances from some Author of Reputation. *Humour* I take, either to be born with us, and so of a Natural Growth; or else to be grafted into us, by some accidental change in the Constitution, or Revolution of the Internal Habit of Body; by which it becomes, if I may so call it, Naturaliz'd.

Humour is from Nature, *Habit* from Custom; and *Affectation* from Industry.

Humour shews us as we *are*.

Habit shews us, as we appear, under a forcible Impression.

Affectation, shews what we would be, under a Voluntary Disguise.

Though here I would observe by the way, that a continued Affectation, may in time become a Habit.

The Character of *Morose* in the *Silent Woman*, I take to be a Character of Humour. And I choose to Instance this Character to you, from many others of the same Author, because I know it has been Condemn'd by many as Unnatural and Farce: And you have yourself hinted some Dislike of it, for the same Reason, in a Letter to me, concerning some of *Jonson*'s Plays.

Let us suppose *Morose* to be a Man Naturally Splenetic and Melancholy; is there any thing more offensive to one of such a Disposition, than Noise and Clamour? Let any Man that has the Spleen (and there are enough in *England*) be Judge. We see common Examples of this Humour in little every day. 'Tis ten to one, but three parts in four of the Company that you dine with, are Discompos'd and

Startled at the Cutting of a Cork, or Scratching a Plate with a Knife: It is a Proportion of the same Humour, that makes such or any other Noise offensive to the Person that hears it; for there are others who will not be disturb'd at all by it. Well; But *Morose* you will say, is so Extravagant, he cannot bear any Discourse or Conversation, above a Whisper. Why, It is his excess of this Humour, that makes him become Ridiculous, and qualifies his Character for Comedy. If the Poet had given him, but a Moderate proportion of that Humour, 'tis odds but half the Audience, would have sided with the Character, and have Condemn'd the Author, for Exposing a Humour which was neither Remarkable nor Ridiculous. Besides, the distance of the Stage requires the Figure represented, to be something larger than the Life; and sure a Picture may have Features larger in Proportion, and yet be very like the Original. If this Exactness of Quantity, were to be observed in Wit, as some would have it in Humour; what would become of those Characters that are design'd for Men of Wit? I believe if a Poet should steal a Dialogue of any length, from the *Extempore* Discourse of the two Wittiest Men upon Earth, he would find the Scene but coldly receiv'd by the Town. But to the purpose.

The Character of Sir *John Daw* in the same Play, is a Character of Affectation. He every where discovers an Affectation of Learning; when he is not only Conscious to himself, but the Audience also plainly perceives, that he is Ignorant. Of this kind are the Characters of *Thraso* in the *Eunuch* of *Terence,* and *Pyrgopolynices* in the *Miles Gloriosus* of *Plautus.*[5] They affect to be thought Valiant, when both themselves and the Audience know they are not. Now such a Boasting of Valour in Men who were really Valiant, would undoubtedly be a *Humour;* for a Fiery Disposition might naturally throw a Man into the same Extravagance, which is only affected in the Characters I have mentioned.

The Character of *Cob* in *Every Man in his Humour,*[6] and most of the under Characters in *Bartholomew Fair,* discover only a Singularity of Manners, appropriated to the several Educations and Professions of the Persons represented. They are not Humours but Habits contracted by Custom. Under this Head may be ranged all Country Clowns, Sailors, Tradesmen, Jockeys, Gamesters and such like, who make use of *Cants* or peculiar *Dialects* in their several Arts and Vocations. One

---

5 See above, Introduction, p. 6.
6 See above, pp. 22–25.

may almost give a Receipt for the Composition of such a Character: For the Poet has nothing to do, but to collect a few proper Phrases and terms of Art, and to make the Person apply them by ridiculous Metaphors in his Conversation, with Characters of different Natures. Some late Characters of this Kind have been very successful; but in my mind they may be Painted without much Art or Labour; since they require little more, than a good Memory and Superficial Observation. But true Humour cannot be shewn, without a Dissection of Nature, and a Narrow Search, to discover the first Seeds, from whence it has its Root and growth.

If I were to write to the World, I should be obliged to dwell longer upon each of these Distinctions and Examples; for I know that they would not be plain enough to all Readers. But a bare hint is sufficient to inform you of the Notions which I have on this Subject: And I hope by this time you are of my Opinion, that Humour is neither Wit, nor Folly, nor personal Defect; nor Affectation, nor Habit; and yet, that each, and all of these, have been both written and received for Humour.

I should be unwilling to venture even on a bare Description of Humour, much more, to make a Definition of it, but now my hand is in, Ile tell you what serves me instead of either. I take it to be, *A singular and unavoidable manner of doing or saying any thing, Peculiar and Natural to one Man only; by which his Speech and Actions are distinguish'd from those of other Men.*

Our *Humour* has Relation to us, and to what proceeds from us, as the Accidents have to a Substance; it is a Colour, Taste, and Smell, Diffused through all; though our Actions are never so many, and different in Form, they are all Splinters of the same Wood, and have Naturally one Complexion; which though it may be disguised by Art, yet cannot be wholly changed: We may Paint it with other Colours, but we cannot change the Grain. So the Natural sound of an Instrument will be distinguish'd, though the Notes expressed by it, are never so various, and the Divisions never so many. Dissimulation, may by Degrees, become more easy to our practice; but it can never absolutely Transubstantiate us into what we would seem: It will always be in some proportion a Violence upon Nature.

A Man may change his Opinion, but I believe he will find it a Difficulty, to part with his Humour, and there is nothing more provoking, than the being made sensible of that difficulty, Sometimes, one shall meet with those, who perhaps, Innocently enough, but at the same time impertinently, will ask the Question; *Why are you not Merry? Why are you not Gay, Pleasant, and Chearful?* then instead of answering, could I ask such a one; *Why are you not handsome? Why have you not Black Eyes, and a better Complexion?* Nature abhors to be forced.

The two Famous Philosophers of *Ephesus* and *Abdera*,[7] have their different Sects at this day. Some Weep, and others laugh at one and the same thing.

I dont doubt, but you have observed several Men Laugh when they are Angry; others who are Silent; some that are Loud: Yet I cannot suppose that it is the passion of *Anger* which is in it self different, or more or less in one than t'other; but that it is the *Humour* of the Man that is Predominant, and urges him to express it in that manner. Demonstrations of pleasure are as Various; one Man has a Humour of retiring from all Company, when any thing has happen'd to please him beyond expectation; he hugs himself alone, and thinks it an Addition to the pleasure to keep it Secret. Another is upon Thorns till he has made Proclamation of it; and must make other People sensible of his happiness, before he can be so himself. So it is in Grief, and other Passions. Demonstrations of Love and the Effects of that Passion upon several Humours, are infinitely different; but here the Ladies who abound in Servants[8] are the best Judges. Talking of the Ladies, methinks something should be observed of the Humour of the Fair Sex; since they are sometimes so kind as to furnish out a Character for Comedy. But I must confess I have never made any observation of what I Apprehend to be true Humour in Women. Perhaps Passions are too powerful in that Sex, to let Humour have its Course; or may be by Reason of their Natural Coldness, Humour cannot Exert it self to that extravagant Degree, which it often does in the Male Sex. For if ever any thing does appear Comical or Ridiculous in a Woman, I think it is little more than an acquir'd Folly, or an Affectation. We may call them the weaker Sex, but I think the true Reason is, because our Follies are stronger, and our Faults are more prevailing.

One might think that the Diversity of Humour, which must be allowed to be diffused throughout Mankind, might afford endless Matter, for the support of Comedies. But when we come closely to

---

[7] Heraclitus and Democritus. Democritus is sometimes known as "the laughing philosopher," in contrast to the melancholy Heraclitus.

[8] I.e., lovers.

consider that point, and nicely to distinguish the Difference of Humours, I believe we shall find the contrary. For though we allow every Man something of his own, and a peculiar Humour; yet every Man has it not in quantity, to become Remarkable by it: Or, if many do become Remarkable by their Humours; yet all those Humours may not be Diverting. Nor is it only requisite to distinguish what Humour will be diverting, but also how much of it, what part of it to shew in Light, and what to cast in Shades; how to set it off by preparatory Scenes, and by opposing other humours to it in the same Scene. Through a wrong Judgment, sometimes, Mens Humours may be opposed when there is really no specific Difference between them; only a greater Proportion of the same, in one than t'other; occasion'd by his having more Flegm, or Choller, or whatever the Constitution is, from whence their Humours derive their Source.

There is infinitely more to be said on this Subject; though perhaps I have already said too much; but I have said it to a Friend, who I am sure will not expose it, if he does not approve of it. I believe the Subject is intirely new, and was never touch'd upon before; and if I would have any one to see this private Essay, it should be some one, who might be provoked by my Errors in it, to Publish a more Judicious Treatise on the Subject. Indeed I wish it were done, that the World being a little acquainted with the scarcity of true Humour, and the difficulty of finding and shewing it, might look a little more favourably on the Labours of them, who endeavour to search into Nature for it, and lay it open to the Public View.

I dont say but that very entertaining and useful Characters, and proper for Comedy, may be drawn from Affectations, and those other Qualities, which I have endeavoured to distinguish from Humour: but I would not have such imposed on the World, for Humour, nor esteem'd of Equal value with it. It were perhaps, the Work of a long Life to make one Comedy true in all its Parts, and to give every Character in it a True and Distinct Humour. Therefore, every Poet must be beholding to other Helps, to make out his Number of ridiculous Characters. But I think such a One deserves to be broke, who makes all false Musters; who does not shew one true Humour in a Comedy, but entertains his Audience to the end of the Play with every thing out of Nature.

I will make but one Observation to you more, and have done; and that is grounded upon an Observation of your own, and which I mention'd at the beginning of my Letter, *viz*, That there is more of

Humour in our English Comic Writers than in any others. I do not at all wonder at it, for I look upon Humour to be almost of English Growth; at least, it does not seem to have found such Encrease on any other Soil. And what appears to me to be the reason of it, is the great Freedom, Privilege, and Liberty which the Common People of *England* enjoy. Any Man that has a Humour, is under no restraint, or fear of giving it Vent; they have a Proverb among them, which, may be, will shew the Bent and Genius of the People, as well as a longer Discourse: *He that will have a May-pole, shall have a May-pole.* This is a Maxim with them, and their Practice is agreeable to it. I believe something Considerable too may be ascribed to their feeding so much on Flesh, and the Grossness of their Diet in general. But I have done, let the Physicians agree that.

Thus you have my Thoughts of *Humour,* to my Power of Expressing them in so little Time and Compass. You will be kind to shew me wherein I have Err'd; and as you are very Capable of giving me Instruction, so, I think I have a very Just title to demand it from you; being without Reserve,

July 10, 1695

Your real Friend,
And humble Servant,
W. CONGREVE

PROLOGUE

TO

The Way of the World

[*1700*]

Spoken by Mr. Betterton[1]

Of those few Fools, who with ill Stars are curs'd,
Sure scribbling Fools, call'd Poets, fare the worst.
For they're a sort of Fools which *Fortune* makes,
And after she has made 'em Fools, forsakes.
With *Nature's* Oafs 'tis quite a diff'rent Case,
For *Fortune* favours all her *Idiot-Race:*
In her own Nest the *Cuckow-Eggs* we find,
O'er which she broods to hatch the *Changling-Kind*.
No Portion for her own she has to spare,
So much she doats on her adopted Care.

Poets are Bubbles, by the Town drawn in,
Suffer'd at first some trifling Stakes to win:
But what unequal Hazards do they run!
Each time they write, they venture all they've won:
The 'Squire that's butter'd still, is sure to be undone.
This Author, heretofore, has found your Favour,
But pleads no Merit from his past Behaviour.
To build on that might prove a vain Presumption,
Should Grants to Poets made, admit Resumption:
And in Parnassus he must lose his Seat,
If that be found a forfeited Estate.

Our text follows the first edition: *The Way of the World, A Comedy.* As it is
Acted at the Theatre in *Lincoln's-Inn-Fields,* By His Majesty's Servants. Written
by Mr. Congreve.... London: Printed for *Jacob Tonson*...1700.

1 Thomas Betterton (1635?–1710), leading actor on the London stage for more
than forty years. He joined Sir William D'Avenant's company at Lincoln's Inn
Fields in 1661 and played Hamlet in that year. In 1700 he played Falstaff in his
own adaptation of Shakespeare's *King Henry IV*. Cf. above, p. 71.

He owns, with Toil, he wrought the following Scenes,
But if they're naught ne're spare him for his Pains:
Damn him the more; have no Commiseration
For Dulness on mature Deliberation.
He swears he'll not resent one hiss'd-off Scene, ⎫
Nor, like those peevish Wits, his Play maintain, ⎬
Who, to assert their Sense, your Taste arraign. ⎭
Some Plot we think he has, and some new Thought;
Some Humour too, no Farce; but that's a Fault.
Satire, he thinks, you ought not to expect,
For so Reform'd a Town, who dares Correct?
To please, this time, has been his sole Pretence,
He'll not instruct least it should give Offence.
Should he by chance a Knave or Fool expose,
That hurts none here, sure here are none of those.
In short, our Play, shall (with your leave to shew it)
Give you one Instance of a Passive Poet.
Who to your Judgments yields all Resignation;
So Save or Damn, after your own Discretion.

JOSEPH ADDISON

[1672–1719]

W e have seen that the playwright and poet William Congreve was a gentleman—witty and fashionable. His peer and fellow member of the Whig Kit Cat Club, Joseph Addison—poet, Latinist, playwright, essayist, secretary of state, and M.P.—was, if it is possible to conceive it, even more a gentleman, with a courtlier accent, courteous, kindly, serious, noble, gentle—in short, a *gentle*man. According to Alexander Pope, who may well have known what he was talking about, this gentleman could be unfriendly and prudently mean: "Willing to wound and yet afraid to strike, Just hint a fault and hesitate dislike." Yet the overall portrait remains, bathed in a light of kindly suggestion. If we look at Addison's chief poetical productions, his smoothly Augustan *Account of the Greatest English Poets*, 1694, for instance, his dutiful verse *Letter from Italy* (to his patron Lord Halifax), 1704, his officially commissioned *Campaign*, 1704, celebrating Marlborough's victory at Blenheim, or his political tragedy that managed to please both Whigs and Tories, *Cato*, acted in 1713, we sense a solemn and carefully eloquent, a moral, meditative, and cheerfully conservative personality—moderately capable in the couplet idiom. If he is on occasion witty, he is yet not a wit, and does not wish to be. He is a minor poet, a duly cautious tragic dramatist.

Addison's major writings are his periodical essays, and especially the 276 papers which he contributed to the total of 635 *Spectators*,[1] published in 1711–1712, with his school friend Richard Steele (Nos. 1–555), and in 1714, without Steele (Nos. 556–635). Some sixty of Addison's *Spectators* deal with themes of literary criticism—in just the temperate, undogmatical, genial, and good-humored way which we might expect of such a gentlemanly philosopher. The *Spectators* in general are a crossroads of London life and conversation, a medley of contemporary learning, thinking, coffee-house and street scenes. Addison's critical speculations, accordingly, are marked less by any

---

[1] *The Spectator,* ed. Donald F. Bond (Oxford, 1965), I, lix, lxxvii.

strong prepossessions or polemic purpose than by a reportorial avidity to get things in, to be fair to the exuberant wealth of phenomena. He is a judiciously enthusiastic appreciator: as in his three pioneer papers on the folk ballad (70, 74, 85), his welcome to Pope's youthful *Essay on Criticism* (254), and his classically oriented *tour de force* on *Paradise Lost* (18 numbers, on Saturdays, starting with No. 267). He is a moderately opinionated analyst of the English literary tradition and situation: as in the five papers on tragedy (in favor of blank verse, but against poetical justice, tragi-comedy, stage spectacles, and butchery—39, 40, 42, 44, 548), the series on true and false wit (58–63), and his extended venture in a new pictorially centered aesthetics, the "pleasures of the imagination" (411–421).

He writes an easy, engaging, conversational style, which, in view of the toughness of some of the problems he tackles, may seem at moments naïve—and perhaps at moments is. "By modern standards," says his most modern editor, many of his critical essays "seem unnecessarily simplified and 'unphilosophical,' but to the contemporary reader they provided just the right amount of critical learning, amply supported with illustrative quotations and without the pedantry of the schools."[2]

English comic writers, from the time of Ben Jonson, had steadily protested the moral intent of their ridiculous, sometimes scandalous, scenes. Thus they tended to assimilate comedy to satire—making an equation which may tempt purists in genre criticism to object, but which is difficult enough to refute, for in truth it would seem impossible to draw a hard line between the two aims and forms. In this profession of moral concern, the English stage had much help from France, and especially from Molière. A kind of generalized moral criticism of society, the reiterated aim of both comedy and satire during the seventeenth century, is to be found at its most refined in a few plays of Molière— *Le Tartuffe, Le Bourgeois Gentilhomme, L'Avare,* and above all *Le Misanthrope.* Molière had defended his ethical aims in a few statements to which we have already alluded.[3] *Le devoir de la comédie est de corriger les hommes en les divertissant.... On veut bien être méchant, mais on ne veut point être ridicule.*[4] This was a plausible and in part justifiable posture, and sometimes innocent enough, as in the following from Shadwell:

> If poets aim at naught but to delight,
> Fiddlers have to the bays as equal right.[5]

---

2 *The Spectator,* ed. Bond, I, lxiii.

3 Above, p. 60.

4 "Comedy aims to reform people while amusing them." "We don't mind being wicked; what we mind is being silly." The two sentences are from the *Premier Placet* to *Le Tartuffe,* 1664, and the *Préface* to *Le Tartuffe,* 1669, respectively.

5 Prologue to *The Squire of Alsatia,* 1688.

In other instances, the poet seems to speak with a sly smile, as when Pope amplifies his "imitation" of Horace's *Epistle to Augustus* with this couplet:

> Hence Satire rose, that just the medium hit,
> And heals with Morals what it hurts with Wit.

There *was* morality in Dryden's or Pope's satires, and there *was* a kind of morality, or social philosophy, in the comedies of Etherege, Wycherley, and Congreve—as advanced academic critics have recently been arguing in a crescendo of ingenuity and ironic reflexiveness.[6] There was also, pretty plainly, much indecency and blasphemy. The norms which the dramatists were interested in promoting—so far as they were promoters or propagandists at all—were those of elegant society and high-varnished manners, certainly not the charity and chastity of the Church and Scriptures. Their unsympathetic derision was directed against the social misfit, the climbing bourgeois or city merchant, the country Tory, the chilly "prude," the conventional prig, the obtuse gull. They ministered to the vanity of the smart aristocratic audience. If in truth they aimed in any way at the discouragement of carnal vices, it was by the dubiously calculated method of the lively and witty painting of their indulgence. We have already noticed Congreve, in his *Amendments* of 1698, rushing (confidently, if not very convincingly[7]) to the defense of his art against the nonjuring divine Jeremy Collier's *Short View of the Immorality and Profaneness of the English Stage*. "*Smuttiness* of *Expression*," says Collier, "...*Swearing, Profainness*, and *Lewd Application* of *Scripture...Abuse* of the *Clergy* ...making their *Top Characters Libertines*, and giving them *Success* in their *Debauchery*"—these are the darling "liberties" of the modern comic stage.[8]

At a later moment in the debate we have the following corroboration of Collier's view from the Tory clergyman and wit Jonathan Swift:

> I do not remember, that our English poets ever suffered a criminal amour to succeed upon the stage, till the reign of King Charles the

---

6 Marvin Mudrick, "Restoration Comedy and Later," in *English Stage Comedy*, ed. W. K. Wimsatt (New York, 1955), pp. 98–125; Dale Underwood, *Etherege and the Seventeenth Century Comedy of Manners* (New Haven, 1957); Norman N. Holland, *The First Modern Comedies* (Cambridge, Mass., 1959); Rose A. Zimbardo, *Wycherley's Drama: A Link in the Development of English Satire* (New Haven, 1965).

7 "He is very angry," says Samuel Johnson, "and, hoping to conquer Collier with his own weapons, allows himself the use of every term of contumely and contempt; but he has the sword without the arm of Scanderbeg" (*Life of Congreve*, in *Lives of the Poets*, ed. G. B. Hill, Oxford, 1905, II, 222).

8 *A Short View of the Immorality and Profaneness of the English Stage: Together with the Sense of Antiquity upon this Argument* (London, 1698), p. 2.

Second. Ever since that time, the alderman is made a cuckold, the
deluded virgin is debauched, and adultery and fornication are supposed
to be committed behind the scenes, as part of the action.[9]

One would not expect Addison to try to blink anything so palpable
as the immorality of the contemporary stage, or to contrive armaments
in the cause of the men of licentious wit. The "true wit," which he
surveyed so judiciously in a series of early *Spectators* and distinguished
so shrewdly from "false wit" and even from "mixed wit" (see No. 62),
was not the laughable "sheer" wit of salon conversation or stage
repartee, but a more refined, if no less agile, thing, the very principle
of vitality in poetry itself, as the discussion of it had come down to
him from the days of Hobbes and Dryden, and as it had been depreci-
ated in the more recent *Essay* of John Locke.

The single *Spectator* which Addison devotes explicitly to the comic
stage (No. 446, reprinted in this volume) is concerned not with laughter
directly but with the moral issue raised by Collier. We may see Addison
here, if we are willing, as for the moment playing the role of a more
urbane and tactful Collier. Though he is scandalized and would work
a reform, he is at the same time more sympathetic to the possibly
virtuous aims of the comic stage. The kind of drama which the furious
divine would in effect have suppressed, the literary moralist would
teach the way of a not unpleasant reform. Nothing indecent, and
nothing malicious. He was probably in the long run more concerned
about the latter kind of fault in laughter. "There is nothing that more
betrays a base, ungenerous Spirit than the giving of secret Stabs to
a Man's Reputation. Lampoons and Satyrs, that are written with
Wit and Spirit, are like poisoned Darts, which not only inflict a Wound,
but make it incurable" (No. 23).[10] Addison later claimed that his
critical persuasions in *The Spectator* had in fact done their part in
a successful campaign to "divert raillery from improper objects" and
to promote the development of the innocent kind of English comedy[11]
with which we shall find his friend Steele and others concerned.

An optimistic theology informs Addison's well-known resistance to
the witty "Gloom of the Tory Satirists."[12] In one *Spectator* essay

---

[9] *A Project for the Advancement of Religion and the Reformation of Manners*
(1709), in *Prose Works,* ed. Temple Scott (London, 1898), III, 39–40. Swift
proposed a government censorship for the stage.

[10] Cf. No. 209: "A Satyr should expose nothing but what is corrigible"; No.
445: "For my own part, I have endeavoured to make nothing Ridiculous that is
not in some measure Criminal"; or No. 249, reprinted in this volume.

[11] *Freeholder* No. 45, Friday, May 25, 1716, an answer to Sir Richard Black-
more's *Essay Upon Wit* in his *Essays Upon Several Subjects,* 1716. See The
Augustan Reprint Society's edition of both essays, Series I, No. 1 (May 1946).

[12] Louis I. Bredvold, "The Gloom of the Tory Satirists," in James L. Clifford
and Louis A. Landa, *Pope and his Contemporaries: Essays Presented to George
Sherburn* (Oxford, 1949), pp. 1–19.

(No. 381) he swings so far in the cause of pious good cheer as, para-doxically, to put fun and laughter into a kind of Baudelairean eclipse. "I have always preferred Chearfulness to Mirth." "Men of austere Principles look upon Mirth as too wanton and dissolute for a State of Probation, and as filled with a certain Triumph and Insolence of Heart. . . . [They] have observed that the sacred Person who was the great Pattern of Perfection was never seen to Laugh." But in the course of 660 *Spectators* there is much room for change of heart. In No. 494, we hear of "Superstitious Fears, and groundless Scruples" against laughter, ". . . as if Mirth was made for Reprobates." "Man," we are instructed, "is distinguished from all other Creatures, by the Faculty of Laughter." And No. 598 asserts a characteristically Addisonian balance:

> Mankind may be divided into the Merry and the Serious, who, both of them, make a very good Figure in the Species, so long as they keep their respective Humours from degenerating into the neighbouring Extreme; there being a natural Tendency in the one to melancholy Moroseness, and in the other to a fantastick Levity.[13]

Three of the four *Spectators* which appear in our text (Nos. 35, 47, 249) give us a kind of interlude or remission from strict attention to the stage. No. 35 deals broadly with the theme of "humor"—not humor in the sense we have read in Jonson, Dryden, Congreve, or Temple, but, as a later amateur would complain,[14] simply in the sense of whatever aims at making us laugh. This essay contrives a sort of agreeable tautology—a foam-rubber "genealogy" of true and false humor. With light aplomb, it manages to make the valuable assertion that "humor" ought to be reasonable and natural, truly witty, sensible, and mirthful, rather than delirious, false, crude, feigned, or nonsensical. In Nos. 47 and 249 we anticipate some classic psychological themes to be noted again on later pages of this volume (Postscript, pp. 284–88): Hobbesian egoism (in the respectable Medieval and Renaissance insti-tutions of fool, droll, and butt), personal "projection" (as human laughter at brutes or inanimate nature), and a kind of "relief" experi-enced through the very "Remissness" and "Dissolution" of laughter (a distinct harbinger of Freudian recathexis). No. 249 charts a dis-tinction between comedy and burlesque which will recur for us in a context of more immediate significance with Fielding's *Joseph Andrews*. The end of the essay stresses the Addisonian allegiance to amiable mirth in quoting twenty-two of the archetypal tetrameters of Milton's

---

13 See below, pp. 239–40, the Victorian version of the Aristotelian theme, by George Meredith.

14 Corbyn Morris, *An Essay Towards Fixing the True Standards of Wit, Humour, Raillery, Satire, and Ridicule,* 1744: The Augustan Reprint Society, Series I, No. 4 (November 1947).

L'Allegro: "...come thou Goddess fair and free, / In Heaven ycleped Euphrosyne."

Despite such efforts as his assimilation of the ballad of *Chevy Chase* to the Virgilian epic and his elaborate appreciation of *Paradise Lost* according to Aristotelian categories, Addison enjoyed in general an attitude of graceful relaxation in the presence of the critical rules. This can be shown in amusingly dramatic style from an early essay, *Tatler* No. 165, which brings a fearsome critic, Sir Timothy Tittle, into conversation with a young lady.

> "But madam," says he, "you ought not to have laughed; and I defy anyone to shew me a single rule that you could laugh by." "Ought not to laugh!" says she; "pray who should hinder me?" "Madam," says he, "there are such people in the world as Rapin, Dacier, and several others, that ought to have spoiled your mirth."[15]

Addison himself was the author of a single comic drama, *The Drummer; or, The Haunted House,* acted anonymously at Drury Lane in 1716, a very correct play, and very moral. Directing its wit (as his *Spectators* had prescribed) to the defense of the decent and praiseworthy (in the institution of marriage), it met with little success. Addison's gentle and reflective wit found its best stage in his periodical essays. Some of these, we know, were even humorous dramatizations of character that show how a tradition from Theophrastus and La Bruyère was already working toward the free narrative play of prose fiction in the novel. The Tory squire Sir Roger de Coverley is Addison's most fondly regarded contribution to the gallery of lovable eighteenth-century humors. Addison reduces Sir Roger to a harmless noddy with the gentlest of strokes.

> The enemy, far from being vilified, is being turned into a dear old man. The thought that he could ever be dangerous has been erased from our minds; but so also the thought that anything he said could ever be taken seriously. We all love Sir Roger. . . . That element in English society which stood against all that Addison's party was bringing in is henceforth seen through a mist of smiling tenderness—as an archaism, a lovely absurdity. What we might have been urged to attack as a fortress we are tricked into admiring as a ruin.[16]

---

[15] Cf. Molière, *La Critique de L'Ecole des Femmes* (1663), scene vi, quoted above, p. 61.

[16] C. S. Lewis, "Addison," in *Essays in Honor of David Nichol Smith,* reprinted in *Eighteenth Century English Literature: Modern Essays in Criticism,* ed. James L. Clifford (New York, 1959), p. 146.

The Spectator

Number 446

Quid deceat, quid non; quo Virtus, quo ferat Error.
                                                    Horace[1]

Friday, August 1, 1712

Since two or three Writers of Comedy who are now living have taken their Farewell of the Stage,[2] those who succeed them finding themselves incapable of rising up to their Wit, Humour and good Sense, have only imitated them in some of those loose unguarded Strokes, in which they complied with the corrupt Taste of the more Vicious Part of their Audience. When Persons of a low Genius attempt this kind of Writing, they know no Difference between being Merry and being Lewd. It is with an Eye to some of these degenerate Compositions that I have written the following Discourse.[3]

Were our *English* Stage but half so virtuous as that of the *Greeks* or *Romans,* we should quickly see the Influence of it in the Behaviour of all the Politer Part of Mankind. It would not be fashionable to ridicule Religion, or its Professors; the Man of Pleasure would not be the compleat Gentleman; Vanity would be out of Countenance, and every Quality which is Ornamental to Human Nature, wou'd meet with that Esteem which is due to it.

If the *English* Stage were under the same Regulations the *Athenian* was formerly, it would have the same Effect that had, in recommending the Religion, the Government, and Publick Worship of its Country. Were our Plays subject to proper Inspections and Limita-

---

The *Spectator* was published from March 1, 1711, to December 20, 1714, a total of 665 folio numbers: London, Printed for Sam Buckley. Our text follows, with a few corrections and normalizations, a bound set of the original numbers in the Beinecke Rare Book and Manuscript Library, Yale University. The annotation of the four *Spectators* which follow owes much to that in the edition by Donald F. Bond, 1965 (see above, p. 87).

[1] *Ars Poetica,* 308: "What fit, what not, what good or evil leads to."
[2] Congreve, Vanbrugh, and Wycherley are perhaps intended.
[3] Cf. Nos. 51 and 65.

tions, we might not only pass away several of our vacant Hours in the highest Entertainments; but should always rise from them wiser and better than we sat down to them.

It is one of the most unaccountable things in our Age, that the Lewdness of our Theatre should be so much complained of, so well exposed, and so little redressed. It is to be hoped, that some time or other we may be at leisure to restrain the Licentiousness of the Theatre, and make it contribute its Assistance to the Advancement of Morality, and to the Reformation of the Age. As Matters stand at present, Multitudes are shut out from this noble Diversion, by reason of those Abuses and Corruptions that accompany it. A Father is often affraid that his Daughter should be ruined by those Entertainments, which were invented for the Accomplishment and Refining of Human Nature. The *Athenian* and *Roman* Plays were written with such a regard to Morality, that *Socrates* used to frequent the one, and *Cicero* the other.

It happened once indeed, that *Cato* dropped into the *Roman* Theatre, when the *Floralia* were to be represented; and as in that Performance, which was a kind of Religious Ceremony, there were several indecent Parts to be acted, the People refused to see them whilst *Cato* was present. *Martial* on this Hint made the following Epigram, which we must suppose was applied to some grave Friend of his, that had been accidentally present at some such Entertainment.

> *Nosses jocosae dulce cum sacrum Florae,*
> *Festosque lusus, et licentiam vulgi,*
> *Cur in Theatrum Cato severe venisti?*
> *An Ideo tantum veneras, ut exires?*[4]

> Why dost thou come, great Censor of thy Age,
> To see the loose Diversions of the Stage?
> With awful Countenance and Brow severe,
> What in the Name of Goodness dost thou here?
> See the mixt Crowd! how Giddy, Lewd and Vain!
> Didst thou come in but to go out again?

An Accident of this Nature might happen once in an Age among the *Greeks* or *Romans;* but they were too wise and good to let the constant Nightly Entertainment be of such a Nature, that People of the most Sense and Virtue could not be at it. Whatever Vices are represented upon the Stage, they ought to be so marked and branded by the Poet, as not to appear either laudable or amiable in the Person

---

4 Martial, *Epigrams,* I.1–4. The translation is Addison's.

who is tainted with them. But if we look into the *English* Comedies
abovementioned, we would think they were formed upon a quite contrary Maxim, and that this Rule, tho' it held good upon the Heathen
Stage, was not to be regarded in Christian Theatres. There is another
Rule likewise, which was observed by Authors of Antiquity, and which
these Modern Genius's have no regard to, and that was never to chuse
an improper Subject for Ridicule. Now a Subject is improper for
Ridicule, if it is apt to stir up Horrour and Commiseration rather than
Laughter. For this Reason, we do not find any Comedy in so polite
an Author as *Terence*, raised upon the Violations of the Marriage Bed.
The Falshood of the Wife or Husband has given Occasion to noble
Tragedies, but a *Scipio* or a *Lelius* would have looked upon Incest or
Murder to have been as proper Subjects for Comedy.[5] On the contrary, Cuckoldom is the Basis of most of our Modern Plays. If an
Alderman appears upon the Stage, you may be sure it is in order to
be Cuckolded. An Husband that is a little grave or elderly, generally
meets with the same Fate. Knights and Baronets, Country Squires,
and Justices of the Quorum, come up to Town for no other Purpose.
I have seen Poor *Doggets* Cuckolded in all these Capacities.[6] In short,
our *English* Writers are as frequently severe upon this Innocent
unhappy Creature, commonly known by the Name of a Cuckold, as
the Ancient Comick Writers were upon an eating Parasite, or a vain-
glorious Soldier.

At the same time the Poet so contrives his Matters, that the two
Criminals are the Favourites of the Audience. We sit still, and wish
well to them through the whole Play, are pleased when they meet
with proper Opportunities, and are out of humour when they are
disappointed. The truth of it is, the accomplished Gentleman upon the
English Stage, is the Person that is familiar with other Mens Wives,
and indifferent to his own; as the Fine Woman is generally a Composition of Sprightliness and Falshood. I do not know whether it
proceeds from Barrenness of Invention, Depravation of Manners, or
Ignorance of Mankind; but I have often wondered that our ordinary
Poets cannot frame to themselves the Idea of a Fine Man that is
not a Whoremaster, or of a Fine Woman that is not a Jilt.

---

5 The friendship between Scipio Africanus the Younger and Laelius is com-
memorated in Cicero's dialogue *Laelius: De Amicitia.* Cf. above p. 6, and below
p. 143.

6 Thomas Doggett (d. 1721) had created the role of Fondle-wife in *The Old
Bachelor* of Congreve. He had appeared in this part at Drury Lane as recently as
May 13 of this year (1712).

I have sometimes thought of compiling a System of Ethics out of the Writings of these corrupt Poets, under the Title of *Stage Morality*. But I have been diverted from this Thought, by a Project which has been executed by an Ingenious Gentleman of my Acquaintance. He has composed, it seems, the History of a young Fellow, who has taken all his Notions of the World from the Stage, and who has directed himself in every Circumstance of his Life, and Conversation, by the Maxims and Examples of the Fine Gentleman in *English* Comedies. If I can prevail upon him to give me a Copy of this new-fashioned Novel, I will bestow on it a Place in my Works, and question not but it may have as good an Effect upon the Drama, as *Don Quixote* had upon Romance.

The Spectator

Number 35

Risu inepto res ineptior nulla est. Martial[1]

Tuesday, April 10, 1711

Among all kinds of Writing, there is none in which Authors are more apt to miscarry than in Works of Humour, as there is none in which they are more ambitous to excell. It is not an Imagination that teems with Monsters, an Head that is filled with extravagant Conceptions, which is capable of furnishing the World with Diversions of this nature; and yet if we look into the Productions of several Writers, who set up for Men of Humour, what wild irregular Fancies, what unnatural Distortions of Thought, do we meet with? If they speak Nonsense, they believe they are talking Humour; and when they have drawn together a Scheme of absurd, inconsistent Idea's, they are not able to read it over to themselves without laughing. These poor Gentlemen endeavour to gain themselves the Reputation of Wits and Humourists, by such monstrous Conceits as almost qualify them for *Bedlam;* not considering that Humour should always lye under the Check of Reason, and that it requires the Direction of the nicest Judgment, by so much the more as it indulges it self in the most boundless Freedoms. There is a kind of Nature that is to be observed in this sort of Compositions, as well as in all other, and a certain Regularity of Thought that must discover the Writer to be a Man of Sense, at the same time that he appears altogether given up to Caprice: For my part, when I read the delirious Mirth of an unskilful Author, I cannot be so barbarous as to divert my self with it, but am rather apt to pity the Man, than to laugh at any thing he writes.

The Deceas'd Mr. *Shadwell,*[2] who had himself a great deal of the Talent, which I am treating of, represents an empty Rake, in one of

---

1 Actually Catullus, *Carmina,* XXXIX.16: "Nothing is sillier than a silly laugh."
2 Thomas Shadwell died in 1692. Cf. above, p. 71, n. 2. Rakish characters in Shadwell's plays (*The Woman-Captain, The Squire of Alsatia, The Scowrers, Epsom Wells*) are often associated with window-breaking.

97

his Plays, as very much surprized to hear one say that breaking of Windows was not Humour; and I question not but several *English* Readers will be as much startled to hear me affirm, that many of those raving incoherent Pieces, which are often spread among us, under odd Chymerical Titles, are rather the Offsprings of a Distempered Brain, than Works of Humour.

It is indeed much easier to describe what is not Humour, than what is; and very difficult to define it otherwise than as *Cowley*[3] has done Wit, by Negatives. Were I to give my own Notions of it, I would deliver them after *Plato's* manner, in a kind of Allegory, and by supposing Humour to be a Person, deduce to him all his Qualifications, according to the following Genealogy. TRUTH was the Founder of the Family, and the Father of GOOD SENSE. GOOD SENSE was the Father of WIT, who married a Lady of a Collateral Line called MIRTH, by whom he had Issue HUMOUR. HUMOUR therefore being the youngest of this Illustrious Family, and descended from Parents of such different Dispositions, is very various and unequal in his Temper; sometimes you see him putting on grave Looks and a solemn Habit, sometimes airy in his Behaviour and fantastick in his Dress: Insomuch that at different times he appears as serious as a Judge, and as jocular as a *Merry-Andrew*. But as he has a great deal of the Mother in his Constitution, whatever Mood he is in, he never fails to make his Company laugh.

But since there are several Impostors abroad, who take upon them the Name of this young Gentleman, and would willingly pass for him in the World; to the end that well-meaning Persons may not be imposed upon by Counterfeits, I would desire my Readers, when they meet with any of these Pretenders, to look into his Parentage, and to examine him strictly, whether or no he be remotely allied to TRUTH, and lineally descended from GOOD SENSE? if not, they may conclude him a Counterfeit. They may likewise distinguish him by a loud and excessive Laughter, in which he seldom gets his Company to join with him. For as TRUE HUMOUR generally looks serious, whilst every Body laughs that is about him; FALSE HUMOUR is always laughing, whilst every Body about him looks serious. I shall only add, if he has not in him a Mixture of both Parents, that is, if he wou'd pass for the Offspring of WIT, you may conclude him to be altogether Spurious, and a Cheat.

---

[3] See Cowley's ode *Of Wit*, stanzas 3–7.

The Impostor of whom I am speaking, descends Originally from FALSEHOOD, who was the Mother of NONSENSE, who was brought to Bed of a Son called FRENZY, who Married one of the Daughters of FOLLY, commonly known by the Name of LAUGHTER, on whom he begot that Monstrous Infant of which I have been here speaking. I shall set down at length the Genealogical Table of FALSE HUMOUR, and, at the same time, place under it the Genealogy of TRUE HUMOUR, that the Reader may at one View behold their different Pedigrees and Relations.

FALSEHOOD.
NONSENSE.
FRENZY——LAUGHTER.
FALSE HUMOUR.

TRUTH.
GOOD SENSE.
WIT——MIRTH.
HUMOUR.

I might extend the Allegory, by mentioning several of the Children of FALSE HUMOUR, who are more in Number than the Sands of the Sea, and might in particular enumerate the many Sons and Daughters which he has begot in this Island. But as this would be a very invidious Task, I shall only observe in general, that FALSE HUMOUR differs from the TRUE, as a Monkey does from a Man.

First of all, He is exceedingly given to little Apish Tricks and Buffooneries.

Secondly, He so much delights in Mimickry, that it is all one to him whether he exposes by it Vice and Folly, Luxury and Avarice; or, on the contrary, Virtue and Wisdom, Pain and Poverty.

Thirdly, He is wonderfully unlucky, insomuch that he will bite the Hand that feeds him, and endeavour to ridicule both Friends and Foes indifferently. For having but small Talents, he must be merry where he *can,* not where he *should.*

Fourthly, Being intirely void of Reason, he pursues no Point either of Morality or Instruction, but is Ludicrous only for the sake of being so.

Fifthly, Being incapable of any thing but Mock-Representations, his Ridicule is always Personal, and aimed at the Vicious Man, or the Writer; not at the Vice, or at the Writing.

I have here only pointed at the whole Species of False Humourists, but as one of my principal Designs in this Paper is to beat down that malignant Spirit, which discovers it self in the Writings of the present Age, I shall not scruple, for the future, to single out any of the small Wits, that infest the World with such Compositions as are ill-natured, immoral and absurd. This is the only Exception which I shall make to the General Rule I have prescribed my self, of *attacking Multitudes*. Since every honest Man ought to look upon himself as in a Natural State of War with the Libeller and Lampooner, and to annoy them where-ever they fall in his way, this is but retaliating upon them and treating them as they treat others.

The Spectator

Number 47

Ride si sapis.—Martial[1]

Tuesday, April 24, 1711

Mr. *Hobbs*,[2] in his Discourse of Human Nature, which, in my humble Opinion, is much the best of all his Works, after some very curious Observations upon Laughter, concludes thus:

> The Passion of Lauhgter is nothing else but sudden Glory arising from some sudden Conception of some Eminency in our selves, by Comparison with the Infirmity of others, or with our own formerly: For Men laugh at the Follies of themselves past, when they come suddenly to Remembrance, except they bring with them any present Dishonour.

According to this Author therefore, when we hear a Man laugh excessively, instead of saying he is very Merry, we ought to tell him he is very Proud. And indeed, if we look into the bottom of this Matter, we shall meet with many Observations to confirm us in his Opinion. Every one laughs at some Body that is in an inferior State of Folly to himself. It was formerly the Custom for every great House in *England* to keep a tame Fool dress'd in Petticoats, that the Heir of the Family might have an opportunity of joking upon him, and divert himself with his Absurdities. For the same Reason Ideots are still in request in most of the Courts of *Germany,* where there is not a Prince of any great Magnificence who has not two or three dress'd, distinguish'd, undisputed Fools in his Retinue, whom the rest of the Courtiers are always breaking their Jests upon.

The *Dutch,* who are more famous for their Industry and Application, than for Wit and Humour, hang up in several of their Streets what they call the Sign of the *Gaper,* that is, the Head of an Ideot dress'd

---

[1] Martial, *Epigrams,* II.xli.1: "Laugh if you are wise."
[2] Thomas Hobbes, *Human Nature* (1650), ix.13 (*Elements of Law,* I.ix.13). Another phrasing of this celebrated thought appears in Hobbes, *Leviathan* (1651), I.vi.

in a Cap and Bells, and gaping in a most-immoderate manner: This is a standing Jest at *Amsterdam*.

Thus every one diverts himself with some Person or other that is below him in Point of Understanding, and triumphs in the Superiority of his Genius, whilst he has such Objects of Derision before his Eyes. Mr. *Dennis* has very well expressed this in a Couple of humorous Lines, which are part of a Translation of a Satire in Monsieur *Boileau*.[3]

> Thus one Fool lolls his Tongue out at another,
> And shakes his empty Noddle at his Brother.

Mr. *Hobb's* Reflection gives us the Reason why the insignificant People above mention'd are Stirrers up of Laughter among Men of a gross Taste: But as the more Understanding Part of Mankind do not find their Risibility affected by such ordinary Objects, it may be worth the while to examine into the several Provocatives of Laughter in Men of superior Sense and Knowledge.

In the first Place I must observe, that there is a Set of merry Drolls, whom the common People of all Countries admire, and seem to love so well, *that they could eat them,* according to the old Proverb: I mean those circumforaneous Wits whom every Nation calls by the Name of that Dish of Meat which it loves best. In *Holland* they are termed *Pickled Herrings;* in *France, Jean Pottages;* in *Italy, Maccaronies;* and in *Great Britain, Jack Puddings.* These merry Wags, from whatsoever Food they receive their Titles, that they may make their Audiences laugh, always appear in a Fool's Coat, and commit such Blunders and Mistakes in every Step they take, and every Word they utter, as those who listen to them would be ashamed of.

But this little Triumph of the Understanding, under the Disguise of Laughter, is no where more visible than in that Custom which prevails every where among us on the First Day of the present Month, when every Body takes it in his Head to make as many Fools as he can. In proportion as there are more Follies discover'd, so there is more Laughter raised on this Day than on any other in the whole Year. A Neighbour of mine, who is a Haberdasher by Trade, and

---

3 Boileau, *Satire* IV. In a reply "To the Spectator upon his Paper on the 24th of April," published in an *Essay on the Genius and Writings of Shakespear* (November 1711), the critic John Dennis (see below pp. 122–27) expressed much annoyance that the author of that *Spectator* (whom he supposed to be Steele) had chosen to quote just that example of his poetic power, rather than something from the Fourth Book of his blank-verse heroic poem *The Battle of Ramillia,* 1706 (*Critical Works of John Dennis,* ed. E. N. Hooker, II, 24, 440).

a very shallow conceited Fellow, makes his Boasts that for these Ten Years successively he has not made less than an Hundred *April* Fools. My Landlady had a falling out with him about a Fortnight ago, for sending every one of her Children upon some *Sleeveless Errand,* as she terms it. Her eldest Son went to buy an Halfpenny worth of Inkle at a Shoemakers; the eldest Daughter was dispatch'd half a Mile to see a Monster; and, in short, the whole Family of innocent Children made *April* Fools. Nay, my Landlady her self did not escape him. This empty Fellow has laughed upon these Conceits ever since.

This Art of Wit is well enough, when confined to one Day in a Twelve-month; But there is an ingenious Tribe of Men sprung up of late Years, who are for making *April* Fools every Day in the Year. These Gentlemen are commonly distinguished by the name of *Biters;* a Race of Men that are perpetually employ'd in laughing at those Mistakes which are of their own Production.

Thus we see, in proportion as one Man is more refined than another, he chuses his Fool out of a lower or higher Class of Mankind; or, to speak in a more Philosophical Language, that secret Elation and Pride of Heart which is generally call'd Laughter, arises in him from his comparing himself with an Object below him, whether it so happens that it be a Natural or an Artificial Fool. It is indeed very possible that the Persons we laugh at may in the main of their Characters be much wiser Men than our selves, but if they would have us laugh at them, they must fall short of us in those Respects which stir up this Passion.

I am afraid I shall appear too Abstracted in my Speculations, if I show that when a Man of Wit makes us laugh, it is by betraying some Oddness or Infirmity in his own Character, or in the Representation which he makes of others; and that when we laugh at a Brute or even an Inanimate thing, it is at some Action or Incident that bears a remote Analogy to any Blunder or Absurdity in reasonable Creatures.

But to come into common Life, I shall pass by the Consideration of those Stage Coxcombs that are able to shake a whole Audience, and take Notice of a particular sort of Men who are such Provokers of Mirth in Conversation, that it is impossible for a Club or Merry-meeting to subsist without them; I mean, those honest Gentlemen that are always exposed to the Wit and Raillery of their Well-wishers and Companions; that are pelted by Men, Women and Children, Friends and Foes, and, in a word, stand as *Butts* in Conversation, for every one to shoot at that pleases. I know several of these *Butts,* who are Men of Wit and Sense, though by some odd turn of Humour, some unlucky Cast in their Person or Behaviour, they have always the Misfortune to make the Company merry. The Truth of it is, a Man is not qualified for a *Butt*, who has not a good deal of Wit and Vivacity, even in the ridiculous side of his Character. A stupid *Butt* is only fit for the Conversation of ordinary People: Men of Wit require one that will give them Play, and bestir himself in the absurd part of his Behaviour. A *Butt* with these Accomplishments, frequently gets the Laugh of his side, and turns the Ridicule upon him that attacks him. Sir *John Falstaff* was an Hero of this Species, and gives a good Description of himself in his Capacity of a *Butt*, after the following manner; *Men of all sorts* (says that merry Knight) *take a pride to gird at me. The Brain of Man is not able to invent any thing that tends to Laughter more than I invent, or is invented on me. I am not only Witty in my self, but the Cause that Wit is in other Men.*[4]

---

[4] *2 Henry IV*, I.ii.7–12.

The Spectator

Number 249

Γέλως ἄκαιρος ἐν Βροτοῖς δεινὸν κακον.
Fragmentum Veteris Poetae[1]

Saturday, December 15, 1711

When I make Choice of a Subject that has not been treated of by others, I throw together my Reflections on it without any Order or Method, so that they may appear rather in the Looseness and Freedom of an Essay, than in the Regularity of a Set Discourse. It is after this manner that I shall consider Laughter and Ridicule in my present Paper.

Man is the merriest species of the Creation, all above and below him are Serious. He sees things in a different Light from other Beings, and finds his Mirth rising from Objects that perhaps cause something like Pity or Displeasure in higher Natures. Laughter is indeed a very good Counterpoise to the Spleen; and it seems but reasonable that we should be capable of receiving Joy from what is no real Good to us, since we can receive Grief from what is no real Evil.

I have in my Forty seventh Paper raised a Speculation on the Notion of a Modern Philosopher, who describes the first Motive of Laughter to be a secret Comparison which we make between our selves and the Persons we laugh at; or in other Words, that Satisfaction which we receive from the Opinion of some Pre-eminence in our selves, when we see the Absurdities of another, or when we reflect on any past Absurdities of our own. This seems to hold in most cases, and we may observe that the vainest part of Mankind are the most addicted to this Passion.

---

[1] "Unseasonable laughter is a grievous ill." Addison perhaps found his motto in Ralph Winterton, *Poetae Minores Graeci* (Cambridge, 1635, 1677), "Sententiae singulis versibus contentae e diversis Poetis" (1677, p. 507). This monostich occurs in a partly apocryphal schoolbook collection of 1,013 one-line moral maxims (Μενάνδρου Γνῶμαι) originating perhaps in the second century A.D. and today reassembled from various sources (John Maxwell Edmonds, *The Fragments of Attic Comedy,* IIIB (Leiden, 1961), 901–2, 910, No. 88.

I have read a Sermon of a Conventual in the Church of *Rome,* on those Words of the Wise Man, *I said of Laughter it is mad, and of Mirth what does it.*[2] Upon which he laid it down as a Point of Doctrine, that Laughter was the effect of Original Sin, and that *Adam* could not laugh before the Fall.[3]

Laughter, while it lasts, slackens and unbraces the Mind, weakens the Faculties and causes a kind of Remissness and Dissolution in all the Powers of the Soul: And thus far it may be looked upon as a Weakness in the Composition of Human Nature. But if we consider the frequent Reliefs that we receive from it, and how often it breaks the Gloom which is apt to depress the Mind, and damp our Spirits with transient unexpected gleams of Joy, one would take care not to grow too Wise for so great a Pleasure of Life.

The Talent of turning Men into Ridicule, and exposing to Laughter those one Converses with, is the Qualification of little ungenerous Tempers. A young Man with this cast of Mind cuts himself off from all manner of Improvement. Every one has his Flaws and Weaknesses; nay, the greatest Blemishes are often found in the most shining Characters; but what an absurd thing is it to pass over all the valuable Parts of a Man, and fix our Attention on his Infirmities; to observe his Imperfections more than his Virtues; and to make use of him for the Sport of others, rather than for our own Improvement.

We therefore very often find that Persons the most accomplished in Ridicule are those who are very shrewd at hitting a Blot, without exerting any thing Masterly in themselves. As there are many eminent Criticks who never writ a good Line, there are may admirable Buffoons that animadvert upon every single Defect in another, without ever discovering the least Beauty of their own. By this means these unlucky Wits often gain Reputation in the Esteem of Vulgar Minds, and raise themselves above Persons of much more laudable Characters.

If the Talent of Ridicule were employed to laugh Men out of Vice and Folly, it might be of some use to the World; but instead of this, we find that it is generally made use of to laugh Men out of Virtue and good Sense, by attacking every thing that is Solemn and Serious, Decent and Praise-worthy in Human Life.

---

2 *Ecclesiastes* II.2.

3 Touring on the Continent in February 1700, Addison had written from Blois to a friend in England, reporting the "Odd opinion of a Holy Father, a Capuchin, who in a discourse on the Vanity of Mirth, told us that he did not question but laughter was the effect of Original Sin and that Adam was not Risible before the Fall" (*Letters,* ed. Walter Graham, Oxford, 1941, p. 20).

We may observe, that in the First Ages of the World, when the great Souls and Master-pieces of Human Nature were produced, Men shined by a noble Simplicity of Behaviour, and were Strangers to those little Embellishments which are so fashionable in our present Conversation. And it is very remarkable, that notwithstanding we fall short at present of the Ancients in Poetry, Painting, Oratory, History, Architecture, and all the noble Arts and Sciences which depend more upon Genius than Experience, we exceed them as much in Doggerel, Humour, Burlesque, and all the trivial Arts of Ridicule. We meet with more Raillery among the Moderns, but more Good Sense among the Ancients.

The two great Branches of Ridicule in Writing are Comedy and Burlesque.[4] The first ridicules Persons by drawing them in their proper Characters, the other by drawing them quite unlike themselves. Burlesque is therefore of two kinds, the first represents mean Persons in the Accoutrements of Heroes, the other describes great Persons acting and speaking, like the basest among the People. *Don Quixote* is an Instance of the first, and *Lucian's* Gods of the second.[5] It is a Dispute among the Criticks, whether Burlesque Poetry runs best in Heroic Verse, like that of the *Dispensary,* or in Doggerel, like that of *Hudibras.*[6] I think where the low Character is to be raised the Heroic is the proper Measure, but when an Hero is to be pulled down and degraded it is done best in Doggerel.

If *Hudibras* had been set out with as much Wit and Humour in Heroic Verse as he is in Doggerel, he would have made a much more agreeable Figure than he does; though the generality of his Readers are so wonderfully pleased with the double Rhimes, that I do not expect many will be of my Opinion in this Particular.

I shall conclude this Essay upon Laughter with observing, that the Metaphor of Laughing, applied to Fields and Meadows when they are in Flower, or to Trees when they are in Blossom, runs through all

---

4 See Fielding's *Preface* to *Joseph Andrews,* reprinted in this volume.

5 The hero of Cervantes' satirical *Don Quixote de la Mancha,* 1605, is a poor gentleman, half-crazed by reading romances of chivalry, who sets out in rusty armor on a ridiculous quest for adventures. Lucian, a Greek writer of the second century A.D., author of several sorts of satirical dialogues and fantastic tales, in his *Dialogues of the Gods* and *Dialogues of the Sea-Gods* makes fun of the classic myths.

6 Samuel Garth's *Dispensary,* 1699, burlesques a war between London physicians and apothecaries, in heroic couplets. Samuel Butler's *Hudibras,* Parts I–III, 1663–1678, written in tetrameter couplets, with fantastic rhymes, satirizes contemporary sectarian squabbles.

Languages; which I have not observed of any other Metaphor, excepting that of Fire, and burning, when they are applied to Love. This
shews that we naturally regard Laughter, as what is in it self both
amiable and beautiful. For this Reason likewise *Venus* has gained the
Title of φιλομμείδης the Laughter-loving Dame, as *Waller* has Translated it, and is represented by *Horace* as the Goddess who delights in
Laughter.[7] *Milton,* in a Joyous Assembly of imaginary Persons, has
given us a very poetical Figure of Laughter. His whole Band of
Mirth is so finely described that I shall set it down at length.

> *But come thou Goddess fair and free,*
> *In Heav'n ycleap'd* Euphrosyne,
> *And by Men, heart-easing Mirth,*
> *Whom lovely* Venus *at a birth*
> *With two Sister Graces more*
> *To Ivy-crowned* Bacchus *bore:*
> *Haste thee Nymph, and bring with thee*
> *Jest and youthful Jollity,*
> *Quips and Cranks, and wanton Wiles,*
> *Nods, and Becks, and Wreathed Smiles,*
> *Such as hang on* Hebe's *Cheek,*
> *And love to live in dimple sleek;*
> *Sport that wrinkled Care derides,*
> *And Laughter holding both his sides.*[8]
> *Come, and trip it as you go*
> *On the light fantastick Toe,*
> *And in thy right hand lead with thee,*
> *The Mountain Nymph, sweet Liberty;*
> *And if I give thee Honour due,*
> *Mirth, admit me of thy Crue*
> *To live with her, and live with thee,*
> *In unreproved Pleasures free.*[9]

---

[7]See Homer, *Iliad* IV.10; V.375; XIV.211 (φιλομμείδης); Edmund Waller, *The
Countess of Carlisle in Mourning,* 13; and Horace, *Odes* II.viii.12.

[8] See below, Meredith, p. 242.

[9] Milton, *L'Allegro,* 11–16, 25–40.

RICHARD STEELE

[1672–1729]

The reform of the English stage demanded by Collier in his *Short View* of 1698 was not his own solitary or sudden inspiration. Certain softenings of the love-game motif, moral ameliorations, concessions to feminine feeling, had appeared, for instance, in the plays of Shadwell.[1] The arrival (1689) of a sober monarch (William III), in place of a merry one, had helped along an already rising tide of bourgeois decent feeling. In 1696 the atmosphere was right for a young hanger-on and actor at Drury Lane Theater, Colley Cibber (guided by a pure dramatic instinct rather than by any aim at moral philosophy) to write, and act a part in, a first comedy entitled *Love's Last Shift*— a play in which a faithful, long-abandoned wife, Amanda, employs the trick of Shakespeare's dark comedies, the disguised mistress, to win back a rakish husband, Loveless. Cibber himself played the coxcomb Sir Novelty Fashion, a distinguished fatuous role imitated from Etherege. And he showed the depth of his moral commitment by accepting next season a promotion as Lord Foppington in another first play, the youthful John Vanbrugh's return to witty, adulterous fun, a reversal of the "last shift," entitled *The Relapse*. This play and Vanbrugh's *Provok'd Wife*, 1697, were fair targets in Collier's *Short View*, and, like Congreve, Vanbrugh satisfied honor in a predictable retort: "What I have done is in general a discouragement of vice and folly. I am sure I intended it, and I hope I have performed it."[2]

A more earnest index of the new moral temper of the times appears when Richard Steele, a young Captain of the Coldstream Guards, discovering in himself an uncomfortable "Propensity towards unwarrantable Pleasures" (or the "Military life exposed to much Irregu-

---

[1] John Harrington Smith, "Shadwell, the Ladies, and the Change in Comedy," *Modern Philology*, XLVI (August 1948), 22–33.

[2] John Vanbrugh, *A Short Vindication of "The Relapse" and "The Provok'd Wife," from Immorality and Profaneness* (1698), ed. W. C. Ward (London, 1893), II, 379. For a modern critical version of the defense, see Chapter 16, "The Critical Failure," in Norman N. Holland, *The First Modern Comedies* (Cambridge, Mass., 1959), pp. 199–209.

larity") and wishing to "fix upon his own Mind a strong Impression of Virtue and Religion," published in 1701 *The Christian Hero, An Argument proving that no Principles but those of Religion are Sufficient to make a great Man.* In one of the most notable passages, he recommended to the literary world of the day a more chivalrous attitude toward women. In the same year, this young Captain brought out his own first play, *The Funeral, or Grief à-la-Mode,* a comedy which attempts a kind of submission to Collier's principles in touches of moral satire (the lugubrious circumstances of a mock-funeral in the first act) and in a providentially ordered ending where a wicked stepmother is exposed and true lovers gain their ladies.

At about the same time, another youthful dramatist, last in the line of Restoration wits, George Farquhar, made his momentary obeisance to the ideal of Collier. A theoretical utterance, his *Discourse upon Comedy,* carelessly thrown together and too much absorbed in topics of the moment, was published in February 1702; it subscribes to poetic justice and to the comic aim of moral ridicule. His comedy *The Twin-Rivals,* acted in December of the same year, resembles Steele's *Funeral* in displaying the just inheritance of wealth and true love rewarded. But Collier's straight moral principles were not really to be those of the New Comedy.[3] Farquhar went on to the realistic merriment of his *Recruiting Officer* in 1706 and his *Beaux' Stratagem* in 1707. Steele's next two comedies, *The Lying Lover,* 1703, and *The Tender Husband* (with Addison's Prologue), 1705, gave up both moral lessons and laughter in favor of yet another primary value, that of simple tears, which about this time became established as a dominant comic mode on the London stage.[4] The following awkwardly versified profession of purpose appears in Steele's Epilogue to *The Lying Lover:*

> OUR too advent'rous Author soar'd to Night
> Above the little Praise, Mirth to excite,
> And chose with Pity to chastise Delight.
> For Laughter's a distorted Passion, born
> Of sudden Self-Esteem, and sudden Scorn;

---

[3] Eric Rothstein, "Farquhar's *Twin-Rivals* and the Reform of Comedy," *PMLA,* LXXIX (March 1964), 33–41.

[4] Even Colley Cibber's *The Careless Husband,* 1704, encloses in the sordid setting of a conventional love-game the tearful reform of an old-fashioned wit and lecher. Cibber works into the text of his play (Act V) a complaint that the "late short-sighted view" of Collier now *prevents* the comic stage from carrying on the business of exposing vice. The Prologue contains a rich expression of the high Restoration idea that the vices of genteel persons only are proper comic targets. Cf. above p. 40, Dryden: "Gentlemen will now be entertained with the follies of each other."

Which, when 'tis o'er, the Men in Pleasure wise,
Both him that mov'd it, and themselves despise:
While gen'rous Pity of a painted Woe
Makes us our selves both more approve and know.

Author of *Tatler* periodical essays (under the pseudonym Isaac
Bickerstaff) in 1709–1711, of *Spectators* in 1711–1712, and of
Guardians in 1713, official Gazetteer, Whig pamphlet writer, M.P.,
justice of the peace, supervisor of Drury Lane Theater on the accession
of George I in 1714, and knight in 1715, Addison's old Charterhouse
schoolmate and fellow Oxonian (generous, convivial, madcap, capricious, improvident) pursued a militant and tumultous career on all
fronts. The cause of morality in the comic theater had not advanced
him very rapidly in early years, but more than once amid his later
strifes and varied interests he returned to it. In an early *Spectator*
(No. 51) he took a seductive phrase from his own comedy *The Funeral*
(recently revived at Drury Lane) as the provocation for a sermon
against "Luscious Expressions" and "lascivious Gestures" on the stage
—angling for the reader's interest with only a moderate clowning of
pretended naïveté and a few more or less delicately guarded winks of
prurience. *Spectator* No. 65 (reprinted in this volume), following close
upon Addison's series on "true wit" (a universal poetic principle, as
we have noted), is Steele's pursuit of the same theme—or at least
the same word—into the playhouse, the very "Seat of Wit, when one
speaks as a Man of the Town and the World." The essay is a strenuous
chop upon one of the "most Applauded Plays" of the Restoration
stage—a very "Pattern of Genteel Comedy"—George Etherege's *Man
of Mode, or Sir Fopling Flutter* (1676), the masterpiece which had
been Cibber's inspiration for Sir Novelty Fashion in *Love's Last Shift*.
"I allow it to be Nature, but it is Nature in its utmost Corruption
and Degeneracy."[5]

Family sorrows (the death of his wife and two of his children),
physical ailments, a quarrel with Addison, and pecuniary difficulties
which in the end drove him from London to retirement in Wales, were
to darken the closing years of Steele's acrobatic life. Nevertheless, a
last major literary effort (after he had been absent from the stage for
seventeen years) produced the best of his demonstrations of a tearful
stage morality, *The Conscious Lovers,* acted at Drury Lane for eighteen
nights in November 1722. It was published with Steele's Preface
(reprinted in this volume) in December.[6] Steele lays some stress upon

---

5 Immorality in plays is again his theme in *Spectator* No. 208. In *Tatler* No. 3
Steele had commended one Restoration comedy of wit, Wycherley's *Country Wife,*
because the portrayal of vice in it was unattractive.

6 The title page was dated 1723.

the power of the play to evoke joyful tears and upon a happy debt
which he owes to a classic of the ancient stage, *The Woman of Andros,*
by Terence. The return to the tenderhearted and tenderly treated
heroine, a motif which the Roman Terence had derived from plays of
Menander long lost to the modern world, was in fact an original and
forward-looking maneuver.[7] At the same time historians of the English
stage see *The Conscious Lovers* as less remarkable for a moderate
sentimentality than for its full-blown moralism. "The chief design. . .
was to be an innocent performance." The morality of dueling might
seem to us a minor issue, hardly the stuff for a fine comedy. But,
says Steele, "the whole was writ for the sake of the scene in the
fourth act wherein Mr. Bevil evades the quarrel with his friend."
Certain snatches of the merely laughable which do find their way into
the play are said to have been prompted by urgent advice from Steele's
Drury Lane associate Colley Cibber,[8] who himself acted the comic
part of the servant Tom. A general prescription for plays, drawn from
a Roman rhetoric, the pseudo-Ciceronian *Ad Herennium,* and inserted
as epigraph upon the title page of the published play, stresses, along
with gaiety of dialogue and diversity of character and events, tenderness, pity, sudden joy, and a happy ending.[9]

---

[7] Cf. below, p. 143 (Dennis) and pp. 256–58 (Meredith).

[8] Theophilus Cibber, *The Lives of the Poets of Great Britain and Ireland* (London, 1753), IV, 120; see also John Loftis, *Steele at Drury Lane* (Berkeley, 1952),
pp. 192–93.

[9] See above, Introduction, p. 15.

The Spectator[1]

Number 65

Demetri, teque, Tigelli,
Discipularum inter Jubeo plorare cathedras. Horace[2]

Tuesday, May 15, 1711.

After having at large explained what Wit is, and described the false Appearances of it, all that Labour seems but an useless Enquiry, without some Time be spent in considering the Application of it. The Seat of Wit, when one speaks as a Man of the Town and the World, is the Play-house; I shall therefore fill this Paper with Reflections upon the Use of it in that Place. The Application of Wit in the Theatre has as strong an Effect upon the Manners of our Gentlemen, as the Taste of it has upon the Writings of our Authors. It may, perhaps, look like a very Presumptuous Work, tho' not Foreign from the Duty of a SPECTATOR, to tax the Writings of such as have long had the general Applause of a Nation: But I shall always make Reason, Truth, and Nature the Measures of Praise and Dispraise; if those are for me, the Generality of Opinion is of no Consequence against me; if they are against me, the General Opinion cannot long support me.

Without further Preface, I am going to look into some of our most Applauded Plays, and see whether they deserve the Figure they at present bear in the Imaginations of Men, or not.

In reflecting upon these Works, I shall chiefly dwell upon that for which each respective Play is most celebrated. The present Paper shall be employed upon *Sir Foplin Flutter.*[3] The Received Character of this Play is, That it is the Pattern of Gentile Comedy.[4] *Dorimant* and

---

1 See above, p. 93.
2 *Satires*, I.x.90–91: "You, Demetrius, and you, Tigellius, I bid you go whine among the armchairs of your lady pupils."
3 Etherege's comedy *The Man of Mode, or Sir Fopling Flutter* (1676) had been acted at Drury Lane as recently as April 20, 1711.
4 A play constructed, as if with deliberate negligence, on a very slender pattern of heartless and immoral love intrigues, a highly varnished picture of the pursuit of

Harriot are the Characters of Greatest Consequence, and if these are Low and Mean, the Reputation of the Play is very Unjust,

I will take for granted, that a fine Gentleman should be honest in his Actions, and refined in his Language. Instead of this, our Hero, in this Piece, is a direct Knave in his Designs, and a Clown in his Language. *Bellair* is his Admirer and Friend, in return for which, because he is forsooth a greater Wit than his said Friend, he thinks it reasonable to perswade him to Marry a young Lady, whose Virtue, he thinks, will last no longer than 'till she is a Wife, and then she cannot but fall to his Share, as he is an irresistible fine Gentleman. The Falshood to Mrs. *Loveit,* and the Barbarity of Triumphing over her Anguish for losing him, is another Instance of his Honesty, as well as his good Nature. As to his fine Language; he calls the Orange Woman, who, it seems, is inclined to grow Fat, *An Over-grown Jade, with a Flasket of Guts before her;* and salutes her with a pretty Phrase of *How now, Double Tripe?*[5] Upon the Mention of a Country Gentlewoman, whom he knows nothing of, (no one can imagine why) he *will lay his Life she is some awkard, ill-fashioned Country Toad, who not having above four Dozen of Hairs on her Head, has adorned her Baldness with a large white Fruz, that she may look Sparkishly in the Fore-front of the King's Box at an old Play.* Unnatural Mixture of senseless Common Place!

As to the Generosity of his Temper, he tells his poor Footman, *If he did not wait better*—he would turn him away, in the insolent Phrase of, *I'll Uncase you.*

Now for Mrs. *Harriot:* She laughs at Obedience to an absent Mother, whose Tenderness *Busie* describes to be so exquisite, *that she is so pleased with finding* Harriot *again, that she cannot chide her for being out of the Way.*[6] This Witty Daughter, and Fine Lady, has so little Respect for this good Woman, that she Ridicules her Air in taking Leave, and cries, *In what Struggle is my poor Mother yonder? See,*

---

pleasure and folly in Restoration Society. The brilliance erupts in the animation of the dialogue and the vividly corrupt characterizations: Dorimant, the insolent young gentleman (said to be a portrait of the rakish court wit Lord Rochester); the object of his admiration, the young country gentlewoman Harriet (his equal in tart repartee and his superior in intelligence—from whom he gallantly conceals his genuine love); and the title portrait, Sir Fopling, "lately arrived piping hot from Paris"—the prototype of all the Restoration and Augustan fops, drawn by Etherege in part from Mascarille, the pretending valet in Molière's *Les Précieuses Ridicules.*

[5] The quotations in this paragraph and the next are from the opening scene.
[6] Act III, Scene iii.

See, her Head tottering, her Eyes staring, and her under Lip trembling.[7]
But all this is atoned for, because *she has more Wit than is usual in
her Sex, and as much Malice, tho' she is as Wild as you would wish
her, and has a Demureness in her Looks that makes it so surprising!*[8]
Then to recommend her as a fit Spouse for his Hero, the Poet makes
her speak her Sense of Marriage very ingeniously. *I Think,* says she,
*I might be brought to endure him, and that is all a reasonable Woman
should expect in an Husband.*[9] It is, methinks, unnatural that we are
not made to understand how she that was bred under a silly pious old
Mother, that would never trust her out of her Sight, came to be so
Polite.

It cannot be denied, but that the Negligence of every thing, which
engages the Attention of the sober and valuable Part of Mankind,
appears very well drawn in this Piece: But it is denied, that it is
necessary to the Character of a Fine Gentleman, that he should in
that manner Trample upon all Order and Decency. As for the Character of *Dorimant,* is it more of a Coxcomb than that of *Foplin.* He says
of one of his Companions,[10] that a good Correspondence between them
is their mutual Interest. Speaking of that Friend, he declares, their
being much together *makes the Women think the better of his Understanding, and judge more favourably of my Reputation. It makes him
pass upon some for a Man of very good Sense, and me upon others
for a very civil Person.*

This whole celebrated Piece is a perfect Contradiction to good
Manners, good Sense, and common Honesty; and as there is nothing
in it but what is built upon the Ruin of Virtue and Innocence, according to the Notion of Merit in this Comedy, I take the Shoemaker to
be, in reality, the fine Gentleman of the Play: For it seems he is an
Atheist, if we may depend upon his Character as given by the Orange
Woman, who is her self far from being the lowest in the Play. She
says of a Fine Man, who is *Dorimant's* Companion, There *is not such
another Heathen in the Town, except the Shoe-maker.* His Pretention
to be the Hero of the *Drama* appears still more in his own Description
of his way of Living with his Lady. *There is,* says he, *never a Man
in Town lives more like a Gentleman with his Wife than I do; I never
mind her Motions; she never enquires into mine. We speak to one*

---

7 Act IV, Scene i.
8 Act I, Scene i.
9 Act III, Scene i.
10 Bellair. The remaining quotations are again from the opening scene.

another civilly, hate one another heartily; and because it is Vulgar to Lye and Soak together, we have each of us our several Settle-Bed. That of *Soaking together* is as good as if *Dorimant* had spoken it himself; and, I think, since he puts Humane Nature in as ugly a Form as the Circumstances will bear, and is a staunch Unbeliever, he is very much Wronged in having no part of the good Fortune bestowed in the last Act.

To speak plainly of this whole Work, I think nothing but being lost to a Sense of Innocence and Virtue can make any one see this Comedy, without observing more frequent Occasion to move Sorrow and Indignation, than Mirth and Laughter. At the same time I allow it to be Nature, but it is Nature in its utmost Corruption and Degeneracy.

PREFACE

TO

The Conscious Lovers

[*1722*]

This Comedy has been receiv'd with universal Acceptance, for it was in every Part excellently perform'd; and there needs no other Applause of the Actors, but that they excell'd according to the Dignity and Difficulty of the Character they represented. But this great Favour done to the Work in Acting, renders the Expectation still the greater from the Author, to keep up the Spirit in the Representation of the Closet, or any other Circumstance of the Reader, whether alone or in Company: To which I can only say, that it must be remember'd a Play is to be Seen, and is made to be Represented with the Advantage of Action, nor can appear but with half the Spirit, without it; for the greatest Effect of a Play in reading is to excite the Reader to go see it; and when he does so, it is then a Play has the Effect of Example and Precept.

The chief Design of this was to be an innocent Performance, and the Audience have abundantly show'd how ready they are to support what is visibly intended that way; nor do I make any Difficulty to acknowledge, that the whole was writ for the sake of the Scene of the Fourth Act, wherein Mr. *Bevill* evades the Quarrel with his Friend,[1] and hope it may have some Effect upon the *Goths* and *Vandals* that frequent the Theatres, or a more polite Audience may supply their Absence.

But this Incident, and the Case of the Father and Daughter, are

---

The Conscious Lovers was first acted at Drury Lane in November 1722 and was published in December (The title page is dated 1723). Our text follows the first edition (London, 1723).

1 Young Bevil, the leading man in Steele's Terentian play, unwilling to accept Lucinda, his father's match for him, makes known to her his difficultly, but, in doing so, offends her lover, his friend Myrtle, who issues him a challenge, which he declines (Act IV, Scene i), thus teaching a lesson in the folly of dueling.

117

esteem'd by some People no Subjects of Comedy; but I cannot be
of their Mind; for any thing that has its Foundation in Happiness
and Success, must be allow'd to be the Object of Comedy, and sure
it must be an Improvement of it, to introduce a Joy too exquisite for
Laughter, that can have no Spring but in Delight, which is the Case
of this young Lady. I must therefore contend, that the Tears which
were shed on that Occasion flow'd from Reason and Good Sense, and
that Men ought not to be laugh'd at for weeping, till we are come to
a more clear Notion of what is to be imputed to the Hardness of the
Head, and the Softness of the Heart; and I think it was very politely
said of Mr. *Wilks* to one who told him there was a *General* weeping
for *Indiana,* I'll warrant he'll fight ne'er the worse for that.[2] To be
apt to give way to the Impressions of Humanity is the Excellence of
a right Disposition, and the natural Working of a well-turn'd Spirit.
But as I have suffer'd by Criticks who are got no farther than to
enquire whether they ought to be pleas'd or not, I would willingly
find them properer Matter for their Employment, and revive here a
Song which was omitted for want of a Performer, and design'd for
the Entertainment of *Indiana;* Signor *Carbonelli* instead of it play'd
on the Fiddle, and it is for want of a Singer that such advantageous
things are said of an Instrument which were design'd for a Voice.
The Song is the Distress of a Love-sick Maid, and may be a fit
Entertainment for some small Criticks to examine whether the Passion
is just, or the Distress Male or Female.

I.

From Place to Place forlorn I go,
  With downcast Eyes a silent Shade;
Forbidden to declare my Woe;
  To speak, till spoken to, afraid.

II.

My inward Pangs, my secret Grief,
  My soft consenting Looks betray:
He Loves, but gives me no Relief:
  Why speaks not he who may?

It remains to say a Word concerning *Terence,* and I am extremely

---

[2] Robert Wilks (1665?–1732), with Steele one of the managers of Drury Lane,
played the part of Myrtle. Indiana (the celebrated actress Anne Oldfield) is at
first, as a supposedly destitute orphan, young Bevil's protegée and the object of his
frustrated affections. Only on turning out to be a long-lost sister of Lucinda and
daughter of the wealthy Mr. Sealand, does she become his eligible fiancée.

surpris'd to find what Mr. *Cibber* told me, prove a Truth, That what I valued my self so much upon, the Translation of him, should be imputed to me as a Reproach.[3] Mr. *Cibber's* Zeal for the Work, his Care and Application in instructing the Actors, and altering the Disposition of the Scenes, when I was, through Sickness, unable to cultivate such Things my self, has been a very obliging Favour and Friendship to me. For this Reason, I was very hardly persuaded to throw away *Terence's* celebrated Funeral,[4] and take only the bare Authority of the young Man's Character, and how I have work'd it into an *Englishman,* and made Use of the same Circumstances of discovering a Daughter, when we least hop'd for one, is humbly submitted to the Learned Reader.

---

[3] *The Conscious Lovers* is based upon Terence's *The Woman of Andros* (167 B.C.). See Introduction, p. 6, and p. 143.

[4] In Terence's *Woman of Andros,* the funeral of the courtesan Chrysis is an occasion when a supposed sister Glycerium, and her secret lover Pamphilus are moved to a spontaneous betrayal of their tenderness for each other. See below, p. 257 for Meredith's appreciation of this scene.

PROLOGUE

By Mr. Welsted[1]

TO

The Conscious Lovers

[*1722*]

To win your Hearts, and to secure your Praise,
The Comic-Writers strive by various Ways:
By subtil Stratagems they act their Game,
And leave untry'd no Avenue to Fame.
One writes the Spouse a beating from his Wife;
And says, Each stroke was Copy'd from the Life.
Some fix all Wit and Humour in Grimace,
Aud make a Livelyhood of Pinkey's[2] *Face:*
Here, One gay Shew and costly Habits tries,
Confiding to the Judgment of your Eyes:
Another smuts his Scene (a cunning Shaver)
Sure of the Rakes and of the Wenches Favour.
Oft have these Arts prevail'd; and one may guess,
If practis'd o'er again, would find Success.
But the bold Sage, the Poet of To-night,
By new and desp'rate Rules resolv'd to Write;
Fain would he give more just Applauses Rise,
And please by Wit that scorns the Aids of Vice;
The Praise be seeks, from worthier Motives springs,
Such Praise, as Praise to those that give, it brings.
Your Aid, most humbly sought, then Britons *lend,*

---

[1] Leonard Welsted (1688–1747) was a clerk in government offices, a miscellaneous poet and satirical writer, a protégé of Steele's, and an opponent of Pope. He would receive attention in Pope's *Dunciad* III (1728–1729) and *Epistle to Arbuthnot* (1735).

[2] William Pinkethman (d. 1725), a popular actor of low, clowning parts.

120

And Lib'ral Mirth, like Lib'ral Men, defend:
No more let Ribaldry, with Licence writ,
Usurp the Name of Eloquence or Wit;
No more let lawless Farce uncensur'd go,
The lewd dull Gleanings of a Smithfield *Show.*[3]
'Tis yours, with Breeding to refine the Age,
To Chasten Wit, and Moralize the Stage.

    Ye Modest, Wise and Good, ye Fair, ye Brave,
To-night the Champion of your Virtues save,
Redeem from long Contempt the Comic Name,
And Judge Politely for your Countrey's Fame.

---

[3] Smithfield, a city district near St. Paul's, was from the twelfth century to 1855 the scene of an annual summertime fair, originally held in honor of St. Bartholomew. Its features of popular humor, drollery, license, and riot are presented in Ben Jonson's farcical comedy *Bartholomew Fayre,* 1614.

JOHN DENNIS

[1657–1734]

A few pages of ruggedly sane comic theory confront us, framed in the frustrations and obscurities of a long subcultural career. Born thirty-one years earlier than the poet Pope, who was to be the most destructive adversary of his later years, John Dennis was, like Pope, a native of London and the son of a well-to-do tradesman.[1] He went to Harrow and then to Cambridge, where he stayed eleven years (until he was about thirty), proceeding B.A. (Caius College, 1679) and M.A. (Trinity Hall, 1683). At Trinity, if we can believe a scrap of a record, he gave an early promise of mature truculence when he stabbed a fellow student with a sword. During the autumn of 1688 he traveled in France and Italy, and on crossing the Alps enjoyed a moment of the "sublime" landscape emotion which in the course of the next century was to become so notable a part of the growing romantic mind—"a delightful Horrour, a terrible Joy," "transporting Pleasures."[2] A few years later the experience was to be repeated more quietly by Addison.

Dennis seems to have come back to London bringing some inheritance from his father and from an uncle (who had been an alderman), and to have frequented the coffee-houses with the deliberate aim of cultivating the chief men of wit and fashion. He succeeded well enough, in fact so well as to be able to publish in 1696 a volume of *Letters upon Several Occasions, between Mr. Dryden, Mr. Wycherley, Mr.———, Mr. Congreve,* and *Mr. Dennis*—from which we have already drawn one of our texts (above pp. 74–84), the now celebrated letter by Congreve on humor. In this dawning phase of his London career,

---

[1] Dennis's father was a saddler, Pope's a linen-draper.

[2] Recorded in a letter from Turin, October 25, 1688, published by Dennis in one of his early bids for a literary name, *Miscellanies in Verse and Prose,* 1693. It is quoted in E. N. Hooker, ed., *The Critical Works of John Dennis,* II (Baltimore, 1939), 380–82; cf. 520. Cf. C. D. Thorpe, "Two Augustans Cross the Alps: Dennis and Addison on Mountain Scenery," *Studies in Philology,* XXXII (1935), 463–82, and review by D. F. Bond, *Philological Quarterly,* XV (April 1936), 171–72. On the early career of Dennis, see Hooker, II, xii ff.

Dennis also wrote and published certain poems "in the Pindaric way,"[3]
and with these he elicited from no less a giant than Dryden a huge
compliment: "...that which we call Pindarique...of this, Sir, you
are certainly one of the greatest Masters."[4]

Poems...letters...and also criticism! Of course Dennis was from
the start an ambitious critic. When the laborious historian Thomas
Rymer delivered his attack on the irregularities of Shakespeare's
Othello in his *Short View of Tragedy,* 1692, Dennis responded with
The Impartial Critick, 1693, an agreeable dialogue which shows the
difference between the casual English manner and the stricter "Grecian
Method" in the Art of the Stage. When Collier denounced the immorality of the English stage, 1698, Dennis, like Congreve and Vanbrugh,
and perhaps with tighter reasoning than they, had a ready answer:
*The Usefulness of the Stage, to the Happiness of Mankind, to Govern-
ment, and to Religion* (1698). He formed a mighty scheme for a total
critical organon—one large block of which actually achieved publication, *The Grounds of Criticism in Poetry,* 1704. Longinus among the
ancients, Milton among the moderns, objects vast, mighty, and threaten-
ing in nature, and in literature blank verse, were his inspirations and
touchstones. "Passion is the Principal thing in Poetry."[5] Not ordinary
or vulgar passions, but passion lifted by meditation or reflection to
the level of consistency with Reason, where it becomes (oddly, according to our own way of using the words) "Enthusiastick Passion,"
which is *par excellence* also Religious Passion. Passion is pleasure, it is
happiness. It is the "sublime."[6] A century later his ideas would come
to the attention of English romantic poets and would make a strong
impression, especially on Wordsworth. In the more immediate future,
he was to be known as "Sir Tremendous Longinus," "the sour Longinus
of the present times," and "Sulky Bathos."[7]

He wrote plays, some eight or nine. One of the worst was a comedy,
The Comical Gallant, or the Amours of Sir John Falstaff, 1702, a
reworking of Shakespeare's *Merry Wives of Windsor.* To a published
edition of this Dennis prefixed a long *apologia* addressed to another
gentlemanly adapter of Shakespeare, the Honorable George Granville

[3] Hooker, II, vii.
[4] In a letter to Dennis, first published in Dennis's volume *Letters upon Several Occasions,* 1696, pp. 53 ff. See *The Letters of John Dryden,* ed. Charles E. Ward (Durham, N.C., 1942), Letter 31, p. 72.
[5] Epistle Dedicatory to *The Advancement and Reformation of Modern Poetry,* 1701.
[6] See especially *Remarks on a Book Entituled "Prince Arthur,"* 1696; *The Usefulness of the Stage,* 1698; *The Advancement and Reformation of Modern Poetry,* 1701; *The Grounds of Criticism in Poetry,* 1704, in *Critical Works,* ed. Hooker, I, 46–47, 148–50, 217, 223, 256–61, 338–39.
[7] *Works,* ed. Hooker, I, lix–xi.

(later Lord Lansdowne). Dennis had a talent for expounding a point
of view with such ruthless and repetitious clarity as inevitably to
betray whatever weakness a more cunning debater might have concealed. In a striking reaction against the aristocratic view which we
have seen flourishing in the era of his early friends Dryden, Wycherley,
and Congreve, Dennis now tells Granville that a comedy ought to
consist, not of high wit, which is only the author himself showing off,
but of low humor, which is a "subordinate," or "less degree" of,
"Passion," and is hence the variety of all life itself. Low humor requires
of the poet a keen eye for observing.

> Humour after the Plot is what is most valuable in Comedy. I desire
> then, Sir, that I may have leave to prove two things: First, that
> Humour is more the business of Comedy than Wit: And secondly, that
> Humour is more to be found in low Characters, than among Persons
> of a higher Rank, and consequently that low Characters are more
> proper for Comedy than high, and that low Comedy is to be preferred
> to the high. . . .
> . . . Humour is the business in Comedy, and not Wit. The business of
> a Comic Poet is to shew his Characters and not himself, to make ev'ry
> one of them speak and act, as such a person in such circumstances
> would probably act and speak. Comedy, is an Image of common Life,
> and in Life, a Man, who has discerning Eyes, may find something
> ridiculous in most People, but something that is witty in very few.
> And a Comic Poet may be certain of this, that the grossest touches
> which are in nature, will please the men of sense, more than the most
> delicate strokes which are out of it. Now that which is truly ridiculous
> in any man is chiefly Humour, or the effect of Humour. . . . Humour
> . . . is harder to write, for the writing Wit is the effect of the Fancy,
> and the writing Humour the work of the Judgment. 'Tis observation
> alone that can qualify a man for it, and observation is the business of
> the Judgment. . . . Tho a fine Imagination is to be met with in few,
> Judgment is to be found in fewer. Humour then is harder to be Written
> than Wit, and that which in any kind of Writing is the hardest to
> be attaind, makes the principal Beauty of that kind of Writing. . . .
> Humour . . . gives a necessary occasion for Action, which Wit does not,
> and Action after all is the very Life and Soul of the Theatre. . . .
> Humour is Passion, as I have shewn in another place,[8] and nothing but
> Action is able to express Passion. . . . Humour . . . distinguishes the
> Characters better. . . . Since Humour distinguishes the Characters, it
> must be always agreeable to men of Sense, whereas Wit must be often
> shocking and nauseous to them, because it destroys and confounds the
> Characters. . . .[9]

8 *Advancement and Reformation of Modern Poetry.* [Dennis's note.]
9 *A Large Account of the Taste in Poetry, And The Causes of the Degeneracy of
It—To George Granville,* in *The Comical Gallant: or The Amours of Sir John
Falstaff* (London, 1702), p. iii.

What is more, there is not only too much wit, there is too much "love" and "gallantry" in high comedies—for "love" itself is not funny and has no special affinity for funniness. "Love is so agreeable in its own Nature, that it can never be made to appear Ridiculous, unless it is joyned with an Humour."[10]

With a degree of seeming absent-mindedness about the special comic virtue which he has located so emphatically in "low" characters and their humors, Dennis now concludes his essay with a very long and very deliberately squared-off Horatian and Miltonic appeal to the few but fit audience (*pauci lectores*). No matter that his comedy failed with the town: Granville will know better—as all those gentlemen of the age of Charles would have known better.

> ...in King *Charles* the Second's time, a considerable part of an Audience were qualified to judge for themselves, and...at present a considerable part of our Audiences are not qualify'd for it.... They who were not qualified to judge in King *Charles* his Reign, were influenced by the authority of those who were; and that is of the Court, which always in a peculiar manner influences the pleasures of the Gentry. And some of the most eminent young Courtiers had then an admirable taste of Comedy, as it must always happen in a Court where the Prince delights in it.[11]

We arrive at what Dryden would have considered the self-contradictory thesis that the humor of low life (the "mechanic humour" of an age "when men were dull and conversation low") will be the comic norm for an audience of elegant, high mentality. By a happy coincidence, the town will cooperate by supplying an excellent brand of lowness for the comic targets.[12] Dennis does not seem to sense any conflict here, either with history or with aesthetic likelihood. We have seen a version of this dilemma as early as the theorizing of Aristotle about the ethics of politely amusing conversation, and we shall see another, perhaps more refined, in George Meredith's retrospect on the luckily mixed milieu of courtiers and bourgeoisie in the age of Molière.

In the year 1705 Dennis got an appointment in the London customs,

---

10 *The Comical Gallant*, p. v. "Love is very often agreeable without being instructive; nay, it very often gives a pernicious pleasure."

11 *The Comical Gallant*, p. xiii. "...In the present Reign, a great part of the Gentlemen have not leisure, because want throws them upon employments, and there are ten times more Gentlemen now in business, than there were in King *Charles* his Reign" (*The Comical Gallant*, p. xiii). See *Works*, I, 491 for a good note by Hooker on the degeneracy of the Augustan theater audience.

12 "All the sheer Originals in Town were known, and in some measure copied. But now the case is vastly different. For all those great and numerous Originals are reduced to one single Coxcomb, and that is the foolish false Politician" (*The Comical Gallant*, p. xii).

and about this time he seems to have retreated into a sort of fiercely independent aloofness from the life of the literary frontier. An increasingly isolated survivor from an older age, he contrived to find himself at odds with nearly all the leading new wits, of both the Whig and the Tory alliances. He revolted against the Augustan norm of good nature and urbanity in criticism and did not flinch from censuring even the poetry of men socially superior to himself. He wrote some political pamphlets and established himself as an enemy not only of rhyme, puns, opera, and sentimental comedy, but of Jacobitism, "priestcraft," France, and Spain.[13]

Unhappily, and to the eclipse of a perhaps fairer posthumous reputation, Dennis is today most widely known through a battle with Pope. This was outrageous on both sides, lasting intermittently almost thirty years and producing the enshrinement of Dennis in Pope's Longinian travesty *Peri Bathous, Or of the Art of Sinking in Poetry,* 1727, and his *Dunciad,* 1728. Pope seems to have jumped on Dennis first, just for the fun of it, in his *Essay on Criticism,* published in May 1711.

> But Appius[14] reddens at each word you speak,
> And stares, tremendous, with a threatening eye,
> Like some fierce Tyrant in old tapestry.

It seems a likely enough picture of the aging and irritable failed poet and opposition critic rising to the rebuttal in some coffee-house contention. Dennis responded with *Reflections* upon Pope's poem, containing a mean portrait of Pope's physical deformity, and later (1728) with equally militant *Remarks* upon the verbal wit of Pope's *Rape of the Lock*. A quarrel with Addison has a far more serious literary content. It centers around *Spectators* Nos. 39 and 40, in which Addison pooh-poohed poetic justice, and Addison's tragedy *Cato,* 1713, with its serene injustice to the virtuous characters. A quarrel with Steele is essentially a quarrel about how Steele and his cronies are ruining the royal theater, and especially about one of their vehicles, the new comedy of morality and sentiment. In the autumn of 1722, hearing reports of Steele's preparations with *The Conscious Lovers,* Dennis anticipated the event (see below, pp. 128–41) in a blast aimed at redressing the ancient wrong of *Spectator* No. 65, Steele's attack on *Sir Fopling Flutter*. This effort quotes a good many key passages of classical Greek and Latin and seventeenth-century French comic

---

13 See *A Proposal for Putting a Speedy End to the War, by Ruining the Commerce of the French and the Spaniards, and Securing Our Own, without Any Additional Expense to the Nation,* 1703 (H. G. Paul, *John Dennis: His Life and Criticism,* New York, 1911, p. 48).

14 Dennis's last play, a tragedy, *Appius and Virginia,* was produced at Drury Lane in 1709.

theory, and thus draws a useful map of the comic issue. The main line of argument is another of Dennis's crystal-clear but apparently unconscious paradoxes: that a writer of comedy succeeds in proportion as he faithfully observes and copies human *nature,* but that if Etherege drew fine gentlemen as rakes and asses, that was for the reason that they happened indeed to be just that—in London, at the moment when he wrote. The "nature" with which Dennis and Etherege are concerned apparently does not enjoy its usual association with the classic universal—"one clear, unchanged, and universal light."

PREFACE

TO

A Defence of Sir Fopling Flutter

[*1722*]

The following Defence of the Comedy of *Sir Fopling Flutter*, not only contains several Remarks upon Comedy in general; Remarks that are equally necessary for the Writing it successfully, and for the Judging of it surely; but every Article of that Defence, is a just Censure of a certain Comedy now in Rehearsal,[1] if I can depend upon the Account which I have had of it, from several who have read it, or to whom it has been read. And that the Account which I have had of it is very just, I am apt to believe, not only from the Judgment and Sincerity of the Persons from whom I had it, but likewise from the scandalous Methods that are us'd, to give it a false and a transitory Reputation.

I have formerly made Mention of Poetical Mountebanks. The Author of the Comedy now in Rehearsal, has all the Marks of an Empiric of *Parnassus:* His Play has trotted as far as *Edinburgh* Northward, and as far as *Wales* Westward, and has been read to more Persons than will be at the Representation of it, or vouchsafe to read it, when it is publish'd.[2]

Our text follows, with a few corrections and normalizations, the original printing of Dennis's essay: *A Defence of "Sir Fopling Flutter," A Comedy Written by Sir George Etheredge. In which Defence is shewn, That Sir Fopling, the merry Knight, was rightly compos'd by the Knight his Father, to answer the Ends of Comedy; and that he has been barbarously and scurrilously attack'd by the Knight his Brother, in the 65th "Spectator." By which it appears, That the latter Knight knows nothing of the Nature of Comedy.* London: Printed for T. Warner... 1722.

[1] Steele's *Conscious Lovers* was first acted on November 7, 1722. Rehearsals were in progress during October.

[2] As a member of the Commission for Forfeited Estates, Steele was in Edinburgh from August to October 1720, and again in October 1721. G. A. Aitken, *Life of Steele* (London, 1889), II, 318, cites a story that Steele wrote *The Conscious Lovers* during a visit to Wales and that the play was first acted there by friends at his own house.

128

Another certain Sign that a Man is an Empiric, is, when he gives high *Encomiums* to himself, and his *Nostrums,* and pretends at the same Time, that those *Encomiums* are given by others. Now, Advertisements have been sent to the News-Papers to this Effect, That the Comedy now in Rehearsal, is, in the Opinion of excellent Judges, the very best that ever came upon the *English* Stage.[3] Now, no Body could send that Advertisement but the Author, or one of his *Zanies,* by his own Contrivance, or, at least, Connivance. No one could send such an Advertisement, or give such a Judgment, but a Fool, or a Knave; a Knave, if he did it with a Design to impose on the World, and a Fool if he did it in the Sincerity of his Heart. For, to declare with Judgment, that a Play is the very best that ever came upon the *English* Stage, requires vast Consideration, profound Reflection, and a long, long Comparison. And what Mortal is qualify'd to pass such a Judgment upon a single momentary Reading? He who sent those Advertisements then, sent them with a Design to impose upon the World, or is an arrant Ass. But 'tis highly improbable, that a Fool who knows nothing of the Matter, should give himself the Trouble to send such an Advertisement; or that any one else should do it but the Author, or the Author's *Zanies* by his Subornation. For whose Interest could it be but theirs, to endeavour to impose upon the World? But now, if it shall appear by the following Treatise, that the Author of the Dramatic Piece in Rehearsal, knows nothing of the Nature of True Comedy, then how foolishly arrogant are those insolent and impudent Advertisements? These very Ways of Proceeding, sufficiently declare the Author's Consciousness of his own Incapacity; for a noble Genius will scorn such infamous Methods, and will resolve to owe his Reputation to his Merit, and not to tricking Artifice. These are some of the Methods which the present Managers of the *Stage* have us'd to ruine the *Dramas,* and with it all other Human Learning, which is in some Measure dependent on it. For since Cabal and Trick, and the Favour and Interest of three or four sordid Wretches,[4] have been found necessary for the obtaining Success; every one who is duly qualify'd to write for the *Stage,* has either with a just Disdain refus'd it, or has undertaken it with extream Reluctancy. The *Drama*

---

[3] On October 2, 1722, a newspaper advertisement announcing that Steele's new comedy would be ready by the 6th of November concluded: "It is thought that this play is the best modern play that has been produced." Cf. Aitken, *Life of Steele,* II, 276, n. 4.

[4] The managers of the Drury Lane playhouse: Colley Cibber, Robert Wilks, and Barton Booth.

therefore is like to be lost, and all the Arts dependent on it; therefore every one who is concern'd for the Honour of his Country, ought to do his utmost Endeavour to prevent a Calamity which will be so great a Disgrace to is: And all who are concern'd for the Honour of the *King,* ought to reflect with Indignation, that by the Malice, and the basest *Breach of Trust* of Persons whom *His Majesty* has appointed to encourage Literature, all the gentle Studies of Humanity are like to be either entirely lost, or extreamly impair'd, in his otherwise auspicious Reign.

A Defence of Sir Fopling Flutter

[*1722*]

A Certain Knight, who has employ'd so much of his empty Labour in extolling the weak Performances of some living Authors, has scurriously and inhumanly in the 65th *Spectator,* attack'd one of the most entertaining Comedies of the last Age, written by a most ingenious Gentleman, who perfectly understood the World, the Court, and the Town, and whose Reputation has now for near thirty Years together, surviv'd his Person, and will, in all Probability, survive it as long as Comedy shall be in vogue; by which Proceeding, this worthy Knight has incurr'd the double Censure, that Olivia in *The Plain Dealer* has cast upon a certain Coxcomb, "Who rather," says she, "than not flatter, will flatter the Poets of the Age, whom none will flatter; and rather than not rail, will rail at the Dead, at whom none besides will rail."[1]

If other Authors have had the Misfortune, to incurr the Censure of ill-nature with unthinking deluded People, for no other so much as pretended Reason, than because to improve a noble Art, they have expos'd the Errors of popular Writers, who ow'd their Success, to the infamous Method of securing an ignorant or a corrupt Cabal; when those Writers were not only living, but in full Prosperity, and at full Liberty to answer for themselves; what Appellation must he deserve, who has basely and scurrilously attack'd the Reputation of a Favourite of the comic Muse, and of the Darling of the Graces, after Death has for so many Years depriv'd him of the Means of answering for himself.

What the Knight falsely and impudently says of the Comedy, may be justly said of the Criticism, and of the whole 65th *Spectator,* that 'tis a perfect Contradiction to good Manners and good Sense. He allows this Comedy, he says, to be in Nature, but 'tis Nature in its utmost Corruption and Degeneracy.

Suppose this were true, I would fain know where he learnt, that

---

1 Wycherley, *The Plain Dealer,* I.i, Olivia's account of Novel.

Nature in its utmost Corruption and Degeneracy, is not the proper
Subject of Comedy? Is not this a merry Person, who, after he has
been writing what he calls Comedy for twenty Years together, shews
plainly to all the World, that he knows nothing of the Nature of true
Comedy, and that he has not learnt the very first Rudiments of an
Art which he pretends to teach? I must confess, the Ridicule in *Sir
Fopling Flutter,* is an Imitation of corrupt and degenerate Nature,
but not the most corrupt and the most degenerate; for there is neither
Adultery, Murder, nor Sodomy in it. But can any Thing but corrupt
and degenerate Nature be the proper Subject of Ridicule? And can
any Thing but Ridicule be the proper Subject of Comedy? Has not
Aristotle told us in the Fifth Chapter of his *Poetics,* that Comedy is
an Imitation of the very worst of Men? Not the worst, says He, in
every Sort of Vice, but the worst in the Ridicule. And has not Horace,
in the Fourth Satire of his First Book,[2] reminded us, that the old
Athenian Comic Poets made it their Business to bring all Sorts of
Villains upon the Stage, Adulterers, Cheats, Thieves, Murderers? But
then they always took Care, says a modern Critic, that those several
Villainies should be envelop'd in the Ridicule, which alone, says he,
could make them the proper Subjects of Comedy.[3] If this facetious
Knight had formerly liv'd at Lacedemon with the same wrong turn'd
Noddle that he has now among us, would he not, do you think, have
inveighed against that People, for shewing their drunken Slaves to
their Children?[4] Would he not have represented it as a Thing of
most pernicious Example? What the Lacedemonians did by Drunken-
ness, the Comic Poet does by that and all other Vices. He exposes
them to the View of his Fellow Subjects, for no other Reason, than
to render them ridiculous and contemptible.

But the Criticism of the Knight in the foresaid *Spectator,* is as
contrary to good Manners, as it is to good Sense. What Aristotle and
his Interpreters say of Tragedy, that 'tis infallibly good, when it
pleases both the Judges and the People, is certainly as true of Comedy;
for the Judges are equally qualify'd to judge of both, and the People
may be suppos'd to be better Judges of Comedy then they are of

---

2 Horace, *Satires* I.iv.1–5.

3 Perhaps André Dacier (1651–1722), Permanent Secretary of the French
Academy, in his commentary on Horace (1681–1689), or in his edition of Aristotle's
Poetics, remark on Chap. V (Paris, 1692, pp. 58–60).

4 Plutarch, *Life of Lycurgus,* Chap. 25, says that at Sparta the ephors brought
drunken helots into the military dining halls as an object lesson; they made them
perform ignoble and ridiculous songs and dances.

Tragedy, because Comedy is nothing but a Picture of common Life, and a Representation of their own Humours and Manners.[5] Now this Comedy of *Sir Fopling Flutter,* has not been only well receiv'd, and believ'd by the People of England to be a most agreeable Comedy for about Half a Century, but the Judges have been still more pleas'd with it than the People. They have justly believ'd (I speak of the Judges) that the Characters, and especially the principal Characters, are admirably drawn, to answer the two Ends of Comedy, Pleasure, and Instruction; and that the Dialogue is the most charming that has been writ by the Moderns: That with Purity and Simplicity, it has Art and Elegance; and with Force and Vivacity, the utmost Grace and Delicacy. This I know very well, was the Opinion of the most eminent Writers, and of the best Judges contemporary with the Author; and of the whole Court of King Charles the Second, a Court the most polite that ever England saw.

Now, after this Comedy has pass'd with the whole People of England, the knowing as well as the Ignorant, for a most entertaining and most instructive Comedy, for fifty Years together, after that long Time comes a Two-Penny Author, who has given a thousand Proofs through the Course of his Rhapsodies, that he understands not a Tittle of all this Matter; this Author comes and impudently declares, that this whole celebrated Piece, that has for half a Century, been admir'd by the whole People of Great Britain, is a perfect Contradiction to good Sense, to good Manners, and to common Honesty. *O Tempora! O Mores!*

The Knight certainly wrote the foremention'd *Spectator,* though it has been writ these ten Years, on Purpose to make Way for his *Fine Gentleman,*[6] and therefore he endeavours to prove, that *Sir Fopling* is not that genteel Comedy, which the World allows it to be. And then, according to his usual Custom, whenever he pretends to criticise, he does, by shuffling and cutting and confounding Notions, impose upon his unwary Reader; for either Sir George Etheredge did design to make this a genteel Comedy, or he did not. If he did not design it, what is it to the Purpose, whether 'tis a genteel Comedy or not? Provided that 'tis a good one: For I hope, a Comedy may be a good one, and yet not a genteel one. The *Alchemist* is an admirable Comedy, and yet it is not a genteel one. We may say the same of *The Fox,* and *The Silent Woman,* and of a great many more. But if Sir George did

---

[5] See Horace, *Epistle to Augustus,* quoted above p. 14.
[6] See below, p. 141, n. 16.

design to make it a genteel one, he was oblig'd do adapt it to that
Notion of Gentility, which he knew very well, that the World at that
Time had, and we see he succeeded accordingly. For it has pass'd for
a very genteel Comedy, for fifty Years together.[7] Could it be expected
that the admirable Author, should accommodate himself, to the wrong
headed Notions of a would be Critic, who was to appear fifty Years
after the first Acting of his Play: A Critic, who writes Criticism, as
Men commit Treason or Murder, by the Instigation of the Devil
himself, whenever the old Gentleman owes the Knight a Shame.

To prove that this Comedy is not a genteel one, he endeavours to
prove that one of the principal Characters, is not a fine Gentleman.
I appeal to every impartial Man, if when he says, that a Man or
a Woman are genteel, he means any Thing more, than that they are
agreeble in their Air, graceful in their Motions, and polite in their
Conversation. But when he endeavours to prove, that Dorimant is
not a fine Gentleman, he says no more to the Purpose, then he said
before, when he affirm'd that the Comedy is not a genteel Comedy;
for either the Author design'd in Dorimant a fine Gentleman, or he
did not. If he did not, the Character is ne'er the less excellent on that
Account, because Dorimant is an admirable Picture of a Courtier in
the Court of King Charles the Second. But if Dorimant was design'd
for a fine Gentleman by the Author, he was oblig'd to accommodate
himself to that Notion of a fine Gentleman, which the Court and the
Town both had at the Time of the writing of this Comedy. 'Tis
reasonable to believe, that he did so, and we see that he succeeded
accordingly. For Dorimant not only pass'd for a fine Gentleman with
the Court of King Charles the Second, but he has pass'd for such
with all the World, for Fifty Years together. And what indeed can
any one mean, when he speaks of a fine Gentleman, but one who is
qualify'd in Conversation, to please the best Company of either Sex.

But the Knight will be satisfy'd with no Notion of a fine Gentleman
but his own. A fine Gentleman, says he, is one who is honest in his
Actions, and refin'd in his Language. If this be a just Description of
a fine Gentleman, I will make bold to draw two Consequences from it.
The first is, That a Pedant is often a fine Gentleman. For I have
known several of them, who have been Honest in their Actions, and
Refin'd in their Language. The second is, That I know a certain

---

7 Steele seems to have been among a small minority in his censure of *Sir Fopling*. After another fifty years Horace Walpole would defend the comedy in nearly the same terms as Dennis. See below p. 198.

Knight, who, though he should be allow'd to be a Gentleman born, yet is not a fine Gentleman. I shall only add, that I would advise for the future, all the fine Gentlemen, who travel to London from Tipperary,[8] to allow us Englishmen to know what we mean, when we speak our native Language.

To give a true Character of this charming Comedy, it must be acknowledg'd, that there is no great Mastership in the Design of it. Sir George had but little of the artful and just Designs of Ben Jonson: But as Tragedy instructs chiefly by its Design, Comedy instructs by its Characters; which not only ought to be drawn truly in Nature, but to be the resembling Pictures of our Contemporaries, both in Court and Town. Tragedy answers to History-Painting, but Comedy to drawing of Portraits.

How little do they know of the Nature of true Comedy, who believe that its proper Business is to set us Patterns for Imitation: For all such Patterns are serious Things, and Laughter is the Life, and the very Soul of Comedy. 'Tis its proper Business to expose Persons to our View, whose Views we may shun, and whose Follies we may despise; and by shewing us what is done upon the Comic Stage, to shew us what ought never to be done upon the Stage of the World.

All the Characters in *Sir Fopling Flutter*, and especially the principal Characters, are admirably drawn, both to please and to instruct. First, they are drawn to please, because they are drawn in the Truth of Nature; but to be drawn in the Truth of Nature, they must be drawn with those Qualities that are proper to each respective Season of Life.

This is the chief Precept given for the forming the Characters, by two Great Masters of the Rules which Nature herself dictated, and which have been received in every Age, for the Standards of writing successfully, and of judging surely, unless it were with Poetasters, and their foolish Admirers. The Words of Horace, in his *Art of Poetry*, are these, v. 153.

> Tu, quid ego et populus mecum desideret, audi.
> Si sessoris eges aulaea manentis, et usque
> Sessuri, donec cantor, vos plaudite, dicat;
> Aetatis cuiusque notandi sunt tibi mores,
> Mobilibusque decor naturis dandus, et annis.

And thus my Lord Roscommon has translated it:

> Now hear what ev'ry Auditor expects,
> If you intend that he should stay to hear

---

[8] Steele was born at Dublin.

> The Epilogue, and see the Curtain fall;
> Mark how our Tempers alter with our Years,
> Then give the Beauty proper to each Age,
> And by this Rule form all your Characters.[9]

And now see the Character that Horace gives of a Person who is in the Bloom of his Years.

> *De Arte Poetica,* v. 161.
> Imberbis tandem juvenis custode remoto,
> Gaudet equis, canibusque, et aprici gramine campi;
> Cereus in vitium flecti, monitoribus asper,
> Utilium tardus provisor, prodigus aeris,
> Sublimis, cupidusque, et amata relinquere pernix.

And thus the 'foresaid Noble Poet translates it:

> A Youth that first casts off his Tutor's Yoke,
> Loves Horses, Hounds, and Sports, and Exercise;
> Prone to all Vice, impatient of Reproof,
> Proud, careless, fond, inconstant, and profuse.

Now, Horace, to shew the Importance of this Precept, as soon as he has done with the Characters of the four Parts of Life, returns to it, repeats it, and enforces it.

> *Ibid.,* v. 176.
> ——————— No forte seniles
> Mandentur juveni partes, pueroque viriles,
> Semper in adjunctis, aevoque morabimur aptis.

"That a Poet may never be guilty of such an Absurdity," says he, "as to give the Character of an Old Man to a Young Man, or of a Boy to a Middle Ag'd Man, let him take Care to adhere to those Qualities, which are necessarily or probably annexed to each respective Season of Life."

If a Dramatic Poet does not observe this Rule, he misses that which gives the Beauty, and the Decorum, which alone can make his Characters please.

As Horace is but an Epitomizer of Aristotle, in giving Rules for the Characters; that Philosopher gives us more at large the Character of a Person in his early Bloom, in the 14th Chapter of the Second Book of his *Rhetoric.*

"Young Men," says he, "have strong Appetites, and are ready to

---

9 Wentworth Dillon, Fourth Earl of Roscommon (1633?–1685), published his blank-verse translation of Horace's *Ars Poetica* in 1680, and in 1684 his more interesting *Essay on Translated Verse,* a couplet poem in the Horatian manner.

undertake any thing, in order to satisfy them; and of all those Appetites which have a Relation to the Body, they are most powerfully sway'd by Venereal ones, in which they are very changeable, and are quickly cloy'd. For their Desires are rather acute than lasting; like the Hunger and Thirst of the Sick. They are prone to Anger, and easily provok'd; vehement in their Anger, and ready to obey the Dictates of it. For by Reason of the Concern which they have for their Honour, they cannot bear the being undervalu'd, but resent an Affront heinously. And as they are desirous of Honour, they are more ambitious of Victory: For Youth is desirous of excelling, and Victory is a Sort of Excellency." Thus far Aristotle.

And here it may not be amiss to shew, that this Rule is founded in Reason and in Nature: In order to which, let us see what Dacier remarks upon that Verse of Horace, which we cited above.

Mobilibusque decor naturis dandus, et annis.

Behold, says he, a very fine, and very significant Verse; which tells us, if we render it Word for Word, "That we ought to give to moveable Natures and Years their proper Beauty." "By moveable Natures," says Dacier, "Horace means Age, which still runs on like a River, and which, as it runs, gives different Inclinations to Men; and those different Inclinations make what he calls *Decor,* the Beauty proper to the Age. For every Part of Man's Life has its proper Beauties, like every Season of the Year. He that gives to Manly Age the Beauties of Youth, or to Youth the Beauties of Manly Age, does like a Painter, who should paint the Autumn with the Ornaments of Summer, or the Summer with the Ornaments of Autumn."[10]

A Comic Poet, who gives to a Young Man the Qualities that belong to a Middle Ag'd Man, or to an Old Man, can answer neither of the Ends of his Art. He cannot please, because he writes out of Nature, of which all Poetry is an Imitation, and without which, no Poem can possibly please. And as he cannot please, he cannot instruct; because, by shewing such a young Man as is not to be seen in the World, he shews a Monster, and not a Man, sets before us a particular Character, instead of an allegorical and universal one, as all his Characters, and especially his principal Characters, ought to be; and therefore can give no general Instruction, having no Moral, no Fable, and therefore no Comedy.

---

[10] This is Dennis's own translation of André Dacier's comment on line 157 of Horace's *Ars Poetica.* See above p. 132, n. 3.

Now if any one is pleased to compare the Character of Dorimant, to which the Knight has taken so much absurd Exception with the two forementioned Descriptions, he will find in his Character all the chief distinguishing Strokes of them. For such is the Force of Nature, and so admirable a Talent had she given Sir George for Comedy, that, though to my certain Knowledge he understood neither Greek nor Latin, yet one would swear, that in drawing his Dorimant, he copy'd the foresaid Draughts, and especially that of Aristotle. Dorimant is a young Courtier, haughty, vain, and prone to Anger, amorous, false, and inconstant. He debauches Loveit, and betrays her; loves Belinda, and as soon as he enjoys her is false to her.

But 2dly, The Characters in *Sir Fopling* are admirably contriv'd to please, and more particularly the principal ones, because we find in those Characters, a true Resemblance of the Persons both in Court and Town, who liv'd at the Time when that Comedy was writ: For Rapin tells us with a great deal of Judgment, "That Comedy is as it ought to be, when an Audience is apt to imagine, that instead of being in the Pit and Boxes, they are in some Assembly of the Neighbourhood, or in some Family Meeting, and that we see nothing done in it, but what is done in the World. For it is," says he, "not worth one Farthing, if we do not discover our selves in it, and do not find in it both our own Manners, and those of the Persons with whom we live and converse."[11]

The Reason of this Rule is manifest: For as 'tis the Business of a Comic Poet to cure his Spectators of Vice and Folly, by the Apprehension of being laugh'd at; 'tis plain that his Business must be with the reigning Follies and Vices. The violent Passions, which are the Subjects of Tragedy, are the same in every Age, and appear with the same Face; but those Vices and Follies, which are the Subjects of Comedy, are seen to vary continually: Some of those that belonged to our Ancestors, have no Relation to us; and can no more come under the Cognisance of our present Comic Poets, than the Sweating and Sneezing Sickness can come under the Practice of our contemporary Physicians. What Vices and Follies may infect those who are to come after us, we know not; 'tis the present, the reigning Vices, and Follies, that must be the Subjects of our present Comedy: The Comic Poet therefore must take Characters from such Persons as are

---

11 René Rapin, *Reflections on Aristotle's Poesie*, Pt. II, Sect. xxv (in *Critical Works*, trans. Basil Kennet, London, 1716, II, 220).

his Contemporaries, and are infected with the foresaid Follies and Vices.

Agreeable to this, is the Advice which Boileau, in his *Art of Poetry*, gives to the Comic Poets:

> Etudiez la Cour, et connoissez la ville,
> L'une et l'autre est toujours en modèles fertile,
> C'est par là que Molière illustrant ses écrits,
> Peut-être de son Art eût remporté la prix, etc.[12]

Now I remember very well, that upon the first acting this Comedy, it was generally believed to be an agreeable Representation of the Persons of Condition of both Sexes, both in Court and Town; and that all the World was charm'd with Dorimant; and that it was unanimously agreed, that he had in him several of the Qualities of Wilmot Earl of Rochester, as, his Wit, his Spirit, his amorous Temper, the Charms that he had for the fair Sex, his Falshood, and his Inconstancy; the agreeable Manner of his chiding his Servants, which the late Bishop of Salisbury takes Notice of in his Life; and lastly, his repeating, on every Occasion, the Verses of Waller, for whom that noble Lord had a very particular Esteem; witness his Imitation of the Tenth Satire of the First Book of Horace:

> Waller, by Nature for the Bays design'd,
> With Spirit, Force, and Fancy unconfind,
> In Panegyrick is above Mankind.[13]

Now, as several of the Qualities in Dorimant's Character were taken from that Earl of Rochester, so they who were acquainted with the late Sir Fleetwood Shepherd,[14] know very well, that not a little of that Gentleman's Character is to be found in Medley.

But the Characters in this Comedy are very well form'd to instruct as well as to please, especially those of Dorimant and of Loveit; and they instruct by the same Qualities to which the Knight has taken so much whimsical Exception; as Dorimant instructs by his Insulting, and his Perfidiousness, and Loveit by the Violence of her Resentment and her Anguish. For Loveit has Youth, Beauty, Quality, Wit, and Spirit. And it was depending upon these, that she repos'd so dangerous a Trust in Dorimant, which is a just Caution to the Fair Sex, never to be so conceited of the Power of their Charms, or their other

---

[12] Boileau, *L'Art Poétique*, III. 391–94.

[13] John Wilmot, Earl of Rochester, *An Allusion to the Tenth Satyr of the First Book of Horace* (1677–1679?), 34–36, slightly misquoted.

[14] Sir Fleetwood Sheppard (1634–1698), courtier and poet.

extraordinary Qualities, as to believe they can engage a Man to be true to them, to whom they grant the best Favour, without the only sure Engagement, without which they can never be certain, that they shall not be hated and despis'd by that very Person whom they have done every Thing to oblige.

To conclude with one General Observation, That Comedy may be qualify'd in a powerful Manner both to instruct and to please, the very Constitution of its Subject ought always to be Ridiculous. Comedy, says Rapin, is an Image of common Life, and its End is to expose upon the Stage the Defects of particular Persons, in order to cure the Defects of the Public, and to correct and amend the People, by the Fear of being laugh'd at. That therefore, says he, which is most essential to Comedy, is certainly the Ridicule.[15]

Every Poem is qualify'd to instruct, and to please most powerfully by that very Quality which makes the Fort and the Characteristic of it, and which distinguishes it from all other Kinds of Poems. As Tragedy is qualify'd to instruct and to please, by Terror and Compassion, which two Passions ought always to be predominant in it, and to distinguish it from all other Poems. Epic Poetry pleases and instructs chiefly by Admiration, which reigns throughout it, and distinguishes it from Poems of every other Kind. Thus Comedy instructs and pleases most powerfully by the Ridicule, because that is the Quality which distinguishes it from every other Poem. The Subject therefore of every Comedy ought to be ridiculous by its Constitution; the Ridicule ought to be of the very Nature and Essence of it. Where there is none of that, there can be no Comedy. It ought to reign both in the Incidents and in the Characters, and especially in the principal Characters, which ought to be ridiculous in themselves, or so contriv'd, as to shew and expose the Ridicule of others. In all the Masterpieces of Ben Jonson, the principal Character has the Ridicule in himself, as Morose in *The Silent Woman,* Volpone in *The Fox,* and Subtle and Face in *The Alchemist:* And the very Ground and Foundation of all these Comedies is ridiculous. 'Tis the very same Thing in the Master-pieces of Molière. The *Misanthrope,* the *Impostor,* the *Avare,* and the *Femmes Savantes.* Nay, the Reader will find, that in most of his other Pieces, the principal Characters are ridiculous; as, *L'Etourdi, Les Précieuses Ridicules, Le Cocu Imaginaire, Les Fâcheux,* and *Monsieur de Pourceaugnac, Le Bourgeois Gentilhomme, L'Ecole des Maris, L'Ecole des Femmes, L'Amour Médecin, Le Médecin*

---

15 See Rapin, *Reflections on Aristotle's Poesie,* Pt. II, Sect. xxv (in *Critical Works,* 1716, II, 219).

Malgré Lui, Le Mariage Forcé, George Dandin, Les Fourberies de Scapin, Le Malade Imaginaire. The Reader will not only find, upon Reflection, that in all these Pieces the principal Characters are ridiculous, but that in most of them there is the Ridicule of Comedy in the very Titles.

'Tis by the Ridicule that there is in the Character of Sir Fopling, which is one of the principal ones of this Comedy, and from which it takes its Name, that he is so very well qualify'd to please and to instruct. What true Englishman is there, but must be pleas'd to see this ridiculous Knight made the Jest and the Scorn of all the other Characters, for shewing, by his foolish aping foreign Customs and Manners, that he prefers another Country to his own? And of what important Instruction must it be to all our Youth who travel, to shew them, that if they so far forget the Love of their Country, as to declare by their espousing foreign Customs and Manners, that they prefer France or Italy to Great Britain, at their Return, they must justly expect to be the Jest and the Scorn of their own Countrymen.

Thus, I hope, I have convinc'd the Reader, that this Comical Knight, Sir Fopling, has been justly form'd by the Knight his Father, to instruct and please, whatever may be the Opinion to the contrary of the Knight his Brother.

Whenever *The Fine Gentleman*[16] of the latter comes upon the Stage, I shall be glad to see that it has all the shining Qualities which recommend *Sir Fopling*, that his Characters are always drawn in Nature, and that he never gives to a young Man the Qualities of a Middle-aged Man, or an old one; that they are the just Images of our Contemporaries, and of what we every Day see in the World; that instead of setting us Patterns for our Imitation, which is not the proper Business of Comedy, he makes those Follies and Vices ridiculous, which we ought to shun and despise; that the Subject of his Comedy is comical by its Constitution; and that the Ridicule is particularly in the Grand Incidents, and in the principal Characters. For a true Comic Poet is a Philosopher, who, like old Democritus, always instructs us laughing.

When Steele's play, with its Preface, was published late in 1722, Dennis resumed his punitive attentions in a verbose pamphlet from

---

16 Apparently a tentative or working title by which Steele's play was known before the production. Compare Steele's criticism of Etherege's "fine gentleman" Dorimant in *Spectator* No. 65 and Dennis above p. 133.

which the following passage of fairly hard theoretical reason deserves quotation.

When Sir Richard says, that any thing that has its Foundation in Happiness and Success must be the Subject of Comedy, he confounds Comedy with that Species of Tragedy which has a happy Catastrophe. When he says, that 'tis an Improvement of Comedy to introduce a Joy too exquisite for Laughter, he takes all the Care that he can to shew, that he knows nothing of the Nature of Comedy. Does he really believe that Molière understood the Nature of it: I say Molière, who, in the Opinion of all Europe, excepting that small Portion of it which is acquainted with Ben Jonson, had born away the Prize of Comedy from all Nations, and from all Ages, if for the sake of his Profit, he had not descended sometimes too much to Buffoonry. Let Sir Richard, or any one, look into that little Piece of Molière, call'd, *La Critique de l'Ecole des Femmes,* and he shall find there, that in Molière's Opinion, 'tis the Business of a Comic Poet to enter into the Ridicule of Men, and to expose the blind Sides of all Sorts of People agreeably; that he does nothing at all, if he does not draw the Pictures of his Contemporaries, and does not raise the Mirth of the sensible Part of an Audience, which, says he, 'tis no easy Matter to do. This is the sense of Molière, tho' the words are not his exactly.

When Sir Richard talks of a Joy too exquisite for Laughter, he seems not to know that Joy, generally taken, is common like Anger, Indignation, Love, to all Sorts of Poetry, to the Epic, the Dramatic, the Lyric; but that that kind of Joy which is attended with Laughter, is the Characteristic of Comedy; as Terror or Compassion, according as one or the other is predominant, makes the Characteristic of Tragedy, as Admiration does of Epic Poetry.

When Sir Richard says, That weeping upon the Sight of a deplorable Object is not a Subject for Laughter, but that 'tis agreeable to good Sense and to Humanity, he says nothing but what all the sensible Part of the World have always granted; but then all that sensible Part of the World have always deny'd, that a deplorable Object is fit to be shewn in Comedy. When Sir George Etherege, in his Comedy of *Sir Fopling Flutter,* shews Loveit in all the Height and Violence of Grief and Rage, the Judicious Poet takes care to give those Passions a Ridiculous Turn by the Mouth of Dorimant. Besides that, the Subject is at the Bottom ridiculous: For Loveit is a Mistress, who has abandon'd her self to Dorimant; and by falling into these violent Passions, only because she fancies that something of which she is very desirous has gone beside her, makes herself truly ridiculous. Thus is this famous Scene in the second Act of *Sir Fopling,* by the character of Loveit, and the dextrous handling the Subject, kept within the Bounds of Comedy: But the Scene of the Discovery in the *Conscious Lovers* is truly tragical. Indiana is strictly virtuous: She had indeed conceiv'd a violent Passion for Bevil; but all young People in full

Health are liable to such a Passion, and perhaps the most sensible and the most virtuous are more than others liable: But besides, that she had kept this Passion within the Bounds of Honour, it was the natural Effect of her Esteem for her Benefactor, and of her Gratitude, that is, of her Virtue. These Considerations render'd her Case deplorable, and the Catastrophe downright tragical, which of a Comedy ought to be the most comical Part, for the same Reason that it ought to be the most tragical Part of a Tragedy.[1]

Another passage of this pamphlet is remarkable for a special attention which Dennis, stimulated by Steele's Preface to *The Conscious Lovers* (cf. above, p. 119), bestows upon the most polished and the most tender of the ancient dramatic poets, Terence. The Romans themselves, he observes, or at least those of the Augustan age, and especially Caesar, were aware of a great defect in the comedies of Terence. For all his subtle merits, he lacked the one thing most necessary for a comic writer, namely "comic Force" (the *vis comica*).[2] A few years earlier, in a letter to a fashionable friend, Dennis had reported his great delight in recently renewing a much earlier acquaintance with Terence and had quoted from the *Life of Terence* by Suetonius, the classic lines in which the Emperor Julius Caesar both "calls Terence a Demy Menander and complains that the *Vis Comica* was wanting" to him.

> Tu quoque, Tu in summis, O dimidiate Menander
> Poneris, et merito, puri Sermonis Amator;
> Lenibus atque utinam scriptis adjuncta foret vis
> Comica, ut aequato virtus polleret Honore
> Cum Graecis, neque in hac despectus parte jaceres.
> Unum hoc maceror, et Doleo tibi deesse Terenti.[3]

---

[1] *Remarks on a Play, Call'd, The Conscious Lovers, a Comedy* (London, 1723), pp. 6–8. See this passage quoted and a further discussion of its theme in Joseph Wood Krutch, *Comedy and Conscience after the Restoration* (New York, 1924), pp. 250–51.

[2] *Remarks on a Play*, p. 9.

[3] "Thou also, O thou demi-Menander! art ranked with the highest, and rightly, lover of pure language that thou art. Would only thy graceful lines had the comic force to rise to the height of the Greeks. Would that in this one respect thou couldst not be looked down upon. This only hurts me, this I grieve to find wanting in thee, Terence!" (Letter to Henry Cromwell, Esq., October 11, 1717, in *Original Letters, Familiar, Moral, and Critical, by Mr. Dennis*, London, 1721, I, 14).

HENRY FIELDING

[1707–1754]

The great comic genius Henry Fielding came of landed gentry in Somerset, was educated at Eton, and studied law for a while at Leyden. At an early age he began his London literary career by writing for the stage, producing some twenty-six pieces (comedies, burlesques, and farces) in a period of about nine years, 1728–1737. He was least successful in a few attempts at the witty mode of Congreve—immensely successful in his burlesque *Tragedy of Tragedies; or, The Life and Death of Tom Thumb the Great,* 1731,[1] a subverted panorama of the English heroic stage from Dryden's *Conquest of Granada* to James Thomson's *Sophonisba.* He gave a preview of later more profound concerns in a blend of burlesque politics and country-inn realism entitled *Don Quixote in England,* 1734. A series of assaults upon the Government reached, in *Pasquin* (opening The Little Theater in the Haymarket, 1736) and *The Historical Register,* 1737, a crescendo which helped to provoke the Theatrical Licensing Act of June 1737 and to drive Fielding himself from the stage. Turning again to law, and to Opposition journalism (as Captain Hercules Vinegar of *The Champion*), he was in uncertain straits when late in 1740 his moral and comic sensibilities were stimulated by the publication and hysterical popular reception of Samuel Richardson's epoch-making epistolary novel *Pamela: or Virtue Rewarded.* Virtue for sale, as some might reword it, a "luscious" celebration of purity in the idiom of lubricity. Formula: servant girl resists master's lewd advances, becomes lady. Fielding made a first anonymous retort to *Pamela* early in 1741 with his burlesque *Apology for the Life of Mrs. Shamela Andrews.* This was a brief, whacking, and slaughterous epistolary narrative—equally prurient with the distinguished original. Fortunately for the annals of the comic spirit, he conceived and wrote—during the course of the following autumn, in poverty and illness,[2] by an extraordinary feat of

---

[1] Expanded from a shorter version, *Tom Thumb,* 1730. The *Tragedy of Tragedies* is said to have made Jonathan Swift laugh for the second time in his life. (Laetitia Pilkington, *Memoirs,* 1754, III, 155.)

[2] Fielding himself, his wife, and elder daughter, five years old, were ill. His daughter was to die in March 1742, and his wife in November 1744.

detachment—his second response to Richardson's novel—*The History
of the Adventures of Joseph Andrews and of his Friend Mr. Abraham
Adams. Written in Imitation of the Manner of Cervantes. Author of
Don Quixote.* This was in fact something far more than a response to
Pamela. It was a demonstration of an alternative species of "true"
fiction. Along with *Pamela,* other targets are conspicuously in sight—
the complacent coxcombery and bad grammar of the aged memorialist
of the theater Colley Cibber,[3] the literary genre of the vast French
prose romance, the newly popular feverish Methodism of faith without
works[4]—more simply and comprehensively, the whole broad spectrum
of human vice, folly, and partly foolish virtue, displayed in a picaresque
and tripartite vista-vision of city, road, and country village.

It is a correct tradition of Fielding criticism to say that he kicked
in or broke out of the closed hothouse of Richardson's forced and
florid world and showed how to conduct a novel in the full outdoor
sunlight, wind, clouds, and storm of the human condition. It is a
commonplace and in a broad sense it is correct to take a serious view
of Fielding's own assertion in his Preface (below pp. 154–56) that he
is by no means writing a burlesque. Burlesque indeed, he says, in the
"diction" (epic similes, lofty apostrophes, heroic descriptions), but in
the "sentiments" and "characters" something far different—that is,
comedy, the faithful portrayal of ridiculous human nature. *Joseph
Andrews* is a playwright's first novel, full of scenes, actions, dialogues,
and characters arranged in striking and funny oppositions. The Preface,
as the author suggests in a boast about his former theatrical successes,
is a playwright's preface. Speedy, energetic, even dramatic, like the
novel itself, this essay contrives to cut rapidly around a few difficulties,
even contradictions. If only in its contrast to the painstaking betrayals
of our immediately preceding authority, John Dennis, Fielding's critical
prose is worth our attention.

A distinction which might not have helped Fielding, as it might well
have made his argument seem less assured, but which might help a
commentator upon him, is one which has sometimes been drawn
between "low" and "high" burlesque, or perhaps better, between
travesty (or parody) and mock-heroic (or heroi-comical).[5] The first
makes fun of, or brings down, some lofty literary work or tradition.
The second is a laughing criticism of life itself. It is true that *both*
travesty and mock-heroic work by an implied contrast with some
established high or heroic (or supposedly high or heroic) work or
tradition. And no doubt there is always something of either extreme

---

3 *An Apology for the life of Mr. Colley Cibber, Comedian,* 1740.
4 See below, p. 146, n.6
5 See Geoffrey Tillotson, ed. *The Rape of the Lock* (London, 1940), pp. 107–8.

(travesty or mock-heroic) in the other. The mirrors of low and high, immediate and remote, reflect each other. The mere "diction," furthermore, can assuredly never, as Fielding seems to believe, be cleanly separated from the "sentiments" and "characters." But a very great difference between travesty and mock-heroic *can* appear in the direction toward which the ridicule is pointed. Paul Scarron's *Virgile Travesti*, or *Aeneid* transformed in comic tetrameter couplets, 1648, was a well-known seventeenth-century instance of fairly simple travesty (or low burlesque). The fun was poked at Virgil or at the epic idea or at whatever was pompous or vulnerable in that idea. Fielding's *Tom Thumb* was of this sort—fun at the expense of the English heroic stage. And so was his *Shamela*—fun at the expense of a parvenu pretender to moral dignity. Doubtless he had these performances of his own much in mind in his Preface to *Joseph Andrews* as he urged the difference between burlesque and comedy, "caricature" and "nature." Pope's *Rape of the Lock* and *Dunciad* are good examples of the opposite end of the low-high burlesque spectrum. Homeric, Virgilian, Biblical, Spenserian, and Miltonic parallels (or contrasts) permeate and slant these poems, but the fun is at the expense, not of those looming literary presences, but of the immediate life-targets represented—Grub Street Dunces or the daintier belles and beaux of Hampton Court. Pope himself called *The Rape of the Lock* "heroi-comical."

Fielding's *Joseph Andrews* grapples with a more robust, raw, riotous life both more handsome and uglier, than Pope's epyllion of the Court, and deals with that varied life by a less steadily and uniformly accentuated method of burlesque than Pope employs in *The Dunciad*. A multiplicity and alternation of literary points of reference in *Joseph Andrews* may be one obstacle to clear analysis. Not only *Pamela* and Cibber's *Apology* as momentary parody targets, and *Don Quixote* as a sympathetic model, and Homer and Virgil for heroic language and patterns of episodic action, and picaresque novels and romances for complications and marvelous denouements—but also, as a recent writer has interestingly shown,[6] the most august work in the western tradition, the Holy Bible. Joseph and Abraham, chaste servant and charitable and pious priest and patriarch, flounder their way, half ridiculous, half admirably serious, through the length of a prose comic version of seventeenth-century Biblical epic. The difficulties for our defining a clear difference between "burlesque" and "comedy" and for the concept of the "comic epic poem in prose" which Fielding would set before

---

6 Martin Battestin, *The Moral Basis of Fielding's Art: A Study of "Joseph Andrews"* (Middletown, Connecticut, 1959), Chaps. 2 and 3; and Battestin, ed. *"Joseph Andrews" and "Shamela"* (Boston, 1961), pp. xxiii–xxvii.

us in his Preface may be further suggested if we notice the one instance of classical comic epic to which he refers, unfortunately no longer extant, the supposedly Homeric *Margites* (epic of *The Mad Fellow*), "which Aristotle tells us, bore the same relation to comedy which his *Iliad* bears to tragedy."[7] But the *Margites* was assuredly a burlesque (whether low or high, travesty or mock-heroic). In spite of Aristotle's opinion, it bore a relation to stage comedy (Aristophanes and Plautus) different from the relation of serious epic[8] to stage tragedy. Classical stage comedy may be some kind of archetypal or ritual analogue or complement of tragedy, but it is not *Tom Thumb*, not a burlesque of tragedy.[9] A "comic epic," as John Dennis would have been glad to assure us (with much reason on his side), is in fact a contradiction in terms—"admiration" being the emotion of epic, ridicule that of comedy. Or, the epic and the ridiculous can be brought together only by the mediation of the element of burlesque—albeit this may be, no doubt, not low, but high burlesque, the heroi-comical.

There was something in the classical tradition called Menippean or Varronian satire,[10] the *spoudaiogeloion,* a burlesque medley or monster both serious and funny, best illustrated in certain second-century prose dialogues by the Greek writer Lucian (one of Fielding's acknowledged mentors). The Menippean was a minor tradition, less known and regarded than the Horatian epistolary and witty conversational satire and not very closely related to the traditions of stage comedy, either the warm comedy of humors or the cool comedy of wit. Dryden in his *Discourse on Satire,* 1693, had supposed that his own narrative satires *Mac Flecknoe* and *Absalom and Achitophel* were of the Menippean sort. The Earl of Shaftesbury in the laughing Platonism of his treatise entitled *Sensus Communis,* or *The Freedom of Wit and Humour* (1709, and in his *Characteristics,* 1711), had cited this raucous idiom, and he coupled it with the Homeric *Margites.* There would seem to

---

[7] Cf. Book III, Chap. 1. Parson Adams expounds, "He was the father of the drama, as well as the epic: not of tragedy only, but of comedy also; for his *Margites,* which is deplorably lost, bore, says Aristotle, the same analogy to comedy as his *Odyssey* and *Iliad* to tragedy."

[8] A Greek writer of the first century A.D. at Rome (Longinus, *Peri Hupsous,* Chap. 9) alludes to the *Odyssey* as Homer's comedy. Fielding too invokes the *Odyssey,* not as comedy, but as a classical verse analogue to Fénelon's prose epic *Télémaque.*

[9] There may be burlesque moments, especially in Old Comedy, but even Old Comedy is not a systematic or sustained burlesque.

[10] The third-century B.C. Cynic philosopher Menippus of Gadara wrote satiric mixtures of prose and verse which are lost. He was imitated by Cicero's friend Marcus Terentius Varro, whose *Saturae Menippeae* survive in fragments amounting to about 600 lines. Menippus figures also in the satiric dialogues of Lucian, written in Attic Greek during the second century A.D. See Gilbert Highet, *The Anatomy of Satire* (Princeton, 1962), pp. 36–37, 163–64.

be little room for doubt that Fielding, at least in his choice of key terms in the Preface to *Joseph Andrews,* was influenced by the Menippean tradition, and most likely he owed an immediate debt to Shaftesbury.[11]

In one of the most celebrated clauses of his Preface, his insistence that affectation, either that of vanity or that of hypocrisy, is the only source of the "true Ridiculous," Fielding invokes an idea which we have seen hinted perhaps as early as Plato's *Philebus* and more than hinted in Ben Jonson's Induction to *Every Man out of his Humour.* In two essays on the laughable in *The Champion* during 1739 and 1740 Fielding himself had pursued the same theme.[12] Perhaps Molière's *Critique de l'Ecole des Femmes,* 1662, was a chief source for similar English ideas about the true ridiculous in Fielding's time, and La Rouchefoucauld's *Maxims,*[13] 1665, another, and yet another, cited by Fielding, the Abbé de Bellegarde's *Réflexions sur le Ridicule,* 1696.[14]

"Affectation," we may suppose, is a relatively shallow vice. In excluding from the range of targets for ridicule all deep human miseries and misfortunes, black villainies, and dreadful calamities—"ugliness, infirmity, or poverty"—Fielding touches the theme of kindly laughter which may be illustrated throughout our tradition—in Aristotle, or in Shadwell or Dennis, and conspicuously in the trend we have already traced, in both life and literature, toward the "amiable" and caressible British humor—the goodnatured cove or codger, the harmless eccentric, the splendid "original," the hobbyhorsical Uncle Toby. Parson Abraham Adams, the "most glaring" character in *Joseph Andrews* and unquestionably the hero of the novel, is manifestly a "humor," and in him Fielding raises the amiable humor to a dignity perhaps not again reached before the tradition peters out in Victorian whimsicalities.

The theme of "humor," more broadly considered, was one to which Fielding would return a decade later, but with something less than enthusiasm for the phenomenon as he then saw it developing in the reality of English life. The middle years of the eighteenth century in London present an excellent scene for the study both of the homely,

---

11 See William B. Coley, "The Background of Fielding's Laughter," *ELH, A Journal of English Literary History,* XXVI (June 1959), 229–52, esp. 239–41.

12 Martin Battestin, ed. *Joseph Andrews* (Middletown, Connecticut, 1967), p. 7, n. 14, citing *The Champion* for November 20, 1739, and April 15, 1740.

13 "Monsieur *de la Rochefoucault* very justly observes, that People are never ridiculous from their real, but from their affected Characters; they can't help being what they are, but they can help attempting to appear what they are not" (*Common Sense; or, the Englishman's Journal,* September 3, 1737).

14 Martin Battestin, ed. *Joseph Andrews,* 1967, p. 7, n. 3. Cf. John W. Draper, "The Theory of the Comic in Eighteenth-Century England," *Journal of English and Germanic Philology,* XXXVII (1938), 219–20.

cheerful cult of humor and of a certain aristocratic reaction against it. Even a passionate and sensitive lyric poet might pay his tribute:

> O *Humour*, Thou whose Name is known
> To *Britain*'s favor'd Isle alone:
> Me too amidst thy Band admit.[15]

From the theatrical point of view, a certain comfortable contrast could be drawn between the humorously varied and natural English character and the supposedly opposite, more artificially controlled, rational, and uniform French character. Thus David Garrick in a letter to a friend in 1769:

> Their Politesse has reduced their Characters to such a sameness, that their Humours and Passions are so curb'd by Habit, that when you have seen a dozen French men and Women you have seen the whole: in England...every Man is a distinct Being and requires a distinct Study.[16]

But on the other hand, the observer might be not a theater manager and actor, but a noble lord, the most elegant diplomat and severe critic of manners in England. Then the comparison between French character and English might be valued the opposite way, with a caustic opinion about the fitness of English women for a salon society.

> ...the conversations of our mixed companies here...if they happen to rise above bragg and whist, infallibly stop short of everything either pleasing or instructive. I take the reason of this to be, that (as women generally give the tone of conversation) our English women are not near so well informed and cultivated as the French; besides that they are naturally more serious and silent.[17]

Lord Chesterfield does not quite say it in that letter, but the whole trend of his thinking and aloofness of his taste were, in a way that we have already glimpsed in Ben Jonson, coldly antagonistic to all that was homely, bumbling, eccentric, bluff, hearty, crazy, and agreeably outlaw in the English cult of the humorous. And this aristocratic severity was closely linked with a distinct aversion to the normal human response to humor—namely, laughter. The agelasm (unfriendliness to laughter) which we have already seen in the enthusiastic Sidney and the classical Jonson has its advanced counterpart in the eighteenth-

---

15 William Collins, *"The Manners an Ode,"* 1747.

16 To Helfrich Peter Sturz, January 3, 1769, in *The Letters of David Garrick*, ed. David M. Little and George H. Kahrl, II (Cambridge, Mass., 1963), pp. 634–35, No. 528.

17 Lord Chesterfield, to his son, January 23, 1752, in *Letters* (New York, 1942), p. 250.

century arbiter—beset as he was by the now triumphant cult of the humorous laughable. "Having mentioned laughter," he wrote in another of his excellent letters to his son, "I must particularly warn you against it: and I could heartily wish you may often be seen to smile, but never heard to laugh while you live."

> Frequent and loud laughter is the characteristic of folly and ill manners. . . . In my mind there is nothing so illiberal, and so ill-bred, as audible laughter. True wit, or sense, never yet made anybody laugh; they are above it: they please the mind, and give a cheerfulness to the countenance. But it is low buffoonery, or silly accidents, that always excite laughter; and that is what people of sense and breeding should show themselves above. . . . I am neither of a melancholy, nor a cynical disposition; and am as willing, and as apt, to be pleased as anybody; but I am sure that, since I have had the full use of my reason, nobody has ever heard me laugh.[18]

The English tradition of "humor" and its correspondent loud guffaw finds its balance in the almost directly opposite tradition of polite witty conversation, which the modern mind is likely not to know was cool and intellectual. Sensitive to the lightest ripples of the laughable, it would nevertheless savor them internally, in the mind, and cultivate its sensitivity precisely by the suppression of the outward commotion. We are likely to think of Swift and Pope as two of the most amusing English writers. And we may be surprised to learn that Swift "stubbornly resisted any tendency to laughter," and that "by no merriment, either of others or of his own, was Pope ever seen excited to laughter."[19]

It may seem to us a paradox of literary and cultural history that Henry Fielding the comic novelist and Philip Dormer Stanhope, Fourth Earl of Chesterfield, most elegant of British peers in his day and most aloof from mere laughter, should have enjoyed a kind of affinity in wit. But it is a fact that Chesterfield was a patronly friend to Fielding, and Fielding pays him a compliment in a theoretical chapter of *Joseph Andrews* (III, 1; reprinted in this volume). A justice of the peace for

---

18 In *Letters,* From Bath, March 9, 1748 (O.S.), p. 49.

19 Samuel Johnson, *Lives of the Poets,* ed. G. B. Hill (Oxford, 1905), III, 56, 202.

In Johnson's *Dictionary* under *risibility* appears this telltale Augustan example: "Whatever the philosophers may talk of their risibility, neighing is a more noble expression than laughing.—Arbuthnot."

Pope and Swift's contemporary Congreve, as we have said, was a partisan of the English "humor," at least in his theory. We know that he was an exceedingly witty comic dramatist. In Congreve we find the rebuff to laughter put in the mouth of an aristocratic and comic stage character, Lord Froth: "There is nothing more unbecoming a man of quality than to laugh, it is such a vulgar expression of the passion. Everybody can laugh" (*The Double Dealer,* I.ii).

Westminster, author of the novels *Tom Jones* (1749) and *Amelia* (1751), and editor in 1752 of his fourth periodical organ, *The Covent-Garden Journal*, Fielding was during his last years engaged in a continual running warfare against both bad morals and bad manners—London crime and Grub-Street duncery. Numbers 55 and 56 of the *Covent-Garden Journal* (July 18 and 25, 1752) pick up from Ben Jonson and Congreve the stage topic of "humours" and turn on it, or on the contemporary vogue of self-gratulation in the humors, the moderately censorious gaze of a practical moralist. (See our text below pp. 167–76.) Fielding's temper was that of an aristocratic wit, even though somewhat softened by the middle-class "good sense" ascendant in his generation. He looks back to Pope and Swift and forward to a time about 1877, the date of the last primary text of this volume, the classic *Essay on Comedy* by George Meredith. The following paragraphs, which open *Covent-Garden Journal* No. 18, are a remarkable statement of a sort of rearguard Augustanism which Fielding maintained against the midcentury rising tide of sentiment and soft humor.

It is from a very common but a very false Opinion, that we constantly mix the Idea of Levity with those of Wit and Humour. The gravest of Men have often possessed these Qualities in a very eminent Degree, and have exerted them on the most solemn Subjects with very eminent Success. These are to be found in many Places in the most serious Works of Plato and Aristotle, of Cicero and Seneca. Not only Swift, but South hath used them on the highest and most important of all Subjects. In the Sermons of the Latter, there is perhaps more Wit, than in the Comedies of Congreve; and in his Controversy with Sherlock on the Trinity, he hath not only exerted great Wit, but many Strokes of the most exquisite Drollery. Not to mention the Instance of St. Paul, whose Writings do in my Opinion contain more true Wit, than is to be found in the Works of the unjustly celebrated Petronius.

In like Manner, and with like Error we unite the Ideas of Gravity with Dulness, as if the former was inseparably annexed to the latter. True indeed it is that Dulness appears in her own Form, and in her proper Dress, when she walks abroad in some tritical Essay on a grave Subject; and many millions of Reams have in all Ages been sacrificed to her by her Votaries in this Manner; but she doth not always preserve this solemn Air. She often appears in public in Essays of Entertainment, as the Booksellers chuse to call them; and sometimes in Print, as well as on the Stage, disguises herself in a Jack-pudding Coat, and condescends to divert her good Friends with sundry Feats of Dexterity and Grimace.

The late ingenious Dr. Swift, who was one of the greatest Enemies that Dulness ever had; and who hath traced her out and exposed her in all her various Disguises, likens these two different Appearances of Dulness to the different Qualities of small Beer in the Barrel, and small Beer in the Bottle. The former of which is well known to be of all Things the most vapid, insipid and heavy; but the latter is altogether as airy, frothy, brisk and bouncing.[20]

---

20 *The Covent-Garden Journal,* No. 18. March 3, 1752. This apparently alludes to a passage in the fourth chapter of Pope's *Peri Bathous: Or of the Art of Sinking in Poetry;* here and elsewhere, Fielding attributes *Peri Bathous* to Swift. The piece first appeared in the third volume of *Miscellanies* (1728) by Pope and Swift. "It is with the *Bathos* as with small Beer, which is indeed vapid and insipid, if left at large and let abroad; but being by our Rules confin'd, and well stopt, nothing grows so frothy, pert and bouncing" (p. 16). Professor W. B. Coley brings to my attention a similar passage in Addison's *Whig-Examiner* No. 4, October 5, 1710. For more on "humours," see below pp. 234–35; and Ronald Paulson, *Satire and the Novel in Eighteenth-Century England* (New Haven, 1967), Chapter 2, "Fielding The Satirist."

PREFACE

TO

Joseph Andrews

[1742]

As it is possible the mere *English* Reader may have a different Idea of Romance with the Author of these little Volumes; and may consequently expect a kind of Entertainment, not to be found, nor which was even intended, in the following Pages; it may not be improper to premise a few Words concerning this kind of Writing, which I do not remember to have seen hitherto attempted in our Language.

The EPIC as well as the DRAMA is divided into Tragedy and Comedy. *Homer,* who was the Father of this Species of Poetry, gave us a Pattern of both these, tho' that of the latter kind is entirely lost; which *Aristotle* tells us, bore the same relation to Comedy which his *Iliad* bears to Tragedy.[1] And perhaps, that we have no more Instances of it among the Writers of Antiquity, is owing to the Loss of this great Pattern, which, had it survived, would have found its Imitators equally with the other Poems of this great Original.

And farther, as this Poetry may be Tragic or Comic, I will not scruple to say it may be likewise either in Verse or Prose: for tho' it wants one particular, which the Critic enumerates in the constituent Parts of an Epic Poem, namely Metre; yet, when any kind of Writing contains all its other Parts, such as Fable, Action, Characters, Sentiments, and Diction, and is deficient in Metre only; it seems, I think,

---

The first edition of *The History of the Adventures of Joseph Andrews, And of his Friend Mr. Abraham Adams. Written in Imitation of The Manner of Cervantes, Author of Don Quixote—* London: Printed for A. Millar, was published in February 1742. Our text of the Preface and of Book III, Chapter I follows that edition. A second edition, corrected by Fielding, published in June 1742, changes these parts of the book only in a few "accidentals." Fielding's name did not appear on the title page until the third edition, March 1743.

1 *Poetics,* IV.9. This is discussed above, pp. 145–47.

reasonable to refer it to the Epic; at least, as no Critic hath thought proper to range it under any other Head, nor to assign it a particular Name to itself.

Thus the *Telemachus* of the ArchBishop of Cambray[2] appears to me of the Epic Kind, as well as the *Odyssey* of Homer; indeed, it is much fairer and more reasonable to give it a Name common with that Species from which it differs only in a single Instance, than to confound it with those which it resembles in no other. Such are those voluminous Works commonly called Romances, namely, *Clelia, Cleopatra, Astræa, Cassandra,* the *Grand Cyrus,*[3] and innumerable other which contain, as I apprehend, very little Instruction or Entertainment.

Now a comic Romance is a comic Epic-Poem in Prose; differing from Comedy, as the serious Epic from Tragedy: its Action being more extended and comprehensive; containing a much larger Circle of Incidents, and introducing a greater variety of Characters. It differs from the serious Romance in its Fable and Action, in this; that as in the one these are grave and solemn, so in the other they are light and ridiculous: it differs in its Characters, by introducing Persons of inferiour Rank, and consequently of inferiour Manners, whereas the grave Romance sets the highest before us; lastly in its Sentiments and Diction; by preserving the Ludicrous instead of the Sublime. In the Diction I think, Burlesque itself may be sometimes admitted; of which many Instances will occur in this Work, as in the Descriptions of the Battles, and some other Places, not necessary to be pointed out to the Classical Reader; for whose Entertainment those Parodies or Burlesque Imitations are chiefly calculated.

But tho' we have sometimes admitted this in our Diction, we have carefully excluded it from our Sentiments and Characters: for there it is never properly introduced, unless in Writings of the Burlesque kind, which this is not intended to be. Indeed, no two Species of Writing can differ more widely than the Comic and the Burlesque: for as the latter is ever the Exhibition of what is monstrous and unnatural, and where our Delight, if we examine it, arises from the surprizing Absurdity, as in appropriating the Manners of the highest

---

2 François de Salignac de la Mothe-Fénelon (1651–1715), archbishop of Cambrai, wrote his *Aventures de Télémaque,* 1699, for the instruction of a royal pupil, the duc de Bourgogne, son of the Dauphin.

3 French prose romances, of heroic length, by Madeleine de Scudéry (*Artamène, ou le Grand Cyrus,* 10 volumes, 1649–1653; *Clélie,* 1656–1660); Gauthier de Costes de la Calprenède (*Cléopatre,* 1646; *Cassandre,* 1642–1645); and Honoré D'Urfé (*Astrée,* 1608–1624).

to the lowest, or *è converso;* so in the former, we should ever confine ourselves strictly to Nature, from the just Imitation of which, will flow all the Pleasure we can this way convey to a sensible Reader. And perhaps, there is one Reason, why a Comic Writer should of all others be the least excused for deviating from Nature, since it may not be always so easy for a serious Poet to meet with the Great and the Admirable; but Life every where furnishes an accurate Observer with the Ridiculous.

I have hinted this little, concerning Burlesque; because, I have often heard that Name given to Performances, which have been truly of the Comic kind, from the Author's having sometimes admitted it in his Diction only; which as it is the Dress of Poetry, doth like the Dress of Men establish Characters, (the one of the whole Poem, and the other of the whole Man,) in vulgar Opinion, beyond any of their greater Excellencies: But surely, a certain Drollery in Style, where the Characters and Sentiments are perfectly natural, no more constitutes the Burlesque, than an empty Pomp and Dignity of Words, where every thing else is mean and low, can entitle any Performance to the Appellation of the true Sublime.

And I apprehend, my Lord Shaftesbury's Opinion[4] of mere Burlesque agrees with mine, when he asserts, "There is no such Thing to be found in the Writings of the Antients." But perhaps, I have less Abhorrence than he professes for it: and that not because I have had some little Success on the Stage this way, but rather, as it contributes more to exquisite Mirth and Laughter than any other; and these are probably more wholesome Physic for the Mind, and conduce better to purge away Spleen, Melancholy and ill Affections, than is generally imagined. Nay, I will appeal to common Observation, whether the same Companies are not found more full of Good-Humour and Benevolence, after they have been sweeten'd for two or three Hours with Entertainments of this kind, than when soured by a Tragedy or a grave Lecture.

But to illustrate all this by another Science, in which, perhaps, we shall see the Distinction more clearly and plainly: Let us examine the Works of a Comic History-Painter,[5] with those Performances which the Italians call *Caricatura;* where we shall find the true Excellence of the former to consist in the exactest Copy of Nature; insomuch, that a judicious Eye instantly rejects any thing *outré;* any Liberty

---

4 Cf. above, p. 147.
5 See below, p. 156, n. 6.

which the Painter hath taken with the Features of that *Alma Mater*.
—Whereas in the *Caricatura* we allow all Licence. Its Aim is to
exhibit Monsters not Men; and all Distortions and Exaggerations
whatever are within its proper Province.

Now what *Caricatura* is in Painting, Burlesque is in Writing; and
in the same manner the Comic Writer and Painter correlate to each
other. And here I shall observe, that as in the former, the Painter seems
to have the Advantage; so it is in the latter infinitely on the side of
the Writer: for the *Monstrous* is much easier to paint than describe,
and the *ridiculous* to describe than paint.

And tho' perhaps this latter Species doth not in either Science so
strongly affect and agitate the Muscles as the other; yet it will be
owned, I believe, that a more rational and useful Pleasure arises to us
from it. He who should call the Ingenious Hogarth[6] a Burlesque Painter,
would, in my Opinion, do him very little Honour: for sure it is much
easier, much less the Subject of Admiration, to paint a Man with
a Nose, or any other Feature of a preposterous Size, or to expose him
in some absurd or monstrous Attitude, than to express the Affections
of Men on Canvas. It hath been thought a vast Commendation of
a Painter, to say his Figures *seem to breathe;* but surely, it is a much
greater and nobler Applause, *that they appear to think*.

But to return——The Ridiculous only, as I have before said, falls
within my Province in the present Work.—Nor will some Explanation
of this Word be thought impertinent by the Reader, if he considers
how wonderfully it hath been mistaken, even by Writers who have
profess'd it: for to what but such a Mistake, can we attribute the
many Attempts to ridicule the blackest Villanies; and what is yet
worse, the most dreadful Calamities? What could exceed the Absurdity
of an Author, who should write *The Comedy of Nero, with the merry
Incident of ripping up his Mother's Belly;* or what would give a greater
Shock to Humanity, than an Attempt to expose the Miseries of
Poverty and Distress to Ridicule? And yet, the Reader will not want
much Learning to suggest such Instances to himself.

Besides, it may seem remarkable, that Aristotle, who is so fond and
free of Definitions, hath not thought proper to define the Ridiculous.

---

6 The painter and engraver William Hogarth (1697–1764) was a good friend of
Fielding. In an etching of 1743, *Characters and Caricaturas,* Hogarth illustrated
the difference between comic art and caricature and referred the viewer to the
Preface to *Joseph Andrews "For a farthar Explanation of the Difference Betwixt*
Character & Caricatura." Cf. Ronald Paulson, "The *Harlot's Progress* and the
Tradition of History Painting," *Eighteenth Century Studies,* I (Fall 1967), 69–92.

Indeed, where he tells us it is proper to Comedy, he hath remarked that Villany is not its Object:[7] but he hath not, as I remember, positively asserted what is. Nor doth the *Abbé Bellegarde,* who hath writ a Treatise on this Subject,[8] tho' he shews us many Species of it, once trace it to its Fountain.

The only Source of the true Ridiculous (as it appears to me) is Affectation. But tho' it arises from one Spring only, when we consider the infinite Streams into which this one branches, we shall presently cease to admire at the copious Field it affords to an Observer. Now Affectation proceeds from one of these two Causes; Vanity, or Hypocrisy: for as Vanity puts us on affecting false Characters, in order to purchase Applause; so Hypocrisy sets us on an Endeavour to avoid Censure by concealing our Vices under an Appearance of their opposite Virtues. And tho' these two Causes are often confounded, (for they require some Difficulty in distinguishing;) yet, as they proceed from very different Motives, so they are as clearly distinct in their Operatons: for indeed, the Affectation which arises from Vanity is nearer to Truth than the other; as it hath not that violent Repugnancy of Nature to struggle with, which that of the Hypocrite hath. It may be likewise noted, that Affectation doth not imply an absolute Negation of those Qualities which are affected: and therefore, tho', when it proceeds from Hypocrisy, it be nearly allied to Deceit; yet when it comes from Vanity only, it partakes of the Nature of Ostentation: for instance, the Affectation of Liberality in a vain Man, differs visibly from the same Affectation in the Avaricious; for tho' the vain Man is not what he would appear, or hath not the Virtue he affects, to the degree he would be thought to have it; yet it sits less aukwardly on him than on the avaricious Man, who is the very Reverse of what he would *seem* to be.

From the Discovery of this Affectation arises the Ridiculous— which always strikes the Reader with Surprize and Pleasure; and that in a higher and stronger Degree when the Affectation arises from Hypocrisy, than when from Vanity: for to discover any one to be the exact Reverse of what he affects, is more surprizing, and consequently more ridiculous, than to find him a little deficient in the Quality he desires the Reputation of. I might observe that our Ben Jonson, who of all Men understood the *Ridiculous* the best, hath chiefly used the hypocritical Affectation.

---

[7] *Poetics,* V.1–2.
[8] Cf. above, p. 148.

Now from Affectation only, the Misfortunes and Calamities of Life, or the Imperfections of Nature, may become the Objects of Ridicule. Surely he hath a very ill-framed Mind, who can look on Uglines, Infirmity, or Poverty, as ridiculous in themselves: nor do I believe any Man living who meets a dirty Fellow riding through the Streets in a Cart, is struck with an Idea of the Ridiculous from it; but if he should see the same Figure descend from his Coach and Six, or bolt from his Chair with his Hat under his Arm, he would then begin to laugh, and with justice. In the same manner, were we to enter a poor House, and behold a wretched Family shivering with Cold and languishing with Hunger, it would not incline us to Laughter, (at least we must have very diabolical Natures, if it would:) but should we discover there a Grate, instead of Coals, adorned with Flowers, empty Plate or China Dishes on the Side-board, or any other Affectation of Riches and Finery either on their Persons or in their Furniture; we might then indeed be excused, for ridiculing so fantastical an Appearance. Much less are natural Imperfections the Objects of Derision: but when Ugliness aims at the Applause of Beauty, or Lameness endeavours to display Agility; it is then that these unfortunate Circumstances, which at first moved our Compassion, tend only to raise our Mirth.

The Poet carries this very far;

> None are for being what they are in Fault,
> But for not being what they would be thought.[9]

Where if the Metre would suffer the Word *Ridiculous* to close the first Line, the Thought would be rather more proper. Great Vices are the proper Objects of our Detestation, smaller Faults of our Pity: but Affectation appears to me the only true Source of the Ridiculous.

But perhaps it may be objected to me, that I have against my own Rules introduced Vices, and of a very black Kind into this Work. To which I shall answer: First, that it is very difficult to pursue a Series of human Actions and keep clear from them. Secondly, That the Vices to be found here, are rather the accidental Consequences of some human Frailty, or Foible, than Causes habitually existing in the Mind. Thirdly, That they are never set forth as the Objects of Ridicule but Detestation. Fourthly, That they are never the principal Figure at that Time on the Scene; and lastly, they never produce the intended Evil.

---

9 From Congreve's poem *Of Pleasing*, 63–64.

Having thus distinguished *Joseph Andrews* from the Productions of Romance Writers on the one hand, and Burlesque Writers on the other, and given some few very short Hints (for I intended no more) of this Species of writing, which I have affirmed to be hitherto unattempted in our Language; I shall leave to my good-natur'd Reader to apply my Piece to my Observations, and will detain him no longer than with a Word concerning the Characters in this Work.

And here I solemnly protest, I have no Intention to vilify or asperse any one: for tho' every thing is copied from the Book of Nature, and scarce a Character or Action produced which I have not taken from my own Observations and Experience, yet I have used the utmost Care to obscure the Persons by such different Circumstances, Degrees, and Colours, that it will be impossible to guess at them with any degree of Certainty; and if it ever happens otherwise, it is only where the Failure characterized is so minute, that it is a Foible only which the Party himself may laugh at as well as any other.

As to the Character of Adams, as it is the most glaring in the whole, so I conceive it is not to be found in any Book now extant. It is designed a Character of perfect Simplicity; and as the Goodness of his Heart will recommend him to the Good-natur'd; so I hope it will excuse me to the Gentlemen of his Cloth; for whom, while they are worthy of their sacred Order, no Man can possibly have a greater Respect. They will therefore excuse me, notwithstanding the low Adventures in which he is engaged, that I have made him a Clergyman; since no other Office could have given him so many Opportunities of displaying his worthy Inclinations.

A device of mingling speculation with narration was to appear at its most amusing in the seventeen essay-chapters, on problems of novel-writing and novel-reading, distributed throughout Fielding's later masterpiece *Tom Jones*. (See, for instance, Book VII, Chapter 1, "A Comparison between the World and the Stage": "...the hypocrite may be said to be a player; and indeed the Greeks called them both by one and the same name.") A few chapters of *Joseph Andrews* take the same license. Book III, Chapter 1 especially is a noteworthy theoretical sprint, in which, moving through several ironic angles with such terms as "history," "romance," "biographer," "topographer," he arrives at a memorable hyperbole concerning the universality of comic character. This statement is a descendant of the Aristotelian emphasis on ethical types in comedy,[1] rather than on the logic of plot which is dominant in tragedy. It is also a distant forerunner of the philosopher Henri Bergson's thesis, in his essay *Laughter* (1901): that the comic is essentially a mechanization of the human in some form of absentmindedness or some moral stereotype.[2]

---

[1] Contrast Dryden on the "noble intrigue" of Jonson's *Epicoene* (above p. 39). Plot, "argument," or "design" was a likely enough neoclassic emphasis. See above p. 124, John Dennis; and E. N. Hooker, ed. *Critical Works of Dennis,* I, 485, citing William Burnaby, 1701. On the other hand, Vanbrugh in his *Short Vindication of "The Relapse,"* 1698, p. 58, says that "Character and Dialogue" are more important in comedy than the "Business and the Event."

[2] Cf. below pp. 287–88.

OF

Joseph Andrews

[*1742*]

Matter Prefatory in Praise of Biography.

Notwithstanding the Preference which may be vulgarly given to the Authority of those Romance-Writers, who intitle their Books, *The History of England, The History of France, of Spain,* &c. it is most certain, that Truth is only to be found in their Works who celebrate the Lives of Great Men, and are commonly called Biographers, as the others should indeed be termed Topographers or Chorographers: Words which might well mark the Distinction between them; it being the Business of the latter chiefly to describe Countries and Cities, which, with the Assistance of Maps, they do pretty justly, and may be depended upon: But as to the Actions and Characters of Men, their Writings are not quite so authentic, of which there needs no other Proof than those eternal Contradictions, occurring between two Topographers who undertake the History of the same Country: For instance, between my Lord Clarendon and Mr. Whitlock, between Mr. Echard and Rapin,[1] and many others; where Facts being set forth in a different Light, every Reader believes as he pleases, but all agree in the Scene, where it is supposed to have happen'd. Now with us Biographers the Case is different, the Facts we deliver may be relied on, tho' we often mistake the Age and Country wherein they happened: For tho' it may be worth the Examination of Critics, whether the Shepherd Chrysostom, who, as Cervantes informs us, died for Love of the fair Marcella, who

---

[1] The Tory point of view concerning politics and rebellion in England under the Stuarts (1642–1689) was represented by Edward Hyde, Earl of Clarendon, in his *Narrative of the Rebellion and Civil Wars in England* (1702–1704), and in Laurence Echard's *History of England* (1707–1718); the Whig point of view, in Bulstrode Whitelocke's *Memorials of the English Affairs* (1682) and Paul de Rapin de Thoyras' *Histoire d'Angleterre* (1723–1725).

hated him, was ever in Spain, will any one doubt but that such a silly Fellow hath really existed. Is there in the World such a Sceptic as to disbelieve the Madness of Cardenio, the Perfidy of Ferdinand, the impertinent Curiosity of Anselmo, the Weakness of Camillo, the irresolute Friendship of Lothario,[2] tho' perhaps as to the Time and Place where those several Persons lived, that good Historian may be deplorably deficient: But the most known Instance of this kind is in the true *History of Gil-Blas*,[3] where the inimitable Biographer hath made a notorious Blunder in the Country of Dr. Sangrado, who used his Patients as a Vintner doth his Wine-Vessels, by letting out their Blood, and filling them up with Water.[4] The same Writer hath likewise erred in the Country of his Archbishop, as well as that of those great Personages whose Understandings were too sublime to taste any thing but Tragedy, and perhaps in many others. The same Mistakes may likewise be observed in Scarron,[5] the *Arabian Nights*,[6] the *History of Marianne* and *Le Paisan Parvenu*,[7] and perhaps some few other Writers of this Class, whom I have not read, or do not at present recollect; for I would by no means be thought to comprehend those great Genius's the Authors of immense Romances, or the modern Novel and *Atalantis*[8] Writers; who without any Assistance from Nature or History, record Persons who never were, or will be, and Facts which never did nor possibly can happen: Whose Heroes are of

---

[2] In the translation of *Don Quixote* by Peter Motteux, revised by John Ozell, 1719, the tale of Chrysostom and Marcella appears at I.ii.4–6; that of Cardenio and Ferdinand at I.iii.9ff.; and that of Anselmo, Camilla, and Lothario ("The Novel of the Curious Impertinent") at I.iv.6–8.

[3] René Lesage's *roman picaresque* (1715–) appeared in English as *The History of Gil Blas* (1732–1737) and in another translation, by Smollett (1749).

[4] Dr. Sangrado comes in *Gil Blas,* II.iii–v(1749); the Archbishop of Granada in VII.ii–iv. The "Personages" are a Marchioness of Chaves and her fashionable literary society, IV.viii. The grounds of Fielding's humorous argument have shifted almost imperceptibly. With *Don Quixote,* he has availed himself of the archetypal character of the incidental fictions with which the novel is embellished, to suggest that Cervantes may well be in error as to the time and place of the actions narrated. But with *Gil Blas,* Fielding, momentarily assuming a naïve posture, seems to imply that Dr. Sangrado could not have been in Spain, no doubt because he is in England this very day.

[5] Paul Scarron's *Roman comique* (1651).

[6] *The Arabian Nights' Entertainments* were translated from Arabic into French by Antoine Galland early in the eighteenth century.

[7] The French dramatist and romance-writer Pierre de Marivaux's *Vie de Marianne* (1731) and *Paysan Parvenu* (1735).

[8] The scandalous *roman à clef, Secret Memoirs and Manners of Several Persons of Quality of Both Sexes. From the New Atalantis* (1709), by Mrs. Mary de la Rivière Manley.

their own Creation, and their Brains the Chaos whence all their Materials are collected. Not that such Writers deserve no Honour; so far otherwise, that perhaps they merit the highest: for what can be nobler than to be as an Example of the wonderful Extent of human Genius. One may apply to them what Balzac says of Aristotle, that they are a second Nature;[9] for they have no Communication with the first; by which Authors of an inferiour Class, who can not stand alone, are obliged to support themselves as with Crutches; but these of whom I am now speaking, seem to be possessed of "those Stilts," which the excellent Voltaire tells us in his *Letters*[10] "carry the Genius far off, but with an irregular Pace."[11] Indeed far out of the sight of the Reader,

Beyond the Realm of Chaos and old Night.[12]

But, to return to the former Class, who are contented to copy Nature, instead of forming Originals from their confused heap of Matter in their own Brains; is not such a Book as that which records the Atchievements of the renowned Don Quixote, more worthy the Name of a History than even *Marianna's*;[13] for whereas the latter is confined to a particular Period of Time, and to a particular Nation; the former is the History of the World in general, at least that Part which is polished by Laws, Arts and Sciences; and of that from the time it was first polished to this day; nay and forwards, as long as it shall so remain.

I shall now proceed to apply these Observations to the Work before us; for indeed I have set them down principally to obviate some Con- structions, which the Good-nature of Mankind, who are always forward to see their Friends Virtues recorded, may put to particular parts. I question not but several of my Readers will know the Lawyer in the Stage-Coach, the Moment they hear his Voice. It is likewise odds,

---

9 Jean-Louis Guez de Balzac, in the second of *Deux discours Envoyez à Rome* (1627), remarks that the Arabian philosopher Averroës had praised Aristotle as the perfection of Nature, and that a later philosopher had extended the hyper- bole, calling him *Une Seconde Nature*.

10 Voltaire's *Letters* were first published at London, in an English translation, 1733.

11 *Letters Concerning the English Nation* (1733), Letter 18. Voltaire alludes to a bombastic style that he believes characteristic of English tragic drama.

12 Fielding misquotes *Paradise Lost*, I.543.

13 Juan de Mariana's *Historia general de España* (1601).

14 Characters who appear in a stagecoach conversation in *Joseph Andrews*, Book I, Chapter 12, the object of certain frosty attitudes and heartless jests on their part being the virtuous footman Joseph, who has been found by the road- side beaten by robbers and stripped of his clothes and money.

but the Wit and the Prude[14] meet with some of their Acquaintance, as well as all the rest of my Characters. To prevent therefore any such malicious Applications, I declare here once for all, I describe not Men, but Manners; not an Individual, but a Species. Perhaps it will be answered, Are not the Characters then taken from Life? To which I answer in the Affirmative; nay, I believe I might aver, that I have writ little more than I have seen. The Lawyer is not only alive, but hath been so these 5000 Years, and I hope G—— will indulge his Life as many yet to come. He hath not indeed confined himself to one Profession, one Religion, or one Country; but when the first mean selfish Creature appeared on the human Stage, who made Self the Centre of the whole Creation; would give himself no Pain, incur no Danger, advance no Money to assist, or preserve his Fellow-Creatures; then was our Lawyer born; and whilst such a Person as I have described, exists on Earth, so long shall he remain upon it. It is therefore doing him little Honour, to imagine he endeavours to mimick some little obscure Fellow, because he happens to resemble him in one particular Feature, or perhaps in his Profession; whereas his Appearance in the World is calculated for much more general and noble Purposes, than to expose one pitiful Wretch, to the small Circle of his Acquaintance; but to hold the Glass to thousands in their Closets, that they may contemplate their Deformity, and endeavour to reduce it, and thus by suffering private Mortification may avoid public Shame. This places the Boundary between, and distinguishes the Satirist from the Libeller; for the former privately corrects the Fault for the Benefit of the Person, like a Parent; the latter publickly exposes the Person himself, as an Example to others, like an Executioner.[15]

There are besides little Circumstances to be considered, as the Drapery of a Picture, which though Fashion varies at different Times, the Resemblance of the Countenance is not by those means diminished. Thus, I believe, we may venture to say, Mrs. Tow-wouse is coeval with our Lawyer, and tho' perhaps during the Changes, which so long an Existence must have passed through, she may in her Turn have stood behind the Bar at an Inn, I will not scruple to affirm, she hath likewise in the Revolution of Ages sat on a Throne. In short where extreme Turbulency of Temper, Avarice, and an Insensibility of human

---

15 Compare Molière's apology for satire in *La Critique de L'Ecole des Femmes,* Scene vi, where the sagacious Uranie talks about the supposed scandals of M. Molière's new comedy, quoted above p. 61.

Misery, with a Degree of Hypocrisy, have united in a female Composition, Mrs. Tow-wouse was that Woman; and where a good Inclination eclipsed by a Poverty of Spirit and Understanding, hath glimmer'd forth in a Man, that Man hath been no other than her sneaking Husband.[16]

I shall detain my Reader no longer than to give him one Caution more of an opposite kind: For as in most of our particular Characters we mean not to lash Individuals, but all of that like sort; so in our general Descriptions, we mean not Universals, but would be understood with many Exceptions: For instance, in our Description of high People, we cannot be intended to include such, as whilst they are an Honour to their high Rank, by a well-guided Condescension, make their Superiority as easy as possible, to those whom Fortune hath chiefly placed below them. Of this number I could name a Peer[17] no less elevated by Nature than by Fortune, who whilst he wears the noblest Ensigns of Honour on his Person, bears the truest Stamp of Dignity on his Mind, adorned with Greatness, enriched with Knowledge, and embelished with Genius. I have seen this Man relieve with Generosity, while he hath conversed with Freedom, and be to the same Person a Patron and a Companion. I could name a Commoner[18] raised higher above the Multitude by superiour Talents, than is in the power of his Prince to exalt him; whose Behaviour to those he hath obliged is more amiable than the Obligation itself, and who is so great a Master of Affability, that if he could divest himself of an inherent Greatness in his Manner, would often make the lowest of his Acquaintance forget who was the Master of that Palace, in which they are so courteously entertained. These are Pictures which must be, I believe, known: I declare they are taken from the Life, nor are intended to exceed it. By those high People therefore whom I have

---

16 Mr. and Mrs. Tow-wouse are the keepers of an inn which is the scene of certain rowdy picaresque adventures in *Joseph Andrews,* Book I, Chapters 12–18; Book II, Chapter 2.

17 Most likely Philip Dormer Stanhope, Fourth Earl of Chesterfield (1694–1773), literary patron, model of good taste and conversational elegance, leader of the Opposition against Walpole's ministry. Like Fielding's friend Ralph Allen (see next note), Chesterfield frequented the city of Bath.

18 Ralph Allen (1694–1764) made a fortune by a system of cross-posts for England and Wales and augmented it by investment in the limestone quarries from which the city of Bath was being built and from which he built his own Palladian mansion nearby at Prior Park. He was the model for Squire Allworthy in Fielding's *Tom Jones.* A close friendship with Allen is recorded in the correspondence of Alexander Pope and in the *Epilogue* to Pope's *Satires,* I.135–36.

described, I mean a Set of Wretches, who while they are a Disgrace to their Ancestors, whose Honours and Fortunes they inherit, (or perhaps a greater to their Mother, for such Degeneracy is scarce credible) have the Insolence to treat those with disregard, who have been equal to the Founders of their own Splendor. It is, I fancy, impossible to conceive a Spectacle more worthy of our Indignation, than that of a Fellow who is not only a Blot in the Escutcheon of a great Family, but a Scandal to the human Species, maintaining a supercilious Behaviour to Men who are an Honour to their Nature, and a Disgrace to their Fortune.

And now, Reader, taking these Hints along with you, you may, if you please, proceed to the Sequel of this our true History.

The Covent-Garden Journal

Number 55

By Sir Alexander Drawcansir, Knight-Censor of Great Britain

——————— *Juvat integros accedere Fontes*
Atque haurire. ———————

Lucretius[1]

——————— *It is pleasant to handle*
An untouched Subject.

Saturday, July 18, 1752

It hath been observed, that Characters of Humour do abound more in this our Island, than in any other Country;[2] and this hath been commonly supposed to arise from that pure and perfect State of Liberty which we enjoy in a degree greatly superior to every foreign Nation.

This Opinion, I know, hath great Sanction, and yet I am inclined to suspect the Truth of it, unless we will extend the Meaning of the Word Liberty, farther than I think it hath been yet carried, and will include in it not only an Exemption from all Restraint of municipal Laws, but likewise from all Restraint of those Rules of Behaviour which are expressed in the general Term of good Breeding. Laws which, tho' not written, are perhaps better understood, and tho' estab-

---

The *Covent-Garden Journal* was published from January 4, 1752, to November 25, 1752, a total of seventy-two numbers: "London: Printed and sold by Mrs. Dodd, at the Peacock, Temple-bar." Fielding was the primary contributor to the journal, writing under the pseudonym "Sir Alexander Drawcansir, Knight-Censor of Great Britain." Our text is taken from a set of rotograph prints from a bound copy of the original numbers in the British Museum (Beinecke Rare Book and Manuscript Library, Yale University).

[1] *De Rerum Natura,* I.927–28. It is pleasant to approach fresh springs and drink.

[2] See above, pp. 73–74, 84, 149–50.

lished by no coercive Power, much better obeyed within the Circle where they are received, than any of those Laws which are recorded in Books, or enforced by public Authority.

A perfect Freedom from these Laws, if I am not greatly mistaken, is absolutely necessary to form the true Character of Humour; a Character which is therefore not to be met with among those People who conduct themselves by the Rules of good Breeding.

For indeed good Breeding is little more than the Art of rooting out all those Seeds of Humour which Nature had originally implanted in our Minds.

To make this evident it seems necessary only to explain the Terms, a Matter in which I do not see the great Difficulty which hath appeared to other Writers. Some of these have spoken of the Word Humour, as if it contained in it some Mystery impossible to be revealed, and no one, as I know of, hath undertaken to shew us expressly what it is, tho' I scarce doubt but it was amply done by Aristotle in his Treatise on Comedy, which is unhappily lost.

But what is more surprizing, is, that we find it pretty well explained in Authors who at the same Time tell us, they know not what it is. Mr. Congreve, in a Letter to Mr. Dennis, hath these Words. "We cannot certainly tell what Wit is, or what Humour is," and within a few Lines afterwards he says, "There is great Difference between a Comedy wherein there are many things humorously, as they call it, which is pleasantly spoken; and one where there are several Characters of Humour, distinguished by the particular and different Humours appropriated to the several Persons represented, and which naturally arise from the different Constitutions, Complexions, and Dispositions of Men." And again "I take Humour to be a singular and unavoidable Manner of saying or doing any thing peculiar and natural to one Man only; by which his Speech and Actions are distinguished from those of other Men. Our Humour hath Relation to us, and to what proceeds from us, as the Accidents have to a Substance; it is a Colour, Taste, and Smell diffused through all; tho' our Actions are ever so many, and different in Form, they are all Splinters of the same Wood, and have naturally one Complexion," &c.

If my Reader hath any doubt whether this is a just Description of Humour, let him compare it with those Examples of humorous Characters which the greatest Masters have given us, and which have been universally acknowledged as such, and he will be perhaps convinced.

Ben Jonson, after complaining of the Abuse of the Word, proceeds thus,[3]

> Why Humour (as 'tis Ens) we thus define it,
> To be a Quality of Air, or Water,
> And in itself holds these two Properties,
> Moisture and Fluxure; as for Demonstration,
> Pour Water on this Floor, 'twill wet and run;
> Likewise the Air forc'd thro' a Horn or Trumpet
> Flows instantly away, and leaves behind
> A kind of Dew; and hence we do conclude,
> That whatsoe'er hath Fluxure and Humidity,
> As wanting Power to contain itself,
> Is Humour. So in every human Body,
> The Choler, Melancholy, Phlegm and Blood,
> By Reason that they flow continually
> In some one Part, and are not continent,
> Receive the Name of *Humours*. Now thus far
> It may, by Metaphor, apply itself
> Unto the general Disposition:
> As when some one peculiar Quality
> Doth so possess a Man, that it doth draw
> All his Effects, his Spirits, and his Powers,
> In their Confluxions all to run one Way,
> *This may be truly said to be a Humour.*
> But that a Rook by wearing a py'd Feather,
> The Cable Hatband, or the three piled Ruff,
> A Yard of Shoe-tie, or the Switzer's Knot
> On his French Garters should affect a Humour!
> O! it is more than most ridiculous.

This Passage is in the first Act of *Every Man out of his Humour;* and I question not but to some Readers, the Author will appear to have been *out of his Wits* when he wrote it; but others I am positive will discern much excellent Ore shining among the Rubbish. In Truth his Sentiment when let loose from that stiff Boddice in which it is laced, will amount to this that as the Term Humour contains in it the Ideas of Moisture and Fluxure, it was applied to certain moist and flux Habits of the Body, and afterwards metaphorically to peculiar Qualities of the Mind, which when they are extremely prevalent, do, like the predominant Humours of the Body, flow all to one Part, and as the latter are known to absorb and drain off all the corporeal Juices and Strength to themselves, so the former are no less

---

[3] See above, pp. 25, 28–29.

certain of engaging the Affections, Spirits, and Powers of the Mind, and of enlisting them as it were, into their own Service, and under their own absolute Command.

Here then we have another pretty adequate Notion of Humour, which is indeed nothing more than a violent Bent or Disposition of the Mind to some particular Point. To enumerate indeed these several Dispositions would be, as Mr. Congreve observes, as endless as to sum up the several Opinions of Men; nay, as he well says, the *Quot homines tot sententiae* may be more properly interpreted of their Humours, than their Opinions.[4]

Hitherto there is no Mention of the Ridiculous, the Idea of which, tho' not essential to Humour, is always included in our Notions of it. The Ridiculous is annexed to it these two ways, either by the Manner or the Degree in which it is exerted.

By either of these the very best and worthiest Disposition of the Human Mind may become ridiculous. Excess, says Horace, even in the Pursuit of Virtue, will lead a wise and good Man into Folly and Vice[5]—— So will it subject him to Ridicule; for into this, says the judicious Abbé Bellegarde, a Man may tumble headlong with an excellent Understanding, and with the most laudable Qualities.[6] Piety, Patriotism, Loyalty, Parental Affection, &c. have all afforded Characters of Humour for the Stage.

By the Manner of exerting itself likewise a Humour becomes ridiculous. By this Means chiefly the Tragic Humour differs from the Comic; it is the same Ambition which raises our Horror in *Macbeth,* and our Laughter at the drunken Sailors in *The Tempest;* the same Avarice which causes the dreadful Incidents in *The Fatal Curiosity* of Lillo,[7] and in *The Miser* of Molière; the same Jealousy which forms an Othello, or a Suspicious Husband.[8] No Passion or Humour of the Mind is absolutely either Tragic or Comic in itself. Nero had the Art of

---

4 See above, p. 76.

5 *Epistles* I.vi.15–16:

> Insani sapiens nomen ferat, aequus iniqui,
> Ultra quam satis est Virtutem si petat ipsam.

6 At the beginning of *Réflexions sur le Ridicule* (1723).

7 *The Fatal Curiosity* by George Lillo (1693–1739) appeared in 1736. Young Wilmot returns from India with a casket of treasure and leaves it with his mother; she, not suspecting his identity, persuades old Wilmot to murder his own child in order to rob him.

8 *The Suspicious Husband,* a comedy by Dr. Benjamin Hoadly, was produced in 1747 at Covent Garden.

making Vanity the Object of Horror;[9] and Domitian, in one Instance, at least, made Cruelty ridiculous.[10]

As these Tragic Modes however never enter into our Notion of Humour, I will venture to make a small Addition to the Sentiments of the two great Masters I have mentioned, by which I apprehend my Description of Humour will pretty well coincide with the general Opinion. By Humour, then I suppose, is generally intended a violent Impulse of the Mind, determining it to some one peculiar Point, by which a Man becomes ridiculously distinguished from all other Men.

If there be any Truth in what I have now said, nothing can more clearly follow than the manifest Repugnancy between Humour and good Breeding. The latter being the Art of conducting yourself by certain common and general Rules, by which Means, if they were universally observed, the whole World would appear (as all Courtiers actually do) to be, in their external Behaviour at least, but one and the same Person.

I have not room at present, if I were able, to enumerate the Rules of good Breeding: I shall only mention one, which is a Summary of them all. This is the most golden of all Rules, no less than that *of doing to all Men as you would they should do unto you.*[11]

In the Deviation from this Law, as I hope to evince in my next, all that we call Humour principally consists. I shall at the same Time, I think, be able to shew, that it is to this Deviation we owe the general Character mentioned in the Beginning of this Paper, as well as to assign the Reasons why we of this Nation have been capable of attracting to ourselves such Merit in Preference to others.

---

[9] He was said to have started the great fire at Rome (A.D. 64) in order to give himself an adequate stage for singing the Homeric hymns.

[10] His customary diversion was catching and torturing flies.

[11] Matthew, VII.12, in the Sermon on the Mount.

The Covent-Garden Journal

Number 56

By Sir Alexander Drawcansir, Knight-Censor of Great Britain:

Hoc Fonte derivata.

Horace[1]

These are the Sources.

Saturday, July 25, 1752

At the Conclusion of my last Paper, I asserted that the Summary of Good Breeding was no other than that comprehensive and exalted Rule, which the greatest Authority hath told us is the Sum Total of all Religion and all Morality.

Here, however, my Readers will be pleased to observe that the subject Matter of good Breeding being only what is called Behaviour, it is this only to which we are to apply it on the present Occasion. Perhaps therefore we shall be better understood if we vary the Word, and read it thus: *Behave unto all Men, as you would they should behave unto you.*

This will most certainly oblige us to treat all Mankind with the utmost Civility and Respect, there being nothing which we desire more than to be treated so by them. This will most effectually restrain the Indulgence of all those violent and inordinate Desires, which, as we have endeavoured to shew, are the true Seeds of Humour in the Human Mind: the Growth of which Good Breeding will be sure to obstruct; or will at least so over-top and shadow, that they shall not appear. The Ambitious, the Covetous, the Proud, the Vain, the Angry, the Debauchee, the Glutton, are all lost in the Character of the Well-Bred Man; or if Nature should now and then venture to peep forth, she

---

[1] Horace, *Odes,* III.vi.19.

withdraws in an Instant, and doth not shew enough of herself to become ridiculous.

Now Humour arises from the very opposite Behaviour, from throwing the Reins on the Neck of our favorite Passion, and giving it a full Scope and Indulgence. The ingenious Abbé, whom I quoted in my former Paper, paints this admirably in the Characters of Ill-Breeding, which he mentions as the very first Scene of the Ridiculous.[2] "Ill-Breeding (*L'Impolitesse*)," says he, "is not a single Defect, it is the Result of many. It is sometimes a gross Ignorance of Decorum, or a stupid Indolence, which prevents us from *giving to others what is due to them*. It is a peevish Malignity which inclines us to oppose the Inclinations of those with whom we converse. It is the Consequence of a foolish Vanity, which hath no Complaisance for any other Person: *The Effect of a proud and whimsical Humour, which soars above all the Rules of Civility;* or, lastly, it is produced by a melancholly Turn of Mind, which pampers itself (*qui trouve du Ragoût*) with a rude and disobliging Behaviour."

Having thus shewn, I think very clearly, that Good Breeding is, and must be, the very Bane of the Ridiculous, that is to say, of all humorous Characters; it will perhaps be no difficult Task to discover why this Character hath been in a singular Manner attributed to this Nation.[3]

For this I shall assign two Reasons only, as these seem to me abundantly satisfactory, and adequate to the Purpose.

The first is that Method so general in this Kingdom of giving no Education to the Youth of both Sexes; I say general only, for it is not without some few Exceptions.

Much the greater Part of our Lads of Fashion return from School at fifteen or sixteen, very little wiser, and not at all the better for having been sent thither. Part of these return to the Place from whence they came, their Fathers Country Seats; where Racing, Cock fighting, Hunting, and other rural Sports, with Smoking, Drinking, and Party become their Pursuit, and form the whole Business and Amusement of their future Lives. The other Part escape to Town in the Diversions, Fashion, Follies and Vices of which they are immediately initiated.

---

[2] Abbé Bellegarde once again, the beginning of the first treatise in *Réflexions sur le Ridicule*.

[3] Once again Fielding follows Congreve's suggestion at the end of his *Letter to Dennis*. See above, p. 84.

In this Academy some finish their Studies, while others by their wiser Parents are sent abroad to add the Knowledge of the Diversions, Fashions, Follies, and Vices of all Europe, to that of those of their own Country.

Hence then we are to derive two great general Characters of Humour, which are the Clown and the Coxcomb, and both of these will be almost infinitely diversified according to the different Passions and natural Dispositions of each Individual; and according to their different Walks in Life. Great will be the Difference; for Instance, whether the Country Gentleman be a Whig or a Tory, whether he prefers Women, Drink, or Dogs; so will it be whether the Town Spark be allotted to serve his Country as a Politician, a Courtier, a Soldier, a Sailor, or possibly a Churchman, (for by Draughts from this Academy, all these Offices are supplied); or lastly whether his Ambition shall be contented with no other Appellation than merely that of a Beau.

Some of our Lads however, are destined to a further Progress in Learning; these are not only confined longer to the Labours of a School, but are sent thence to the University. Here if they please, they may read on, and if they please they may (as most of them do) let it alone, and betake themselves as their Fancy leads, to the Imitation of their elder Brothers either in Town or Country.

This is a Matter which I shall handle very tenderly, as I am clearly of an Opinion that an University Education is much the best we have; for here at least there is some Restraint laid on the Inclinations of our Youth. The Sportsman, the Gamester, and the Sot, cannot give such a Loose to their Extravagance, as if they were at home and under no manner of Government; nor can our Spark who is disposed to the Town Pleasures, find either Gaming-houses or Play-houses, nor half the Taverns or Bawdy-houses which are ready to receive him in Covent-Garden.

So far however I hope I may say without Offence, that among all the Schools at the Universities, there is none where the Science of Good-Breeding is taught; no Lectures like the excellent Lessons on the Ridiculous, which I have quoted above, and which I do most earnestly recommend to all my young Readers. Hence the learned Professions produce such excellent Characters of Humour; and the Rudeness of Physicians, Lawyers, and Parsons, however dignified or distinguished, affords such pleasant Stories to divert private Companies, and sometimes the Public.

I come now to the beautiful Part of thè Creation, who, in the Sense I here use the Word, I am assured can hardly (for the most Part) be said to have any Education.

As to the Counterpart of my Country Squire, the Country Gentle-woman, I apprehend, that except in the Article of the Dancing-Master, and perhaps in that of being barely able to read and write, there is very little Difference between the Education of many a Squire's Daughter, and that of his Dairy Maid, who is most likely her principal Companion; nay the little Difference which there is, is, I am afraid, not in the Favour of the Former; who, by being constantly flattered with her Beauty and her Wealth, is made the vainest and most selfconceited Thing alive, at the same Time that such Care is taken to instil into her the principles of Bashfulness and Timidity, that she becomes ashamed and afraid of she knows not what.

If by any Chance this poor Creature drops afterwards, as it were, into the World, how absurd must be her Behaviour! If a Man looks at her, she is confounded, and if he speaks to her, she is frightened out of her Wits. She acts, in short, as if she thought the whole Sex was engaged in a Conspiracy to possess themselves of her Person and Fortune.

This poor Girl, it is true, however she may appear to her own Sex, especially if she is handsome, is rather an Object of Compassion, than of just Ridicule; but what shall we say when Time or Marriage have carried off all this Bashfulness and Fear, and when Ignorance, Aukwardness, and Rusticity, are embellished with the same Degree, tho' perhaps not the same kind of Affectation, which are to be found in a Court. Here sure is a plentiful Source of all that various Humour which we find in the Character of a Country Gentlewoman.

All this, I apprehend, will be readily allowed; but to deny Good-Breeding to the Town-Lady, may be the more Dangerous Attempt. Here, besides the Professors of Reading, Writing, and Dancing, the French and Italian Masters, the Music Master, and of Modern Times, the Whist Master, all concur in forming this Character. The Manners Master alone I am afraid is omitted. And what is the Consequence? not only Bashfulness and Fear are intirely subdued, but Modesty and Discretion are taken off at the same Time. So far from running away from, she runs after the Men; and instead of blushing when a modest Man looks at her, or speaks to her, she can bear, without any such Emotion to stare an impudent Fellow in the Face, and sometimes to utter what, if he be not very impudent indeed, may put him to the

Blush.—— Hence all those agreable Ingredients which form the Humour of a Rampant Woman of—— the Town.

I cannot puit this Part of my Subject, in which I have been obliged to deal a little more freely than I am inclined with the loveliest Part of the Creation, without preserving my own Character of Good-Breeding, by saying that this last Excess, is by much the most rare; and that every Individual among my Female Readers, either is already, or may be, when she pleases, an Example of a contrary Behaviour.

The second general Reason why Humour so much abounds in this Nation, seems to me to arise from the great Number of People, who are daily raised by Trade to the Rank of Gentry, without having had any Education at all; or, to use no improper Phrase, Without having served an Apprenticeship to this Calling. But I have dwelt so long on the other Branch, that I have no Room at present to animadvert on this; nor is it indeed necessary I should, since most Readers with the Hints I have already given them, will easily suggest to themselves, a great Number of humorous Characters with which the Public have been furnished this Way. I shall conclude by wishing, that this excellent Source of Humour may still continue to flow among us, since tho' it may make us a little laughed at, it will be sure to make us the Envy of all the Nations of Europe.

OLIVER GOLDSMITH

[c. 1731–1774]

DAVID GARRICK

[1717–1779]

Sir Richard Steele's success with his moral comedy *The Conscious Lovers* at Drury Lane in 1722 was followed by the burlesque morality of Gay's *Beggar's Opera* at Lincoln's Inn Fields in 1728 and then by a spell of nearly fifty years on the London stage during which nobody wrote any new plays of great distinction, either tragedies or comedies. In the same year as Fielding's burlesque *Tragedy of Tragedies* (1731), a very popular domestic and pathetic prose tragedy, *The London Merchant,* by an actual London merchant, George Lillo, showed one kind of influence which the new sentimental school of comedy could exert.[1] During this period, farce, harlequinade, and pantomime did much to set the tone of the laughing theater, and sheer funniness enjoyed a correspondingly low degree of theoretical prestige. At the same time, old comedies of all kinds were constantly played, and the newer trend of "sentimental" comedy was countered by managers and actors in putting on more performances of the older "manners" comedy than of any other kind.[2] Above all, the acting of the manager of Drury Lane, David Garrick, was a redemptive force in comedy for nearly thirty years (1747–1776). He had to exercise some care in choosing his "low" or ludicrous roles, but he not only acted Shakespearean tragic roles with maximum acclaim—his Richard III, his Hamlet, his

---

[1] The play revived a form that had scarcely been seen since Elizabethan examples like *Arden of Feversham* and *A Woman Killed with Kindness.*

[2] G. W. Stone, Jr., estimates that during Garrick's management of Drury Lane, 1747–1776, there were 266 performances of comedies of humors, 392 performances of comedies of intrigue, 491 performances of Shakespearian comedies, 690 performances of sentimental comedies, and 1,102 performances of comedies of manners. At Covent Garden during the same period, 384 performances of sentimental comedies were outdone by 840 performances of comedies of manner. (*The London Stage, 1660–1800, Part 4: 1747–1776,* Carbondale, Ill., 1962), I, clxiii, clxv.

Macbeth, his Lear—he also scintillated as Abel Drugger in Jonson's *Alchemist,* as the poet Bayes in Buckingham's classic burlesque *The Rehearsal,* as Sir John Brute in Vanbrugh's *Provok'd Wife.*[3] In 1766 Garrick and his friend George Colman (soon to be rival manager of Covent Garden) were revealed as joint authors of *The Clandestine Marriage,* a confection of social comedy, both sentimental and witty,[4] derived from Hogarth's satiric picture series *Marriage-à-la-Mode.* It was very successfully acted at Drury Lane. Two years later (1768) there appeared a very fine shading of the sentimental-moral, Hugh Kelly's high-aphoristic, half "put-on" *False Delicacy,* with a Prologue by Garrick making fun of the genre. (This was, in effect, an eighteenth-century "problem" play.) In 1771, another of Garrick's productions, *The West Indian,*[5] by Richard Cumberland, was a marvel of thirty nights, a climactic demonstration of morality, with fun, in the tradition of *The Conscious Lovers.*

Meanwhile, however, a new, if at first somewhat bumbling and ineffective, champion of laughter was on the scene. Oliver Goldsmith, an Irish adventurer who had studied medicine at Edinburgh and Leyden and had wandered for a year through France, Switzerland, and Italy, had arrived destitute in London in 1756. But he had made his way so quickly as a journalist and popular philosophical essayist that within five years he was the friend of such littérateurs as the anti-quarian Thomas Percy and the great moralist and lexicographer Samuel Johnson and was an original member of the Literary Club in 1764. Very early in his London career he showed a talent for a certain easy, Addisonian conversational style in arguing commonplaces of literary theory. His first sizable literary performance, *An Enquiry into the Present State of Polite Learning in Europe,* 1759, urges some insistent grumbles about the learning and taste of contemporary Britain.

> . . .by the power of one single monosyllable, our critics have almost got the victory over humour amongst us. Does the poet paint the absurdities of the vulgar; then he is *low:* does he exaggerate the features of folly, to render it more thoroughly ridiculous, he is then very *low.* In short, they have proscribed the comic or satyrical muse from every walk but high life, which, though abounding in fools as well as the humblest station, is by no means so fruitful in absurdity. Among well-bred fools we may despise much, but have little to laugh at; nature

---

[3] Another of Garrick's favorite comic roles was that of the rattlepated young blade Ranger in a contemporary play, Benjamin Hoadly's *Suspicious Husband,* 1747.

[4] Colman's earlier comedy *The Jealous Wife,* acted at Drury Lane in 1761, had been another reaction against sentiment.

[5] *The West Indian* is a youthful Jamaica merchant of mysterious parentage who comes back to London.

seems to present us with an universal blank of silk, ribbands, smiles and whispers; absurdity is the póet's game, and good breeding is the nice concealment of absurdities. The truth is, the critic generally mistakes humour for wit, which is a very different excellence. Wit raises human nature above its level; humour acts a contrary part, and equally depresses it. To expect exalted humour, is a contradiction in terms; and the critic, by demanding an impossibility from the comic poet, has, in effect, banished new comedy from the stage.

When a thing is humorously described...we compare the absurdity of the character represented with our own, and triumph in our conscious superiority. No natural defect can be a cause of laughter, because it is a misfortune to which ourselves are liable; a defect of this kind, changes the passion into pity or horror; we only laugh at those instances of moral absurdity, to which we are conscious we ourselves are not liable.

Thus, then, the pleasure we receive from wit, turns on the admiration of another; that which we feel from humour, centers in the admiration of ourselves. The poet, therefore, must place the object he would have the subject of humour in a state of inferiority; in other words, the subject of humour must be low.[6]

Goldsmith went on to increasing successes—his series of humorous essays entitled *Chinese Letters,* giving some exotic perspectives on London life, 1762; his pensive Alpine panorama in couplets, *The Traveller,* 1764; and his pastoral romance *The Vicar of Wakefield,* rescued by Dr. Johnson from the shelf in order to get the author out of debt, 1766. By 1767 he was ready to invade the theater. His first play, a moderatedly undistinguished comedy, *The Good-Natured Man,* was rejected by Garrick (Chapter XII of the *Enquiry into Polite Learning* had been hard on actors and managers) and was only with great reluctance put on by Coleman in January 1768. Garrick's success a week earlier with Kelly's *False Delicacy* contributed no doubt to the near failure at Covent Garden.

The point of Goldsmith's *Good-Natured Man* is that the hero is much too good-natured (for his own good or anybody else's) in throwing his money around, and much too self-effacing to respond to the hopes of an amiable fair one. As a reaction against sheer sentimentalism this was rather tame compared to the French finesses and twittery falsehoods of Kelly's *Delicacy.* Goldsmith's boldest effort to be funny was a scene in Act III where two bailiffs move in on the

---

6 *An Enquiry into the Present State of Learning in Europe* (London, 1774), pp. 121–22, 123, 124. This edition contains extensive revisions. The passages quoted above, from a chapter entitled *Of the Marks of Literary Decay in France and England,* occur in the edition of 1759 in almost the same form in a chapter entitled *Of Criticism.*

hero young Honeywood at his home and, upon the subsequent arrival of his sweetheart Miss Richland, are introduced to her as his guests. But this scene was too "low" for Colman and was omitted after the first performance, appearing only in the printed editions and on the stage again only in May 1773.[7]

---

[7] Arthur Friedman, ed. *Collected Works of Oliver Goldsmith* (Oxford, 1966), V, 5–6.

PREFACE

TO

The Good-Natur'd Man

[*1768*]

When I undertook to write a comedy, I confess I was strongly prepossessed in favour of the poets of the last age, and strove to imitate them. The term, *genteel comedy,* was then unknown amongst us, and little more was desired by an audience, than nature and humour, in whatever walks of life they were most conspicuous. The author of the following scenes never imagined that more would be expected of him, and therefore to delineate character has been his principal aim. Those who know any thing of composition, are sensible, that in pursuing humour, it will sometimes lead us into the recesses of the mean; I was even tempted to look for it in the master of a spunging-house:[1] but in deference to the public taste, grown of late, perhaps, too delicate; the scene of the bailiffs was retrenched in the representation. In deference also to the judgment of a few friends, who think in a particular way, the scene is here restored. The author submits it to the reader in his closet; and hopes that too much refinement will not banish humour and character from our's, as it has already done from the French theatre. Indeed the French comedy is now become so very elevated and sentimental, that it has not only banished humour and *Molière* from the stage,[2] but it has banished all spectators too.

The Good-Natur'd Man: A Comedy. As performed at the Theatre-Royal in Covent-Garden. By Mr. Goldsmith. London: printed for W. Griffin, in Catherine-Street, Strand. 1768. See Arthur Friedman, ed. *Collected Works of Oliver Goldsmith,* V, 9, for a description of the early editions.

1 A squeezing house, i.e., a house where a bailiff held a person arrested for debt.

2 Classical French comedy in the Molièresque way had yielded to tearful strains (*comédie larmoyante*) in the semi-serious works of Nivelle de la Chausée (1691?–1754), who wrote under the influence of Rousseau and Richardson, and in "bourgeois" plays by the French *philosophes* Voltaire and Diderot. The climax of the trend came in two masterpieces of emotive intrigue and social criticism, by

Upon the whole, the author returns his thanks to the public for the favourable reception which *The Good Natur'd Man* has met with: and to Mr. Colman in particular, for his kindness to it. It may not also be improper to assure any, who shall hereafter write for the theatre, that merit, or supposed merit, will ever be a sufficient passport to his protection.

"I loves to hear him sing, bekeays he never gives us nothing that's *low.*" Thus the *Second Fellow,* appreciating Tony Lumpkin's song in the tavern scene of Goldsmith's masterpiece *She Stoops to Conquer,* in March 1773. *Third Fellow:* "O damn anything that's *low,* I cannot bear it!" *Fourth Fellow:* "The genteel thing is the genteel thing at any time. If so be that a gentleman bees in a concatenation accordingly."

Like his earlier and less inspired effort (and partly because that effort had been what it was), Goldsmith's *She Stoops to Conquer* had hard going with the theatrical management, Garrick keeping clear of it, and Colman only after more than a year's delay, and upon the intervention of Dr. Johnson with "a kind of force," at length putting it into rehearsal. It was during the course of Colman's long hesitation that Goldsmith himself brought some theoretical argument to bear on the question by publishing anonymously in *The Westminster Magazine* (December 1772) *An Essay on the Theatre, or a Comparison between Laughing and Sentimental Comedy* (reprinted in this volume). This is an essay remarkable less for any toughness of theoretical sinew than for Goldsmith's usual easy and picturesque expression of an attitude. Invoking the

---

Beaumarchais, *Le Barbier de Séville,* 1775, and its sequel *Le Mariage de Figaro,* 1784. For a good defense of *comédie sérieuse,* see Diderot's essay *De la Poésie Dramatique* (first published with his play *Le Père de Famille,* Amsterdam, 1758). "Duties performed," he says, "are just as fertile a ground for drama as folly and vice. Sober and serious dramatic works will always succeed, and even more in a corrupt society than elsewhere. At the theater, people will be rescued from the bad company that otherwise surrounds them; they'll see the kind of human beings they'd like to live with; they'll see the human species as it really is, and they'll be reconciled with it.... Virtue!...The sight of virtue touches us so much more intimately, and pleasantly, than wickedness and nonsense do.... What a great day for humanity it would be if all the arts were to set themselves but a single goal— if they all worked in harmony with the law, to persuade us to love virtue" (*Oeuvres Complètes de Diderot,* ed. J. Assézat, Paris, 1875, VII, 309, 312, 313).

authority of Aristotle, he can say that comedy is a picture of the "lower part of mankind," and hence ought to be a laughing picture of the frailties and follies of that part, rather than a weeping picture of its calamities and its goodness of heart. True calamities belong in fact only to the great, and only what affects the great can strongly affect *us*. "As the hero is but a tradesman, it is indifferent to me whether he be turned out of his counting-house on Fish-street Hill, since he will still have enough left to open shop in St. Giles's." We shall move only a little way in the good Dr. Goldsmith's canon (to the ordeals of the country Vicar and his family, or to the sad citizens of *The Deserted Village*, 1770) before we discover that at heart he himself did not believe in the *Essay on Comedy*. The *Essay* itself is hardly a self-protecting statement. By the "great" we gather that Goldsmith means only royalty and the nobility. By the "low," all the rest of us. For, as he says in his first paragraph, following Horace and Molière and Fielding, "all have sat for the picture." Goldsmith stands astride the ridge of a great historical watershed. He is almost the last man of tolerable education who will be able to express, even carelessly or perfunctorily, that view of the tradesman on Fish-street Hill.[1] His respected senior friend Dr. Samuel Johnson, to whom he dedicated *She Stoops to Conquer*, had already in a *Rambler* essay on the subject of biography (No. 60, October 13, 1750) and an *Idler* essay on the same subject (No. 84, November 24, 1759) propounded the thesis that "vice" and "folly" are best displayed "by those relations which are levelled with the general surface of life." "The sensations are the same in all, though produced by very different occasions."

In another *Rambler* (No. 125, May 28, 1751), Dr. Johnson had

---

1 The same orientation appears only superficially in the following discrimination by Charles Lamb: "You shall hear the same persons say that George Barnwell is very natural, and Othello is very natural, that they are both very deep; and to them they are the same kind of thing. At the one they sit and shed tears, because a good sort of young man is tempted by a naughty woman to commit *a trifling peccadillo*, the murder of an uncle or so, that is all, and so comes to an untimely end, which is *so moving;* and at the other, because a blackamoor in a fit of jealousy kills his innocent white wife: and the odds are that ninety-nine out of a hundred would willingly behold the same catastrophe to both the heroes, and have thought the rope more due to Othello than to Barnwell. For of the texture of Othello's mind, the inward construction marvellously laid open with all its strengths and weaknesses, its heroic confidences and its human misgivings, its agonies of hate springing from the depths of love, they see no more than the spectators at a cheaper rate, who pay their pennies a-piece to look through the man's telescope in Leicester-fields, see into the inner plot and topography of the moon" (*On the Tragedies of Shakespeare, Considered with Reference to Their Fitness for Stage Representation*, in *The Reflector*, 1811, 10th paragraph).

thrown out the following terse sketch of the classic distinction
between tragedy and comedy and of difficulties that arose in a
"mixed way" of writing.

Comedy has been particularly unpropitious to definers; for though
perhaps they might properly have contented themselves, with declaring
it to be *such a dramatick representation of human life, as may excite
mirth,* they have embarrassed their definition with the means by which
the comick writers attain their end, without considering that the various methods of exhilarating their audience, not being limited by nature,
cannot be comprised in precept. Thus, some make comedy a representation of mean, and others of bad men; some think that its essence
consists in the unimportance, others in the fictitiousness of the trans-
action. But any man's reflections will inform him, that every dramatick
composition which raises mirth, is comick; and that, to raise mirth, it
is by no means universally necessary, that the personages should be
either mean or corrupt, nor always requisite, that the action should be
trivial, nor ever, that it should be fictitious.

If the two kinds of dramatick poetry had been defined only by their
effects upon the mind, some absurdities might have been prevented,
with which the compositions of our greatest poets are disgraced, who,
for want of some settled ideas and accurate distinctions, have unhappily confounded tragick with comick sentiments. They seem to have
thought, that as the meanness of personages constituted comedy, their
greatness was sufficient to form a tragedy; and that nothing was necessary but that they should crowd the scene with monarchs, and generals,
and guards; and make them talk, at certain intervals, of the downfal
of kingdoms, and the rout of armies. They have not considered, that
thoughts or incidents, in themselves ridiculous, grow still more
grotesque by the solemnity of such characters; that reason and nature
are uniform and inflexible; and that what is despicable and absurd, will
not, by any association with splendid titles, become rational or great;
that the most important affairs, by an intermixture of an unseasonable
levity, may be made contemptible; and that the robes of royalty can
give no dignity to nonsense or to folly.

Goldsmith's comic masterpiece *She Stoops to Conquer* opened on
March 15, 1773, under sufficiently auspicious circumstances. A
month before that first night, a mimic actor, manager, and rival
dramatist, Samuel Foote, had helped promote a return of laughing
comedy by devoting his "Primitive Puppet Shew" at the Haymarket Theater to a burlesque of genteel sentiment called *The
Handsome Housemaid, or Piety in Pattens.* Even Garrick helped
Goldsmith's play, contributing a good Prologue (reprinted in this
volume), a lament for the laughing muse, spoken by one of the
comic actors, Mr. Woodward, in mourning dress. The play was
applauded to success by a claque of friends led by Dr. Johnson.
Earlier that year Johnson had written a sort of proto-criticism in

a letter to his young Scots friend and future biographer James
Boswell: "Dr. Goldsmith has a new comedy, which is expected in
the spring. No name is yet given it. The chief diversion arises from
a stratagem by which a lover is made to mistake his future father-in
law's house for an inn. This, you see, borders upon farce. The
dialogue is quick and gay, and the incidents are so prepared as
not to seem improbable." After the play's success, Johnson said
to Boswell: "I know of no comedy for many years that has so much
exhilarated an audience, that has answered so much the great end
of comedy, making an audience merry."[2] Far away in Edinburgh,
at the time of the play's performance, James Boswell, who kept up
eagerly with theatrical news, was thinking about his annual jaunt
to the great world of London. On March 29th, a few hours before
setting out, he renewed and improved a somewhat careless relation
with Goldsmith in a letter[3] which is an adroit reflection, and for us a
neat epitome, of the crisis of sentimentalism in the London theater
of 1773.

Dear Sir.
    I sincerely wish you joy on the great success of your new Comedy:
She stoops to conquer, or the Mistakes of a Night. The English Nation
was just falling into a lethargy. Their blood was thickened and their
minds *creamed and mantled like a standing Pool;* and no wonder,—
when their Comedies which should enliven them, like sparkling
Champagne, were become mere syrup of poppies gentle soporifick
draughts. Had there been no interruption to this, our audiences must
have gone to the Theatres with their night caps. In the Opera houses
abroad, the Boxes are fitted up for teadrinking. Those at Drury Lane
& Covent Garden must have been furnished with settees, and com-
modiously adjusted for repose. I am happy to hear that you have
waked the spirit of mirth which has so long layn dormant, and revived
natural humour and hearty laughter. It gives me pleasure that our
friend Garrick has written the Prologue for you. It is at least lending
you a Postilion since you have not his coach; and I think it is a
very good one, admirably adapted both to the Subject and to the
Authour of the Comedy.
    You must know my wife was safely delivered of a daughter, the
very evening that *She stoops to conquer* first appeared. I am fond of
the coincidence. My little daughter is a fine healthy lively child, and
I flatter myself shall be blest with the cheerfullness of your Comick
Muse. She has nothing of that wretched whining and crying which we
see childen so often have; nothing of the *Comedie Larmoyante....*

---

[2] April 29, 1773.
[3] From the autograph letter in the Hyde Collection, Four Oaks Farm, Somer-
ville, New Jersey. By kind permission of Mrs. Donald F. Hyde.

An Essay on the Theatre

or

A Comparison Between Laughing and Sentimental Comedy

[*1773*]

The Theatre, like all other amusements, has its Fashions and its Prejudices; and when satiated with its excellence, Mankind begin to mistake Change for Improvement. For some years, Tragedy was the reigning entertainment; but of late it has entirely given way to Comedy, and our best efforts are now exerted in these lighter kinds of composition. The pompous Train, the swelling Phrase, and the unnatural Rant, are displaced for that natural portrait of Human Folly and Frailty, of which all are judges, because all have sat for the picture.

But as in describing Nature it is presented with a double face, either of mirth or sadness, our modern Writers find themselves at a loss which chiefly to copy from; and it is now debated, Whether the Exhibition of Human Distress is likely to afford the mind more Entertainment than that of Human Absurdity?

Comedy is defined by Aristotle to be a picture of the Frailties of the lower part of Mankind, to distinguish it from Tragedy, which is an exhibition of the Misfortunes of the Great.[1] When Comedy therefore ascends to produce the Characters of Princes or Generals upon the Stage, it is out of its walk, since Low Life and Middle Life are entirely its object. The principal question therefore is, Whether in describing Low or Middle Life, an exhibition of its Follies be not preferable to a detail of its Calamities? Or, in other words, Which deserves the preference? The Weeping Sentimental Comedy, so much

---

Our text follows *The Westminster Magazine or the Pantheon of Taste*...of the Year 1773...Vol. I. London: Printed for W. Goldsmith, pp. 4–6.
[1] See above, Introduction, pp. 8–9.

in fashion at present, or the Laughing and even Low Comedy, which seems to have been last exhibited by Vanbrugh and Cibber?

If we apply to authorities, all the Great Masters in the Dramatic Art have but one opinion. Their rule is, that as Tragedy displays the Calamities of the Great; so Comedy should excite our laughter by ridiculously exhibiting the Follies of the Lower Part of Mankind. Boileau, one of the best modern Critics, asserts, that Comedy will not admit of Tragic Distress.

> *Le Comique, ennemi des soupirs et des pleurs,*
> *N'admet point dans ses vers de tragiques douleurs.*[2]

Nor is this rule without the strongest foundation in Nature, as the distresses of the Mean by no means affect us so strongly as the Calamities of the Great. When Tragedy exhibits to us some Great Man fallen from his height, and struggling with want and adversity, we feel his situation in the same manner as we suppose he himself must feel, and our pity is increased in proportion to the height from whence he fell. On the contrary, we do not strongly sympathize with one born in humbler circumstances, and encountering accidental distress: so that while we melt for Belisarius,[3] we scarce give halfpence to the Beggar who accosts us in the street. The one has our pity; the other our contempt. Distress, therefore, is the proper object of Tragedy, since the Great excite our pity by their fall; but not equally so of Comedy, since the Actors employed in it are originally so mean, that they sink but little by their fall.

Since the first origin of the Stage, Tragedy and Comedy have run in distinct channels, and never till of late encroached upon the provinces of each other. Terence, who seems to have made the nearest approaches, yet always judiciously stops short before he comes to the downright pathetic; and yet he is even reproached by Caesar for wanting the *vis comica.*[4] All the other Comic Writers of antiquity aim only at rendering Folly or Vice ridiculous, but never exalt their characters into

---

2 "Comedy is hostile to sighs and tears; its verses will not entertain any tragic distress"—*L'Art Poétique*, III.401–2.

3 The great military commander Belisarius was accused of conspiring against the emperor Justinian (A.D. 563), and, according to tradition, his eyes were put out, and he wandered as a beggar about the streets of Constantinople. He was the subject of Jean-François Marmontel's romance *Bélisaire*, translated into English in 1767.

4 See above p. 143, Caesar's verses on Terence quoted from Suetonius by John Dennis.

buskined pomp, or make what Voltaire humourously calls a *Trades-man's Tragedy*.[5]

Yet, notwithstanding this weight of authority, and the universal practice of former ages, a new species of Dramatic Composition has been introduced under the name of *Sentimental* Comedy, in which the virtues of Private Life are exhibited, rather than the Vices exposed; and the Distresses, rather than the Faults of Mankind, make our interest in the piece. These Comedies have had of late great success, perhaps from their novelty, and also from their flattering every man in his favourite foible. In these Plays almost all the Characters are good, and exceedingly generous; they are lavish enough of their *Tin* Money of the Stage, and though they want Humour, have abundance of Sentiment and Feeling. If they happen to have Faults or Foibles, the Spectator is taught not only to pardon, but to applaud them, in consideration of the goodness of their hearts; so that Folly, instead of being ridiculed, is commended, and the Comedy aims at touching our Passions without the power of being truly pathetic: in this manner we are likely to lose one great source of Entertainment on the Stage; for while the Comic Poet is invading the province of the Tragic Muse, he leaves her lovely Sister quite neglected. Of this, however, he is noway solicitous, as he measures his fame by his profits.

But it will be said, that the Theatre is formed to amuse Mankind, and that it matters little, if this end be answered, by what means it is obtained. If Mankind find delight in weeping at Comedy, it would be cruel to abridge them in that or any other innocent pleasure. If those Pieces are denied the name of Comedies; yet call them by any other name, and if they are delightful, they are good. Their success, it will be said, is a mark of their merit, and it is only abridging our happiness to deny us an inlet to Amusement.

These objections, however, are rather specious than solid. It is true, that Amusement is a great object of the Theatre; and it will be allowed, that these Sentimental Pieces do often amuse us: but the question is, Whether the True Comedy would not amuse us more? The question is, Whether a Character supported throughout a Piece with its Ridicule still attending, would not give us more delight than

---

[5] Voltaire's article *Art Dramatique* had appeared in his *Dictionnaire Philosophique,* 1770. Cf. his *Oeuvres Complètes,* ed. Louis Moland, XVII (Paris, 1878), 419. He himself wrote a few comedies in the category of the sentimental or bourgeois. Cf. above p. 181, n. 2.

this species of Bastard Tragedy, which only is applauded because it is new?

A friend of mine who was sitting unmoved at one of these Sentimental Pieces, was asked, how he could be so indifferent. "Why, truly," says he, "as the Hero is but a Tradesman, it is indifferent to me whether he be turned out of his Counting-house on Fish-street Hill, since he will still have enough left to open shop in St. Giles's."

The other objection is as ill-grounded; for though we should give these Pieces another name, it will not mend their efficacy. It will continue a kind of *mulish* production, with all the defects of its opposite parents, and marked with sterility. If we are permitted to make Comedy weep, we have an equal right to make Tragedy laugh, and to set down in Blank Verse the Jests and Repartees of all the Attendants in a Funeral Procession.[6]

But there is one Argument in favour of Sentimental Comedy which will keep it on the Stage in spite of all that can be said against it. It is, of all others, the most easily written. Those abilities that can hammer out a Novel, are fully sufficient for the production of a Sentimental Comedy. It is only sufficient to raise the Characters a little, to deck out the Hero with a Ribband, or give the Heroine a Title; then to put an Insipid Dialogue, without Character or Humour, into their mouths, give them mighty good hearts, very fine cloaths, furnish a new sett of Scenes, make a Pathetic Scene or two, with a sprinkling of tender melancholy Conversation through the whole, and there is no doubt but all the Ladies will cry and all the Gentlemen applaud.

Humour at present seems to be departing from the Stage, and it will soon happen, that our Comic Players will have nothing left for it but a fine Coat and a Song. It depends upon the Audience whether they will actually drive those poor Merry Creatures from the Stage, or sit at a Play as gloomy as at the Tabernacle. It is not easy to recover an art when once lost; and it would be but a just punishment that when, by our being too fastidious, we have banished Humour from the Stage, we should our selves be deprived of the art of Laughing.

---

6 Cf. above p. 156, Fielding's Preface to *Joseph Andrews*.

PROLOGUE

By David Garrick, Esq.

TO

She Stoops to Conquer

[March 15, 1773]

Enter Mr. Woodward[1]
Dressed in Black, and holding a Handkerchief to his Eyes.

Excuse me, Sirs, I pray— I can't yet speak—
I'm crying now— and have been all the week!
'Tis not alone this mourning suit, good masters;
I've that within[2]— for which there are no plaisters!
Pray wou'd you know the reason why I'm crying?
The Comic muse, long sick, is now a dying!
And if she goes, my tears will never stop;
For as a play'r, I can't squeeze out one drop:
I am undone, that's all— shall lose my bread—
I'd rather, but that's nothing— lose my head.
When the sweet maid is laid upon the bier,
Shuter[3] and *I* shall be chief mourners here.
To *her* a mawkish drab of spurious breed,
Who deals in *sentimentals* will succeed!
Poor *Ned* and *I* are dead to all intents,
We can as soon speak *Greek* as sentiments!
Both nervous grown, to keep our spirits up,

Our text follows that of the first edition of the play, published by F. Newbery on March 25, 1773. See Arthur Friedman, *Collected Works of Oliver Goldsmith,* V. 92, 96, 102–3.

[1] Henry Woodward (1714–1777), veteran comic actor at London and Dublin theaters, had refused to act the low-comic part of Tony Lumpkin.

[2] A parody of *Hamlet,* I.ii.76–85.

[3] Edward Shuter (1728?–1776).

We now and then take down a hearty cup.[4]
What shall we do?— If Comedy forsake us!
They'll turn us out, and no one else will take us.
But why can't I be moral?— Let me try—
My heart thus pressing— fix'd my face and eye—
With a sententious look, that nothing means,
(Faces are blocks, in sentimental scenes)
Thus I begin— *All is not gold that glitters,*
Pleasure seems sweet, but proves a glass of bitters.
When ign'rance enters, folly is at hand;
Learning is better far than house and land.
Let not your virtue trip, who trips may stumble,
And virtue is not virtue, if she tumble.
   I give it up— morals won't do for me;
To make you laugh I must play tragedy.
One hope remains— hearing the maid was ill,
A *doctor*[5] comes this night to shew his skill.
To cheer her heart, and give your muscles motion,
He in *five draughts* prepar'd, presents a potion:
A kind of magic charm— for be assur'd,
If you will *swallow* it, the maid is cur'd:
But desperate the Doctor, and her case is,
If you reject the dose, and make wry faces!
This truth he boasts, will boast it while he lives,
No *pois'nous drugs* are mix'd in what he gives;
Should he succeed, you'll give him his degree;
If not, within he will receive no fee!
The college *you*, must his pretenisons back,
Pronounce him regular, or dub him quack.

---

[4] Shuter sometimes came on the stage drunk.
[5] "Doctor Goldsmith" had studied medicine at Edinburgh and Leyden, was said to have received a medical degree at some foreign university, had supported himself for a while in Southwark as a physician, and had failed in 1758 to qualify for a medical appointment in India.

HORACE WALPOLE

[1717–1797]

Johnson's *Life of Gray,* "or rather criticism on his *Odes,*" wrote the eminent litterateur Horace Walpole early in 1781, "is come out; a most wretched, dull, tasteless, *verbal* criticism." "Dr. Johnson has indubitably neither taste nor ear, criterion of judgement, but his old woman's prejudices."[1] Walpole himself had published Gray's Pindaric *Odes* in 1757, and Johnson now wrote of the *Odes:* " 'Double, double, toil and trouble.' He has a kind of strutting dignity, and is tall by walking on tiptoe." This juncture of opinions relates mainly to lyric poetry, rather than to stage comedy, but it well illustrates a kind of general oppositeness which prevailed between the middle-class world of such working persons as London journalists, playwrights, and actors —Johnson, Goldsmith, Garrick—and the world of rank and privilege, the *beau monde* of elegance, virtuosity, tone, taste, and frolic, inhabited by the author of our next essay on comedy.

Horace Walpole was the fourth son of the Prime Minister whose government was the target of Pope and Fielding *circa* 1737. After Eton and Cambridge and two years in Italy with Thomas Gray and other friends, Walpole returned to England in 1741, the holder of certain "little patent-places" (or lucrative sinecures) and a member of the Parliament which was about to "put a period to his father's administration."[2] In 1747 (two years after his father's death) he leased, and later bought, a small house on the Thames at Twickenham, Strawberry Hill, just upstream from Pope's Villa. Rebuilt as a Gothic castle, and with the adjunct of his own printing press, 1757, this home became a kind of "central passion" and focus of all his interests

---

[1] Letters to William Mason, the biographer of Gray, January 27 and February 19, 1781, *Horace Walpole's Correspondence,* ed. W. S. Lewis, XXIX–II (New Haven, 1955), 97, 111.

[2] The phrases quoted are from Walpole's own "Short Notes of My Life," a "long extract" from which appears in W. S. Lewis's *Selection of the Letters of Horace Walpole,* (New York, 1926). On retiring from office, Sir Robert Walpole became First Earl of Orford. In 1791, on the death of a nephew, Horace Walpole became Fourth Earl.

for the rest of his life. One thinks very readily of Walpole in his political, social, antiquarian, historical, Gothic, romantic, and virtuoso associations, the author of the thousands of letters[3] in which, deliberately and methodically addressing select correspondents, he devoted his life to the record of himself and his times—for posterity.

He was the author also of such published works as his Gothic romance *The Castle of Otranto,* 1764, his *Historic Doubts on Richard the Third,* 1768, his *Anecdotes of Painting in England,* 1762–1771. He was one of the most accomplished prose writers of the age. One of his favorite epistolary assertions was that "this world is a comedy to those who think, a tragedy to those who feel."[4] One is less likely to remember offhand his connections with the stage. But he did write a sort of comedy, *Nature Will Prevail, A Moral Entertainment in One Act,* a small piece of "moonstruck nonsense" which Colman produced with success in 1778 at The Little Theater in the Haymarket. And he wrote also a tragedy of incestuous passion (unfit for the stage), *The Mysterious Mother,* which he printed at Strawberry Hill in 1768 and published in 1781. And in 1781, when a friend, Robert Jephson, turned *The Castle of Otranto* into a tragedy *The Count of Narbonne,* Walpole implored the actress Mrs. Pope to take a part in it and was behind the scenes at Covent Garden when it was put on with éclat.[5] Walpole's dramatic sensibility and genius for comic observation are prominent in the idiom of social reporting which flashes in so many of the most celebrated scenes and episodes of his letters. From the varied allusions in his letters, we may infer a more or less constant and life-long awareness of the London theater and, it need hardly be argued, of the comic stage.

Walpole's most recent biographer gives us an engaging *lanterne* of the young man about town, shortly after his return from Italy—whirling in his round of balls, masquerades, concerts, cards, water parties, Ranelagh, Vauxhall, the park, the Opera, the theater. He was not much impressed by the rising star of the stage, David Garrick, preferred to have breakfast and reminiscences with the aged actress

---

3 The Yale Edition of *Horace Walpole's Correspondence,* ed. W. S. Lewis and several others, reached volume XXXIV in 1966, the third volume of Walpole's correspondence with the Countess of Upper Ossory. It is estimated that the complete edition will include more than 7,000 letters from and to Walpole.

4 For an early and a late example: Walpole to Mann, December 31, 1769; to Lady Ossory, August 26, 1784 (*Correspondence,* XXIII, 166; XXXIII, 444); cf. *Detached Thoughts (The Works of Horatio Walpole,* London, 1798, IV, 369).

5 R. W. Ketton-Cremer, *Horace Walpole: A Biography* (London, 1940; revised ed., 1964). Quoted phrases not otherwise identified in the text above are from Ketton-Cremer. A short discourse by Walpole entitled *Thoughts on Tragedy* is written in the form of three letters to Jephson on the occasion of his successful tragedy *Braganza,* 1775 (*Works,* 1798, II, 304–14).

Mrs. Bracegirdle (the heroine of Congreve's plays). Once he went to Drury Lane when Fleetwood the manager happened to have packed the pit with "great numbers of Bear-garden *bruisers*" to put down the audience when they hissed the pantomime. During the riot which ensued, the curtain flew up and revealed the stage also "filled with blackguards armed with bludgeons and clubs." One of the actors came forward and began to make an apology for the manager: "Mr. Fleet-wood———" when Walpole himself, sitting in a box, called out, "with a most audible voice and dignity of anger:...'He is an impudent rascal!'" The crowd cheered, and while Walpole's "shadow of a person was dilating to the consistence of a hero," one of the leaders came up and, pulling off his hat, asked, "Mr. W., what would you please to have us do next?" The town rang with his name for several days. And one of his friends gave him the nickname "Wat Tyler."[6]

Some years later, in 1753, a year after the end of Johnson's *Rambler* and a few months after Fielding's *Covent-Garden Journal,* Walpole joined the Earl of Chesterfield and other gentlemen in beginning a series of periodical essays addressed to the fashionable world. *The World* was the title. The first of Walpole's nine contributions, No. 6 (February 8, 1753), uniting the "world" and its epitome the "theatre" in the epigraph *Totum mundum agit histrio,* commented, with sure taste and Aristotelian insight, on a certain kind of "Progress" recently "made towards Nature in the Theatres."

> I allude to those excellent exhibitions of the animal or inanimate part of the creation, which are furnished by the worthy philosophers Rich and Garrick; the latter of whom has refined on his competitor; and having perceived that art was become so perfect that it was necessary to mimic it by nature, he has happily introduced a cascade of real water.... They tell you that the town...was in raptures last year with one of tin at Vauxhall.[7]

Everything considered, one might have thought it likely enough that Walpole would not be among the most vociferous applauders of Goldsmith's homely merriment in March 1773.

> What play makes you laugh very much, and yet is a very wretched comedy? Dr. Goldsmith's *She Stoops to Conquer.* Stoops indeed!— so she does, that is the Muse; she is draggled up to the knees, and has trudged, I believe, from Southwark Fair. The whole view of the piece is low humour, and no humour in it. All the merit is in the situations, which are comic; the heroine has no more modesty than Lady Bridget,

---

6 Ketton-Cremer, pp. 89–90. The description of the riot in the theater occurs in Walpole's letter of November 11, 1744, to his friend Sir Horace Mann, British Minister at Florence.

7 *The British Essayists,* ed. A. Chalmers (London, 1817), XXVI, 27–28.

and the author's wit is as much *manqué* as the lady's; but some of the
characters are well acted, and Woodward speaks a poor prologue,
written by Garrick, admirably.[8]

According to the editor[9] of Walpole's *Works* published posthumously
in 1798, his essay *Thoughts on Comedy* (reprinted in this volume)
was written only a few years after Goldsmith's vulgar triumph and
just at the time of Garrick's retirement from Drury Lane, or "in 1775
and 1776." Probably, however, he kept the manuscript in a drawer
and added to it from time to time, for there are two footnotes that
look like afterthoughts, and the last paragraph refers to a play of 1786
and to *The School for Scandal*, 1777. The latter was the climax of
a very notable episode in London theatrical history, the beginning of
which had been R. B. Sheridan's earlier success with *The Rivals* in
1775. In 1776 Sheridan succeeded Garrick as manager of Drury Lane.
Here was a revival of laughing comedy about which Walpole did
have some reservations, but which was on the whole much more to
his taste.

> I have seen Sheridan's new comedy *School for Scandal* and liked it
> much better than any I have seen since *The Provoked Husband*. There
> is a great deal of wit and good situations; but it is too long, has two
> or three bad scenes that might easily be omitted, and seemed to me to
> want nature and truth of character; but I have not read it, and sat
> too high to hear it well. It is admirably acted.[10]

Sheridan's plays were a renascence of high Restoration "manners" and
wit, somewhat rouged, however, and sweetened to suit the need of a
new audience, a generation which had, inevitably, if we consider the
history of the times, been more or less improved in morals and softened
in heart—"sentimentalized," no doubt. The triumph of a new kind of
laughter during the last decades of Walpole's life was summarized in
one of the prologues of the day—that written by George Colman
for Miss Sophia Lee's *Chapter of Accidents*, 1780.

> When Fielding, Humour's fav'rite child appear'd,
> *Low* was the word— a word each author fear'd!
> 'Till chac'd at length, by Pleasantry's bright ray,

---

[8] To the Countess of Upper Ossory, March 27, 1773, *Correspondence*, XXXII–I,
108–9. In a letter to William Mason written on the same day, he calls the play
"the lowest of all farces" (*Correspondence*, XXVIII–I, 79). John Forster (*The
Life and Times of Oliver Goldsmith*, 6th ed., London, 1877, II, 327) suggests that
Goldsmith had earned this severity by repeated slights to the memory of Walpole's
father, the great minister.

[9] This was Miss Mary Berry (1763–1852), the darling protégée of Walpole's last
years and his literary executrix.

[10] Letter to William Mason, May 16, 1777, *Correspondence*, XXVIII–I, 309.
The School for Scandal was first acted at Drury Lane, May 8, 1777.

Nature and Mirth resum'd their legal sway;
And Goldsmith's Genius bask'd in open day.

To-night, our Author's is a mixt intent—
Passion and Humour— *Low* and *Sentiment:*
Smiling in tears— a Serio-comick Play—
Sunshine and show'r— a kind of April-Day![11]

Horace Walpole sometimes wrote hastily and carelessly, even incorrectly, ungrammatically, and obscurely—but almost never (except perhaps in moments of a Gothic romance or an Elizabethan-sounding tragedy) pompously or tediously. An editor who has recently republished the *Thoughts on Comedy* remarks that Walpole's essay is the best account he knows of "the English comedy of manners by an 'insider,' one who shared its presuppositions, even if the genre was already moribund."[12] "Why," asked Walpole himself in 1787, "are there so few genteel comedies but because most comedies are written by men not of that sphere [of high life]? Etherege, Congreve, Vanbrugh and Cibber wrote genteel comedy, because they lived in the best company, and Mrs. Oldfield played it so well, because she not only followed, but often set the fashion. General Burgoyne has written the best modern comedy for the same reason."[13] In the *Thoughts on Comedy,* Walpole speeds along, touching on nearly all the main events in the history of English stage comedy, all the vogues and opinions which we have noted from the time of Ben Jonson:—passion, humor, and wit, the individual and society, the eccentric and the civilized.

---

[11] George Colman, *Prose on Several Occasions; Accompanied with Some Pieces in Verse* (1787), III, 227–28. Miss Lee's comedy was based on Diderot's *Le Père de Famille.*

[12] F. W. Bateson, in *Essays in Criticism,* XV (April 1965), 162–70.

[13] To Lady Ossory, June 14, 1787, *Correspondence,* XXXIII–II, 563–64. Walpole continues: "and Mrs. Farren is as excellent as Mrs. Oldfield, because she has lived with the best style of men in England; whereas Mrs. Abington can never go beyond Lady Teazle, which is a second-rate character, and that rank of women are always aping women of fashion without arriving at the style." Anne Oldfield (1683–1730), leading London actress of high roles in both comedy and tragedy, was buried in Westminster Abbey beneath Congreve's monument. She had played Narcissa in Colley Cibber's *Love's Last Shift* and appears under that name in Pope's *Moral Essays* I and II, 1734–1735. Frances Abington (1737–1815) was in girlhood a flower-seller, street-singer, domestic servant, and cook-maid. She came to Drury Lane in 1764 at Garrick's invitation and in 1777 was the original Lady Teazle, frivolous and headstrong young country-bred wife of an elderly wealthy husband, Sir Peter, in Sheridan's *The School for Scandal.* Elizabeth Farren (1759?–1829), in 1797 Countess of Derby, first appeared at Drury Lane in 1778. Hazlitt praised her for her "fine-lady airs and graces." See, below p. 222, Lamb's allusion to Mrs. Abington and Mrs. Farren. John Burgoyne (1722–1792), Gentleman Johnny, the British general who capitulated to the Americans at Saratoga in 1777, was author of a successful high comedy, *The Heiress,* 1786, mentioned by Walpole at the end of *Thoughts on Comedy* (below p. 205).

He gets into most of the critical difficulties intrinsic to the tradition, and gets out of them no more adroitly, rather more by a cool absent-mindedness, than most of his forerunners. He knows enough to contrast the English with the French (Molièresque) tradition in comedy, and hence he is a forerunner of the final and longest statement in the present volume, the end of the tradition, Meredith's *Essay* of 1877. At one moment he arrives at what we may come very close to accepting actually as a brief formula of the comic: "The comic writer's art consists in seizing and distinguishing these shades, which have rendered man a fictitious animal, without destroying his original composition." But within a few paragraphs he slides into his denial, or at least into grave difficulties. "Half the time of the Chinese is passed in ceremony. I conclude their comedies cannot be very striking. Where one kind of polish runs through a whole nation, the operation of the passions must be less discernible." Walpole here anticipates a paradox which a pundit of the romantic age, William Hazlitt, in his *Characters of Shakespeare's Plays,* 1817, would wrap in a much heavier protection of verbalism:

There is a certain stage of society in which people become conscious of their peculiarities and absurdities, affect to disguise what they are, and set up pretensions to what they are not. This gives rise to a corresponding style of comedy, the object of which is to detect the disguise of self-love, and to make reprisals on these preposterous assumptions of vanity, by marking the contrast between the real and the affected character as severely as possible, and denying to those, who would impose on us for what they are not, even the merit which they have. This is the comedy of artificial life, of wit and satire, such as we see it in Congreve, Wycherley, Vanbrugh, etc. To this succeeds a state of society from which the same sort of affectation and pretence are banished by a greater knowledge of the world or by their successful exposure on the stage; and which by neutralising the materials of comic character, both natural and artificial, leaves no comedy at all— but *the sentimental.* Such is our modern comedy. There is a period in the progress of manners anterior to both these, in which the foibles and follies of individuals are of nature's planting, not the growth of art or study; in which they are therefore unconscious of them themselves, or care not who knows then, if they can but have their whim out; and in which, as there is no attempt at imposition, the spectators rather receive pleasure from humouring the inclination of the persons they laugh at, than wish to give them pain by exposing their absurdity. This may be called the comedy of nature, and it is the comedy which we generally find in Shakespeare.[14]

---

[14] *Characters of Shakespeare's Plays* (London, 1848), pp. 251–52, "Twelfth Night, or, What You Will." Cf. the same writer's *Lectures on the English Comic Writers* (London, 1819), Lecture VIII, "On the Comic Writers of the Last Century," pp. 302–6.

Thoughts on Comedy

[*1798*]

Our old comedies are very valuable from their variety of characters, and for preserving customs and manners; but they are more defective in plans and conduct than excellent in particular parts. Some are very pedantic, the greater part gross in language and humour, the latter of which is seldom true. Ben Jonson was more correct, but still more pedantic. *Volpone* is faulty in the moral, and too elevated in the dialogue: *The Alchemist* is his best play: *The Silent Woman,* formed on an improbable plan, is unnaturally loaded with learning. Beaumont and Fletcher are easier than Jonson, but less happy in executing a plan than in conceiving it.

The next age dealt in the intricacies of Spanish plots, enlivened by the most licentious indecency. Dryden and the fair sex rivalled each other in violating all decorum. Wycherley naturalized French comedy, but prostituted it too. That chaste stage blushed at our translations of its best pieces. Yet Wycherley was not incapable of easy dialogue. The same age produced almost the best comedy we have, though liable to the same reprehension: *The Man of Mode* shines as our first genteel comedy; the touches are natural and delicate, and never overcharged. Unfortunately the tone of the most fashionable people was extremely indelicate; and when Addison, in *The Spectator,*[1] anathematised this play, he forgot that it was rather a satire on the manners of the court, than an apology for them. Less licentious conversation would not have painted the age. Vanbrugh, the best writer of dialogue we have seen, is more blameless in his language, than in his images. His expressions are sterling, and yet unstudied: his wit is not owing to description or caricature; neither sought nor too abundant. We are pleased both with the duration of his scenes and with the result of them. We are entertained, not surprised or struck.

From *The Works of Horatio Walpole* (London, 1798), II, 315–22. Written in 1775–1776.

[1] It was Steele who wrote the attacks on Etherege's play in *Spectator* No. 65, reprinted in this volume.

We are in good company while with him; and have neither adventures nor bons mots to repeat afterwards. It is proof of consummate art in a comic writer, when you seem to have passed your time at the theatre as you might have done out of it—it proves he has exactly hit the style, manners, and character of his cotemporaries. Plot, the vital principle of Spanish and female plays, ought to be little laboured; nor is scarcely more necessary than to put the personages into action and to release them. Vanbrugh's plays, *The Man of Mode,* and *The Careless Husband,*[2] have no more intrigue than accounts for the meeting of the characters, as a passion or an intended marriage may do. *The Double Dealer,*[3] the groundwork of which is almost serious enough for tragedy in private life, perplexes the attention; and the wit of the subordinate characters is necessary to enliven the darkness of the back ground.

Congreve is undoubtedly the most witty author that ever existed. Though sometimes his wit seems the effort of intention, and, though an effort, never failed; it was so natural, that, if he split it into ever so many characters, it was a polypus that soon grew perfect in each individual. We may blame the universality of wit in all his personages, but nobody can say which ought to have less. It assimilated with whatever character it was poured into: and, as Congreve would certainly have had wit in whatever station of life he had been born; as he would have made as witty a footman or old lady, as a fine gentleman; his gentlemen, ladies old or young, his footmen, nay his coxcombs (for they are not fools but puppies) have as much wit, and wit as much their own, as his men of most parts and best understandings. No character drops a sentence that would be proper in any other mouth. Not only Lady Wishfor't and Ben are characteristically marked, but Scandal, Mrs. Frail, and every fainter personage, are peculiarly distinct from each other. Sir Wilful Witwoud is unlike Sir Joseph Wittol. Witwoud is different from Tattle, Valentine from Mellefont, and Cynthia from Angelica.[4] That still each play is unnatural, is only because four assemblages of different persons could never have so much wit as Congreve has bestowed on them. We want breath or

---

2 A comedy by Cibber, published in 1715.
3 By Congreve, produced in 1694.
4 Lady Wishfor't, Witwoud, and his half-brother, Sir Wilful Witwoud, are characters in *The Way of the World* (1700); Mellefont and Cynthia appear in *The Double Dealer* (1694); Sir Joseph Wittol appears in Congreve's earliest comedy, *The Old Bachelor* (1693); Mrs. Frail, Tattle, Angelica, Valentine, and his younger brother, Ben, are all characters in *Love for Love* (1695). Walpole's spelling of "Wishfor't" calls attention to a pun in the name. Early editions have "Wishfort."

attention to follow their repartees; and are so charmed with what every body says, that we have not leisure to be interested in what any does. We are so pleased with each person, that we wish success to all; and our approbation is so occupied, that our passions cannot be engaged. We even do not believe that a company who seem to meet only to show their wit, can have any other object in view. Their very vices seem affected, only to furnish subject for gaiety: thus the intrigue of Careless and Lady Pliant[5] does not strike us more than a story that we know is invented to set off the talents of the relator. For these reasons, though they are something more, I can scarce allow Congreve's to be true comedies. No man would be corrected, if sure that his wit would make his vices or ridicules overlooked.

The delicate and almost insensible touches of *The Careless Husband* are the reverse of Congreve's ungovernable wit. The affected characters of Lady Betty Modish and Lord Foppington are marked with the pencil of nature as much as Sir Charles, Lady Easy, and Lady Graveairs. It is in drawing *refined* or *affected nature* that consists the extreme difficulty of painting what is called *high life*, where affection, politeness, fashion, art, interest, and the attentions exacted by society, restrain the sallies of passion, colour over vice, disguise crimes, and confine man to an uniformity of behaviour, that is composed to the standard of not shocking, alarming, or offending those who profess the same rule of exterior conduct. Good breeding conceals their sensations, interest their crimes, and fashion legitimates their follies. Good sense forms the plan, education ripens it, conversation gives the varnish, and wit the excuse. Yet under all these disguises nature lets out its symptoms. Protestations are so generally the marks of falsehood, that the more liberally they are dealt, the more they indicate what they mean to conceal. Ceremonious behaviour is the substitute for pride, and equally demands return of respect. A fashionable man banters those whom in a state of nature he would affront. Thus good company have the same passions with low life, and have only changed the terms and moderated the display. The first instance of good breeding in the world was complimenting the fair sex with substituting the word *love* for *lust*. Courts and society have changed all the other denominations of our passions, and regulated their appearance. The feuds of great barons are now marked by not bowing to each other, or not visiting. The rancour is not decreased, but society could not

---

5 Careless and Lady Pliant are characters in *The Double Dealer*.

subsist if they fought whenever they met. In former days fields of battle were the only public places; but since wealth and luxury and elegance, and unrestrained conversation with the other sex, have softened our manners, nature finds its account in less turbulent gratification of the passions; and good-breeding, which seems the current coin of humanity, is no more than bank bills[6] real treasure: but it increases the national fund of politeness, and is taken as current money; though the acceptor knows it is no more addressed to him than the bill to the first person to whom it was made payable; but he can pay it away, and knows it will always be accepted.

The comic writer's art consists in seizing and distinguishing these shades, which have rendered man a fictitious animal, without destroying his original composition. The French, who have carried the *man of society* farther than other nations, no longer exhibit the naked passions. Their characters are all graduated. The *misanthrope* and the *avare* are exploded personages. *L'homme du jour ou les dehors trompeurs,*[7] *Le Glorieux,*[8] *Le Méchant,*[9] are the beings of artificial habitude, not the entities that would exist in a state of nature.[10] If any vice pre-

---

6 I.e., bank notes, paper currency. These had appeared in one form or another since late in the seventeenth century.

7 Comedy by Louis de Boissy, 1740.

8 Comedy by Destouches (Philippe Néricault), 1732.

9 By Jean-Baptiste-Louis Gresset, 1747.

10 This is so true, that the French, observing how much general passions are exhausted, have of late written pieces on compound characters, as the *Bourru Bienfaisant, L'Avare Fastueux,* &c. Such characters must arise in the advanced state of society, and may even be natural; but it requires great address and delicacy to manage them: and though it may not be universally true that there is a *ruling passion* in every man, it is still very improbable that two predominant passions should be so equally balanced as to produce such a contrast or opposition as the business of comedy may require: and yet unless the two contending passions are nearly equal in force, the superior or predominant one will relapse into the old comedy, which exhibited such a single passion or vice. The difficulty will be increased by these reflections; one of the passions in the compounded character may be, and probably is, an affected one; especially if the latter is at war with the ruling passion: for instance, an ostentatious miser can only *affect* generosity; for a generous man is not likely to act avarice, because, generosity being a quality esteemed, and covetousness held in aversion, the latter may be glad to conceal a vice; but few men are such good Christians as to disguise the beauty of their minds beneath an ugly mask. The parsimony then of the miser will certainly preponderate; and the poet's art must distinguish between his natural sordidness and adopted liberality, and must take care not to make the opposition farcical. Another difficulty will be, that compound characters cannot be general; and, therefore, when an author blends two passions, he will seem to draw a portrait rather than a character. Yet such compound of passions may open a new field, and enrich the province of comedy. The extensive mischiefs of ambition have appropriated that

dominates, it acts according to the rules within which it is circum-scribed by the laws of society. Ambition circumvents, not invades; lust tempts, but does not ravish. Ill-nature whispers, rather than accuses. Husbands and wives can hate, without scolding. A duel is transacted as civilly as a visit. Kings, instead of challenging, mourn for each other, though in open war.

Even the lower ranks of people could not be brought on the stage in this age, without softening the outline. A shopkeeper's daughter is a *young lady with a handsome fortune* and necessary *accomplishments*. Her brother *acts plays* for his diversion, is of a club, and games. Footmen have all the graces of their masters; and even highwaymen die genteelly.

One reads that in China even carmen make excuses to one another for stopping up the way. Half the time of the Chinese is passed in ceremony. I conclude their comedies cannot be very striking. Where one kind of polish runs through a whole nation, the operation of the passions must be less discernible. All common characters are not only exhausted, but concealed. In this nation we have certainly more characters than are seen in any other, owing perhaps to two causes, our liberty and the uncertainty of our climate. But this does not help the comic writer. Though he may every day meet with an original character, he cannot employ it—for, to be tasted, the humour must be common enough to be understood by the generality. Peculiarities in character are commonly affectations, and the affectation of a private or single person is not prey for the stage. I take Cimberton in *The Conscious Lovers* to be a portrait; probably a very resembling one— but as nobody knows the original, nobody can be much struck with the copy. Still, while the liberty of our government exists, there will be more originality in our manners than in those of other nations, though an inundation of politeness has softened our features as well as weakened our constitution. Englishmen used to exert their inde-pendence by a certain brutality, that was *not* honesty, but often produced it; for a man that piques himself on speaking truth grows to have a pride in not disgracing himself.

---

passion to tragedy; but might not very comic scenes be produced by representing *an ambitious miser* perpetually destroying his own views by grudging and saving the money, which, if expended, would promote his ambition? [Walpole's note. The two plays referred to, *The Kindly Boor* and *The Luxurious Miser,* are comedies derived from Carlo Goldoni, acted at Fontainebleau and Paris, 1771 and 1776. See Clarence D. Brenner, *A Bibliographical List of Plays in the French Language, 1700–1789,* Berkeley, 1947.]

As the great outlines of the passions are softened down by urbanity, fashionable follies usurp the place which belonged to criticism on characters; and when fashions are the object of ridicule, comedies soon grow obsolete and cease to be useful. Alchemy was the pursuit in vogue in the age of Ben Jonson; but, being a temporary folly, satire on it is no longer a lesson. Fashions pushed to excess produce a like excess in the reproof; and comedies degenerate into farce and buffoonery, when follies are exaggerated in the representation. The traits in *The Miser* that exhibit his extreme avarice are within the operation of the passions: in *The Alchemist* an epidemic folly, grown obsolete, is food for a commentator, not for an audience.

In fact, exaggeration is the fault of the author. If he is master enough of his talent to seize the precise truth of either passion or affectation, he will please more, though perhaps not at the first representation. Falstaff is a fictitious character, and would have been so had it existed in real life: yet his humour and his wit are so just, that they never have failed to charm all who are capable of tasting him in his own tongue.

Some lessons of the drama, or at least the shortness of its duration, have reduced even Shakespeare to precipitate his catastrophe. The reformation of the termagant wife in *The Taming of the Shrew* is too sudden. So are those of Margarita in *Rule a Wife and have a Wife*,[11] and of Lady Townly in *The Provoked Husband*.[12] Time or grace only operates such miracles.

In my own opinion, a good comedy, by the passions being exhausted, is at present the most difficult of all compositions, if it represents either nature or fictitious nature; I mean mankind in its present state of civilised society.

The enemies of *sentimental comedy* (or, as the French, the inventors, called it, *comédie larmoyante*) seem to think that the great business of comedy is to make the audience laugh. *That* may certainly be effected without nature or character. A Scot, an Irishman, a Mrs. Slipslop,[13] can always produce a laugh, at least from half the audience. For my part, I confess I am more disposed to weep than to laugh at such poor artifices. The advocates of merry comedy appeal to Molière. I appeal to him too. Which is his better comedy, The *Misanthrope,* or

---

11 By John Fletcher, produced in 1624.

12 *The Provok'd Husband, or a Journey to London* was written largely by Vanbrugh but finished by Cibber and produced in 1728.

13 The malapropian attendant of Lady Booby in Fielding's *Joseph Andrews*.

The *Bourgeois Gentilhomme?* The *Tartuffe,* or The *Etourdi?*[14] In reality, did not Molière in The *Misanthrope* give a pattern of serious comedy? What is finer than the serious scenes of Maskwell and Lady Touchwood in *The Double Dealer?* I do not take the *comédie larmoyante* to have been so much a deficience of pleasantry in its authors, as the effect of observation and reflection. Tragedy had been confined to the distresses of kings, princesses, and heroes; and comedy restrained to making us laugh at passions pushed to a degree of ridicule. In the former, as great personages only were concerned, language was elevated to suit their rank, rather than their sentiments; for real passion rarely talks in heroics. Had tragedy descended to people of subordinate stations, authors found the language would be too pompous. I should therefore think that the first man who gave a *comédie larmoyante,* rather meant to represent a melancholy story in private life, than merely to produce a comedy without mirth. If he had therefore not married two species then reckoned incompatible, that is tragedy and comedy, or, in other words, distress with a cheerful conclusion; and, instead of calling it *comédie larmoyante,* had named his new genus *tragédie mitigée,*[15] or, as the same purpose has since been styled, *tragédie bourgeoise;* he would have given a third species to the stage.

The French, who feel themselves and their genius cramped by the many impertinent shackles they have invented for authors, have taught these to escape, in those pieces which shake off all fetters, and leave genius and imagination at full liberty—I mean in their *comédie Italienne,* where under the *cannon* of Harlequin, and in defiance of all rules, they indulge their gaiety and invention. In short, a man who declares he writes without rules, may say what he pleases. If he invents happily, he succeeds, is indulged, and his piece lasts in spite of Aristotle and Bossu.[16] If he does not compensate by originality, fancy, wit, or nature, for scorning rule, the author is deservedly damned, at the sole expence to the public of having been tired by dulness for one evening.

I will finish this rhapsodical essay with remarking, that comedy is infinitely more difficult to an English than to a French man. Not only their language, so inferior in numbers, harmony and copiousness, to ours for poetry and eloquence, is far better adapted to conversation

---

14 *The Blunderer.*

15 Soft tragedy.

16 René le Bossu's *Traité du Poëme Epique,* 1675, was the most authoritative summation of neoclassic epic theory.

and dialogue; but all the French, especially of the higher ranks,[17] pique themselves on speaking their own language correctly and elegantly; the women especially. It was not till of late years with us that the language has been correctly spoken even in both houses of parliament. Before Addison and Swift, style was scarce aimed at even by our best authors. Dryden, whose prose was almost as harmonious and beautiful as his poetry, was not always accurate. Lord Shaftesbury[18] proved that when a man of quality soared above his peers, he wrote bombastly, turgidly, poetically. Lord Chatham[19] gave the tone to fine language in oratory. Within these very few years, our young orators are correct in their common conversation. Our ladies have not yet adopted the patronage of our language. Thence correct language in common conversation sounds pedantic or affected. Mr. Gray was so circumspect in his usual language, that it seemed unnatural, though it was only pure English. My inference is, that attention to the style in comedy runs a risk of not appearing easy. Yet I own *The Careless Husband* and Vanbrugh are standards—and *The School for Scandal* and *The Heiress*[20] have shewn that difficulties are no impediments to genius; and that, however passions and follies may be civilised, refined, or complicated, subjects for comedy are not wanting, and can be exhibited in the purest language of easy dialogue, without swelling to pedantry, or sinking to incorrectness. The authors of those two comedies have equalled Terence in the graces of style, and excelled him in wit and character: consequently we have better comedies than Greece or Rome enjoyed. It is even remarkable that the Grecians, who perfected poetry and eloquence, and invented tragedy and comedy, should have made so little progress in the last. Terence's plays, copied from Menander, convey little idea of that author's talent; and when so many of the farces of Aristophanes have been preserved, it is difficult to conceive that only a few scraps of Menander would have been transmitted to us, if his merit had been in proportion to the excellence of their tragic writers. Molière will probably be as immortal as Corneille and Racine.

---

[17] I include men of learning in the higher ranks, because in France they are admitted into the best company, who certainly give the tone to the elegance of any language, and in that sense only the highest company are the best company; for the term *best* has been ravished from the lowest ranks of men, who I doubt are the most virtuous of the community, and given to, or usurped by, the richest and most noble. [Walpole's note.]

[18] Cf. above, pp. 147–48.

[19] William Pitt, First Earl of Chatham (1708–78), great Whig statesman and orator.

[20] By John Burgoyne, 1786. Cf. above, p. 196.

CHARLES LAMB

[1775-1834]

A t the north end of Cross Court there yet stands a portal, of some architectural pretensions, though reduced to humble use, serving at present for an entrance to a printing-office. This old door-way, if you are young, reader, you may not know was the identical pit entrance to Old Drury—Garrick's Drury—all of it that is left. I never pass it without shaking some forty years from off my shoulders, recurring to the evening when I passed through it to see *my first play*. . . .

. . . When we got in, and I beheld the green curtain that veiled a heaven to my imagination, which was soon to be disclosed—the breathless anticipation I endured!

The orchestra lights at length arose, those "fair Auroras!" Once the bell sounded. It was to ring out yet once again—and, incapable of the anticipation, I reposed my shut eyes in a sort of resignation upon the maternal lap. It rang the second time. The curtain drew up—I was not past six years old—and the play was *Artaxerxes!*

My third play followed in quick succession. It was *The Way of the World*. I think I must have sat at it as grave as a judge; for, I remember, the hysteric affectations of good Lady Wishfort affected me like some solemn tragic passion.

I saw these plays in the season 1781–2, when I was from six to seven years old.

Charles Lamb, the child whose earliest experiences at Drury Lane we have just been quoting, from his reminiscence of forty years later, became, soon after those experiences, the schoolfellow of Samuel Taylor Coleridge at Christ's Hospital, where he stayed for his next seven years and saw no more plays ("for at school all play-going was inhibited"). The same essay, however, tells us, engagingly, not only of certain humble associations of his family with John Palmer, the comic actor, and Sheridan, the manager of Drury Lane, but of Lamb's return to the theater in his teens and, after the first shock given to his new rationalism by the realities of "a certain quantity of green baize" and the mere "clumsy machinery" of the orchestra lights, the

206

more considered and settled attraction which the scene came to exercise for him.

The most whimsically surefooted, the most playful, and yet the most serious of romantic prose writers, and today perhaps still the best loved of all English essayists, Lamb led a life of severe limitation, patient unambition, and tough endurance. Two years in the South Sea House, and he moved up (at the age of seventeen) to the Accountant's Office of the East India Company, where he worked at his job as a clerk until he was pensioned at the age of fifty (in 1825). "I have left the d———d India House for Ever!"[1] When he was twenty-one, his sister, Mary Ann, who did dressmaking jobs at home, had run amok with a knife in the family lodging in Little Queen Street, Holborn, and stabbed their invalid mother to the heart. Lamb himself a few months before had spent some time in a "lunatic asylum" recovering from a disappointment in love. He became the main support of his father and an aunt and for the rest of his life the guardian of his sister. A friend and early biographer gives us this well-known pathetic vignette:

> Whenever the approach of one of her fits of insanity was announced by some irritability or change of manner, he would take her under his arm to Hoxton Asylum...the young brother and sister walking together (weeping) on this painful errand, Mary herself, although sad, very conscious of the necessity of a temporary separation from her only friend. They used to carry a strait jacket with them.[2]

Lamb was short ("*petit* and ordinary in his person and appearance") and lame. He "stammered abominably" and was sometimes difficult in conversation, given, it would seem, either to reserved silences (perhaps when in the wrong company) or to spattering out jokes, "quaint aphorisms," and "poor quibbles," "senseless puns." He was exceedingly fond of gin-and-water.[3] He eked out his income by writing newspaper squibs. With his sister he wrote children's books: *Tales from Shakespear: Designed for the Use of Young Persons* (six tragedies by Charles, fourteen comedies by Mary), 1807; *The Adventures of Ulysses,* 1808. He was, at the same time, the friend of the poets

[1] To Henry Crabb Robinson, March 29, 1825 (*The Letters of Charles Lamb to Which Are Added Those of His Sister, Mary Lamb,* ed. E. V. Lucas, New Haven, 1935, II, 465). "I came home for ever on Tuesday in last week" (to William Wordsworth, April 6, 1825, *Letters,* II, 466).

[2] Bryan Waller Procter ("Barry Cornwall"), *Charles Lamb: A Memoir,* 1866, quoted in E. V. Lucas, *The Life of Charles Lamb* (London, 1921), I, 210–11.

[3] Details conflated from Lamb's Preface to *Last Essays of Elia* and from an autobiographical sketch contained in a letter of 1827 (to William Upcott, *Letters,* III, 82). The Preface is in a sense fictional but seems in the main corroborated as an autobiographical document by the letter.

Coleridge, Wordsworth, Southey, and Leigh Hunt, the essayist William Hazlitt, the painter Benjamin Haydon, and many more—a tireless and nervously interesting correspondent, and celebrated in an inner circle for his Wednesday evenings at home.[4]

His bent was antiquarian, and especially Elizabethan, and, as we have seen, theatrical. Such interests, such reading, shaped the now famous style which in the Preface to *Last Essays of Elia*, he imputes to that "poor gentleman," his "late friend," the author. "Crude," he says these writings are, "a sort of unlicked, incondite things—villainously pranked in an affected array of antique modes and phrases. They had not been *his,* if they had been other than such." He was (or liked to seem) prone to whimsical impulse or prejudice, snatches and moods. "There is an order of imperfect intellects (under which mine must be content to rank)...minds rather suggestive than comprehensive. They have no pretences to much clearness or precision in their ideas, or in their manner of expressing them...."[5] He tried his hand at a serious blank-verse drama, *John Woodvil,* published in 1802, and at a farce, *Mr. H.* (December 1806), hissed at Drury Lane. (Lamb himself joined in the hissing—perhaps was a leader.[6]) He wrote critical commentaries for a volume of favorite passages entitled *Specimens of English Dramatic Poets who Lived about the Time of Shakespeare,* published in 1808, and then a sustained, and for its time paradoxical, essay on *The Tragedies of Shakespeare Considered with Reference to their Fitness for Stage Representation,* published in Leigh Hunt's *Reflector,* No. IV, 1812.

In 1818 he brought out a collection of his own miscellaneous verse and prose under the title *The Works of Charles Lamb: in Two Volumes* [crown octavo]. "Pompously christened his Works," he said, "though in fact, they were his recreations; and his true works may be found on the shelves of Leaden Hall Street, filling some hundred folios."[7] It might have seemed to some that he had wound up a slender literary career. But in 1820 a new organ of the Cockney School and a rival to *Blackwood's,* the *London Magazine,* elicited the whimsically reflective vein for which Lamb is best known to posterity, in the series of his essays signed "Elia."[8] The recollections of his "First Play," from which

---

4 Hazlitt's essay "On the Conversation of Authors" (*London Magazine,* September 1820) looks back to "lively skirmishes" at Lamb's in a bygone era [c. 1806, *Letters,* II, 29, 59] and expatiates on Lamb's own peculiar powers as a conversationalist. "No one ever stammered out such fine, pregnant, deep, eloquent things in half a dozen half-sentences as he does. His jests scald like tears: and he probes a question with a play upon words."

5 *Imperfect Sympathies,* in *The Essays of Elia.*

6 Henry Crabb Robinson's *Diary,* cited in *Letters,* II, 31.

7 Sketch of 1827.

8 "The fact is, a person of that name, an Italian, was a fellow clerk of mine at the South Sea House, thirty...years ago, when the characters I described there

we have already quoted, were followed by three essays on "old actors" and the "artificial comedy" of the last century[9] (one of them in this volume). *The Essays of Elia* were collected as a volume in 1823. A further series, appearing in 1823–1825 and collected as *Last Essays of Elia* in 1833, includes an essay on *Stage Illusion* (in this volume).

Lamb's essays on the stage are reminiscential, in a mildly sad, nostalgic way, for the very good reason that by the time he wrote, in his mid-forties, the London stage was already far on the way toward a spectacular decline. True, it was an era of famous acting, and especially of Shakespearean acting—as we can read in Lamb's own reports. It was the fortune of Lamb and his friends to see John Philip Kemble as Hamlet, as Iago, as Romeo,[10] his sister Mrs. Siddons as Belvidera, as Lady Macbeth, as Jane Shore,[11] and their younger brother Charles Kemble as Charles Surface, as Falstaff, and as Mercutio.[12] They saw

---

existed" (to John Taylor, 30 June 1821, *Letters*, II, 302). The South Sea House was the topic of Lamb's first Elian essay.

[9] See below p. 215, n.

[10] Kemble played Hamlet, Macbeth, Iago, and Romeo during his long engagement at Drury Lane (1783–1802), and Hamlet and Iago again during his engagement at Covent Garden before the fire of 1808. For Lamb's estimate of Kemble's ability see *On the Artificial Comedy of the Last Century,* in this volume.

[11] Sarah Kemble Siddons first acted the part of Belvidera in Otway's *Venice Preserved* at Cheltenham in 1774, and again at Drury Lane in 1782. She first performed Lady Macbeth, triumphantly, in 1785. A sonnet by Lamb and Coleridge which appeared in the *Morning Chronicle* for December 29, 1794, testifies to Lamb's high opinion of her histrionic abilities, presumably in the part of Lady Macbeth:

> As when a child on some long Winter's night
> Affrighted clinging to its Grandam's knees
> With eager wond'ring and perturb'd delight
> Listens strange tales of fearful dark decrees
>   Mutter'd to wretch by necromantic spell;
> Or of those hags, who at the witching time
> Of murky Midnight ride the air sublime,
> And mingle foul embrace with fiends of Hell:
>   Cold Horror drinks its blood! Anon the tear
> More gentle starts, to hear the Beldame tell
> Of pretty Babes, that lov'd each other dear,
>   Murder'd by cruel Uncle's mandate fell:
>   Even such the shiv'ring joys thy tones impart,
>   Even so thou, *Siddons!* meltest my sad heart!

[12] Charles Kemble first played Charles Surface at Drury Lane in 1800. He began managing Covent Garden in 1822, where he played Falstaff in 1824. In 1829 his daughter Fanny Kemble played Juliet to her father's Mercutio at Covent Garden. See A. M. Nagler, *A Source Book in Theatrical History* (New York, 1952), pp. 451–59, for reports by the actor William Charles Macready, by Leigh Hunt, and by William Hazlitt, on the majestic classical style of John Philip Kemble and the romantic energy of his supplanter Edmund Kean. "We believe it was the opinion of a great many besides ourselves that Kean did extinguish Kemble" (Hunt).

Edmund Kean as Shylock (1814), his son Charles John as Young
Norval in *Douglas* (1819) and soon after as King Lear. It was an era
too of physical expansiveness. Drury Lane had been rebuilt in progressive grandeur in 1792–1794, and in 1812, after a fire of 1809.
Covent Garden had been enlarged as early as 1787 and rebuilt in
1792, and again in 1809, after a fire the year before.[13] In the vast
spaces of these two royally licensed "major" theaters—with their poor
illumination and lofty galleries and hence boldly fronted apron stages—
the productions ran to immense scenic effects (gorgeous tableaux and
ensembles), powerful choruses and music, and strenuously declamatory
acting. Even Shakespeare's characters seemed designed primarily as
vehicles for the assertive personality and rhetoric of those mighty
Thespians.

Such external magnification was in obvious ways not a scrupulous
correlative of any internal or aesthetic finesse—as Lamb and some
other literary spirits of the time were heard to complain. During these
latter years of the reign of the aged George III and the Regency, the
theaters, in one respect reverting to Elizabethan and Restoration
phases, became once more places of fashionable debauchery and much
ill repute. A dissolute part of the *bourgeoisie* aped an upper class that
was libertine and vulgar. A biography of John Philip Kemble, published
in 1825, two years after the actor-manager's death, gives us the vignette
of an evening at Covent Garden in 1806 when an apple arrived on the
stage, falling just between Kemble, playing the part of the conqueror
Coriolanus, and his distinguished sister Mrs. Siddons, playing that of
his mother Volumnia, at the height of her impassioned plea *pro patria*.
A person in the audience had launched this missile at some "disorderly
females in the boxes."

The dominant forms of original writing for the stage (already
established toward the end of the eighteenth century) were romantic
(or Gothic) melodrama (on German models), domestic drama (sentimental, humanitarian, heavily moral), and, complementing these in
the department of the laughable, comic opera (the sprawling descendant
of Gay's masterpiece), burlesque, farce, and pantomime. Charles
Lamb's friend Leigh Hunt in his *Autobiography* (1850) recollected
of the year 1805 that the theater had gone "commercial" in its subjects—"nothing but gentlemen in distress and hard landlords, and
generous interferers, and fathers who got a great deal of money, and
sons who spent it."[14] Lamb himself complained of an "insipid levelling
morality...a puritanical obtuseness of sentiment, a stupid infantile

---

[13] See Nagler, *Source Book,* pp. 447–51, on Covent Garden (1808) and Drury
Lane (1812).

[14] *Autobiography,* ed. Edmund Blunden (Oxford, 1928), p. 196.

goodness." "Our audiences come to the theatre to be complimented on their goodness. They compare notes with the amiable characters in the play, and find a wonderful sympathy of disposition between them."[15] It was a time when men of letters and men of the theater drew apart to an unprecedented distance from each other. The best poets *all* tried their hand at dramas, but the genius of these poets was in fact lyric, meditative, and descriptive. Lamb's Elizabethan tragedy *Woodvil*, to which we have alluded, is part of a cycle of such unactable and mostly unacted serious plays running through two generations of English literature, from Wordsworth to Tennyson.[16]

The circumstance of his writing in nostalgic reminiscence of a bygone (and now almost dreamlike) era had much to do with a second central feature of Lamb's thought about the stage—his preoccupation with problems of physical illusion and reality. This was a theme established as a classic of English speculation from the time of Dryden's debate with his brother-in-law Sir Robert Howard about the supposedly verisimilitudinous unities of time and place. Shrewdly skeptical arguments had been urged by George Farquhar in his *Discourse on Comedy* of 1702,[17] and by Samuel Johnson in his Shakespeare *Preface* of 1765. ("Time is, of all modes of existence, most obsequious to the imagination.") A sort of balance in favor of illusion in a broader sense had been asserted by Coleridge in Chapter XIV of his *Biographia Literaria* (1817), with his memorable phrase: "that willing suspension of disbelief for the moment, which constitutes poetic faith." The simple truth for Lamb was that he did not relish a very stark confrontation with verisimilitude, either in tragedy or in comedy. In what is probably

---

15 Note on Thomas Middleton's *A Fair Quarrel,* in Lamb's *Specimens of English Dramatic Poets Who Lived about the Time of Shakespeare,* 1808, rearranged for Lamb's *Works,* 1818 (*The Works of Charles and Mary Lamb,* ed. E. V. Lucas, London, 1903, I, 46).

16 Allardyce Nicoll, *British Drama* (New York, 1933), pp. 301–33, surveys this period in English theatrical history. See p. 302, the incident from Boaden's *Life of Kemble* adduced above, and pp. 313–15, his assessment of Shelley's *Cenci* (1819) and Byron's dramas. See also Harold Child, "Nineteenth Century Drama," *The Cambridge History of English Literature,* XIII, ed. A. W. Ward and A. R. Waller (Cambridge, 1916), 257.

17 "Why should a Poet fetter the Business of his Plot, and starve his Action, for the nicety of an Hour or the Change of a Scene; since the Thought of Man can fly over a Thousand Years with the same Ease, and in the same Instant of Time, that your Eye glances from the Figure of Six, to Seven, on the Dial-Plate; and can glide from the *Cape of Good-Hope* to the *Bay of St. Nicholas,* which is quite cross the World, with the same Quickness and Activity, as between *Covent-Garden Church,* and *Will's Coffee-House*" (*Critical Essays of the Eighteenth Century,* ed. W. H. Durham, New Haven, 1915, p. 285). See Sylvan Barnet, "Charles Lamb's Contribution to the Theory of Dramatic Illusion," *PMLA,* LXIX (December 1954), 1150–59.

his most celebrated critical essay, that on the acting of Shakespeare's tragedies (1811), he expounds the view that stage production only externalizes and superficializes Shakespeare's plays, purchasing the cheap effects of vividness and violence at the expense of interior spiritual values.

> ...When we no longer read it in a book, when we have given up that vantage-ground of abstraction which reading possesses over seeing, and come to see a man [Macbeth] in his bodily shape before our eyes actually preparing to commit a murder, if the acting be true and impressive, as I have witnessed it in Mr. K.'s[18] performance of that part, the painful anxiety about the act...the two close pressing semblance of reality, give a pain and an uneasiness which totally destroy all the delight which the words in the book convey.

> So to see Lear acted,—to see an old man tottering about the stage with a walking-stick, turned out of doors by his daughters in a rainy night, has nothing in it but what is painful and disgusting.... But the Lear of Shakespeare cannot be acted.... The greatness of Lear is not in corporal dimension, but in intellectual: the explosions of his passion are terrible as a volcano.[19]

At the end of this Shakespeare essay Lamb ventures: "It would be no very difficult task to extend the enquiry to his comedies; and to shew why Falstaff, Shallow, Sir Hugh Evans, and the rest, are equally incompatible with stage representation." If this statement were repeated at the beginning of the Elian essay on *Artificial Comedy*, it would imply or require a very marked distinction between Shakespeare and Congreve or Sheridan in respect to fitness for the stage. For the essay on comedy not only concedes, it seems to insist on, the role of Lamb's "old actors" in conjuring up the kind of unreality and release from practical life norms which either was the condition of his aesthetic response to these "immoral" plays or was in fact the essence of that happily delusive experience. The two essays, on the whole, if taken together, may require indeed some further explanation or apology, for in the earlier, as we have just seen, tragedy, through the sheer shock of its outward content, is unfit for physical presentation (*incredulus odi*), but in the later, tragedy makes a seriously emotive appeal which *needs* the immediacy of physical realization— even as comedy in the old days, but for an opposite reason, had seemed to benefit by that realization. In yet another essay, entitled at first *Imperfect Dramatic Illusion*, and then more simply *Stage*

---

18 John Philip Kemble (1757–1823), dean of declamatory actors, opened the rebuilt Drury Lane theater in 1794 in the title role of *Macbeth*. His younger brother Charles Kemble played Malcolm.

19 *Works,* ed. Lucas, I, 107.

Illusion, in his later series *Last Essays of Elia,* Lamb would return to the congenial theme of the comic actor's connivance with the audience. (See below, pp. 224–27.) The masterly and now celebrated treatise on the actor's detachment by the French philosopher Diderot, *Paradoxe sur le Comédien,* had been written (in a first draft) as early as 1770 but was not published until 1830.

It is probably best to try to look into Lamb's delicate insights only so far as they extend, and not to try too hard to systematize him. For litterateurs of the Victorian tradition he was a critic who opened vistas for the soul. For that reason his ideas about the old comedy of manners have not been the most highly relished. They have often been avoided by the compilers, or more than his other ideas have been assigned to his amateurishness, his caprice, his narrow range, his quaintness. It is not an issue to be argued very earnestly, with proof or counterproof. More than most mortals, Lamb had known something both of harder reality and of certain kinds of pathological escape from reality—he had known "weakness...reliance, and the shadow of imbecility."[20] As Elia he wrote not only about "stage illusion" but about the "sanity of genius." In his essay on comedy he contrives a cunning intimation of a view which metaphysicians from the time at least of Kant's third *Critique* (1790), if not indeed from the time of Aquinas or Aristotle, have labored to promote. Favorite modern names of what Lamb is talking about are "disinterest," "distance," "detachment."

A year before Lamb began his essays signed "Elia" in *The London Magazine,* his friend William Hazlitt, a lecturer and essayist of much deeper resonance, delivered at the Surrey Institution in London his *Lectures on the English Comic Writers* to which we have already alluded.[21] Lamb disliked listening to lectures and probably did not attend these.[22] But they were available in print in the same year. Hazlitt was a scholar who more than Lamb was likely to be interested in the dialectic of history, in cycles of culture and literature—after the manner of Lamb's "genteel" writer Sir William Temple, or of the more recent historian of English poetry Thomas Warton. In his fourth lecture of the series, *On Wycherley, Congreve, Vanbrugh, and Farquhar,* Hazlitt manages to see Restoration comedy in a shimmering double light, both as airy fantasy and as satiric copy of the vices indigenous to that age.

---

[20] See *Dream Children* in *Essays of Elia* (*Works,* ed. Lucas, II, 100). Lamb's essay *On the Genius and Character of Hogarth* (1811) is a loving vindication of the pictorial comic vision which we have seen recognized briefly by Fielding in the Preface to *Joseph Andrews* (1742; above p. 156).

[21] Above p. 197, n. 14.

[22] *Letters,* II, 227, alluding to Coleridge's lectures of 1818 on Shakespeare and Hazlitt's *On the English Poets.*

Comedy is a "graceful ornament to the civil order; the Corinthian
capital of polished society." Like the mirrors which have been added
to the sides of one of our theatres, it reflects the images of grace, of
gaiety, and pleasure double, and completes the perspective of human
life. To read a good comedy is to keep the best company in the world,
where the best things are said, and the most amusing happen. The
wittiest remarks are always on the tongue, and the liveliest occasions
are always at hand to give birth to the happiest conceptions. Sense
makes strange havoc of nonsense. Refinement acts as a foil to affectation,
and affectation to ignorance. Sentence after sentence tells. We don't know
which to admire most, the observation, or the answer to it. We would
give our fingers to be able to talk so ourselves, or to hear others talk
so. In turning over the pages of the best comedies, we are almost transported to another world, and escape from this dull age to one that was
all life, and whim, and mirth, and humour. The curtain rises, and a
gayer scene presents itself, as on the canvas of Watteau. We are
admitted behind the scenes like spectators at courts, on a levee or
birth-day; but it is the court, the gala day of wit and pleasure, of
gallantry and Charles II! What an air breathes from the name! what
a rustling of silks and waving of plumes! what a sparkling of diamond
ear-rings and shoe-buckles! What bright eyes, (ah, those were Waller's
Sacharissa's[23] as she passed!) what killing looks and graceful motions!
How the faces of the whole ring are dressed in smiles! how the repartee
goes round! how wit and folly, elegance and awkward imitation of it,
set one another off! Happy, thoughtless age, when kings and nobles led
purely ornamental lives; when the utmost stretch of a morning's study
went no farther than the choice of a sword-knot, or the adjustment of
a side-curl; when the soul spoke out in all the pleasing eloquence of
dress; and beaux and belles, enamoured of themselves in one another's
follies, fluttered like gilded butterflies, in giddy mazes, through the
walks of St. James's Park![24]

---

[23] Lady Dorothy Sidney, before her marriage to Henry Lord Spencer in 1639,
had been courted at her ancestral home Penshurst by the poet Edmund Waller
(1606–1687). She became famous as "Sacharissa," the object of celebration in many
of his love lyrics.

[24] William Hazlitt, *Lectures on the English Comic Writers. Delivered at the
Surrey Institution* (London, 1819), pp. 133–34, Lecture IV, first paragraph.

On the Artificial Comedy
of the Last Century

[*1822*]

The artificial Comedy, or Comedy of manners, is quite extinct on our stage. Congreve and Farquhar show their heads once in seven years only, to be exploded and put down instantly. The times cannot bear them. Is it for a few wild speeches, an occasional licence of dialogue? I think not altogether. The business of their dramatic characters will not stand the moral test. We screw every thing up to that. Idle gallantry in a fiction, a dream, the passing pageant of an evening, startles us in the same way as the alarming indications of profligacy in a son or ward in real life should startle a parent or guardian. We have no such middle emotions as dramatic interests left. We see a stage libertine playing his loose pranks of two hours' duration, and of no after consequence, with the severe eyes which inspect real vices with their bearings upon two worlds. We are spectators to a plot or intrigue (not reducible in life to the point of strict morality) and take it all for truth. We substitute a real for a dramatic person, and judge him accordingly. We try him in our courts, from which there is no appeal to the *dramatis personæ,* his peers. We have been spoiled with—not sentimental comedy—but a tyrant far more pernicious to our pleasures which has succeeded to it, the exclusive and all-devouring drama of common life; where the moral point is every thing; where, instead of the fictitious half-believed personages of the stage (the phantoms of old comedy) we recognise ourselves, our brothers, aunts, kinsfolk, allies, patrons, enemies,—the same as in life,—with an interest in what

---

Lamb's three essays on the old comedies originally appeared in the *London Magazine* in February, April, and October 1822, under the single title *The Old Actors.* They were revised and somewhat shortened for the collected *Essays* of 1823, under three new titles:—*On Some of the Old Actors, On the Artificial Comedy of the Last Century,* and *On the Acting of Munden.* The essays have always been republished in the revised form. Our text follows the first edition of *Elia, Essays which have Appeared under That Signature in the London Magazine.* London: Printed for Taylor and Hessey...1823.

is going on so hearty and substantial, that we cannot afford our moral judgment, in its deepest and most vital results, to compromise or slumber for a moment. What is *there* transacting, by no modification is made to affect us in any other manner than the same events or characters would do in our relationships of life. We carry our fireside concerns to the theatre with us. We do not go thither, like our ancestors, to escape from the pressure of reality, so much as to confirm our experience of it; to make assurance double, and take a bond of fate.[1] We must live our toilsome lives twice over, as it was the mournful privilege of Ulysses to descend twice to the shades. All that neutral ground of character, which stood between vice and virtue; or which in fact was indifferent to neither, where neither properly was called in question; that happy breathing-place from the burthen of a per-petual moral questioning—the sanctuary and quiet Alsatia[2] of hunted casuistry—is broken up and disfranchised, as injurious to the interests of society. The privileges of the place are taken away by law. We dare not dally with images, or names, of wrong. We bark like foolish dogs at shadows. We dread infection from the scenic representation of disorder; and fear a painted pustule. In our anxiety that our morality should not take cold, we wrap it up in a great blanket surtout of precaution against the breeze and sunshine.

I confess for myself that (with no great delinquencies to answer for) I am glad for a season to take an airing beyond the diocese of the strict conscience,—not to live always in the precincts of the law-courts,—but now and then, for a dream-while or so, to imagine a world with no meddling restrictions—to get into recesses, whither the hunter cannot follow me—

——————— Secret shades
Of woody Ida's inmost grove,
While yet there was no fear of Jove—[3]

I come back to my cage and my restraint the fresher and more healthy for it. I wear my shackles more contentedly for having respired the breath of an imaginary freedom. I do not know how it is with others,

---

[1] *Macbeth,* IV.i.83–84:

But yet I'll make assurance double sure,
And take a bond of fate.

[2] "Alsatia" was a name for the precinct of Whitefriars in London, until 1697 a sanctuary for debtors and lawbreakers—from Alsace, the debatable area between France and Germany. This is the Alsatia of Shadwell's play *The Squire of Alsatia* (1688; cf. above p. 63).

[3] *Il Penseroso,* 28–30.

but I feel the better always for the perusal of one of Congreve's—
nay, why should I not add even of Wycherley's—comedies. I am the
gayer at least for it; and I could never connect those sports of a witty
fancy in any shape with any result to be drawn from them to imitation
in real life. They are a world of themselves almost as much as fairyland.
Take one of their characters, male or female (with few exceptions they
are alike), and place it in a modern play, and my virtuous indignation
shall rise against the profligate wretch as warmly as the Catos[4] of the
pit could desire; because in a modern play I am to judge of the right
and the wrong. The standard of *police* is the measure of *political
justice*. The atmosphere will blight it, it cannot live here. It has got
into a moral world, where it has no business, from which it must needs
fall head long; as dizzy, and incapable of making a stand, as a
Swedenborgian bad spirit that has wandered unawares into the sphere
of one of his Good Men, or Angels.[5] But in its own world do we feel
the creature is so very bad?—The Fainalls and the Mirabels,[6] the
Dorimants[7] and the Lady Touchwoods,[8] in their own sphere, do not
offend my moral sense; in fact they do not appeal to it at all. They
seem engaged in their proper element. They break through no laws,
or conscientious restraints. They know of none. They have got out of
Christendom into the land—what shall I call it?—of cuckoldry—the
Utopia of gallantry, where pleasure is duty, and the manners perfect
freedom. It is altogether a speculative scene of things, which has no
reference whatever to the world that is. No good person can be justly
offended as a spectator, because no good person suffers on the stage.
Judged morally, every character in these plays—the few exceptions
only are *mistakes*—is alike essentially vain and worthless. The great
art of Congreve is especially shown in this, that he has entirely excluded
from his scenes,—some little generosities in the part of Angelica[9]
perhaps excepted,—not only any thing like a faultless character, but
any pretensions to goodness or good feelings whatsoever. Whether he
did this designedly, or instinctively, the effect is as happy, as the

---

4 Cato the Roman Censor (234–149 B.C.) was famous for his opposition to
luxurious fashions.
5 In the system of Emanuel Swedenborg (1688–1772), Swedish visionary philosopher, there are three heavens and three hells, the first three peopled by good
spirits, the second by evil.
6 Fainall and Mirabel are charatcers in Congreve's *The Way of the World*
(1700).
7 A character in Etherege's *The Man of Mode* (1676).
8 In Congreve's *The Double Dealer* (1694).
9 In Congreve's *Love for Love* (1695).

design (if design) was bold. I used to wonder at the strange power which his *Way of the World* in particular possesses of interesting you all along in the pursuits of characters, for whom you absolutely care nothing—for you neither hate nor love his personages—and I think it is owing to this very indifference for any, that you endure the whole. He has spread a privation of moral light, I will call it, rather than by the ugly name of palpable darkness,[10] over his creations; and his shadows flit before you without distinction or preference. Had he introduced a good character, a single gush of moral feeling, a revulsion of the judgment to actual life and actual duties, the impertinent Goshen[11] would have only lighted to the discovery of deformities, which now are none, because we think them none.

Translated into real life, the characters of his, and his friend Wycherley's dramas, are profligates and strumpets,—the business of their brief existence, the undivided pursuit of lawless gallantry. No other spring of action, or possible motive of conduct, is recognised; principles which, universally acted upon, must reduce this frame of things to a chaos. But we do them wrong in so translating them. No such effects are produced in *their* world. When we are among them, we are amongst a chaotic people. We are not to judge them by our usages. No reverend institutions are insulted by their proceedings,—for they have none among them. No peace of families is violated,—for no family ties exist among them. No purity of the marriage bed is stained,—for none is supposed to have a being. No deep affections are disquieted,— no holy wedlock bands are snapped asunder,—for affection's depth and wedded faith are not of the growth of that soil. There is neither right nor wrong,—gratitude or its opposite,—claim or duty,—paternity or sonship. Of what consequence is it to virtue, or how is she at all concerned about it, whether Sir Simon, or Dapperwit, steal away Miss Martha;[12] or who is the father of Lord Froth's, or Sir Paul Pliant's children.[13]

The whole is a passing pageant, where we should sit as unconcerned at the issues, for life or death, as at a battle of the frogs and mice. But, like Don Quixote, we take part against the puppets, and quite

---

10 *Paradise Lost,* I.63:
              No light, but rather darkness visible.
11 Land of plenty allotted to the Israelites (Exodus, VIII.22).
12 In Wycherley's *Love in a Wood* (1671).
13 In *The Double Dealer.*

as impertinently. We dare not contemplate an Atlantis,[14] a scheme, out of which our coxcombical moral sense is for a little transitory ease excluded. We have not the courage to imagine a state of things for which there is neither reward nor punishment. We cling to the painful necessities of shame and blame. We would indict our very dreams.

Amidst the mortifying circumstances attendant upon growing old, it is something to have seen *The School for Scandal* in its glory. This comedy grew out of Congreve and Wycherley, but gathered some allays of the sentimental comedy which followed theirs. It is impossible that it should be now *acted,* though it continues, at long intervals, to be announced in the bills. Its hero, when Palmer[15] played it at least, was Joseph Surface. When I remember the gay boldness, the graceful solemn plausibility, the measured step, the insinuating voice—to express it in a word—the downright *acted* villainy of the part, so different from the pressure of conscious actual wickedness,—the hypocritical assumption of hypocrisy,—which made Jack so deservedly a favourite in that character, I must needs conclude the present generation of play-goers more virtuous than myself, or more dense. I freely confess that he divided the palm with me with his better brother; that, in fact, I liked him quite as well. Not but there are passages,—like that, for instance, where Joseph is made to refuse a pittance to a poor relation, —incongruities which Sheridan was forced upon by the attempt to join the artificial with the sentimental comedy, either of which must destroy the other—but over these obstructions Jack's manner floated him so lightly, that a refusal from him no more shocked you, than the easy compliance of Charles gave you in reality any pleasure; you got over the paltry question as quickly as you could, to get back into the regions of pure comedy, where no cold moral reigns. The highly artificial manner of Palmer in this character counteracted every disagreeable impression which you might have received from the contrast, supposing them real, between the two brothers. You did not believe in Joseph with the same faith with which you believed in Charles. The latter was a pleasant reality, the former a no less pleasant poetical foil to it. The comedy, I have said, is incongruous; a mixture of Congreve with sentimental incompatibilities: the gaiety upon the

---

14 In Plato's *Timaeus,* a fabulous, beautiful, and prosperous island in the ocean west of the Pillars of Hercules.

15 John Palmer (1742?–1798), celebrated actor of high comedy, an associate of Lamb's "godfather F.," as Lamb tells us in the essay on his *First Play.*

whole is buoyant; but it required the consummate art of Palmer to reconcile the discordant elements.

A player with Jack's talents, if we had one now, would not dare to do the part in the same manner. He would instinctively avoid every turn which might tend to unrealise, and so to make the character fascinating. He must take his cue from his spectators, who would expect a bad man and a good man as rigidly opposed to each other as the death-beds of those geniuses are contrasted in the prints, which I am sorry to say have disappeared from the windows of my old friend Carrington Bowles, of St. Paul's Church-yard memory—(an exhibition as venerable as the adjacent cathedral, and almost coeval) of the bad and good man at the hour of death; where the ghastly apprehensions of the former,—and truly the grim phantom with his reality of a toasting fork is not to be despised,—so finely contrast with the meek complacent kissing of the rod,—taking it in like honey and butter,—with which the latter submits to the scythe of the gentle bleeder, Time, who wields his lancet with the apprehensive finger of a popular young ladies' surgeon. What flesh, like loving grass, would not covet to meet half-way the stroke of such a delicate mower?—John Palmer was twice an actor in this exquisite part. He was playing to you all the while that he was playing upon Sir Peter and his lady.[16] You had the first intimation of a sentiment before it was on his lips. His altered voice was meant to you, and you were to suppose that his fictitious co-flutterers on the stage perceived nothing at all of it. What was it to you if that half-reality, the husband, was over-reached by the puppetry —or the thin thing (Lady Teazle's reputation) was persuaded it was dying of a plethory? The fortunes of Othello and Desdemona were not concerned in it. Poor Jack has past from the stage in good time, that he did not live to this our age of seriousness. The pleasant old Teazle *King*,[17] too, is gone in good time. His manner would scarce have past current in our day. We must love or hate—acquit or condemn— censure or pity—exert our detestable coxcombry of moral judgment upon every thing. Joseph Surface, to go down now, must be a downright revolting villain—no compromise—his first appearance must shock and give horror—his specious plausibilities, which the pleasurable faculties of our fathers welcomed with such hearty greetings, knowing

16 A similar encomium of Palmer and of John Bannister as Ben in Congreve's *Love for Love* appears near the end of the first of Lamb's three essays, *On Some of the Old Actors.*

17 Thomas King (1730–1805) played Sir Peter Teazle in the first production of *The School for Scandal* in 1777.

that no harm (dramatic harm even) could come, or was meant to come of them, must inspire a cold and killing aversion. Charles (the real canting person of the scene—for the hypocrisy of Joseph has its ulterior legitimate ends, but his brother's professions of a good heart centre in downright self-satisfaction) must be *loved,* and Joseph *hated.* To balance one disagreeable reality with another, Sir Peter Teazle must be no longer the comic idea of a fretful old bachelor bride-groom, whose teasings (while King acted it) were evidently as much played off at you, as they were meant to concern any body on the stage,— he must be a real person, capable in law of sustaining an injury— a person towards whom duties are to be acknowledged—the genuine crim-con antagonist of the villainous seducer Joseph. To realise him more, his sufferings under his unfortunate match must have the down-right pungency of life—must (or should) make you not mirthful but uncomfortable, just as the same predicament would move you in a neighbour or old friend. The delicious scenes which give the play its name and zest, must affect you in the same serious manner as if you heard the reputation of a dear female friend attacked in your real presence. Crabtree, and Sir Benjamin—those poor snakes that live but in the sunshine of your mirth—must be ripened by this hot-bed process of realisation into asps or amphisbænas;[18] and Mrs. Candour—O! frightful!—become a hooded serpent. Oh who that remembers Parsons[19] and Dodd[20]—the wasp and butterfly of *The School for Scandal*—in those two characters; and charming natural Miss Pope,[21] the perfect gentlewoman as distinguished from the fine lady of comedy, in this latter part—would forego the true scenic delight—the escape from life —the oblivion of consequences—the holiday barring out of the pedant Reflection—those Saturnalia of two or three brief hours, well won from the world—to sit instead at one of our modern plays—to have his coward conscience (that forsooth must not be left for a moment) stimulated with perpetual appeals—dulled rather, and blunted, as a faculty without repose must be—and his moral vanity pampered with images of notional justice, notional beneficence, lives saved without the

---

18 *Paradise Lost,* X.524:
                  Scorpion and Asp, and Amphisbaena dire.
19 William Parsons (1736–1795) was associated with the Drury Lane Theater after 1762.
20 James William Dodd (1740?–1795) first appeared at the Drury Lane Theater in 1765. Lamb praised him elsewhere for his Sir Andrew Aguecheek in *Twelfth Night.*
21 Jane Pope (1742–1818) first appeared at Drury Lane in 1756; she remained until her retirement in 1808. Hazlitt and Leigh Hunt also praised her.

spectators' risk, and fortunes given away that cost the author nothing?

No piece was, perhaps, ever so completely cast in all its parts as this *manager's comedy*.[22] Miss Farren[23] had succeeded to Mrs. Abington[24] in Lady Teazle; and Smith,[25] the original Charles, had retired, when I first saw it. The rest of the characters, with very slight exceptions, remained. I remember it was then the fashion to cry down John Kemble,[26] who took the part of Charles after Smith; but, I thought, very unjustly. Smith, I fancy, was more airy, and took the eye with a certain gaiety of person. He brought with him no sombre recollections of tragedy. He had not to expiate the fault of having pleased beforehand in lofty declamation. He had no sins of Hamlet or of Richard to atone for. His failure in these parts was a passport to success in one of so opposite a tendency. But, as far as I could judge, the weighty sense of Kemble made up for more personal incapacity than he had to answer for. His harshest tones in this part came steeped and dulcified in good humour. He made his defects a grace. His exact declamatory manner, as he managed it, only served to convey the points of his dialogue with more precision. It seemed to head the shafts to carry them deeper. Not one of his sparkling sentences was lost. I remember minutely how he delivered each in succession, and cannot by any effort imagine how any of them could be altered for the better. No man could deliver brilliant dialogue—the dialogue of Congreve or of Wycherley—because none understood it—half so well as John Kemble. His Valentine, in *Love for Love*, was, to my recollection, faultless. He flagged sometimes in the intervals of tragic passion. He would slumber over the level parts of an heroic character. His Macbeth has been known to nod. But he always seemed to me to be particularly alive to pointed and witty dialogue. The relaxing levities of tragedy have not been touched by any since him—the playful court-bred spirit in which he condescended to the players in Hamlet—the sportive relief which he threw into the darker shades of Richard—disappeared with him.

---

22 Sheridan replaced Garrick as manager of Drury Lane in 1776, the year before he produced *The School for Scandal*. Cf. above, p. 195.

23 Elizabeth Farren, later Countess of Derby, appeared at Drury Lane in 1778. See above p. 196, n. 13.

24 Mrs. Abington had moved from Drury Lane to Covent Garden in 1782.

25 William Smith (1730?–1819) was considered unsurpassable in the part of Charles Surface at the Drury Lane Theater in 1788.

26 John Philip Kemble (1757–1823) made his reputation as a tragic actor. From 1782 to 1802 he acted more than 120 characters, including Charles Surface, at the Drury Lane Theater.

He had his sluggish moods, his torpors—but they were the halting-stones and resting-places of his tragedy—politic savings, and fetches of the breath—husbandry of the lungs, where nature pointed him to be an economist—rather, I think, than errors of the judgment. They were, at worst, less painful than the eternal tormenting unappeasable vigilance, the "lidless dragon eyes,"[27] of present fashionable tragedy.

---

[27] From Coleridge's *Ode on the Departing Year,* Stanza VIII.

Stage Illusion

[*1825*]

A play is said to be well or ill acted in proportion to the scenical illusion produced. Whether such illusion can in any case be perfect, is not the question. The nearest approach to it, we are told, is, when the actor appears wholly unconscious of the presence of spectators. In tragedy—in all which is to affect the feelings—this undivided attention to his stage business, seems indispensable. Yet it is, in fact, dispensed with every day by our cleverest tragedians; and while these references to an audience, in the shape of rant or sentiment, are not too frequent or palpable, a sufficient quantity of illusion for the purposes of dramatic interest may be said to be produced in spite of them. But, tragedy apart, it may be inquired whether, in certain characters in comedy, especially those which are a little extravagant, or which involve some notion repugnant to the moral sense, it is not a proof of the highest skill in the comedian when, without absolutely appealing to an audience, he keeps up a tacit understanding with them; and makes them, unconsciously to themselves, a party in the scene. The utmost nicety is required in the mode of doing this; but we speak only of the great artists in the profession.

The most mortifying infirmity in human nature, to feel in ourselves, or to contemplate in another, is, perhaps, cowardice. To see a coward *done to the life* upon a stage would produce anything but mirth. Yet we most of us remember Jack Bannister's cowards.[1] Could any thing be more agreeable, more pleasant? We loved the rogues. How was this effected but by the exquisite art of the actor in a perpetual sub-insinuation to us, the spectators, even in the extremity of the shaking fit, that he was not half such a coward as we took him for? We saw all the common symptoms of the malady upon him; the quivering lip,

---

Stage Illusion first appeared in the *London Magazine* for August 1825 under the title *Imperfect Dramatic Illusion*. It was apparently Lamb's last contribution. Our text follows the essay in *The Last Essays of Elia,* London: Edward Moxon, 1833.

[1] John Bannister (1760–1836) retired from the stage in 1815. His Bob Acres in *The Rivals* was famous.

224

the cowering knees, the teeth chattering; and could have sworn "that man was frightened."[2] But we forgot all the while—or kept it almost a secret to ourselves—that he never once lost his self-possession; that he let out by a thousand droll looks and gestures—meant at *us,* and not at all supposed to be visible to his fellows in the scene, that his confidence in his own resources had never once deserted him. Was this a genuine picture of a coward? or not rather a likeness, which the clever artist contrived to palm upon us instead of an original; while we secretly connived at the delusion for the purpose of greater pleasure, than a more genuine counterfeiting of the imbecility, helplessness, and utter self-desertion, which we know to be concomitants of cowardice in real life, could have given us?

Why are misers so hateful in the world, and so endurable on the stage, but because the skilful actor, by a sort of sub-reference, rather than direct appeal to us, disarms the character of a great deal of its odiousness, by seeming to engage *our* compassion for the insecure tenure by which he holds his money bags and parchments? By this subtle vent half of the hatefulness of the character—the self-closeness with which in real life it coils itself up from the sympathies of men— evaporates. The miser becomes sympathetic; *i.e.* is no genuine miser. Here again a diverting likeness is substituted for a very disagreeable reality.

Spleen, irritability—the pitiable infirmities of old men, which produce only pain to behold in the realities, counterfeited upon a stage, divert not altogether for the comic appendages to them, but in part from an inner conviction that they are *being acted* before us; that a likeness only is going on, and not the thing itself. They please by being done under the life, or beside it; not *to the life.* When Gattie[3] acts an old man, is he angry indeed? or only a pleasant counterfeit, just enough of a likeness to recognise, without pressing upon us the uneasy sense of reality?

Comedians, paradoxical as it may seem, may be too natural. It was the case with a late actor. Nothing could be more earnest or true than the manner of Mr. Emery; this told excellently in his Tyke, and

[2] In Fielding's *Tom Jones,* Book XVI, Chapter v, the country schoolmaster Partridge sees Garrick act Hamlet and at the ghost scene becomes frightened. "You may call me coward if you will; but if that little man there upon the stage is not frightened, I never saw any man frightened in my life."

[3] Henry Gattie (1774–1844) was the best Dr. Caius of his day in Shakespeare's *Merry Wives of Windsor.*

characters of a tragic cast.[4] But when he carried the same rigid exclusiveness of attention to the stage business, and wilful blindness and oblivion of everything before the curtain into his comedy, it produced a harsh and dissonant effect. He was out of keeping with the rest of the *Personae Dramatis*. There was as little link between him and them as betwixt himself and the audience. He was a third estate, dry, repulsive, and unsocial to all. Individually considered, his execution was masterly. But comedy is not this unbending thing; for this reason, that the same degree of credibility is not required of it as to serious scenes. The degrees of credibility demanded to the two things may be illustrated by the different sort of truth which we expect when a man tells us a mournful or a merry story. If we suspect the former of falsehood in any one tittle, we reject it altogether. Our tears refuse to flow at a suspected imposition. But the teller of a mirthful tale has latitude allowed him. We are content with less than absolute truth. 'Tis the same with dramatic illusion. We confess we love in comedy to see an audience naturalised behind the scenes, taken in into the interest of the drama, welcomed as by-standers however. There is something ungracious in a comic actor holding himself aloof from all participation or concern with those who are come to be diverted by him. Macbeth must see the dagger, and no ear but his own be told of it; but an old fool in farce may think he *sees something*, and by conscious words and looks express it, as plainly as he can speak, to pit, box, and gallery. When an impertinent in tragedy, an Osric,[5] for instance, breaks in upon the serious passions of the scene, we approve of the contempt with which he is treated. But when the pleasant impertinent of comedy, in a piece purely meant to give delight, and raise mirth out of whimsical perplexities, worries the studious man with taking up his leisure, or making his house his home, the same sort of contempt expressed (however *natural*) would destroy the balance of delight in the spectators. To make the intrusion comic, the actor who plays the annoyed man must a little desert nature; he must, in short, be thinking of the audience, and express only so much dissatisfaction and peevishness as is consistent with the pleasure of comedy. In other words, his perplexity must seem half put on. If he repel the intruder with the sober set face of a man in earnest, and more

---

4 John Emery (1777–1822), thought the best actor of country types in his day. The role of Tyke was in Thomas Morton's *School of Reform*, produced in 1805.

5 *Hamlet*, v.ii.80 ff. Osric is a foppish minor functionary sent by the king to invite Hamlet to the fencing match with Laertes.

especially if he deliver his expostulations in a tone which in the world must necessarily provoke a duel; his real-life manner will destroy the whimsical and purely dramatic existence of the other character (which to render it comic demands an antagonist comicality on the part of the character opposed to it), and convert what was meant for mirth, rather than belief, into a downright piece of impertinence indeed, which would raise no diversion in us, but rather stir pain, to see inflicted in earnest upon any unworthy person. A very judicious actor (in most of his parts) seems to have fallen into an error of this sort in his playing with Mr. Wrench in the farce of *Free and Easy*.[6]

Many instances would be tedious; these may suffice to show that comic acting at least does not always demand from the performer that strict abstraction from all reference to an audience, which is exacted of it; but that in some cases a sort of compromise may take place, and all the purposes of dramatic delight be attained by a judicious understanding, not too openly announced, between the ladies and gentlemen—on both sides of the curtain.

---

[6] Benjamin Wrench (1778–1843), an energetic comedian, played Sir John Freeman in Samuel J. Arnold's *Free and Easy,* produced in 1816.

GEORGE MEREDITH

[1828–1909]

Charles Lamb died in 1833, four years before the accession of Queen Victoria. In 1840 the aging romantic Leigh Hunt brought out an edition of *The Dramatic Works of Wycherley, Congreve, Vanbrugh and Farquhar, with Biographical and Critical Notices*. How far the gentle fancies of Elia concerning "artificial comedy" had drifted apart from the prevailing literary mind of the mid-century may be illustrated in a review of Hunt's work which the M. P. for Edinburgh and secretary of war T. B. Macaulay, mainstay of the *Edinburgh Review*, published in its pages for July 1841. It was all right for Hunt to have reprinted the plays, but he should at least have committed himself to some "gentle rebuke" of their immorality—and this in spite of the mistaken efforts of Mr. Charles Lamb to "set up a defence" for them. "For in truth this part of our literature is a disgrace to our language and our national character."

...During the forty years which followed the Restoration, the whole body of the dramatists invariably represent adultery, we do not say as a peccadillo, we do not say as an error which the violence of passion may excuse, but as the calling of a fine gentleman, as a grace without which his character would be imperfect.

The hero is in all superficial accomplishments exactly the fine gentleman whom every youth in the pit would gladly resemble. The heroine is the fine lady whom every youth in the pit would gladly marry.... And the immorality is of a sort which never can be out of date, and which all the force of religion, law, and public opinion united can but imperfectly restrain.

In the name of art, as well as in the name of virtue, we protest against the principle that the world of pure comedy is one into which no moral enters. If comedy be an imitation, under whatever conventions, of real life, how is it possible that it can have no reference to the great rule which directs life, and to feelings which are called forth by every incident of life? If what Mr. Charles Lamb says were correct, the

228

inference would be that these dramatists did not in the least understand the first principles of their craft.[1]

Macaulay's confident and punishing observations were supplemented
not many years later by a humorist and newly eminent novelist,
W. M. Thackeray, speaking on Congreve in a lecture delivered at
London in the spring of 1851. Thackeray might agree with Lamb
about the unreality of that drama—but with how different an accent!

> I have read two or three of Congreve's plays over before speaking of
> him; and my feelings were rather like those, which I dare say most of
> us here have had, at Pompeii, looking at Sallust's house and the relics
> of an orgy; a dried wine-jar or two, a charred supper-table, the breast
> of a dancing girl pressed against the ashes, the laughing skull of a
> jester: a perfect stillness round about, as the Cicerone twangs his
> moral, and the blue sky shines calmly over the ruin. The Congreve
> Muse is dead, and her song choked in Time's ashes. Reading in these
> plays now, is like shutting your ears and looking at people dancing.
> What does it mean? the measures, the grimaces, the bowing, shuffling
> and retreating, the *cavalier seul* advancing upon those ladies. . . . It has
> a jargon of its own quite unlike life; a sort of moral of its own quite
> unlike life too.[2]

The arguments of Macaulay and Thackeray are in a sense unanswer-
able. It is always difficult to decide just what a literary philosopher
means when he says that art ought to be moral, or even when he says
that in order to be art it ought to be moral. And difficult to know
what the opposite statement means. The post-Kantian movement of
Art for Art's Sake sweeps through the century, crossing from France
to England in the third quarter. The date of Gautier's *Premières
Poésies* was 1832, that of Baudelaire's *Fleurs du Mal,* 1857, and that
of Swinburne's *Poems and Ballads,* 1866. Lamb's essay on the "artificial
comedy" may be taken as a very early, and isolated, instance of
English thinking in the vein of aestheticism, all the more an anomaly
because directed upon the unlikely material of stage comedy. The
subject of our present section, George Meredith, will provide us with
the most highly sophisticated English version of a counter-aesthetic,
an intrinsically, if ever so politely, moral argument.

Meredith's lecture *On the Idea of Comedy and of the Uses of the
Comic Spirit* (reprinted in this volume) was delivered at the London
Institution on February 1, 1877, and a revision of it was published in
April in *The New Quarterly Magazine.* This brilliantly sustained sur-

---

[1] T. B. Macaulay, *Critical and Historical Essays* (London, 1961), II, 414–18.
[2] "On Congreve and Addison," *The English Humorists. The Four Georges*
(London, 1929), pp. 55–56.

vey, and reassertion and enhancement, of the classic idea of comedy does not proceed from any close connections with the contemporary theater. We may, however, locate it, if we wish, in relation to the depressed theatrical history of the time, by saying that he delivered it thirty-six years after the opening of Dion L. Boucicault's immensely successful updating of the manners tradition, *London Assurance* (put on, magnificently, with the earliest wall-and-ceiling box set known in London, by Mme. Vestris at Covent Garden in 1841); thirty-four years after the Theater Act which destroyed the monopoly of the two great royal-patent houses and thus opened the way for a more intimate theater in more numerous smaller houses; ten years after *Caste,* 1867, the best of the six comedies for the Prince of Wales's Theatre, by which T. W. Robertson became celebrated for returning to English life of the day as it really (or almost) was; two years after the comic opera *Trial by Jury,* the first of the masterpieces of mock-Victorian mentality written for the company of Richard D'Oyly Carte by Gilbert[3] and Sullivan; and fifteen years before the brief resurgence of witty (if sentimental) manners comedy begun in Oscar Wilde's *Lady Windermere's Fan,* 1892—and the nearly simultaneous birth of the Ibsenesque social problem drama, Shaw's *Widowers' Houses,* 1892, and Arthur Wing Pinero's *Second Mrs. Tanqueray,* 1893.

Meredith was a novelist and poet and, for thirty-three years, from 1862 to 1894, a reader for the publishing house of Chapman and Hall. He was in his later years a celebrated and influential literary lion. A more solemn and metaphysically earnest side of the man, connected with Comtean positivistic philosophy and "fetishes" of earth, blood, brain, and spirit (a kind of Neoplatonic mythology), peeps out at places in his comic theory but is more apparent and more dated in a number of his doctrinaire poems.[4] His novels are high comedy of contemporary English life, narrated in a style of astonishing amplitude, speed, and power. Like Wilde and Gilbert, he had one indispensable talent for the writing of high comedy. He had wit. Thus when the story required that a certain character display wit (Sir Austin Feverel in the aphorisms of his confessional *Pilgrim's Scrip,* his nephew Adrian Harley in the intimation of some Mephistophelian scheme, or the lovely and heartbreakingly elusive Diana, heroine of the *Crossways*) Meredith could supply that character with wit. There was wit enough, and to spare, too, for the editorial voice. Acute personal

---

[3] In Meredith's lecture as delivered, but not in the text published, a passage near the end paid a compliment to "the late Mr. Robertson, Mr. Tom Taylor, Mr. Gilbert, and Mr. Burnand" (*The Times,* London, February 5, 1877, quoted by Lane Cooper, ed., *An Essay on Comedy,* Ithaca, N.Y., 1956, p. 33).

[4] See, for instance, *The Woods of Westermain* in *Poems and Lyrics of the Joy of Earth,* 1883. On his philosophy see Lane Cooper, ed., *An Essay on Comedy,* pp. 10–13.

suffering also went into some of his novels and poems. A fiercely unhappy first marriage[5] (1849–1861) produced perhaps his most intense book of poetry, the sonnet sequence *Modern Love*, published the year after his wife's death. The inept and at length sorely frustrated relations of a father to his son (Arthur Gryffydh, 1853–1890) seem foreshadowed or even expressed by premonition in *The Ordeal of Richard Feverel*, 1859, in which the comedy[6] of a baronet father, deserted by his wife, yet fortified in self-gratulatory prepossessions and superbly confident educational vision, produces the tragedy of his son's ruin.[7] In *The Egoist*, 1877, the same self-focused complacencies are examined in the phase of a young baronet's search for a wife. Self-indulgent sentiment, solemn righteousness, egoism, snobbery, certain related vices of optimism and epicurism, and always a counter spirit of reality, sanity, and laughter, are Meredith's preoccupations in various novels.[8] Such life experiences and fictional realizations seem to have confronted and fused with a wide and receptive reading of the comedy of England, France, and other continental countries, and of ancient Athens and Rome, to erupt in the brilliancies of his lecture.[9]

---

[5] He married an older woman, the widowed daughter of the "jolly old worldling" and satirical novelist Thomas Love Peacock, Lamb's contemporary at the India Office. She went off to Capri with a painter Henry Wallis in 1858, but, deserted by Wallis, returned to England the next year, to die in 1861. It would seem that Meredith remained aloof and kept her from seeing their eight-year-old child.

[6] *The Ordeal of Richard Feverel* in the version of 1859 (readily available today in the Modern Library edition of this work) had comic episodes which are excised or altered in Meredith's revisions which produced the version now usually read. See Hugh Chisolm, "Mr. Meredith's Revision of *Richard Feverel,*" *The Academy,* LXVIII (June 3, 1905), 589–90.

[7] A recent biographer, while allowing that Meredith may have drawn on his relations with his own father in creating the tragic father-son situation in *The Ordeal of Richard Feverel,* thinks it more likely that the novel arose out of Meredith's intense misgivings about his own fitness as father and sole guardian of his son (Lionel Stevenson, *The Ordeal of George Meredith,* New York, 1953, pp. 63–64).

[8] See Joseph W. Beach, *The Comic Spirit in George Meredith,* New York, 1911.

[9] As a boy he had lived and studied in Germany, and he knew something of the novelist Jean Paul (J. P. F. Richter). But he seems not to be in touch with the high doctrine of the laughable in Jean Paul's *Vorschule der Ästhetik,* 1804, or with such sublimations of the comic as are found in Schiller's *Naïve and Sentimental Poetry,* 1795, or Hegel's *Ästhetik,* 1835. One may note certain parallel refinements, however, such as the following from Hegel.

A democratic folk, with egotistic citizens, litigious, frivolous, conceited, without faith or knowledge, always intent on gossip, boasting and vanity—such a folk is past praying for; it can only dissolve in its folly.... People only too often in this respect confound the merely *ridiculous* with the true comic. Every contrast between what is essential and its appearance, the object and its instrument, may be ridiculous, a contradiction in virtue of which the appearance is absolutely cancelled, and the end is stultified in its realization.

If we remember the severe strictures of Macaulay upon the immorality of the old comedy, and the patronizing jokes of Thackeray, we may expect that Meredith's large celebration of comedy and the comic spirit will be in part a retort to these pundits of the immediately preceding generation. Not so. Surprisingly for us perhaps, if we think of the literary lustre which attaches to the name of Meredith and to his Lecture, he turns out to be as thorough a moralist as either Macaulay or Thackeray, pronouncing emphatic censures upon the English Comedy of Manners ("or Comedy of the manners of South-Sea Islanders under city veneer") and even a mild rebuke to Elia for not seeing the difference between "raw realism" and reality "stamped...in the idea." "It is unwholesome for men and women to see themselves as they are, if they are no better than they should be: and they will not, when they have improved in manners, care much to see themselves as they once were." That sentence might almost occur in Macaulay—except for the note of confidence in an improvement of manners. Meredith is indeed a moralist, if not of the pulpit. He is a moralist in a seductively wider sense, secular and full of social-evolutionary optimism. He is perhaps too refined, too "exalted" (as he himself would put it), to feel deeply or painfully enough that "battle" of women with men and of men with women, that rooted perversity in the heterosexual relation, about which he likes to talk.[10]

Amid the violence and the clamor of what we shall see has come to be the laughing preference of our own midcentury, he may seem a pallidly aloof conceptualist or Socratic. But for his own time, his moralism enjoys a fairly easy assimilation with the dramatic and

---

A profounder significance is, however, implied in the comic. There is, for instance, nothing comic in human crime. . . . Satire affords a proof of this, to the point of extreme aridity, no matter how emphatic may be the colours in which it depicts the condition of the actual world in its contrast to all that the man of virtue ought to be. There is nothing in mere folly, stupidity, or nonsense, which in itself necessarily partakes of the comic, though we all of us are ready enough to laugh at it. And as a rule it is extraordinary what a variety of wholly different things excite human laughter. Matters of the dullest description and in the worst possible taste will move men in this way; and their laughter may be excited quite as much by things of the profoundest importance, if only they happen to notice some entirely unimportant feature, which may conflict with habit and ordinary experience. Laughter is consequently little more than an expression of self-satisfied shrewdness; a sign that they have sufficient wit to recognize such a contrast and are aware of the fact. In the same way we have the laughter of mockery, of disdain, of desperation and the like. What on the other hand is inseparable from the comic is an infinite geniality and confidence capable of rising superior to its own contradiction, and experiencing therein no taint of bitterness or sense of misfortune whatever. [*Hegel on Tragedy,* ed. Anne and Henry Paolucci (Garden City, N.Y., 1962), pp. 52–53, from *The Philosophy of Fine Art,* trans. F. P. B. Osmaston, (London, 1920), IV, 248–348.]

10 *Essay,* ed. Cooper, pp. 23–24.

aesthetic. He does not debate with Macaulay or Thackeray. He assumes a transcendence, in both taste and morals, over their whole preoccupation. He gives up English manners comedy—with the single partial exception of Congreve's *Way of the World*. With a gesture, he consigns all that to a limbo of the vulgar, brash, raw, and bumptiously immoral. ("The men and women who sat through the acting of Wycherley's *Country Wife* were past blushing.") He shifts the scene of his inquiry to the superior model and inspiration of the whole English travesty, the comedies of Molière and above all his masterpiece *Le Misanthrope*, with its sparkling heroine Célimène. (The good part of Congreve's *Way of the World*, aside from the general vigorous style, is, as with Molière, the brilliance of its heroine, adorable Millamant.[11]) Molière looked to a wider spectrum of themes than fornication, adultery, and cuckoldry. He had an eye for avarice, for false piety and hypocrisy, for salon preciosité and bourgeois pretensions to gentility, and above all for the delicate but mortal clash of the sexes in a social medium complicated of coquetry, artistic slander, and all-but-justifiable misanthropy.

Meredith drives a thesis about the need for a cultivated society to nourish comedy—to provide both its matter—aristocratic follies and foibles—and its audience, a bourgeoisie sharpened by contact with the superior aristocracy. (Perhaps here he fudges a bit, to cover a certain inconsistency in the argument.) He drives a companion thesis, as we have just suggested, about the high role of women in civilizing both society and comedy, and another about the role of comic laughter itself in that program of civilization. The comic scene is not a house-party where skittish girl wives of elderly foolish Fondlewoulds play an insatiable game of contributing to the adolescent English obsession with horns. It is, rather, an exquisite salon, suitably stocked with a coterie of fops and noodles, in the center of which reign jointly one savage, aloof male philosopher (a "Jean Jacques of the Court") and his not-quite-consenting sweetheart and schoolmistress, the wickedest tongue and coolest head of the assembly. Like Steele and Dennis and others in our tradition, Meredith looks back, wistfully, to the she-comedies of Terence and through Terence, by shrewd conjecture, to Menander, who was then not known even in the lucky fragments of the since-discovered papyri.[12] Unlike Caesar, he finds in Terence no

---

[11] Meredith has a hard time fitting Aristophanes, Rabelais, and Shakespeare into his scheme—though of course he admires all such spirits extravagantly.

[12] The emergence of a nearly complete *Duskolos* or *Curmudgeon* from the Bodmer Library in Geneva a few years ago (1958) reveals something too near to slapstick humors to have greatly enhanced our appreciation of Menander. Still, the theme may be described as the victory of the comic spirit of Pan over the misanthropy of the curmudgeon. See Herbert Musurillo, *Symbol and Myth in Ancient Poetry* (New York, 1961), p. 43.

deficiency of the *vis comica* through the preoccupation of his tenderness
—but all the opposite.

Meredith's quarrel is with nothing, really, in the ethical part of the
classical tradition. Rather, he shows a surprising approach to Aristo-
telianism in his reiterated concern to separate kindly and thoughtful
laughter from all the varieties of the gross and cruel. He draws an
opening distinction between underlaughers and overlaughers, *misogelasts*
and *hypergelasts*, as he calls them, Puritans and Bacchanalians. He
might just as well have said *agroikoi* (boors) and *bōmolochoi* (buffoons),
as Aristotle does in the *Ethics*.[13] He does not, however, refer to
Aristotle—only to Rabelais, in support of *agelast*, a weaker relative of
misogelast. Meredith catalogues the pretending rivals to comic laughter
under several headings of the violent or the self-indulgent: the cruel
laughter of derision, the carrion beak of satire, the semi-caress of
irony, the rouge of sentiment, and the pathos which is inevitably a
component of humor. He mounts a vigorous campaign against one of
the most fondly prized parts of the national tradition—something we
have already noticed a century earlier—the heavy English investment
in the principles of originality, eccentricity,[14] and humor, and in the
hearty, sympathetic laughter which was considered the appropriate
response to the last of these. Though he explicitly disavows nonlaughing,
no less than overlaughing, the brunt of his argument falls against the
latter. He is of the party of Jonson, Swift, Pope, and Chesterfield.
The "smile" in which Lord Chesterfield was willing to be seen indulging
himself was the aristocratic sensible Augustan man's anticipation
of the silvery intelligent laughter volleyed down from overhead upon
the whole preposterous human spectacle by Meredith's "luminous and
watchful," "humanely malign," Olympian, and evolutionary Comic
Spirit. That laughter is "of the order of the smile, finely tempered,
showing sunlight of the mind. . . ."[15]

It was not as if Meredith had to invent or imagine his special
opponents. Humor and kindly, pathetic, boisterous laughter had
flourished in England prodigiously during the years since Sterne and
Smollett, and more than ever after the turn of the century. It was
the era of *John Bull; or the Englishman's Fireside*. We may take as
typical, and a milepost, that title of a play which George Colman

---

[13] See above, Introduction, p. 10.

[14] Edith Sitwell, *The English Eccentrics* (London, 1933). Any few pages of this
helter-skelter book will make its point. See, for instance, the drunken hunting and
horse-loving squire John Mytton (1796–1834), pp. 124–31.

[15] In real life, apparently, Meredith was not a Chesterfield. "His laugh was
something to hear; it was of short duration, but it was a roar" (Francis Burnand,
quoted by Thomas Seccombe, *George Meredith*, in *The Dictionary of National
Biography, Supplement 1901–1911*, London, 1912–1927, p. 609).

the younger (son of Garrick's friend and rival) gave to his countrymen in 1803, a comedy of amiable misanthropy, a blunt yet lovable trades-man's eccentricity and misfortune, which critics of the day, the veteran Walter Scott and the youthful Leigh Hunt, celebrated especially for its power of provoking audiences to simultaneous tears and laughter (the "humorous pathetic").[16] In real life, among literary men them-selves, Charles Lamb, whose gentle combinations of pathos and levity we have recently sampled, was loved by his public as an incomparably amiable-crotchety commentator upon the motley human spectacle.[17] Lamb was succeeded by Thackeray and Dickens. Having passed through several phases, as Aristotle said of tragedy, "humor" at the outset of the Victorian era seemed to have found its ultimately truest shape and sphere in the everyday caricatures of Dickens, and most notably in his *Pickwick Papers* (1836–1837), an early creation so successful that readers complained when Dickens in later works explored ways beyond the cheerful confines of humor. In the wilder-ness of *Little Dorrit,* "we sit down and weep when we remember thee, O *Pickwick!*"[18]

An eminent Victorian man of letters who looked much in the same direction as Meredith, from a similar lofty vantage point, was the "Professor of Poetry in the University of Oxford" (1857–1867), Matthew Arnold. A battle cry of "high seriousness" heard unceasingly in his warfare against the "Philistine" middle class did not imply any very direct concern with the comic. But in such proclamations as his lecture entitled *The Function of Criticism at the Present Time,* pub-lished as the opening essay of his first volume of *Essays in Criticism,* 1865, he turned a disapproving hauteur upon the grotesque and ugly side of the national complacency.

...This paragraph on which I stumbled in a newspaper immediately after reading Mr. Roebuck:[19]—"A shocking child murder has just been

---

16 Stuart M. Tave, *The Amiable Humorist* (Chicago, 1960), pp. 228–32.

17 Tave, pp. 177, 236–37.

18 Tave, p. 243. Theater managers had been exceedingly prompt in extracting dramatic entertainments from the novels of Dickens. "The proof-sheets were snatched as they came from the press; as many as half a dozen separate dramatic versions of one of his novels were produced within a week of its publication" (Allardyce Nicoll, *British Drama,* New York, 1933, p. 329). Graphic versions of the humor appeared in such works as the illustrations of Dickens by George Cruik-shank, the heir of earlier satirical caricaturists like Rowlandson and Gillray.

19 John Arthur Roebuck, 1801–1879, was a liberal politician. Arnold had just read a speech in which Roebuck proclaimed: "I look around me and ask what is the state of England? Is not property safe? Is not every man able to say what he likes? Can you not walk from one end of England to the other in perfect security? I ask you whether, the world over or in past history, there is anything like it? Nothing. I pray that our unrivalled happiness may last." (*Essays in Criticism, First Series,* London, 1902, p. 21).

committed at Nottingham. A girl named Wragg left the workhouse there ...with her young illegitimate child. The child was soon afterwards found dead on Mapperly Hills, having been strangled. Wragg is in custody." Nothing but that...*Wragg!*...has anyone reflected what a touch of grossness in our race, what an original shortcoming in the more delicate spiritual perceptions, is shown by the natural growth amongst us of such hideous names. Higginbottom, Stiggins, Bugg! In Ionia and Attica they were luckier in this respect than "the best race in the world;" by the Ilissus there was no Wragg, poor thing! And "our unrivalled happiness"—what an element of grimness, bareness, and hideousness mixes with it.... Mr. Roebuck will have a poor opinion of an adversary who replies to his defiant songs of triumph only by murmuring under his breath, *Wragg is in custody;* but in no other way will these songs of triumph be induced gradually to moderate themselves, to get rid of what in them in excessive and offensive, and to fall into a softer and truer key.[20]

And in his essay *Sweetness and Light,* the first chapter of his magisterial *Culture and Anarchy,* 1869:

"May not every man in England say what he likes?" Mr. Roebuck perpetually asks; and that, he thinks, is quite sufficient, and when every man may say what he likes, our aspirations ought to be satisfied. But the aspirations of culture, which is the study of perfection, are not satisfied, unless what men say, when they may say what they like, is worth saying,—has good in it, and more good than bad. In the same way the *Times,* replying to some foreign strictures on the dress, looks, and behaviour of the English abroad, urges that the English ideal is that everyone should be free to do and to look just as he likes. But culture indefatigably tries, not to make what each raw person may like, the rule by which he fashions himself; but to draw ever nearer to a sense of what is indeed beautiful, graceful, and becoming, and to get the raw person to like that.[21]

Meredith's sage novel *The Egoist, A Comedy in Narrative,* was published in 1879,[22] only two years after he had delivered his Lecture on the comic spirit. He supplied this novel with a Prelude, a few sentences of which are a nervous resumé of the Lecture. He lays a strong, if almost laconic and unexplained, emphasis upon the difference between

---

[20] *Essays in Criticism, First Series,* pp. 23–25.

[21] Matthew Arnold, *Culture and Anarchy: An Essay in Political and Social Criticism,* 2nd ed. (London, 1875), pp. 15–16.

[22] Serially first, in the *Glasgow Weekly Herald.* Meredith's *Emilia in England,* 1864 (later renamed *Sandra Belloni*) is sometimes said to contain the first formulation of his belief in the purifying flame of the Comic Spirit. But *Richard Feverel,* 1859, is surely an important anticipation. He returned to the theme, more awkwardly, in a poem entitled *The Two Masks* (in *Ballads and Poems of Tragic Life,* 1887) and in his *Ode to the Comic Spirit* (in *A Reading of Earth,* 1892).

plodding realism and the "survey" or "vision" enjoyed by the Comic Spirit, and thus he intimates a near relation, or identity, between the comic laughable and the created reality of the poetic imagination. Not many English critics had advanced such a bold claim for the comic. Lamb, no doubt, and Fielding had looked in the same direction. Dryden, long ago, in a memorable climactic passage of his *Essay of Dramatic Poesy,* had come out for what was "lively" in drama—initially distinguished from the "just" or lifelike—and had calmly asserted that liveliness is the only true source of the lifelike. "Those beauties of the French poesy are...indeed the beauties of a statue, but not of a man, because not animated with the soul of Poesy, which is imitation of humour and passions."[23] And now Meredith, in his Prelude of 1879:

> Comedy is a game played to throw reflections upon social life, and it deals with human nature in the drawing-room of civilized men and women, where we have no dust of the struggling outer world, no mire, no violent crashes, to make the correctness of the representation convincing. Credulity is not wooed through the impressionable senses; nor have we recourse to the small circular glow of the watchmaker's eye to raise in bright relief minutest grains of evidence for the routing of incredulity. The Comic Spirit conceives a definite situation for a number of characters, and rejects all accessories in the exclusive pursuit of them and their speech. For, being a spirit, he hunts the spirit in men; vision and ardour constitute his merit: he has not a thought of persuading you to believe in him.

> Shall we read it [the Book of Earth, the Book of Egoism, the Book of our common wisdom] by the watchmaker's eye...or...under the broad Alpine survey of the spirit born of our united social intelligence, which is the Comic Spirit? Wise men say the latter.

> Comedy...is our means of reading swiftly and comprehensively. She it is who proposes the correcting of pretentiousness, of inflation, of dulness, and of the vestiges of rawness and grossness to be found among us. She is the ultimate civilizer, the polisher, a sweet cook. If...she watches over sentimentalism with a birch rod, she is not opposed to romance.... In Comedy is the singular scene of charity issuing of disdain under the stroke of honourable laughter: an Ariel released by Prospero's wand from the fetters of the damned witch Sycorax. And this laughter of reason refreshed is floriferous, like the magical great gale of the shifty Spring deciding for Summer. You hear it giving the delicate spirit his liberty. Listen, for comparison, to an unleavened society: a low as of the udderful cow past milking hour!

---

23 *Essays of John Dryden,* ed. W. P. Ker, I, 68.

On the Idea of Comedy
and of the
Uses of the Comic Spirit

An Essay on Comedy

[*1877*]

Good Comedies are such rare productions that, notwithstanding the wealth of our literature in the Comic element, it would not occupy us long to run over the English list. If they are brought to the test I shall propose, very reputable Comedies will be found unworthy of their station, like the ladies of Arthur's Court when they were reduced to the ordeal of the mantle.[1]

There are plain reasons why the Comic poet is not a frequent apparition; and why the great Comic poet remains without a fellow. A society of cultivated men and women is required, wherein ideas are current and the perceptions quick, that he may be supplied with matter and an audience. The semi-barbarism of merely giddy communities, and feverish emotional periods, repel him; and also a state

---

Meredith's lecture was delivered at the London Institution on February 1, 1877, and appeared in *The New Quarterly Magazine* for April, with the title *On the Idea of Comedy, and of the Uses of the Comic Spirit.* In 1897 the lecture was published in book form, with the title *An Essay on Comedy and the Uses of the Comic Spirit,* by Archibald Constable & Co., Westminster, and by Charles Scribner's Sons, New York. (A copy of *The New Quarterly Magazine* printing and also page proofs of the Constable 1897 edition, both with revisions throughout in Meredith's hand, may be seen at Yale University in the Beinecke Rare Book and Manuscript Library.) Our text normalizes italics and quotation marks and makes a few improvements in spelling and punctuation, but otherwise follows the edition of Archibald Constable & Co. The edition by Lane Cooper was first published by Charles Scribner's Sons, 1918, and was republished by the Cornell University Press, 1956. The present editing is considerably indebted to Cooper's annotations.

[1] In the old ballad of *The Boy and the Mantle,* a boy visits the Court of King Arthur, bringing a mantle which will exactly fit a wife who has been faithful and will betray one who has not.

238

of marked social inequality of the sexes; nor can he whose business is to address the mind be understood where there is not a moderate degree of intellectual activity.

Moreover, to touch and kindle the mind through laughter demands, more than sprightliness, a most subtle delicacy. That must be a natal gift in the Comic poet. The substance he deals with will show him a startling exhibition of the dyer's hand, if he is without it.[2] People are ready to surrender themselves to witty thumps on the back, breast, and sides; all except the head: and it is there that he aims. He must be subtle to penetrate. A corresponding acuteness must exist to welcome him. The necessity for the two conditions will explain how it is that we count him during centuries in the singular number.

C'est une étrange entreprise que celle de faire rire les honnêtes gens,[3] Molière says; and the difficulty of the undertaking cannot be overestimated.

Then again, he is beset with foes to right and left, of a character unknown to the tragic and the lyric poet, or even to philosophers.

We have in this world men whom Rabelais would call agelasts;[4] that is to say, non-laughers; men who are in that respect as dead bodies, which if you prick them do not bleed. The old gray boulderstone that has finished its peregrination from the rock to the valley, is as easily to be set rolling up again as these men laughing. No collision of circumstances in our mortal career strikes a light for them. It is but one step from being agelastic to misogelastic, and the μισόγελως, the laughter-hating, soon learns to dignify his dislike as an objection in morality.

We have another class of men, who are pleased to consider themselves antagonists of the foregoing, and whom we may term hypergelasts; the excessive laughters, ever-laughing, who are as clappers of a bell, that may be rung by a breeze, a grimace; who are so loosely put together that a wink will shake them.

...C'est n'estimer rien qu'estimer tout le monde,[5]

---

2 Shakespeare, *Sonnet* 111:
    And almost thence my nature is subdued
    To what it works in, like the dyer's hand.
3 Molière, *La Critique de L'Ecole des Femmes,* Scene vi. See above pp. 61–62.
4 Meredith has perhaps seen this word from Rabelais in a French article to which he soon makes an allusion (E. Littré, *Aristophane et Rabelais,* in *Littérature et Histoire,* 1877, p. 173). See below p. 240, n. 8. See Rabelais, *Pantagruel,* IV, Dedication; V, xxv.
5 Molière, *Le Misanthrope,* I.i.58.

and to laugh at everything is to have no appreciation of the Comic of Comedy.

Neither of these distinct divisions of non-laughers and over-laughters would be entertained by reading *The Rape of the Lock,* or seeing a performance of *Le Tartuffe.* In relation to the stage, they have taken in our land the form and title of Puritan and Bacchanalian. For though the stage is no longer a public offender, and Shakespeare has been revived on it, to give it nobility, we have not yet entirely raised it above the contention of these two parties. Our speaking on the theme of Comedy will appear almost a libertine proceeding to one, while the other will think that the speaking of it seriously brings us into violent contrast with the subject.

Comedy, we have to admit, was never one of the most honoured of the Muses. She was in her origin, short of slaughter, the loudest expression of the little civilization of men. The light of Athene over the head of Achilles illuminates the birth of Greek tragedy.[6] But comedy rolled in shouting under the divine protection of the Son of the Wine-jar, as Dionysus is made to proclaim himself by Aristophanes.[7] Our second Charles was the patron, of like benignity, of our Comedy of Manners, which began similarly as a combative performance, under a licence to deride and outrage the Puritan, and was here and there Bacchanalian beyond the Aristophanic example: worse, inasmuch as a cynical licentiousness is more abominable than frank filth. An eminent Frenchman[8] judges from the quality of some of the stuff dredged up for the laughter of men and women who sat through an Athenian Comic play, that they could have had small delicacy in other affairs when they had so little in their choice of entertainment. Perhaps he does not make sufficient allowance for the regulated licence of plainspeaking proper to the festival of the god, and claimed by the Comic poet as his inalienable right, or for the fact that it was a festival in a season of licence, in a city accustomed to give ear to the boldest utterance of both sides of a case. However that may be, there can be no question that the men and women who sat through the acting of Wycherley's *Country Wife*[9] were past blushing. Our tenacity of national impressions has caused the word theatre since then to prod

---

6 *Iliad,* XVIII.203–27.

7 *The Frogs,* 22.

8 Maximilien Paul Emile Littré (1801–1881), lexicographer, professor of history and geography, friend of the positivist philosopher Auguste Comte. The judgment to which Meredith alludes appears at p. 152 of his *Littérature et Histoire,* 1877.

9 1675, a coarse parallel to Molière's *L'Ecole des Femmes.* Cf. above pp. 58–59.

the Puritan nervous system like a satanic instrument; just as one has known Anti-Papists, for whom Smithfield was redolent of a sinister smoke, as though they had a later recollection of the place than the lowing herds.[10] Hereditary Puritanism, regarding the stage, is met, to this day, in many families quite undistinguished by arrogant piety. It has subsided altogether as a power in the profession of morality; but it is an error to suppose it extinct, and unjust also to forget that it had once good reason to hate, shun, and rebuke our public shows.

We shall find ourselves about where the Comic spirit would place us, if we stand at middle distance between the inveterate opponents and the drum-and-fife supporters of Comedy: *Comme un point fixe fait remarquer l'emportement des autres,* as Pascal says.[11] And were there more in this position, Comic genius would flourish.

Our English idea of a Comedy of Manners might be imaged in the person of a blowsy country girl—say Hoyden, the daughter of Sir Tunbelly Clumsey,[12] who, when at home, "never disobeyed her father except in the eating of green gooseberries"—transforming to a varnished City madam; with a loud laugh and a mincing step; the crazy ancestress of an accountably fallen descendant. She bustles prodigiously and is punctually smart in her speech, always in a fluster to escape from Dulness, as they say the dogs on the Nile-banks drink at the river running to avoid the crocodile.[13] If the monster catches her, as at times he does, she whips him to a froth, so that those who know Dulness only as a thing of ponderousness, shall fail to recognize him in that light and airy shape.

When she has frolicked through her five Acts to surprise you with the information that Mr. Aimwell[14] is converted by a sudden death in the world outside the scenes into Lord Aimwell, and can marry the lady in the light of day, it is to the credit of her vivacious nature that she does not anticipate your calling her Farce. Five is dignity with a trailing robe; whereas one, two, or three Acts would be short skirts, and degrading. Advice has been given to householders, that they should follow up the shot at a burglar in the dark by hurling the pistol after it, so that if the bullet misses, the weapon may strike and assure the

---

10 Site of a historic cattle market in London, associated with public executions of Protestants in the reign of Queen Mary.

11 Misquoted from Pascal. See *Pensées,* ed. Brunschwicg (1904), II, 291–92.

12 Sir John Vanbrugh, *The Relapse, or Virtue in Danger* (1696), IV.i.

13 The story goes back to Claudius Aelianus (c. 200 A.D.), *Variae Historiae,* I.iv.

14 A character in *The Beaux' Stratagem* (1707), by George Farquhar.

rascal he has it. The point of her wit is in this fashion supplemented by the rattle of her tongue, and effectively, according to the testimony of her admirers. Her wit is at once, like steam in an engine, the motive force and the warning whistle of her headlong course; and it vanishes like the track of steam when she has reached her terminus, never troubling the brains afterwards; a merit that it shares with good wine, to the joy of the Bacchanalians. As to this wit, it is warlike. In the neatest hands it is like the sword of the cavalier in the Mall, quick to flash out upon slight provocation, and for a similar office—to wound. Commonly its attitude is entirely pugilistic; two blunt fists rallying and countering. When harmless, as when the word "fool" occurs, or allusions to the state of husband, it has the sound of the smack of harlequin's wand upon clown, and is to the same extent exhilarating. Believe that idle empty laughter is the most desirable of recreations, and significant Comedy will seem pale and shallow in comparison. Our popular idea would be hit by the sculptured group of Laughter holding both his sides,[15] while Comedy pummels, by way of tickling him. As to a meaning, she holds that it does not conduce to making merry: you might as well carry cannon on a racing-yacht. Morality is a duenna to be circumvented. This was the view of English Comedy of a sagacious essayist, who said that the end of a Comedy would often be the commencement of a Tragedy, were the curtain to rise again on the performers. In those old days female modesty was protected by a fan, behind which, and it was of a convenient semi-circular breadth, the ladies present in the theatre retired at a signal of decorum, to peep, covertly askant, or with the option of so peeping, through a prettily fringed eyelet-hole in the eclipsing arch.

> Ego limis specto sic per flabellum clanculum.
> —TERENCE.[16]

That fan is the flag and symbol of the society giving us our so-called Comedy of Manners, or comedy of the manners of South-Sea Islanders under city veneer; and as to Comic idea, vacuous as the mask without the face behind it.

Elia, whose humour delighted in floating a galleon paradox and wafting it as far as it would go, bewails the extinction of our artificial Comedy, like a poet sighing over the vanished splendour of Cleopatra's

---

15 Milton, *L'Allegro,* 32.
16 *Eunuchus,* 601–2. "I furtively take a squint at her, thus, through the fan."

Nile-barge;[17] and the sedateness of his plea for a cause condemned even in his time to the penitentiary, is a novel effect of the ludicrous. When the realism of those "fictitious half-believed personages," as he calls them, had ceased to strike, they were objectionable company, uncaressable as puppets. Their artifices are staringly naked, and have now the effect of a painted face viewed, after warm hours of dancing, in the morning light. How could the Lurewells and the Plyants ever have been praised for ingenuity in wickedness? Critics, apparently sober, and of high reputation, held up their shallow knaveries for the world to admire. These Lurewells, Plyants, Pinchwifes, Fondlewifes, Miss Prue, Peggy, Hoyden, all of them save charming Millamant,[18] are dead as last year's clothes in a fashionable fine lady's wardrobe, and it must be an exceptionally abandoned Abigail of our period that would look on them with the wish to appear in their likeness. Whether the puppet show of Punch and Judy inspires our street-urchins to have instant recourse to their fists in a dispute, after the fashion of every one of the actors in that public entertainment who gets possession of the cudgel, is open to question: it has been hinted; and angry moralists have traced the national taste for tales of crime to the smell of blood in our nursery-songs. It will at any rate hardly be questioned that it is unwholesome for men and women to see themselves as they are, if they are no better than they should be: and they will not, when they have improved in manners, care much to see themselves as they once were. That comes of realism in the Comic art; and it is not public caprice, but the consequence of a bettering state.[19] The same of an immoral may be said of realistic exhibitions of a vulgar society.

The French make a critical distinction in *ce qui remue* from *ce qui émeut*—that which agitates from that which touches with emotion. In the realistic comedy it is an incessant *remuage*, no calm, merely

---

[17] Cf. Shakespeare, *Antony and Cleopatra*, II.ii.191–223. For Elia, see above pp. 206–13.

[18] Lady Lurewell in Farquhar's *The Constant Couple, or a Trip to the Jubilee* (1699), and its sequel, *Sir Harry Wildair* (1701); Sir Paul Plyant, "an uxorious, foolish old knight," in Congreve's *The Double-Dealer* (1693); Pinchwife in Wycherley's *The Country Wife* (1675); Fondlewife, an uxorious banker in Congreve's *The Old Bachelor* (1693); Miss Prue, an awkward country girl in Congreve's *Love for Love* (1695); Peg, maid to Lady Wishfort in Congreve's *The Way of the World* (1700); Millamant, heroine of the same play.

[19] Realism in the writing is carried to such a pitch in *The Old Bachelor* that husband and wife use imbecile connubial epithets to one another. [Meredith's note.]

bustling figures, and no thought. Excepting Congreve's *Way of the World*, which failed on the stage, there was nothing to keep our comedy alive on its merits; neither, with all its realism, true portraiture, nor much quotable fun, nor idea; neither salt nor soul.

The French have a school of stately comedy to which they can fly for renovation whenever they have fallen away from it; and their having such a school is mainly the reason why, as John Stuart Mill pointed out, they know men and women more accurately than we do.[20] Molière followed the Horatian precept,[21] to observe the manners of his age and give his characters the colour befitting them at the time. He did not paint in raw realism. He seized his characters firmly for the central purpose of the play, stamped them in the idea, and by slightly raising and softening the object of study (as in the case of the ex-Huguenot, Duke de Montausier, for the study of the Misanthrope,[22] and, according to Saint-Simon, the Abbé Roquette for Tartuffe[23]), generalized upon it so as to make it permanently human. Concede that it is natural for human creatures to live in society, and Alceste is an imperishable mark of one, though he is drawn in light outline, without any forcible human colouring. Our English school has not clearly imagined society; and of the mind hovering above congregated men and women, it has imagined nothing. The critics who praise it for its downrightness, and for bringing the situations home to us, as they admiringly say, cannot but disapprove of Molière's comedy, which appeals to the individual mind to perceive and participate in the social. We have splendid tragedies, we have the most beautiful of poetic plays, and we have literary comedies passingly pleasant to read, and occasionally to see acted. By literary comedies, I mean comedies of classic inspiration, drawn chiefly from Menander

---

20 It is difficult to identify the place in Mill's writings to which Meredith refers. Cf. *Dissertations and Discussions* (New York, 1882), I, 259, 261, 328, 333.

21 Horace, *Ars Poetica,* 156–57.

22 Tallemant des Réaux, in his rough portrait of the Duke, shows the foundation of the character of Alceste. [Meredith's note. The portrait of the Duc de Montausier (Charles de Sainte-Mauve, 1610–1690, tutor to the Dauphin) by Gédéon Tallemant des Réaux (1619–1692) in his *Historiettes* (Paris, 1864, II, 528) is quoted by Sainte-Beuve in his essay *Tallemant et Bussy* in *Causeries du Lundi* (1857), XIII, 187. See Molière, *Le Misanthrope* (1666) and above pp. 57–59.

23 Louis de Rouvroy, Duc de Saint-Simon, memorialist of the Court of Louis XIV, identified the protagonist of Molière's *Le Tartuffe* (see above p. 60) as the Abbé Gabriel de Roquette, Bishop of Autun, who died in 1707 (*Mémoires de Saint-Simon,* Paris, 1879–1916, XIV, 293–94). But the identification has been rejected by nineteenth-century French scholars.

and the Greek New Comedy through Terence; or else comedies of the poet's personal conception, that have had no model in life, and are humorous exaggerations, happy or otherwise. These are the comedies of Ben Jonson, Massinger, and Fletcher. Massinger's Justice Greedy[24] we can all of us refer to a type, "with fat capon lined,"[25] that has been and will be; and he would be comic, as Panurge[26] is comic, but only a Rabelais could set him moving with real animation. Probably Justice Greedy would be comic to the audience of a country booth and to some of our friends. If we have lost our youthful relish for the presentation of characters put together to fit a type, we find it hard to put together the mechanism of a civil smile at his enumeration of his dishes. Something of the same is to be said of Bobadill, swearing "by the foot of Pharaoh";[27] with a reservation, for he is made to move faster, and to act. The comic of Jonson is a scholar's excogitation of the comic; that of Massinger a moralist's.

Shakespeare is a well-spring of characters which are saturated with the comic spirit; with more of what we will call blood-life than is to be found anywhere out of Shakespeare; and they are of this world, but they are of the world enlarged to our embrace by imagination, and by great poetic imagination. They are, as it were—I put it to suit my present comparison—creatures of the woods and wilds, not in walled towns, not grouped and toned to pursue a comic exhibition of the narrower world of society. Jaques,[28] Falstaff and his regiment, the varied troop of clowns, Malvolio,[29] Sir Hugh Evans[30] and Fluellen[31]— marvellous Welshmen!—Benedick and Beatrice, Dogberry,[32] and the rest, are subjects of a special study in the poetically comic.

His Comedy of incredible imbroglio belongs to the literary section.[33] One may conceive that there was a natural resemblance between him and Menander, both in the scheme and style of his lighter plays. Had Shakespeare lived in a later and less emotional, less heroical period

---

[24] In *A New Way to Pay Old Debts* (1625).
[25] Misquoted from Shakespeare, *As You Like It,* II.vii.153–54.
[26] Jester and rogue in *Pantagruel,* by François Rabelais, 1532.
[27] Ben Jonson, *Every Man in his Humor* (1598), I.iv.
[28] Melancholy contemplative courtier in Shakespeare's *As You Like It.*
[29] Pompous steward in Shakespeare's *Twelfth Night.*
[30] Welsh parson in Shakespeare's *Merry Wives of Windsor.*
[31] Choleric Welsh soldier in Shakespeare's *King Henry V.*
[32] The witty, warring lovers and the bumbling constable in Shakespeare's *Much Ado About Nothing.*
[33] *A Comedy of Errors,* built on situations that go back to the *Menaechmi* and *Amphitruo* of Plautus.

of our history, he might have turned to the painting of manners as well as humanity. Euripides would probably, in the time of Menander, when Athens was enslaved but prosperous, have lent his hand to the composition of romantic comedy. He certainly inspired that fine genius.

Politically it is accounted a misfortune for France that her nobles thronged to the Court of Louis Quatorze. It was a boon to the comic poet. He had that lively quicksilver world of the animalcule passions, the huge pretensions, the placid absurdities, under his eyes in full activity; vociferous quacks and snapping dupes, hypocrites, posturers, extravagants, pedants, rose-pink ladies and mad grammarians, son-netteering marquises, highflying mistresses, plain-minded maids, inter-threading as in a loom, noisy as at a fair. A simply bourgeois circle will not furnish it, for the middle class must have the brilliant, flippant, independent upper for a spur and a pattern; otherwise it is likely to be inwardly dull as well as outwardly correct. Yet, though the King was benevolent toward Molière, it is not to the French Court that we are indebted for his unrivalled studies of mankind in society. For the amusement of the Court the ballets and farces were written, which are dearer to the rabble upper, as to rabble lower, class than intellectual comedy. The French bourgeoisie of Paris were sufficiently quick-witted and enlightened by education to welcome great works like *Le Tartuffe*, *Les Femmes Savantes*, and *Le Misanthrope*, works that were perilous ventures on the popular intelligence, big vessels to launch on streams running to shallows. The *Tartuffe* hove into view as an enemy's vessel; it offended, not *Dieu, mais les dévots*, as the Prince de Condé explained the cabal raised against it to the King.[34]

The *Femmes Savantes* is a capital instance of the uses of comedy in teaching the world to understand what ails it. The farce of the *Précieuses*[35] ridiculed and put a stop to the monstrous romantic jargon made popular by certain famous novels. The comedy of the *Femmes Savantes* exposed the later and less apparent but more finely comic absurdity of an excessive purism in grammar and diction, and the

---

[34] In his *Préface* to the first edition of *Le Tartuffe*, 1669, Molière alludes to such a conversation between the King and the Prince. An irreverent and licentious Italian play *Scaramouche Ermite* had recently been performed without protest, whereas Molière's *Tartuffe* had been suppressed. The Italian play, explained the Prince, mocks "Heaven and religion," for which certain censorious gentlemen care little, but Molière's play mocks these gentlemen themselves. The words quoted by Meredith are closer to a version of the anecdote given later, without source, by Voltaire (*Oeuvres Complètes*, Paris, 1879, XXIII, 117).

[35] See above p. 57.

tendency to be idiotic in precision. The French had felt the burden of this new nonsense; but they had to see the comedy several times before they were consoled in their suffering by seeing the cause of it exposed.

The *Misanthrope* was yet more frigidly received. Molière thought it dead. "I can not improve on it, and assuredly never shall," he said.[36] It is one of the French titles to honour that this quintessential comedy of the opposition of Alceste and Célimène was ultimately understood and applauded. In all countries the middle class presents the public which, fighting the world, and with a good footing in the fight, knows the world best. It may be the most selfish, but that is a question leading us into sophistries. Cultivated men and women, who do not skim the cream of life, and are attached to the duties, yet escape the harsher blows, make acute and balanced observers. Molière is their poet.

Of this class in England, a large body, neither Puritan nor Bacchanalian, have a sentimental objection to face the study of the actual world. They take up disdain of it, when its truths appear humiliating: when the facts are not immediately forced on them, they take up the pride of incredulity. They live in a hazy atmosphere that they suppose an ideal one. Humorous writing they will endure, perhaps approve, if it mingles with pathos to shake and elevate the feelings. They approve of Satire, because, like the beak of the vulture, it smells of carrion, which they are not. But of Comedy they have a shivering dread, for Comedy enfolds them with the wretched host of the world, huddles them with us all in an ignoble assimilation, and cannot be used by any exalted variety as a scourge and a broom. Nay, to be an exalted variety is to come under the calm curious eye of the Comic Spirit, and be probed for what you are. Men are seen among them, and very many cultivated women. You may distinguish them by a favourite phrase: "Surely we are not so bad!" and the remark: "If that is human nature, save us from it!" as if it could be done: but in the peculiar Paradise of the wilful people who will not see, the exclamation assumes the saving grace.

Yet should you ask them whether they dislike sound sense, they vow they do not. And question cultivated women whether it pleases them to be shown moving on an intellectual level with men, they will answer

---

36 The story appears in *La Vie de Mr de Molière,* 1705, by J.-L. le Gallois, Sieur de Grimarest (Paris, 1877), pp. 98–99. But the play in fact had a very successful first public run during June and July 1666.

that it does; numbers of them claim the situation. Now, Comedy is the fountain of sound sense; not the less perfectly sound on account of the sparkle: and Comedy lifts women to a station offering them free play for their wit, as they usually show it, when they have it, on the side of sound sense. The higher the Comedy, the more prominent the part they enjoy in it. Dorine in the *Tartuffe* is common-sense incarnate, though palpably a waiting-maid. Célimène is undisputed mistress of the same attribute in the *Misanthrope;* wiser as a woman than Alceste as man. In Congreve's *Way of the World*, Millamant overshadows Mirabell, the sprightliest male figure of English comedy.

But those two ravishing women, so copious and so choice of speech, who fence with men and pass their guard, are heartless! Is it not preferable to be the pretty idiot, the passive beauty, the adorable bundle of caprices, very feminine, very sympathetic, of romantic and sentimental fiction? Our women are taught to think so. The Agnès of the *Ecole des Femmes*[37] should be a lesson for men. The heroines of Comedy are like women of the world, not necessarily heartless from being clear-sighted: they seem so to the sentimentally-reared only for the reason that they use their wits, and are not wandering vessels crying for a captain or a pilot. Comedy is an exhibition of their battle with men, and that of men with them: and as the two, however divergent, both look on one object, namely, Life, the gradual similarity of their impressions must bring them to some resemblance. The Comic poet dares to show us men and women coming to this mutual likeness; he is for saying that when they draw together in social life their minds grow liker; just as the philosopher discerns the similarity of boy and girl, until the girl is marched away to the nursery. Philosopher and Comic poet are of a cousinship in the eye they cast on life: and they are equally unpopular with our wilful English of the hazy region and the ideal that is not to be disturbed.

Thus, for want of instruction in the Comic idea, we lose a large audience among our cultivated middle class that we should expect to support Comedy. The sentimentalist is as averse as the Puritan and as the Bacchanalian.

Our traditions are unfortunate. The public taste is with the idle laughers, and still inclines to follow them. It may be shown by an analysis of Wycherley's *Plain Dealer,* a coarse prose adaption of the *Misanthrope,* stuffed with lumps of realism in a vulgarized theme to

---

[37] See above p. 58. Agnès, a young girl reared by a middle-aged guardian to be his wife, breaks loose and marries a nice young man instead.

hit the mark of English appetite, that we have in it the keynote of the Comedy of our stage. It is Molière travestied, with the hoof to his foot and hair on the pointed tip of his ear. And how difficult it is for writers to disentangle themselves from bad traditions is noticeable when we find Goldsmith, who had grave command of the Comic in narrative, producing an elegant farce for a Comedy; and Fielding, who was a master of the Comic both in narrative and in dialogue, not even approaching to the presentable in farce.[38]

These bad traditions of Comedy affect us not only on the stage, but in our literature, and may be tracked into our social life. They are the ground of the heavy moralizings by which we are outwearied, about Life as a Comedy, and Comedy as a jade,[39] when popular writers, conscious of fatigue in creativeness, desire to be cogent in a modish cynicism: perversions of the idea of life, and of the proper esteem for the society we have wrested from brutishness, and would carry higher. Stock images of this description are accepted by the timid and the sensitive, as well as by the saturnine, quite seriously; for not many look abroad with their own eyes, fewer still have the habit of thinking for themselves. Life, we know too well, is not a Comedy, but something strangely mixed; nor is Comedy a vile mask. The corrupted importation from France was noxious; a noble entertainment spoilt to suit the wretched taste of a villainous age; and the later imitations of it, partly drained of its poison and made decorous, became tiresome, notwithstanding their fun, in the perpetual recurring of the same situations, owing to the absence of original study and vigour of conception. Scene V Act 2, of the *Misanthrope,* owing, no doubt, to the fact of our not producing matter for original study, is repeated in succession by Wycherley, Congreve, and Sheridan, and as it is at second hand, we have it done cynically—or such is the tone; in the manner of "below stairs."[40] Comedy thus treated may be accepted as

---

[38] See above pp. 144–45. The Licensing Act of 1737 turned Fielding away from his relatively inferior stage comedies and burlesques and helped to make him a novelist.

[39] See *Tom Jones,* Book 8, chapter 1, for Fielding's opinion of our Comedy. But he puts it simply; not as an exercise in the quasi-philosophical bathetic. [Meredith's note. The heroes of "our modern authors of Comedy," writes Fielding, "generally are notorious rogues, and their heroines abandoned jades, during the first four acts; but in the fifth, the former become very courtly gentlemen, and the latter women of virtue and discretion."]

[40] Molière's classic salon of the scandal-mongers is echoed in Wycherley's *The Plain Dealer,* II.i; Congreve's *The Way of the World,* I.i–ii; II.ii; and Sheridan's *The School for Scandal,* I.i; II.ii.

a version of the ordinary worldly understanding of our social life; at
least, in accord with the current dicta concerning it. The epigrams
can be made; but it is uninstructive, rather tending to do disservice.
Comedy justly treated, as you find it in Molière, whom we so clown-
ishly mishandled, the Comedy of Molière throws no infamous reflection upon life. It is deeply conceived, in the first place, and therefore
it cannot be impure. Meditate on that statement. Never did man
wield so shrieking a scourge upon vice, but his consummate self-mastery
is not shaken while administering it. Tartuffe and Harpagon,[41] in
fact, are made each to whip himself and his class, the false pietists,
and the insanely covetous. Molière has only set them in motion. He
strips Folly to the skin, displays the imposture of the creature, and is
content to offer her better clothing, with the lesson Chrysale reads to
Philaminte and Bélise.[42] He conceives purely, and he writes purely, in
the simplest language, the simplest of French verse. The source of his
wit is clear reason: it is a fountain of that soil; and it springs to
vindicate reason, common-sense, rightness and justice; for no vain
purpose ever. The wit is of such pervading spirit that it inspires a pun
with meaning and interest.[43] His moral does not hang like a tail, or
preach from one character incessantly cocking an eye at the audience,
as in recent realistic French plays: but is in the heart of his work,
throbbing with every pulsation of an organic structure. If Life is
likened to the comedy of Molière, there is no scandal in the comparison.

Congreve's *Way of the World* is an exception to our other comedies,
his own among them, by virtue of the remarkable brilliancy of the
writing, and the figure of Millamant. The comedy has no idea in it,
beyond the stale one, that so the world goes; and it concludes with
the jaded discovery of a document at a convenient season for the
descent of the curtain. A plot was an afterthought with Congreve. By
the help of a wooden villain (Maskwell) marked gallows to the flattest
eye, he gets a sort of plot in *The Double-Dealer*.[44] His *Way of the*

---

41 Protagonist of Molière's *L'Avare* (1667).

42 Molière, *Les Femmes Savantes*, II.vii. Chrysale is an honest tradesman of
strong common sense; Philaminte, his wife, has discharged an excellent cook for
faulty grammar; Bélise, his sister, detects subtle love-making in the speeches of
all her acquaintance.

43 *Femmes Savantes* [II.vi.64–65]:
   BÉLISE: Veux-tu toute ta vie offenser la grammaire?
   MARTINE: Qui parle d'offenser grand'mère ni grand-père?
The pun is delivered in all sincerity, from the mouth of a rustic. [Meredith's note.]

44 Maskwell seems to have been carved on the model of Iago, as by the hand
of an enterprising urchin. He apostrophizes his "invention" repeatedly: "Thanks,

World might be called "The Conquest of a Town Coquette," and Millamant is a perfect portrait of a coquette, both in her resistance to Mirabell and the manner of her surrender, and also in her tongue. The wit here is not so salient as in certain passages of *Love for Love,* where Valentine feigns madness or retorts on his father,[45] or Mrs. Frail rejoices in the harmlessness of wounds to a woman's virtue, if she "keep them from air."[46] In *The Way of the World,* it appears less prepared in the smartness, and is more diffused in the more characteristic style of the speakers. Here, however, as elsewhere, his famous wit is like a bully-fencer, not ashamed to lay traps for its exhibition, transparently petulant for the train between certain ordinary words and the powder-magazine of the improprieties to be fired. Contrast the wit of Congreve with Molière's. That of the first is a Toledo blade, sharp, and wonderfully supple for steel; cast for duelling, restless in the scabbard, being so pretty when out of it. To shine, it must have an adversary. Molière's wit is like a running brook, with innumerable fresh lights on it at every turn of the wood through which its business is to find a way. It does not run in search of obstructions, to be noisy over them; but when dead leaves and viler substances are heaped along the course, its natural song is heightened. Without effort, and with no dazzling flashes of achievement, it is full of healing, the wit of good breeding, the wit of wisdom.

"Genuine humor and true wit," says Landor, "require a sound and capacious mind, which is always a grave one.[47] Rabelais and La Fontaine are recorded by their countrymen to have been *rêveurs.* Few men have been graver than Pascal. Few men have been wittier."

To apply the citation of so great a brain as Pascal's to our countryman would be unfair. Congreve had a certain soundness of mind; of capacity, in the sense intended by Landor, he had little. Judging him by his wit, he performed some happy thrusts, and taking it for genuine, it is a surface wit, neither rising from a depth nor flowing from a spring.

On voit qu'il se travaille à dire de bons mots.[48]

---

my Invention." He hits on an invention ,to say: "Was it my Brain or Providence? —no matter which." It is no matter which, but it was not his brain. [Meredith's note. See Congreve, *The Double Dealer,* III.i; V.iv.]

[45] Congreve, *Love for Love,* IV.ii; II.i.

[46] *Love for Love,* II.ii.

[47] *Imaginary Conversations, Alfieri and the Jew Salomon.* [Meredith's note. See *The Works and Life of Walter Savage Landor,* ed. John Forster (London, 1876), IV, 269.]

[48] Molière, *Le Misanthrope,* II.v.78: Célimène draws a character sketch.

He drives the poor hack word, "fool," as cruelly to the market for wit as any of his competitors. Here is an example, that has been held up for eulogy:

WITWOUD. He has brought me a letter from the fool my brother, etc. etc.
MIRABELL. A fool, and your brother, Witwoud?
WITWOUD. Ay, ay, my half-brother. My half-brother he is; no nearer, upon my honour.
MIRABELL. Then 'tis possible he may be but half a fool.[49]

By evident preparation. This is a sort of wit one remembers to have heard at school, of a brilliant outsider; perhaps to have been guilty of oneself a trifle later. It was, no doubt, a blaze of intellectual fireworks to the bumpkin squire, who came to London to go to the theatre and learn manners.

Where Congreve excels all his English rivals is in his literary force, and a succinctness of style peculiar to him. He had correct judgment, a correct ear, readiness of illustration within a narrow range, in snapshots of the obvious at the obvious, and copious language. He hits the mean of a fine style and a natural in dialogue. He is at once precise and voluble. If you have ever thought upon style you will acknowledge it to be a signal accomplishment. In this he is a classic, and is worthy of treading a measure with Molière. *The Way of the World* may be read out currently at a first glance, so sure are the accents of the emphatic meaning to strike the eye, perforce of the crispness and cunning polish of the sentences. You have not to look over them before you confide yourself to him; he will carry you safe. Sheridan imitated, but was far from surpassing him. The flow of boudoir Billingsgate[50] in Lady Wishfort is unmatched for the vigour and pointedness of the tongue. It spins along with a final ring, like the voice of Nature in a fury, and is, indeed, racy eloquence of the elevated fishwife.

Millamant is an admirable, almost a lovable heroine. It is a piece of genius in a writer to make a woman's manner of speech portray her. You feel sensible of her presence in every line of her speaking. The stipulations with her lover in view of marriage, her fine lady's delicacy, and fine lady's easy evasions of indelicacy, coquettish airs, and playing with irresolution, which in a common maid would be bashfulness, until she submits to "dwindle into a wife," as she says,[51] form a picture

---

[49] *The Way of the World*, I.ii.
[50] "Billingsgate," originally one of the gates of London near the river, later the fishmarket there—and hence foul language, as of a fishwife.
[51] *The Way of the World*, IV.i.

that lives in the frame, and is in harmony with Mirabell's description of her:

> Here she comes, i' faith, full sail, with her fan spread, and her streamers out, and a shoal of fools for tenders.

And, after an inerview:

> Think of you! To think of a whirlwind, though 'twere in a whirlwind, were a case of more steady contemplation, a very tranquillity of mind and mansion.[52]

There is a picturesqueness, as of Millamant and no other, in her voice, when she is encouraged to take Mirabell by Mrs. Fainall,[53] who is "sure she has a mind to him":

> MILLAMANT. Are you? I think I have—and the horrid man looks as if he thought so too, etc. etc.

One hears the tones, and sees the sketch and colour of the whole scene in reading it.

Célimène is behind Millamant in vividness. An air of bewitching whimsicality hovers over the graces of this Comic heroine, like the lively conversational play of a beautiful mouth.

But in wit she is no rival of Célimène. What she utters adds to her personal witchery, and is not further memorable. She is a flashing portrait, and a type of the superior ladies who do not think, not of those who do. In representing a class, therefore, it is a lower class, in the proportion that one of Gainsborough's full-length aristocratic women is below the permanent impressiveness of a fair Venetian head.[54]

Millamant side by side with Célimène is an example of how far the realistic painting of a character can be carried to win our favour; and of where it falls short. Célimène is a woman's mind in movement, armed with an ungovernable wit; with perspicacious clear eyes for the world, and a very distinct knowledge that she belongs to the world, and is most at home in it. She is attracted to Alceste by her esteem for his honesty; she cannot avoid seeing where the good sense of the man is diseased.

Rousseau, in his letter to D'Alembert on the subject of the *Misanthrope*, discusses the character of Alceste, as though Molière had

---

[52] *The Way of the World*, II.ii.

[53] *The Way of the World*, IV.i.

[54] Thomas Gainsborough (1727–1788), English painter of lacy tall ladies standing against leafy backgrounds (e.g., his Duchess of Devonshire, exhibited in 1783). Titian (1477–1576), Venetian master, idealizer of the blonde type of northern Italy.

put him forth for an absolute example of misanthropy;[55] whereas
Alceste is only a misanthrope of the circle he finds himself placed
in: he has a touching faith in the virtue residing in the country, and
a critical love of sweet simpleness. Nor is he the principal person of
the comedy to which he gives a name. He is only passively comic.
Célimène is the active spirit. While he is denouncing and railing, the
trial is imposed upon her to make the best of him, and control herself,
as much as a witty woman, eagerly courted, can do. By appreciating
him she practically confesses her faultiness, and she is better disposed
to meet him half way than he is to bend an inch: only she is *une âme
de vingt ans*,[56] the world is pleasant, and if the gilded flies of the
Court are silly, uncompromising fanatics have their ridiculous features
as well. Can she abandon the life they make agreeable to her, for
a man who will not be guided by the common sense of his class; and
who insists on plunging into one extreme—equal to suicide in her
eyes—to avoid another? That is the comic question of the *Misanthrope*.
Why will he not continue to mix with the world smoothly, appeased
by the flattery of her secret and really sincere preference of him, and
taking his revenge in satire of it, as she does from her own not very
lofty standard, and will by and by do from his more exalted one?

Célimène is worldliness: Alceste is unworldliness. It does not quite
imply unselfishness; and that is perceived by her shrewd head. Still,
he is a very uncommon figure in her circle, and she esteems him,
l'homme aux rubans verts,[57] "who sometimes diverts but more often
horribly vexes her," as she can say of him when her satirical tongue
is on the run. Unhappily the soul of truth in him, which wins her
esteem, refuses to be tamed, or silent, or unsuspicious, and is the
perpetual obstacle to their good accord. He is that melancholy person,
the critic of everybody save himself; intensely sensitive to the faults
of others, wounded by them; in love with his own indubitable honesty,
and with his ideal of the simpler form of life befitting it: qualities
which constitute the satirist. He is a Jean Jacques of the Court. His
proposal to Célimène when he pardons her, that she should follow

---

[55] *J. J. Rousseau, Citoyen de Genève, à M. D'Alembert, de l'Académie Française*
...1758, is a protest against D'Alembert's article "Genève" in Volume VII of the
Encyclopédie and especially against the idea of establishing a *Théâtre de Comédie*
at Geneva. Comedy is the sort of writing that ridicules an upright man like Alceste,
"who detests the morals of his age...who, precisely because he loves mankind,
despises in them the wrongs they inflict upon one another...."

[56] *Le Misanthrope*, V.vii.42.

[57] *Le Misanthrope*, V.iv.

him in flying humankind, and his frenzy of detestation of her at her refusal, are thoroughly in the mood of Jean Jacques.[58] He is an impracticable creature of a priceless virtue; but Célimène may feel that to fly with him to the desert: that is from the Court to the country,

Où d'être homme d'honneur on ait la liberté,[59]

she is likely to find herself the companion of a starving satirist, like that poor princess who ran away with the waiting-man, and, when both were hungry in the forest, was ordered to give him flesh. She is a *fieffée*[60] coquette, rejoicing in her wit and her attractions, and distinguished by her inclination for Alceste in the midst of her many other lovers; only she finds it hard to cut them off—what woman with a train does not?—and when the exposure of her naughty wit has laid her under their rebuke, she will do the utmost she can: she will give her hand to honesty, but she cannot quite abandon worldliness. She would be unwise if she did.

The fable is thin. Our pungent contrivers of plots would see no indication of life in the outlines. The life of the comedy is in the idea. As with the singing of the skylark out of sight, you must love the bird to be attentive to the song, so in this highest flight of the Comic Muse, you must love pure Comedy warmly to understand the *Misanthrope*: you must be receptive of the idea of Comedy. And to love Comedy you must know the real world, and know men and women well enough not to expect too much of them, though you may still hope for good.

Menander[61] wrote a comedy called *Misogynes,* said to have been the most celebrated of his works. This misogynist is a married man, according to the fragment surviving, and is a hater of women through hatred of his wife. He generalizes upon them from the example of this lamentable adjunct of his fortunes, and seems to have got the worst of it in the contest with her, which is like the issue in reality, in the polite world. He seems also to have deserved it, which may be as true to the copy. But we are unable to say whether the wife was a good voice of her sex: or how far Menander in this instance raised the idea of woman from the mire it was plunged into by the comic poets, or rather satiric dramatists, of the middle period of Greek comedy preced-

---

58 *Le Misanthrope,* V.vii.
59 *Le Misanthrope,* V.viii.72–74.
60 "Feudally established," i.e., "out and out."
61 See above Introduction, pp. 5–6.

ing him and the New Comedy, who devoted their wit chiefly to the abuse, and for a diversity, to the eulogy of extra-mural ladies of conspicuous fame. Menander idealized them without purposely elevating. He satirized a certain Thais, and his Thais of the *Eunuchus* of Terence is neither professionally attractive nor repulsive; his picture of the two Andrians, Chrysis and her sister, is nowhere to be matched for tenderness.[62] But the condition of honest women in his day did not permit of the freedom of action and fencing dialectic of a Célimène, and consequently it is below our mark of pure Comedy.

Sainte-Beuve conjures up the ghost of Menander, saying: "For the love of me love Terence."[63] It is through love of Terence that moderns are able to love Menander; and what is preserved of Terence has not apparently given us the best of the friend of Epicurus. $M\iota\sigma o\acute{\upsilon}\mu\epsilon\nu o\varsigma$, the lover taken in horror,[64] and $\Pi\epsilon\rho\iota\kappa\epsilon\iota\rho o\mu\acute{\epsilon}\nu\eta$, the damsel shorn of her locks, have a promising sound for scenes of jealousy and a too masterful display of lordly authority, leading to regrets, of the kind known to intemperate men who imagined they were fighting with the weaker, as the fragments indicate.[65]

Of the six comedies of Terence, four are derived from Menander; two, the *Hecyra* and the *Phormio,* from Apollodorus.[66] These two are inferior in comic action and the peculiar sweetness of Menander to the *Andria,* the *Adelphi,* the *Heautontimorumenos,* and the *Eunuchus:*[67] but Phormio is a more dashing and amusing convivial parasite than the Gnatho of the last-named comedy. There were numerous rivals

---

[62] Preserved in the adaptation by Terence, *The Lady of Andros (Andria).*

[63] Charles Augustin Sainte-Beuve (1804–1869), *Nouveaux Lundis,* V (Paris, 1866), 339: "Terence," August 3, 1863.

[64] Probably, rather, *The Jilted Lover.*

[65] Meredith makes brilliant guesses which in 1905, before his death, were to be partly confirmed by the discovery of the Cairo Papyrus, containing large portions of four of Menander's plays, *Epitrepontes (The Arbitrants), Samia (The Girl from Samos), Perikeiromenē (The Girl who Gets Her Hair Cut Short),* and *Hērōs (The Hero).* The subsequent appearance of a complete play, *Duskulos (The Curmudgeon),* in the Bodmer Library, Geneva, published in 1958, has done less for Menander's stature.

[66] Terence's *Hecyra (The Mother-in-law)* and *Phormio* are derived from plays by Apollodorus Carystius.

[67] Terence's *Andria (The Lady of Andros)* is drawn from two plays by Menander, one having the same title; his *Eunuchus (The Eunuch)* is likewise from two by Menander, one having the same title; his *Heautontimorumenos (The Self-Tormentor),* from one play by Menander of the same title; his *Adelphoe (The Brothers)* from an *Adelphoi* by Menander and in part, too, from a play by Diphilus of Sinope.

of whom we know next to nothing—except by the quotations of Athenaeus and Plutarch,[68] and the Greek grammarians who cited them to support a dictum—in this as in the preceding periods of comedy in Athens, for Menander's plays are counted by many scores, and they were crowned by the prize only eight times. The favourite poet with critics, in Greece as in Rome, was Menander; and if some of his rivals here and there surpassed him in comic force,[69] and outstripped him in competition by an appositeness to the occasion that had previously in the same way deprived the genius of Aristophanes of its due reward in *Clouds* and *Birds,* his position as chief of the comic poets of his age was unchallenged. Plutarch very unnecessarily drags Aristophanes into a comparison with him, to the confusion of the older poet. Their aims, the matter they dealt in, and the times, were quite dissimilar. But it is no wonder that Plutarch, writing when Athenian beauty of style was the delight of his patrons, should rank Menander at the highest.[70] In what degree of faithfulness Terence copied Menander, whether, as he states of the passage in the *Adelphi* taken from Diphilus, *verbum de verbo*[71] in the lovelier scenes—the description of the last words of the dying Andrian, and of her funeral, for instance—remains conjectural. For us Terence shares with his master the praise of an amenity that is like Elysian speech, equable and ever gracious; like the face of the Andrian's young sister:

Adeo modesto, adeo venusto, ut nihil supra.[72]

The celebrated *flens quam familiariter,* of which the closest rendering grounds hopelessly on harsh prose, to express the sorrowful confidingness of a young girl who has lost her sister and dearest friend, and has but her lover left to her; she turned and flung herself on his

---

68 The Greek biographer and moral philosopher Plutarch of Chaeronea (c. A.D. 46–c. 120) quotes Greek plays in several of his eighty-three miscellaneous treatises known as *Moralia.* Athenaeus (c. A.D. 200) was a Greek writer of Naucratis in Egypt; his *Deipnosophistai,* or *Connoisseurs in Dining,* in fifteen books, is a source of much information about the literature of classical Greece.

69 See above pp. 5–6, 143.

70 Plutarch's *Moralia* as known today includes an abstract by another hand from a treatise which he wrote comparing Aristophanes and Menander, much to the advantage of the latter. He considered Aristophanes merely theatrical—sordid, coarse, malicious, and lewd. The Emperor Hadrian (who reigned A.D. 117–138) promoted a great renaissance of Greek culture in the Roman Empire.

71 Prologue to the *Adelphoe* of Terence, 6–11.

72 "So modest, so charming, that it couldn't be surpassed" (Terence, *Andria,* 120, slightly misquoted by Meredith).

bosom, weeping as though at home there";[73] this our instinct tells us
must be Greek, though hardly finer in Greek. Certain lines of Terence,
compared with the original fragments, show that he embellished them;
but his taste was too exquisite for him to do other than devote his
genius to the honest translation of such pieces as the above. Menander,
then; with him, through the affinity of sympathy, Terence; and
Shakespeare and Molière have this beautiful translucency of language:
and the study of the comic poets might be recommended, if for that
only.

A singular ill fate befell the writings of Menander. What we have of
him in Terence was chosen probably to please the cultivated Romans;[74]
and is a romantic play with a comic intrigue, obtained in two instances,
the *Andria* and the *Eunuchus,* by rolling a couple of his originals into
one. The titles of certain of the lost plays indicate the comic illumining
character; a *Self-Pitier,* a *Self-Chastiser,* an *Ill-tempered Man,* a
Superstitious, an *Incredulous,*[75] etc., point to suggestive domestic
themes. Terence forwarded manuscript translations from Greece, that
suffered shipwreck; he, who could have restored the treasure, died on
the way home. The zealots of Byzantium completed the work of
destruction. So we have the four comedies of Terence, numbering six
of Menander, with a few sketches of plots—one of them, the *Thesaurus,*
introduces a miser, whom we should have liked to contrast with
Harpagon—and a multitude of small fragments of a sententious cast,
fitted for quotation. Enough remains to make his greatness felt.

Without undervaluing other writers of Comedy, I think it may
be said that Menander and Molière stand alone specially as comic
poets of the feelings and the idea. In each of them there is a conception
of the Comic that refines even to pain, as in the Menedemus of the
Heautontimorumenos, and in the Misanthrope. Menander and Molière
have given the principal types to Comedy hitherto. The Micio and
Demea of the *Adelphi,* with their opposing views of the proper management of youth, are still alive; the Sganarelles and Arnolphes of the

---

[73] Terence, *Andria,* 135–36:

   tum illa, ut consuetum facile amorem cerneres,
   reiecit se in eum flens quam familiariter!

[74] Terence did not please the rough old conservative Romans; they liked Plautus
better, and the recurring mention of the *"vetus poeta"* in his prologues, who
plagued him with the crusty critical view of his productions, has in the end a
comic effect on the reader. [Meredith's note.]

[75] See J. M. Edmonds, *The Fragments of Attic Comedy,* IIIB (Leiden, 1961),
572 (*Ho Auton Penthōn*), 602 (*Ho Eauton Timōroumenos*), 700 (*Orgē*), 590
(*Ho Deisidaimōn*), 566 (*Ho Apistos*).

Ecole des Maris and the *Ecole des Femmes,* are not all buried. Tartuffe is the father of the hypocrites; Orgon of the dupes; Thraso[76] of the braggadocios; Alceste of the "Manlys";[77] Davus and Syrus[78] of the intriguing valets, the Scapins[79] and Figaros.[80] Ladies that soar in the realms of Rose-Pink, whose language wears the nodding plumes of intellectual conceit, are traceable to Philaminte and Bélise of the *Femmes Savantes;* and the mordant witty women have the tongue of Célimène. The reason is, that these two poets idealized upon life: the foundation of their types is real and in the quick, but they painted with spiritual strength, which is the solid in Art.

The idealistic conception of Comedy gives breadth and opportunities of daring to Comic genius, and helps to solve the difficulties it creates. How, for example, shall an audience be assured that an evident and monstrous dupe is actually deceived without being an absolute fool? In *Le Tartuffe* the note of high Comedy strikes when Orgon on his return home hears of his idol's excellent appetite. *Le pauvre homme!* he exclaims. He is told that the wife of his bosom has been unwell. *Et Tartuffe?*[81] he asks, impatient to hear him spoken of, his mind suffused with the thought of Tartuffe, crazy with tenderness, and again he croons, *Le pauvre homme!* It is the mother's cry of pitying delight at a nurse's recital of the feats in young animal gluttony of her cherished infant. After this masterstroke of the Comic, you not only put faith in Orgon's roseate prepossession, you share it with him by comic sympathy, and can listen with no more than a tremble of the laughing muscles to the instance he gives of the sublime humanity of Tartuffe:

> Un rien presque suffit pour le scandaliser,
> Jusque-là qu'il se vint l'autre jour accuser
> D'avoir pris une puce en faisant sa prière,
> Et de l'avoir tuée avec trop de colère.[82]

---

76 See above, Introduction, p. 6.

77 Manly is the hero of Wycherley's *The Plain Dealer.*

78 Names commonly given to slaves in Roman comedy. See Terence, *Andria, Adelphoe, Heautontimorumenos.*

79 Scapin, whose original was found in Italian comedy, is the central figure in *Les Fourberies de Scapin* (1671), by Molière.

80 Figaro is the hero of *Le Barbier de Séville* and *Le Mariage de Figaro,* by Beaumarchais (1732–1799) ; in the first a barber, in the second a valet de chambre, in both a witty intriguer.

81 *Le Tartuffe,* I.v.

82 "A mere nothing suffices to scandalize him—to the point that, just the other day, he accused himself of having caught a flea while he was praying, and of having killed it too wrathfully."—*Le Tartuffe,* I.vi.49–52.

"And to have killed it too wrathfuly"! Translating Molière is like humming an air one has heard performed by an accomplished violinist of the pure tones without flourish.

Orgon, awakening to find another dupe in Madame Pernelle, incredulous of the revelations which have at last opened his own besotted eyes, is a scene of the double Comic, vivified by the spell previously cast on the mind.[83] There we feel the power of the poet's creation; and in the sharp light of that sudden turn the humanity is livelier than any realistic work can make it.

Italian Comedy gives many hints for a Tartuffe; but they may be found in Boccaccio, as well as in Machiavelli's *Mandragola*. The Frate Timoteo of this piece is only a very oily friar, compliantly assisting an intrigue with ecclesiastical sophisms (to use the mildest word) for payment. Frate Timoteo has a fine Italian priestly pose.

> Donna. Credete voi, che 'l Turco passi questo anno in Italia?
> Frate Timoteo. Se voi non fate orazione, sì.[84]

Priestly arrogance and unctuousness, and trickeries and casuistries, cannot be painted without our discovering a likeness in the long Italian gallery. Goldoni sketched the Venetian manners of the decadence of the Republic with a French pencil,[85] and was an Italian Scribe in style.[86]

The Spanish stage is richer in such Comedies as that which furnished the idea of the *Menteur* to Corneille.[87] But you must force yourself to believe that this liar is not forcing his vein when he piles lie upon lie. There is no preceding touch to win the mind to credulity. Spanish Comedy is generally in sharp outline, as of skeletons; in quick movement, as of marionettes. The Comedy might be performed by a troop of the *corps de ballet;* and in the recollection of the reading it resolves to an animated shuffle of feet. It is, in fact, something other than the true idea of Comedy. Where the sexes are separated, men and

---

83 *Le Tartuffe,* V.iii.

84 Niccolò Machiavelli (1469–1527), *La Mandragola,* I.iii:

> Lady. Do you believe that the Turk will come to Italy this year?
> Frate Timoteo. If you do not pray, yes.

85 Carlo Goldoni (1707–1793) settled at Venice, his birthplace, in 1740 and in 1761 at Paris. He wrote more than 120 comedies in the Molièresque manner.

86 Eugène Scribe (1791–1861), Parisian author of numerous capably constructed, if not profound, plays.

87 Pierre Corneille (1606–1684), famous tragic poet, and author of the comedy *Le Menteur* (1644). In his Epître and *Examen* for this play he says it is in part translated from a Spanish play, *La Verdad Sospechosa.* At first he attributed this to Lope de Vega but later, and correctly, to Juan Ruiz de Alarcón y Mendoya (1581–1639).

women grow, as the Portuguese call it, *afaimados* of one another, famine-stricken; and all the tragic elements are on the stage. Don Juan[88] is a comic character that sends souls flying: nor does the humour of the breaking of a dozen women's hearts conciliate the Comic Muse with the drawing of blood.

German attempts at comedy remind one vividly of Heine's image of his country in the dancing of Atta Troll.[89] Lessing tried his hand at it, with a sobering effect upon readers.[90] The intention to produce the reverse effect is just visible, and therein, like the portly graces of the poor old Pyrenean bear poising and twirling on his right hind-leg and his left, consists the fun. Jean Paul Richter[91] gives the best edition of the German Comic in the contrast of Siebenkäs with his Lenette.[92] A light of the Comic is in Goethe; enough to complete the splendid figure of the man, but no more.

The German literary laugh, like the timed awakenings of their Barbarossa in the hollows of the Untersberg,[93] is infrequent, and rather monstrous—never a laugh of men and women in concert. It comes of unrefined abstract fancy, grotesque or grim, or gross, like the peculiar humours of their little earth-men. Spiritual laughter they have not yet attained to: sentimentalism waylays them in the flight. Here and there a *Volkslied* or *Märchen* shows a national aptitude for stout animal laughter; and we see that the literature is built on it, which is hopeful so far; but to enjoy it, to enter into the philosophy

---

88 Heartless libertine hero of Tirso de Molina's *Burlador de Sevila* (printed in 1630), forerunner of the protagonist in Molière's tragicomedy *Le Festin de Pierre* (1665).

89 Heinrich Heine's politico-satirical poem *Atta Troll,* in twenty-seven chapters, was published in 1843–1846. Atta Troll is a dancing bear in a village marketplace in the Pyrenees.

90 Gotthold Ephraim Lessing (1729–1781) in his earlier life wrote comedies modeled upon the French. His *Minna von Barnhelm* (1767) is commonly regarded as the first serious German comedy.

91 Johann Paul Friedrich Richter (1763–1825), better known by his pen name, "Jean Paul," a German humorist of vast imagination and sentiment.

92 Siebenkäs is the gifted and idealistic but impecunious husband of a loving but earthbound wife Lenette, in a comic novel by Jean Paul: *Flower-, Fruit-, and Thorn-Pieces, or the Married State, Death, and Wedding of the Counsel for the Indigent, F. St. Siebenkäs, of the Imperial Market-Town of Kuhschnappel,* Berlin, 1796–1797.

93 Frederick I (1123?–1190), Emperor of the Holy Roman Empire, called Barbarossa, died abroad during the Third Crusade. According to one version of a legend, he lies with his knights in enchanted sleep in a cavern high in the valley of Berchtesgaden, waiting the hour of return—and, according to another version, every hundred years, half awake, he sends out a dwarf to see if the time is ripe.

of the Broad Grin, that seems to hesitate between the skull and the embryo, and reaches its perfection in breadth from the pulling of two square fingers at the corners of the mouth, one must have aid of "the good Rhine wine," and be of German blood unmixed besides. This treble-Dutch lumbersomeness of the Comic Spirit is of itself exclusive of the idea of Comedy, and the poor voice allowed to women in German domestic life will account for the absence of comic dialogues reflecting upon life in that land. I shall speak of it again in the second section of this lecture.

Eastward you have total silence of Comedy among a people intensely susceptible to laughter, as the *Arabian Nights* will testify. Where the veil is over women's faces, you cannot have society, without which the senses are barbarous and the Comic Spirit is driven to the gutters of grossness to slake its thirst. Arabs in this respect are worse than Italians —much worse than Germans; just in the degree that their system of treating women is worse.

M. Saint-Marc Girardin,[94] the excellent French essayist and master of critical style, tells of a conversation he had once with an Arab gentleman on the topic of the different management of these difficult creatures in Orient and in Occident: and the Arab spoke in praise of many good results of the greater freedom enjoyed by Western ladies, and the charm of conversing with them. He was questioned why his countrymen took no measures to grant them something of that kind of liberty. He jumped out of his individuality in a twinkling, and entered into the sentiments of his race, replying, from the pinnacle of a splendid conceit, with affected humility of manner: "*You* can look on them without perturbation—but *we!* . . ." And after this profoundly comic interjection, he added, in deep tones, "The very face of a woman!" Our representative of temperate notions demurely consented that the Arab's pride of inflammability should insist on the prudery of the veil as the civilizing medium of his race.

There has been fun in Bagdad. But there never will be civilization where Comedy is not possible; and that comes of some degree of social equality of the sexes. I am not quoting the Arab to exhort and disturb the somnolent East; rather for cultivated women to recognize that the Comic Muse is one of their best friends. They are blind to their interests in swelling the ranks of the sentimentalists. Let them

---

[94] François Auguste Marc Girardin (1801–1873), French journalist, politician, and traveler in the Orient, author of several books of reminiscence and reflections.

look with their clearest vision abroad and at home. They will see that where they have no social freedom, Comedy is absent: where they are household drudges, the form of Comedy is primitive: where they are tolerably independent, but uncultivated, exciting melodrama takes its place and a sentimental version of them. Yet the Comic will out, as they would know if they listened to some of the private conversations of men whose minds are undirected by the Comic Muse: as the sentimental man, to his astonishment, would know likewise, if he in similar fashion could receive a lesson. But where women are on the road to an equal footing with men, in attainments and in liberty—in what they have won for themselves, and what has been granted them by a fair civilization—there, and only waiting to be transplanted from life to the stage, or the novel, or the poem, pure Comedy flourishes, and is, as it would help them to be, the sweetest of diversions, the wisest of delightful companions.

Now, to look about us in the present time, I think it will be acknowledged that in neglecting the cultivation of the Comic idea, we are losing the aid of a powerful auxiliar. You see Folly perpetually sliding into new shapes in a society possessed of wealth and leisure, with many whims, many strange ailments and strange doctors. Plenty of commonsense is in the world to thrust her back when she pretends to empire. But the first-born of common-sense, the vigilant Comic, which is the genius of thoughtful laughter, which would readily extinguish her at the outset, is not serving as a public advocate.

You will have noticed the disposition of common-sense, under pressure of some pertinacious piece of light-headedness, to grow impatient and angry. That is a sign of the absence, or at least of the dormancy, of the Comic idea. For Folly is the natural prey of the Comic, known to it in all her transformations, in every disguise; and it is with the springing delight of hawk over heron, hound after fox, that it gives her chase, never fretting, never tiring, sure of having her, allowing her no rest.

Contempt is a sentiment that cannot be entertained by comic intelligence. What is it but an excuse to be idly-minded, or personally lofty, or comfortably narrow, not perfectly humane? If we do not feign when we say that we despise Folly, we shut the brain. There is a disdainful attitude in the presence of Folly, partaking of the foolishness to Comic perception: and anger is not much less foolish than disdain. The struggle we have to conduct is essence against essence. Let no one doubt of the sequel when this emanation of what is firmest

in us is launched to strike down the daughter of Unreason and Sentimentalism: such being Folly's parentage, when it is respectable.

Our modern system of combating her is too long defensive, and
carried on too ploddingly with concrete engines of war in the attack.
She has time to get behind entrenchments. She is ready to stand a siege,
before the heavily-armed man of science and the writer of the leading
article or elaborate essay have primed their big guns. It should be
remembered that she has charms for the multitude; and an English
multitude seeing her make a gallant fight of it will be half in love
with her, certainly willing to lend her a cheer. Benevolent subscriptions
assist her to hire her own man of science, her own organ in the Press.
If ultimately she is cast out and overthrown, she can stretch a finger
at gaps in our ranks. She can say that she commanded an army and
seduced men, whom we thought sober men and safe, to act as her
lieutenants. We learn rather gloomily, after she has flashed her lantern,
that we have in our midst able men and men with minds for whom
there is no pole-star in intellectual navigation. Comedy, or the Comic
element, is the specific for the poison of delusion while Folly is passing
from the state of vapour to substantial form.

O for a breath of Aristophanes, Rabelais, Voltaire, Cervantes, Fielding, Molière! These are spirits that, if you know them well, will come
when you do call.[95] You will find the very invocation of them act on
you like a renovating air—the South-west coming off the sea, or a cry
in the Alps.

No one would presume to say that we are deficient in jokers. They
abound, and the organization directing their machinery to shoot them
in the wake of the leading article and the popular sentiment is good.

But the Comic differs from them in addressing the wits for laughter;
and the sluggish wits want some training to respond to it, whether in
public life or private, and particularly when the feelings are excited.
The sense of the Comic is much blunted by habits of punning and of
using humouristic phrase: the trick of employing Johnsonian polysyl-
lables to treat of the infinitely little. And it really may be humorous,
of a kind, yet it will miss the point by going too much round about it.

A certain French Duke Pasquier died, some years back, at a very
advanced age.[96] He had been the venerable Duke Pasquier in his later

---

95 Cf. Shakespeare, *1 King Henry IV*, III.i.53–55.
96 Etienne Denis, Duc de Pasquier (1767–1862), French statesman who lived
through the Revolution and held office under the Empire and was chancellor and
duke under Louis-Philippe. His *Memoirs* appeared posthumously (1893–1894).
Meredith had perhaps consulted *Souvenirs* published by Pasquier's *Dernier Secré-
taire*, Louis Favre (Paris, 1870), pp. 438ff.

years up to the period of his death. There was a report of Duke Pasquier that he was a man of profound egoism. Hence an argument arose, and was warmly sustained, upon the excessive selfishness of those who, in a world of troubles, and calls to action, and innumerable duties, husband their strength for the sake of living on. Can it be possible, the argument ran, for a truly generous heart to continue beating up to the age of a hundred? Duke Pasquier was not without his defenders, who likened him to the oak of the forest—a venerable comparison.

The argument was conducted on both sides with spirit and earnestness, lightened here and there by frisky touches of the polysyllabic playful, reminding one of the serious pursuit of their fun by truant boys, that are assured they are out of the eye of their master, and now and then indulge in an imitation of him. And well might it be supposed that the Comic idea was asleep, not overlooking them! It resolved at last to this, that either Duke Pasquier was a scandal on our humanity in clinging to life so long, or that he honored it by so sturdy a resistance to the enemy. As one who has entangled himself in a labyrinth is glad to get out again at the entrance, the argument ran about to conclude with its commencement.

Now, imagine a master of the Comic treating this theme, and particularly the argument on it. Imagine an Aristophanic comedy of the Centenarian, with choric praises of heroical early death, and the same of a stubborn vitality, and the poet laughing at the chorus; and the grand question for contention in dialogue, as to the exact age when a man should die, to the identical minute, that he may preserve the respect of his fellows, followed by a systematic attempt to make an accurate measurement in parallel lines, with a tough rope-yarn by one party, and a string of yawns by the other, of the veteran's power of enduring life, and our capacity for enduring *him,* with tremendous pulling on both sides. Would not the Comic view of the discussion illumine it and the disputants like very lightning? There are questions, as well as persons, that only the Comic can fitly touch.

Aristophanes would probably have crowned the ancient tree, with the consolatory observation to the haggard line of long-expectant heirs of the Centenarian, that they live to see the blessedness of coming of a strong stock. The shafts of his ridicule would mainly have been aimed at disputants. For the sole ground of the argument was the old man's character, and sophists are not needed to demonstrate that we can very soon have too much of a bad thing. A Centenarian does not necessarily provoke the Comic idea, nor does the corpse of a duke. It is not provoked in the order of nature, until we draw its penetrating attentiveness to some circumstance with which we have been mixing our private interests, or our speculative obfuscation. Dulness, insensible to the Comic, has the privilege of arousing it; and the laying of a dull finger on matters of human life is the surest method of establishing electrical communications with a battery of laughter—where the Comic idea is prevalent.

But if the Comic idea prevailed with us, and we had an Aristophanes to barb and wing it, we should be breathing air of Athens. Prosers now pouring forth on us like public fountains would be cut short in the street and left blinking, dumb as pillar-posts, with letters thrust into their mouths. We should throw off incubus, our dreadful familiar—by some called boredom—whom it is our present humiliation to be just alive enough to loathe, never quick enough to foil. There would be a bright and positive, clear Hellenic perception of facts. The vapours of Unreason and Sentimentalism would be blown away before they were productive. Where would Pessimist and Optimist be? They would in any case have a diminished audience. Yet possibly the change of despots, from good-natured old obtuseness to keen-edged intelligence, which is by nature merciless, would be more than we could bear. The rupture of the link between dull people, consisting in the fraternal agreement that something is too clever for them, and a shot beyond them, is not to be thought lightly; for, slender though the link may seem, it is equivalent to a cement forming a concrete of dense cohesion, very desirable in the estimation of the statesman.

A political Aristophanes, taking advantage of his lyrical Bacchic licence, was found too much for political Athens.[97] I would not ask to have him revived, but that the sharp light of such a spirit as his might be with us to strike now and then on public affairs, public themes, to make them spin along more briskly.

He hated with the politician's fervor the Sophist who corrupted simplicity of thought,[98] the poet who destroyed purity of style,[99] the demagogue, "the saw-toothed monster,"[100] who, as he conceived, chicaned the mob, and he held his own against them by strength of laughter, until fines, the curtailing of his Comic licence in the chorus,

---

[97] See *The Acharnians,* 377ff., 497–504, allusions to an attack on the poet by the politician Cleon in response to an earlier comedy which does not survive, *The Babylonians.*

[98] See below p. 267, n. 104.

[99] He made fun of Euripides several times, especially in *The Frogs.*

[100] Cleon, in *The Wasps,* 1031; an allusion to the poet's earlier attack on him in *The Knights,* 1017.

and ultimately the ruin of Athens, which could no longer support the expense of the chorus,[101] threw him altogether on dialogue, and brought him under the law. After the catastrophe, the poet, who had ever been gazing back at the men of Marathon and Salamis, must have felt that he had foreseen it; and that he was wise when he pleaded for peace,[102] and derided military coxcombry, and the captious old creature Demus,[103] we can admit. He had the Comic poet's gift of common-sense—which does not always include political intelligence; yet his political tendency raised him above the Old Comedy turn for uproarious farce. He abused Socrates,[104] but Xenophon, the disciple of Socrates, by his trained rhetoric saved the Ten Thousand.[105] Aristophanes might say that if his warnings had been followed there would have been no such thing as a mercenary Greek expedition under Cyrus. Athens, however, was on a landslip, falling; none could arrest it. To gaze back, to uphold the old times, was a most natural conservatism, and fruitless. The aloe had bloomed.[106] Whether right or wrong in his politics and his criticism, and bearing in mind the instruments he played on and the audience he had to win, there is an idea in his comedies: it is the Idea of Good Citizenship.

---

101 After the defeat of Athens by the Spartan Lysander in 404, leading Athenian citizens were no longer rich enough to underwrite the chorus. In the last two of the extant plays of Aristophanes, the *Ecclesiazusae* and *Plutus,* the chorus is much reduced.

102 The defeat of the Persians by the Greeks under Miltiades at Marathon in 490 B.C. and the destruction of the Persian fleet of Xerxes by the Greeks at Salamis in 480 were great national events reflected in the spirit of the classic tragedies by the soldier-poet Aeschylus. Aristophanes alludes to the heroes of Marathon in *The Acharnians,* 181, and to Marathon and Salamis in *The Knights,* 781–85. *The Babylonians,* a play now lost, produced by Aristophanes in 426, *The Acharnians,* produced at the Lenaea in 425, and *The Knights,* 424, are attacks on the war-leader Cleon and pleas for the end of the Peloponnesian War (431–404 B.C.). After the death of Cleon in 424, the theme continues in *The Peace,* 421, celebrating the approach of the short-lived Peace of Nicias, and in the fiction of the successful women's stratagem in *Lysistrata,* 411. The downfall of Athens followed soon after the naval victory of the Spartans under Lysander at Aegospotami in 405.

103 A personification of the Athenian people in Aristophanes' *Knights:* the John Bull of Athens.

104 Aristophanes satirized Socrates in *The Clouds.*

105 Xenophon, soldier of fortune and miscellaneous writer, records his recollections of Socrates in his *Memorabilia, Apology,* and *Symposium.* He organized the ten thousand Greek mercenaries, and brought them home, after the defeat of Cyrus by Artaxerxes in the battle of Cūnaxa near Babylon in 401 B.C. He tells the story in what is today perhaps the best known of his numerous works, his *Anabasis.* See especially III.i and ii.

106 The aloe, or century plant, according to popular notion, shoots up once every hundred years, blooms, and sinks down.

He is not likely to be revived. He stands, like Shakespeare, an unapproachable. Swift says of him, with a loving chuckle:

> But as for Comic Aristophanes,
> The dog too witty and too profane is.[107]

Aristophanes was "prófane," under satiric direction, unlike his rivals Cratinus, Phrynichus, Ameipsias, Eupolis, and others, if we are to believe him, who in their extraordinary Donnybrook Fair[108] of the day of Comedy, thumped one another and everybody else with absolute heartiness, as he did, but aimed at small game, and dragged forth particular women, which he did not. He is an aggregate of many men, all of a certain greatness. We may build up a conception of his powers if we mount Rabelais upon *Hudibras*,[109] lift him with the songfulness of Shelley, give him a vein of Heinrich Heine, and cover him with the mantle of the *Anti-Jacobin*,[110] adding (that there may be some Irish in him) a dash of Grattan,[111] before he is in motion.

But such efforts at conceiving one great one by incorporation of minors are vain, and cry for excuse. Supposing Wilkes[112] for leading man in a country constantly plunging into war under some plumed Lamachus,[113] with enemies periodically firing the land up to the gates of London, and a Samuel Foote,[114] of prodigious genius, attacking him with ridicule, I think it gives a notion of the conflict engaged in by Aristophanes. This laughing bald-pate, as he calls himself,[115] was a Titanic pamphleteer, using laughter for his political weapon; a laughter without scruple, the laughter of Hercules.[116] He was primed with wit, as with the garlic he speaks of giving to the gamecocks to make them fight the better.[117] And he was a lyric poet of aerial delicacy, with

---

107 Misquoted from Swift's lines *To Dr. Sheridan*, 1718.

108 A riot or free-for-all fight, named after a fair formerly held at Donnybrook, Ireland. Aristophanes refers to his rivals in the parabasis of *The Knights*, 507–46; and in that of *The Clouds*, 518–62; and in *The Frogs*, 14.

109 An anti-Puritan burlesque poem in tetrameter couplets with comic rhyme, by Samuel Butler (1612?–1680), published in three parts (1663, 1664, 1678).

110 A periodical founded in 1797 by the statesmen George Canning (1770–1827) and edited by the satirist William Gifford.

111 Henry Grattan (1746–1820), Irish statesman and brilliant invective orator.

112 John Wilkes (1727–1797)),)English politician, libelous and licentious writer, five times expelled from the House of Commons, Lord Mayor of London in 1774.

113 An Athenian general in the Peloponnesian war, colleague of Alcibiades and Nicias in the ill-fated Sicilian expedition, 415 B.C.

114 London playwright and actor (1720–1777), distinguished for his powers of comic mimicry, sometimes called the "English Aristophanes."

115 *The Peace*, 771.

116 *The Frogs*, 42–46.

117 *The Acharnians*, 166; *The Knights*, 497.

the homely song of a jolly national poet, and a poet of such feeling that the comic mask is at times no broader than a cloth on a face to show the serious features of our common likeness. He is not to be revived; but if his method were studied, some of the fire in him would come to us, and we might be revived.

Taking them generally, the English public are most in sympathy with this primitive Aristophanic comedy, wherein the comic is capped by the grotesque, irony tips the wit, and satire is a naked sword. They have the basis of the Comic in them: an esteem for common-sense. They cordially dislike the reverse of it. They have a rich laugh, though it is not the *gros rire* of the Gaul tossing *gros sel,* nor the polished Frenchman's mentally digestive laugh. And if they have now, like a monarch with a troop of dwarfs, too many jesters kicking the dictionary about,[118] to let them reflect that they are dull, occasionally, like the pensive monarch surprising himself with an idea of an idea of his own, they look so. And they are given to looking in the glass. They must see that something ails them. How much even the better order of them will endure, without a thought of the defensive, when the person afflicting them is protected from satire, we read in Memoirs of a Preceding Age, where the vulgarly tyrannous hostess of a great house of reception shuffled the guests and played them like a pack of cards, with her exact estimate of the strength of each one printed on them: and still this house continued to be the most popular in England; nor did the lady ever appear in print or on the boards as the comic type that she was.[119]

It has been suggested that they have not yet spiritually comprehended the signification of living in society; for who are cheerfuller, brisker of wit, in the fields, and as explorers, colonizers, backwoodsmen? They are happy in rough exercise, and also in complete repose. The intermediate condition, when they are called upon to talk to one another, upon other than affairs of business or their hobbies, reveals them wearing a curious look of vacancy, as it were the socket of an eye wanting. The Comic is perpetually springing up in social life, and it oppresses them from not being perceived.

Thus, at a dinner-party, one of the guests, who happens to have

---

118 He is saying that the English comic writers of the day are too much given to word-play. His friend F. C. Burnand, editor of *Punch,* 1880–1906, wrote *Antony and Cleopatra, or His-tory and Her-story in a Modern Nilo-metre,* 1866, and *F. M. Julius Cnaesar, the Irregular Rum'un,* 1870.

119 This lady has not been securely identified. It is not important that she should be.

enrolled himself in a Burial Company, politely entreats the others to inscribe their names as shareholders, expatiating on the advantages accruing to them in the event of their very possible speedy death, the salubrity of the site, the aptitude of the soil for a quick consumption of their remains, etc.; and they drink sadness from the incongruous man, and conceive indigestion, not seeing him in a sharply defined light, that would bid them taste the comic of him. Or it is mentioned that a newly elected member of our Parliament celebrates his arrival at eminence by the publication of a book on cab fares, dedicated to a beloved female relative deceased, and the comment on it is the word "Indeed." But, merely for a contrast, turn to a not uncommon scene of yesterday in the hunting-field, where a brilliant young rider, having broken his collar-bone, trots away very soon after, against medical interdict, half put together in splinters, to the most distant meet of his neighborhood, sure of escaping his doctor, who is the first person he encounters. "I came here purposely to avoid you," says the patient. "I came here purposely to take care of you," says the doctor. Off they go, and come to a swollen brook. The patient clears it handsomely: the doctor tumbles in. All the field are alive with the heartiest relish of every incident and every cross-light on it; and dull would the man have been thought who had not his word to say about it when riding home.

In our prose literature we have had delightful Comic writers. Besides Fielding and Goldsmith, there is Miss Austen, whose Emma and Mr. Elton[120] might walk straight into a comedy, were the plot arranged for them. Galt's neglected novels have some characters and strokes of shrewd comedy.[121] In our poetic literature the comic is delicate and graceful above the touch of Italian and French. Generally, however, the English elect excel in satire, and they are noble humourists. The national disposition is for hard-hitting, with a moral purpose to sanction it; or for a rosy, sometimes a larmoyant, geniality, not unmanly in its verging upon tenderness, and with a singular attraction for thick-headedness, to decorate it with asses' ears and the most beautiful sylvan haloes. But the Comic is a different spirit.

You may estimate your capacity for Comic perception by being able to detect the ridicule of them you love, without loving them less:

---

[120] Clever and well-intentioned but officious and bungling young heroine and aspiring but hapless country vicar in Jane Austen's *Emma*, 1816.

[121] John Galt (1779–1839), a novelist who dealt with aspects of Scottish rural life.

and more by being able to see yourself somewhat ridiculous in dear eyes, and accepting the correction their image of you proposes.

Each one of an affectionate couple may be willing, as we say, to die for the other, yet unwilling to utter the agreeable word at the right moment; but if the wits were sufficiently quick for them to perceive that they are in a comic situation, as affectionate couples must be when they quarrel, they would not wait for the moon or the almanac, or a Dorine,[122] to bring back the flood-tide of tender feelings, that they should join hands and lips.

If you detect the ridicule, and your kindliness is chilled by it, you are slipping into the grasp of Satire.

If instead of falling foul of the ridiculous person with a satiric rod, to make him writhe and shriek aloud, you prefer to sting him under a semi-caress, by which he shall in his anguish be rendered dubious whether indeed anything has hurt him, you are an engine of Irony.

If you laugh all round him, tumble him, roll him about, deal him a smack, and drop a tear on him, own his likeness to you and yours to your neighbor, spare him as little as you shun, pity him as much as you expose, it is a spirit of Humour that is moving you.

The Comic, which is the perceptive, is the governing spirit, awakening and giving aim to these powers of laughter, but it is not to be confounded with them: it enfolds a thinner form of them, differing from satire, in not sharply driving into the quivering sensibilities, and from humour, in not comforting them and tucking them up, or indicating a broader than the range of this bustling world to them.

Fielding's Jonathan Wild presents a case of this peculiar distinction, when that man of eminent greatness remarks upon the unfairness of a trial in which the condemnation has been brought about by twelve men of the opposite party; for it is not satiric, it is not humorous; yet it is immensely comic to hear a guilty villain protesting that his own "party" should have a voice in the Law. It opens an avenue into villains' ratiocination.[123] And the Comic is not cancelled though we should suppose Jonathan to be giving play to his humour. I may have

---

122 Molière, *Le Tartuffe,* II.iv.
123 The exclamation of Lady Booby, when Joseph defends himself—*"Your virtue!...* I shall never survive it!" etc.—is another case.—*Joseph Andrews.* Also that of Miss Matthews in her narrative to Booth: "But such are the friendships of women."—*Amelia.* [Meredith's note. See *Joseph Andrews* (1742), I.viii; *Amelia* (1752), I.viii.]

dreamed this or had it suggested to me, for on referring to *Jonathan Wild,* I do not find it.[124]

Apply the case to the man of deep wit, who is ever certain of his condemnation by the opposite party, and then it ceases to be comic, and will be satiric.

The look of Fielding upon Richardson is essentially comic.[125] His method of correcting the sentimental writer is a mixture of the comic and the humorous. Parson Adams is a creation of humour.[126] But both the conception and the presentation of Alceste and of Tartuffe, of Célimène and Philaminte, are purely comic, addressed to the intellect: there is no humour in them, and they refresh the intellect they quicken to detect their comedy, by force of the contrast they offer between themselves and the wiser world about them; that is to say, society, or that assemblage of minds whereof the Comic Spirit has its origin.

Byron had splendid powers of humour, and the most poetic satire that we have example of, fusing at times to hard irony. He had no strong comic sense, or he would not have taken an anti-social position, which is directly opposed to the Comic; and in his philosophy, judged by philosophers, he is a comic figure, by reason of this deficiency. *Sobald er philosophirt ist er ein Kind,*[127] Goethe says of him. Carlyle sees him in this comic light, treats him in the humorous manner.[128]

The Satirist is a moral agent, often a social scavenger, working on a storage of bile.

The Ironist is one thing or another, according to his caprice. Irony is the humour of satire; it may be savage, as in Swift,[129] with a moral

---

124 See *The Life of Mr. Jonathan Wild the Great* (1743), I.ii. During the reign of Charles I, a felonious ancestor of Jonathan's named James Wild "was, contrary to the law of arms, put basely and cowardly to death by a combination between twelve men of the enemy's party." Jonathan Wild, a notorious felon, was executed, after a celebrated trial, at Tyburn on May 24, 1725.

125 Fielding's *Joseph Andrews,* 1742, seems to begin as a parody of Richardson's prurient and commercial moralism in *Pamela,* 1740, but it quickly expands into an exuberantly original comic novel.

126 Mr. Abraham Adams, the kindly, ingenuous, eccentric country curate in *Joseph Andrews.* Cf. above, pp. 146, 148, 159.

127 Slightly misquoted from a conversation of Goethe's with Eckermann, January 18, 1825. See *Goethes Gespräche,* ed. von Biedermann, III, 156: "the moment he tries to think he is a child."

128 See, e.g., *Past and Present,* III.iv.

129 See *A Modest Proposal for Preventing the Children of Poor People from Being a Burthen to their Parents, or Country, and for Making Them Beneficial to the Publick,* Dublin, 1729. Swift's *persona* argues the advantage that would arise,

object, or sedate, as in Gibbon,[130] with a malicious. The foppish irony fretting to be seen, and the irony which leers, that you shall not mistake its intention, are failures in satiric effort pretending to the treasures of ambiguity.

The Humourist of mean order is a refreshing laugher, giving tone to the feelings and sometimes allowing the feelings to be too much for him. But the Humourist of high has an embrace of contrasts beyond the scope of the Comic poet.

Heart and mind laugh out at Don Quixote, and still you brood on him. The juxtaposition of the knight and squire is a Comic conception, the opposition of their natures most humorous. They are as different as the two hemispheres in the time of Columbus, yet they touch and are bound in one by laughter. The knight's great aims and constant mishaps, his chivalrous valiancy exercised on absurd objects, his good sense along the high road of the craziest of expeditions; the compassion he plucks out of derision, and the admirable figure he preserves while stalking through the frantically grotesque and burlesque assailing him, are in the loftiest moods of humour, fusing the Tragic sentiment with the Comic narrative.

The stroke of the great humourist is world-wide, with lights of Tragedy in his laughter.

Taking a living great, though not creative, humourist to guide our description: the skull of Yorick is in his hands in our seasons of festival; he sees visions of primitive man capering preposterously under the gorgeous robes of ceremonial.[131] Our souls must be on fire when we wear solemnity, if we would not press upon his shrewdest nerve. Finite and infinite flash from one to the other with him, lending him a two-edged thought that peeps out of his peacefullest lines by fits, like the lantern of the fire-watcher at windows, going the rounds at night. The comportment and performances of men in society are to him, by the vivid comparison with their mortality, more grotesque than

given the depressed condition of Ireland, if the young children of the poor were to be sold as food for the rich.

[130] Meredith is thinking, no doubt, of such a passage in Gibbon as his "solemn sneer" at Christianity in chapter XV of *The Decline and Fall of the Roman Empire*.

[131] Thomas Carlyle (1795–1881) published his metaphysical and autobiographical fantasy *Sartor Resartus* [The Tailor Re-patched]: *The Life and Opinions of Herr Teufelsdröckh*, in *Fraser's Magazine* during 1833–1834. For the philosophy of clothes, see, e.g., I.v, ix. Carlyle was more than eighty-one years old when Meredith delivered the lecture.

respectable. But ask yourself, Is he always to be relied on for justness? He will fly straight as the emissary eagle back to Jove[132] at the true Hero. He will also make as determined a swift descent upon the man of his wilful choice, whom we cannot distinguish as a true one. This vast power of his, built up of the feelings and the intellect in union, is often wanting in proportion and in discretion. Humourists touching upon History or Society are given to be capricious. They are, as in the case of Sterne, given to be sentimental;[133] for with them the feelings are primary, as with singers. Comedy, on the other hand, is an interpretation of the general mind, and is for that reason of necessity kept in restraint. The French lay marked stress on *mesure et goût*, and they own how much they owe to Molière for leading them in simple justness and taste. We can teach them many things; they can teach us in this.

The Comic poet is in the narrow field, or enclosed square, of the society he depicts; and he addresses the still narrower enclosure of men's intellects, with reference to the operation of the social world upon their characters. He is not concerned with beginnings or endings or surroundings, but with what you are now weaving. To understand his work and value it, you must have a sober liking of your kind and a sober estimate of our civilized qualities. The aim and business of the Comic poet are misunderstood, his meaning is not seized nor his point of view taken, when he is accused of dishonouring our nature and being hostile to sentiment, tending to spitefulness and making an unfair use of laughter. Those who detect irony in Comedy do so because they choose to see it in life. Poverty, says the satirist, has nothing harder in itself than that it makes men ridiculous.[134] But poverty is never ridiculous to Comic perception until it attempts to make its rags conceal its bareness in a forlorn attempt at decency, or foolishly to rival ostentation. Caleb Balderstone, in his endeavour to keep up the honour of a noble household in a state of beggary, is an exquisitely comic character.[135] In the case of "poor relatives," on the other hand, it is the rich, whom they perplex, that are really comic; and to laugh at the former, not seeing the comedy of the latter, is to betray dulness

---

132 In classical writers, the eagle is the herald of Zeus. See, e.g., *Iliad,* XXIV.310; Euripides, *Ion,* 158–60.

133 Sterne's *Sentimental Journey through France and Italy* appeared in the winter of 1768, just after the insolvent author had died of pleurisy in London lodgings.

134 Juvenal, *Satires,* III.152–53.

135 Aged and devoted family butler in *The Bride of Lammermoor* (1819), by Sir Walter Scott.

of vision. Humourist and Satirist frequently hunt together as Ironists in pursuit of the grotesque, to the exclusion of the Comic. That was an affecting moment in the history of the Prince Regent, when the First Gentleman of Europe burst into tears at a sarcastic remark of Beau Brummell's on the cut of his coat.[136] Humour, Satire, Irony, pounce on it altogether as their common prey. The Comic Spirit eyes but does not touch it. Put into action, it would be farcical. It is too gross for Comedy.

Incidents of a kind casting ridicule on our unfortunate nature instead of our conventional life, provoke derisive laughter, which thwarts the Comic idea. But derision is foiled by the play of the Intellect. Most of doubtful causes in contest are open to Comic interpretation, and any intellectual pleading of a doubtful cause contains germs of an Idea of Comedy.

The laughter of satire is a blow in the back or the face. The laughter of Comedy is impersonal and of unrivalled politeness, nearer a smile; often no more than a smile. It laughs through the mind, for the mind directs it; and it might be called the humour of the mind.

One excellent test of the civilization of a country, as I have said, I take to be the flourishing of the Comic idea and Comedy; and the test of true comedy is that it shall awaken thoughtful laughter.

If you believe that our civilization is founded in common-sense (and it is the first condition of sanity to believe it), you will, when contemplating men, discern a Spirit overhead; not more heavenly than the light flashed upward from glassy surfaces, but luminous and watchful; never shooting beyond them, nor lagging in the rear; so closely attached to them that it may be taken for a slavish reflect, until its features are studied. It has the sage's brows, and the sunny malice of a faun lurks at the corners of the half-closed lips drawn in an idle wariness of half tension. That slim feasting smile, shaped like the long-bow, was once a big round satyr's laugh, that flung up the brows like a fortress lifted by gunpowder. The laugh will come again, but it will be of the order of the smile, finely tempered, showing sunlight of the mind, mental richness rather than noisy enormity. Its common aspect is one of unsolicitous observation, as if surveying a full field and

---

136 George Bryan, known as "Beau," Brummell (1778–1840) was a leader of fashion in London and for a time friend of the Prince Regent (later George IV). The anecdote seems to be Meredith's memorial transformation of a slightly different incident. See Florence Ellicott, "Beau Brummell," *Temple Bar*, XXXV (1872), 236.

having leisure to dart on its chosen morsels, without any fluttering eagerness. Men's future upon earth does not attract it; their honesty and shapeliness in the present does; and whenever they wax out of proportion, overblown, affected, pretentious, bombastical, hypocritical, pedantic, fantastically delicate; whenever it sees them self-deceived or hoodwinked, given to run riot in idolatries, drifting into vanities, congregating in absurdities, planning short-sightedly, plotting dementedly; whenever they are at variance with their professions, and violate the unwritten but perceptible laws binding them in consideration one to another; whenever they offend sound reason, fair justice; are false in humility or mined with conceit, individually, or in the bulk—the Spirit overhead will look humanely malign and cast an oblique light on them, followed by volleys of silvery laughter. That is the Comic Spirit.

Not to distinguish it is to be bull-blind to the spiritual, and to deny the existence of a mind of man where minds of men are in working conjunction.

You must, as I have said, believe that our state of society is founded in common-sense, otherwise you will not be struck by the contrasts the Comic Spirit perceives, or have it to look to for your consolation. You will, in fact, be standing in that peculiar oblique beam of light, yourself illuminated to the general eye as the very object of chase and doomed quarry of the thing obscure to you. But to feel its presence and to see it is your assurance that many sane and solid minds are with you in what you are experiencing: and this of itself spares you the pain of satirical heat, and the bitter craving to strike heavy blows. You share the sublime of wrath, that would not have hurt the foolish, but merely demonstrate their foolishness. Molière was contented to revenge himself on the critics of the *Ecole des Femmes,* by writing the *Critique de L'Ecole des Femmes,* one of the wisest as well as the playfullest of studies in criticism.[137] A perception of the Comic Spirit gives high fellowship. You become a citizen of the selecter world, the highest we know of in connection with our old world, which is not supermundane. Look there for your unchallengeable upper class! You feel that you are one of this our civilized community, that you cannot escape from it, and would not if you could. Good hope sustains you; weariness does not overwhelm you; in isolation you see no charms for vanity; personal pride is greatly moderated. Nor shall your title of citizenship exclude you from worlds of imagination or of devotion. The

---

137 See above p. 61.

Comic Spirit is not hostile to the sweetest songfully poetic. Chaucer bubbles with it: Shakespeare overflows: there is a mild moon's ray of it (pale with super refinement through distance from our flesh and blood planet) in *Comus*. Pope has it, and it is the daylight side of the night half obscuring Cowper.[138] It is only hostile to the priestly element, when that, by baleful swelling, transcends and overlaps the bounds of its office: and then, in extreme cases, it is too true to itself to speak, and veils the lamps: as, for example, the spectacle of Bossuet over the dead body of Molière:[139] at which the dark angels may, but men do not, laugh.

We have had comic pulpits,[140] for a sign that the laughter-moving and the worshipful may be in alliance: I know not how far comic, or how much assisted in seeming so by the unexpectedness and the relief of its appearance: at least they are popular, they are said to win the ear. Laughter is open to perversion, like other good things; the scornful and the brutal sorts are not unknown to us; but the laughter directed by the Comic Spirit is a harmless wine, conducing to sobriety in the degree that it enlivens. It enters you like fresh air into a study; as when one of the sudden contrasts of the comic idea floods the brain like reassuring daylight. You are cognizant of the true kind by feeling that you take it in, savour it, and have what flowers live on, natural air for food. That which you give out—the joyful roar—is not the better part; let that go to good fellowship and the benefit of the lungs. Aristophanes promises his auditors that if they will retain the ideas of the comic poet carefully, as they keep dried fruits in boxes, their garments shall smell odoriferous of wisdom throughout the year.[141] The boast will not be thought an empty one by those who have choice

---

138 The poet William Cowper (1731–1800) suffered from periodic attacks of religious melancholy, which produced such poems as *Lines Written during a Period of Insanity*, 1763, and *The Castaway*, 1799. In serener moments he could write a comical ballad, *The Diverting History of John Gilpin*, 1782, or the finely tempered couplet satire of his *Table Talk*, 1782, and his mellow and whimsical georgic in Miltonic blank verse, *The Task*, 1784.

139 See above, p. 58, the death of Molière. Jacques Bénigne Bossuet (1672–1704) was the court preacher and reigning pulpit orator of the day. In 1693 he published *Maximes et Réflexions sur la Comédie*, in which (Chapter III) he comes down on the immorality and impiety of Molière and alludes to his having "expired, so to speak, before our eyes."

140 Isaac Barrow (1630–1677) and Robert South (1634–1716) were noted as witty, even humorous, preachers, but in a manner more metaphysical than comic. Laurence Sterne published his four volumes of sermons as *Sermons of Mr. Yorick*, 1760–1767.

141 *The Wasps*, 1051–59.

friends that have stocked themselves according to his directions. Such treasuries of sparkling laughter are wells in our desert. Sensitiveness to the comic laugh is a step in civilization. To shrink from being an object of it is a step in cultivation. We know the degree of refinement in men by the matter they will laugh at, and the ring of the laugh; but we know likewise that the larger natures are distinguished by the great breadth of their power of laughter, and no one really loving Molière is refined by that love to despise or be dense to Aristophanes, though it may be that the lover of Aristophanes will not have risen to the height of Molière. Embrace them both, and you have the whole scale of laughter in your breast. Nothing in the world surpasses in stormy fun the scene in *The Frogs*,[142] when Bacchus and Xanthias receive their thrashings from the hands of businesslike Aeacus, to discover which is the divinity of the two, by his imperviousness to the mortal condition of pain, and each, under the obligation of not crying out, makes believe that' his horrible bellow—the god's *iou iou* being the lustier—means only the stopping of a sneeze, or horseman sighted, or the prelude to an invocation to some deity: and the slave contrives that the god shall get the bigger lot of blows. Passages of Rabelais, one or two in *Don Quixote,* and the Supper in the Manner of the Ancients, in *Peregrine Pickle*,[143] are of a similar cataract of laughter. But it is not illuminating; it is not the laughter of the mind. Molière's laughter, in his purest comedies, is ethereal, as light to our nature, as colour to our thoughts. The *Misanthrope* and the *Tartuffe* have no audible laughter; but the characters are steeped in the comic spirit. They quicken the mind through laughter, from coming out of the mind; and the mind accepts them because they are clear interpretations of certain chapters of the Book lying open before us all.[144] Between these two stand Shakespeare and Cervantes, with the richer laugh of heart and mind in one; with much of the Aristophanic robustness, something of Molière's delicacy.

The laughter heard in circles not pervaded by the Comic idea, will

---

142 *The Frogs,* 612–73.

143 See Tobias George Smollett, *The Adventures of Peregrine Pickle,* 1751, Chapter XLIV: "The Doctor prepares an Entertainment in the Manner of the Ancients, which is attended with divers ridiculous Circumstances."

144 "The Book of Earth," "the Book of Egoism," a "book full of the world's wisdom"—the book "in which the generations have written ever since they took to writing." "The Book needs a powerful compression." And Comedy is its best compressor or interpreter. That is, we need wit more than volumes of information (Meredith's Prelude to *The Egoist,* 1879).

sound harsh and soulless, like versified prose, if you step into them with a sense of the distinction. You will fancy you have changed your habitation to a planet remoter from the sun. You may be among powerful brains too. You will not find poets—or but a stray one, over-worshipped. You will find learned men undoubtedly, professors, reputed philosophers, and illustrious dilettanti. They have in them, perhaps, every element composing light, except the Comic. They read verse, they discourse of art; but their eminent faculties are not under that vigilant sense of a collective supervision, spiritual and present, which we have taken note of. They build a temple of arrogance; they speak much in the voice of oracles; their hilarity, if it does not dip in grossness, is usually a form of pugnacity.

Insufficiency of sight in the eye looking outward has deprived them of the eye that should look inward. They have never weighed themselves in the delicate balance of the Comic idea so as to obtain a suspicion of the rights and dues of the world; and they have, in consequence, an irritable personality. A very learned English professor crushed an argument in a political discussion, by asking his adversary angrily: "Are you aware, sir, that I am a philologer?"

The practice of polite society will help in training them, and the professor on a sofa with beautiful ladies on each side of him, may become their pupil and a scholar in manners without knowing it: he is at least a fair and pleasing spectacle to the Comic Muse. But the society named polite is volatile in its adorations, and to-morrow will be petting a bronzed soldier, or a black African, or a prince, or a spiritualist: ideas cannot take root in its ever-shifting soil. It is besides addicted in self-defence to gabble exclusively of the affairs of its rapidly revolving world, as children on a whirligoround bestow their attention on the wooden horse or cradle ahead of them, to escape from giddiness and preserve a notion of identity. The professor is better out of a circle that often confounds by lionizing, sometimes annoys by abandoning, and always confuses. The school that teaches gently what peril there is lest a cultivated head should still be coxcomb's, and the collisions which may befall high-soaring minds, empty or full, is more to be recommended than the sphere of incessant motion supplying it with material.

Lands where the Comic Spirit is obscure overhead are rank with raw crops of matter. The traveller accustomed to smooth highways and people not covered with burrs and prickles is amazed, amid so much that is fair and cherishable, to come upon such curious barbarism. An

Englishman paid a visit of admiration to a professor in the Land of Culture, and was introduced by him to another distinguished professor, to whom he took so cordially as to walk out with him alone one afternoon. The first professor, an erudite entirely worthy of the sentiment of scholarly esteem prompting the visit, behaved (if we exclude the dagger) with the vindictive jealousy of an injured Spanish beauty. After a short prelude of gloom and obscure explosions, he discharged upon his faithless admirer the bolts of passionate logic familiar to the ears of flighty caballeros:—"Either I am a fit object of your admiration, or I am not. Of these things, one—either you are competent to judge, in which case I stand condemned by you; or you are incompetent, and therefore impertinent, and you may betake yourself to your country again, hypocrite!" That admirer was for persuading the wounded scholar that it is given to us to be able to admire two professors at a time. He was driven forth.

Perhaps this might have occurred in any country, and a comedy of The Pedant, discovering the greedy humanity within the dusty scholar, would not bring it home to one in particular. I am mindful that it was in Germany, when I observe that the Germans have gone through no comic training to warn them of the sly, wise emanation eyeing them from aloft, nor much of satirical. Heinrich Heine[145] has not been enough to cause them to smart and meditate. Nationally, as well as individually, when they are excited they are in danger of the grotesque, as when, for instance, they decline to listen to evidence, and raise a national outcry because one of German blood had been convicted of crime in a foreign country. They are acute critics, yet they still wield clubs in controversy. Compare them in this respect with the people schooled in La Bruyère,[146] La Fontaine,[147] Molière; with the people who have the figures of a Trissotin[148] and a Vadius[149] before them for a comic warning of the personal vanities of the caressed professor. It is more than difference of race. It is the difference of traditions, temper, and style, which comes of schooling.

The French controversialist is a polished swordsman, to be dreaded

---

145 See above p. 261, n. 89.

146 Jean de la Bruyère (1645–1696) published his shrewdly drawn Theophrastan *Caractères* in 1688.

147 Jean de la Fontaine (1621–1695), dramatic and satiric poet, best known for his comic verse tales (*Contes et Nouvelles,* 1665) and his delicately cynical *Fables* (1668, 1678–9, 1694).

148 Poetaster and coxcomb in Molière's *Les Femmes Savantes* (1672).

149 A grand and heavy "savant" in the same comedy.

in his graces and courtesies. The German is Orson,[150] or the mob, or a marching army, in defence of a good case or a bad—a big or a little. His irony is a missile of terrific tonnage: sarcasm he emits like a blast from a dragon's mouth. He must and will be Titan. He stamps his foe underfoot, and is astonished that the creature is not dead, but stinging; for, in truth, the Titan is contending, by comparison, with a god.

When the Germans lie on their arms, looking across the Alsatian frontier at the crowds of Frenchmen rushing to applaud *L'Ami Fritz*[151] at the Théâtre Français, looking and considering the meaning of that applause, which is grimly comic in its political response to the domestic moral of the play—when the Germans watch and are silent, their force of character tells. They are kings in music, we may say princes in poetry, good speculators in philosophy, and our leaders in scholarship. That so gifted a race, possessed moreover of the stern good sense which collects the waters of laughter to make the wells, should show at a disadvantage, I hold for a proof, instructive to us, that the discipline of the Comic Spirit is needful to their growth. We see what they can reach to in that great figure of modern manhood, Goethe. They are a growing people; they are conversable as well; and when their men, as in France, and at intervals at Berlin tea-tables, consent to talk on equal terms with their women, and to listen to them, their growth will be accelerated and be shapelier. Comedy, or in any form the Comic Spirit, will then come to them to cut some figures out of the block, show them the mirror, enliven and irradiate the social intelligence.

Modern French comedy is commendable for the directness of the study of actual life, as far as that, which is but the early step in such a scholarship, can be of service in composing and colouring the picture. A consequence of this crude, though well-meant, realism is the collision of the writers in their scenes and incidents, and in their characters. The Muse of most of them is an *Aventurière*.[152] She is clever, and a certain diversion exists in the united scheme for con-

---

150 One of twin brothers in the old French romance of Valentine and Orson; he was suckled by a bear and had the uncouth manners of the forest, whereas his brother Valentine was reared by their uncle, King Pepin, and grew to be a courtier.

151 A comedy by Erckmann-Chatrian (Emile Erckmann and Alexandre Chatrian), first produced in 1876. It is based upon their novel of the same name (1864), which represents Alsatian life before the war of 1870.

152 "Adventuress," an allusion to *L'Aventurière* (1848), a bourgeois and moralistic play by Emile Augier (1820–1889).

founding her. The object of this person is to reinstate herself in the decorous world; and either, having accomplished this purpose through deceit, she has a *nostalgie de la boue*,[153] that eventually casts her back into it, or she is exposed in her course of deception when she is about to gain her end. A very good, innocent young man is her victim, or a very astute, goodish young man obstructs her path. This latter is enabled to be the champion of the decorous world by knowing the indecorous well. He has assisted in the progress of *Aventurières* downward; he will not help them to ascend. The world is with him; and certainly it is not much of an ascension they aspire to; but what sort of a figure is he? The triumph of a candid realism is to show him no hero. You are to admire him (for it must be supposed that realism pretends to waken some admiration) as a credibly living young man; no better, only a little firmer and shrewder, than the rest. If, however, you think at all, after the curtain has fallen, you are likely to think that the *Aventurières* have a case to plead against him.[154] True, and the author has not said anything to the contrary; he has but painted from the life; he leaves his audience to the reflections of unphilosophic minds upon life, from the specimen he has presented in the bright and narrow circle of a spy-glass.[155]

I do not know that the fly in amber is of any particular use, but the Comic idea enclosed in a comedy makes it more generally perceptible and portable, and that is an advantage. There is a benefit to men in taking the lessons of Comedy in congregations, for it enlivens the wits; and to writers it is beneficial, for they must have a clear scheme, and even if they have no idea to present, they must prove that they have made the public sit to them before the sitting to see the picture. And writing for the stage would be a corrective of a too-incrusted scholarly style, into which some great ones fall at times. It keeps minor writers to a definite plan, and to English. Many of them now swelling a plethoric market, in the composition of novels, in pun-manufactories and in journalism; attached to the machinery forcing perishable matter on a public that swallows voraciously and groans; might, with encour-

---

153 "Homesickness for the mire." See Augier's *Le Mariage d'Olympe* (1855), I.i. Augier was concerned to rebuff the romantic ideas that license is justified by the supreme passion, and that a softening of heart effectually restores the innocence of courtesans.

154 An idea more or less illustrated in Meredith's novel *Rhoda Fleming,* 1865, where the daughter of a Kentish farmer, seduced by an unscrupulous banker's son, retains her purity of heart despite severe trials.

155 This image occurs twice in the Prelude to *The Egoist,* 1879.

agement, be attending to the study of art in literature. Our critics appear to be fascinated by the quaintness of our public, as the world is when our beast-garden has a new importation of magnitude, and the creature's appetite is reverently consulted. They stipulate for a writer's popularity before they will do much more than take the position of umpires to record his failure or success. Now the pig supplies the most popular of dishes, but it is not accounted the most honored of animals, unless it be by the cottager. Our public might surely be led to try other, perhaps finer, meat. It has good taste in song. It might be taught as justly, on the whole, and the sooner when the cottager's view of the feast shall cease to be the humble one of our literary critics, to extend this capacity for delicate choosing in the direction of the matter arousing laughter.

POSTSCRIPTS

I

If we imagine ourselves as drawing a somewhat erratic line down through a chart of the history of Western ideas, and if we let it start with Plato and then pass through the names of such moderns as Hobbes, Shaftesbury, Kant, Hegel, Schopenhauer, Kierkegaard, Baudelaire, Bergson, Freud, we shall indicate roughly the course by which speculations about the nature of what is laughable and about the nature of laughter itself have, apart from theories of comic drama, arrived at their modern development—an exceedingly rich complex of ideas concerning freedom, energy, and egoism, the titanic, the disastrous, and the absurd. The shrewd observations about the impure pleasure of laughter which we have already (above, Inrtoduction, pp. 7–8) quoted from the *Philebus* of Plato may be looked on as very distant harbingers of two closely related ideas which gained an early modern currency, one in a pregnant short formulation by Hobbes, and the other in an overly discursive treatise by Shaftesbury: that we laugh because we experience a sudden elated feeling of superiority over some person, or that we laugh as a way of asserting our superiority to, or freedom from, the tyranny of bad ideas.

> *Sudden Glory,* is the passion which maketh those *Grimaces* called LAUGHTER; and is caused either by some sudden act of their own, that pleaseth them; or by the apprehension of some deformed thing in another, in comparison whereof they suddenly applaud themselves.[1]

> The natural free spirits of ingenious man, if imprisoned or controlled, will find out other ways of motion to relieve themselves in their constraint; and whether it be in burlesque, mimicry or buffoonery, they will be glad at any rate to vent themselves, and be revenged on their constrainers. . . . 'Tis the persecuting spirit has raised the bantering one.[2]

We have seen Hobbes's self-enhancement quoted in a *Spectator* by

---

[1] *Leviathan* (1651), I.vi.
[2] *Sensus Communis: An Essay on the Freedom of Wit and Humour* (1709), I.iv.

284

Addison. We have alluded to Shaftesbury's probable influence on Fielding (above, pp. 147–48). The subversive intimations of Shaftesbury were debated by English moralists throughout the eighteenth century.[3] German romantic metaphysics produced both more severely abstract views of the laughable object and more subtly internalized versions of the laughing self. Kant, who drew much on English empirical thinking, but always rarefied it, generalized the laughable so that it included anything sensuous or physical so far as it precipitates a disappointing contrast to the perfection of an *a priori* idea about it. "Laughter is an affection arising from the sudden transformation of a strained expectation into nothing."[4] This metaphysics of contrast reappears with, for us, perhaps even more startling attenuation in the *World as Will and Idea* of Schopenhauer. All laughter is excited by paradox.

> The cause of laughter in every case is simply the sudden perception of the incongruity between a concept and the real objects which have been thought through it in some relation.

> If we...have present to our minds the abstract conviction of the impossibility of an angle between the circumference of a circle and its tangent; and if now such an angle lies visibly before us upon the paper, this will easily excite a smile. The ludicrousness in this case is exceedingly weak.[5]

The novelist and literary philosopher Jean Paul, drawing much from English writers, Shaftesbury, Fielding, Sterne, and others, had meanwhile (*Vorschule der Ästhetik,* 1804–1813) dwelt with intent reflexiveness on the analogy of the human in every subhuman object of laughter ("Nothing physical can in itself be ridiculous—nothing inanimate, except through personification") and on the corresponding projection of our own wisdom or smartness which occurs in our laughter at even human objects—the naïve or stupid or absentminded.

> We lend *his* efforts *our* insight and perspective, and through such a contradiction produce the infinite absurdity. Our imagination—which in this instance, as with the sublime, is the mediator between subject and object—is able to make this transfer only through the sensuous clarity of the mistake. *Our* own self-deception—by which we attribute to another's efforts a certain understanding which they do not, in fact, enjoy—is what creates that minimum of understanding, that perceived lack of understanding at which we laugh; so that the comic, like the

[3] A. O. Aldridge, "Shaftesbury and the Test of Truth," *PMLA,* LX (1945), 129–56.

[4] *Critique of Judgement* (1790), I.i.ii.54.

[5] *The World as Will and Idea* (1836–1854), trans. R. B. Haldane and J. Kemp, I.i.13; II.viii (London, n.d., 7th ed., pp. 76–77, 272).

sublime, never dwells in the object, but in the subject.... It is the cogency and speed of the sensuous perception that pulls us into this false game.[6]

The element of the ego in laughter and a twist toward the superego are suggested in the darkly brilliant romantic "irony" of Friedrich Schlegel, which is a progressive sardonic self-transcendence. We pity and smile at the poor little result of our former, or other, moments of genius. And Hegel, taking irony in this way, saw it as an apex of pride and "Satanic impertinence." It should be evident that laughter and the laughable and a related cluster of notions had by now arrived at a status of intense reflexiveness and hence of uncertainty, indefinability, and instability. Movement of the dialectic might readily be either up or down. The American essayist Ralph Waldo Emerson, in one of the simpler and more lucid statements on the theme, said laughter erupted whenever a human being in a flash of insight was able to contemplate finite affairs in the perspective of the cosmic or infinite. (And yet laughter was a violent and gross commotion—"pleasant spasms... peculiar explosions...violent convulsions...obstreperous roarings." The comic itself must be seen in the light of the cosmic. "Reason does not joke."[7]) And the Danish theologian Kierkegaard, if anything so simple may in any sense be said to correspond to the simplest aspect of his thought, said that by irony the merely aesthetic man, the earthiest sort of thinking man, was transcended in the ethical man, and in turn the ethical man was by "humor" transcended in the religious man.[8] But on the other hand, the poet of the Flowers of Evil, Baudelaire, meditating on the more egoistic aspect of laughter, noticed by such forerunners as Plato, Hobbes, Schlegel, and Hegel, arrived at the unqualified pronouncement that laughter is diabolical self-assertion.

> Laughter and tears...are both equally the children of woe...the comic
> is a damnable element, and one of diabolic origin.... It would be

---

6 J. P. F. Richter, *Vorschule der Ästhetik* (1804–1813), Part I, Program vi, No. 28, in *Sämtliche Werke,* Part I, Vol. 11 (Weimar, 1935), 97–98. The best commentary in English on Jean Paul's theory is to be found in René Wellek, *A History of Modern Criticism 1750–1950,* II (New Haven, 1955), 100–9. S. T. Coleridge's Lecture IX of 1818, on "Wit and Humour," known today through manuscript notes, a newspaper report, and the *Literary Remains* edited by H. N. Coleridge, borrowed much from Jean Paul's *Vorschule,* I, vi, 26–32, 43–48. (*Coleridge's Miscellaneous Criticism,* ed. T. M. Raysor, Cambridge, Mass., 1936, pp. 111–30, 440–46).

7 See Joseph Jones, "Emerson and Bergson on the Comic," *Comparative Literature,* I (Winter 1949), 63–71, quoting Emerson's *Complete Works* (Centenary Edition), VIII, 158–73.

8 Søren Kierkegaard, *Concluding Unscientific Postscript,* trans. David F. Swenson (Princeton, 1944), p. 450.

rying to cope with life in literature. Dionysus, Freud, Bergson (if
nly he knew it), dreams, surrealism, Marx and society, bombs, arson,
nd looting all tell against it. Only "comedy" in a much bigger sense,
he whole range of human sobs and laughter—from the icy pinnacles
Molière to the base of all comedy, the dirty joke (special praise
ways for the eternally human dirty joke)—is sufficiently deep and
ide and thus relevant to modern man's sense of the deeply inherent
bsurdity of his lonely suffering in a world gone mad. Salvation is
longer acceptable. Nor even any tragic vision. "I think we should
ad only those books that bite and stab," said the fabulist Franz
afka, our "modern Jeremiah," prophetically writing the depraved
tory of our times. "We need books that affect us like a blow on the
ull, a disaster, a suicide, the death of a best friend."[18] Tragedy has
ways had the crippling limitation of being only *high*. Comedy (or
least a range of several things called "comedy") can be either high
low. "Comedy" is our only true, inclusive mirror of the all-but-
mal, would-be angelic human spectacle. It is the metaphor of a
re universal human condition than tragedy. We are all of us much
re likely to be found in the condition of a Quixote, a Micawber,
Malvolio, a Benedick, a Tartuffe, than in that of a Macbeth
an Othello. Echoes of the Medieval grotesque, from Dante to
ronymus Bosch, are vastly amplified in this modern argument. Our
rite commentator on laughter among English romantics will not
amiable, sympathetic Charles Lamb, but metaphysically tough
ridge, pondering the terrible and ludicrous in *Hamlet* and *Lear*.[19]
e ought to recognize a closer union than we do between the comic
the tragic. The simply tragic accent requires a reasonable world
r, notions of responsibility and guilt—and of nobility. At the same
tragedy uses only one half of the primitive violence of the ritual
(birth, struggle, death), whereas comedy uses also resurrection
though the modern version can scarcely be happy). Our commen-
boasts that he has lived amid the "dust and crashes" of the
ieth century; this gives him a special rapport with the remotest
es of the past. Harking back to the deepest caverns of the racial
onsciousness, he *cries out* for a sense of archaic cruelty in the

---

ranz Kafka, Letter to Oskar Pollak, January 27, 1904, *Gesammelte
en,* ed. Max Brod, VI (Prague, 1937), 263. I am following the main lines of
quent exposition by Wylie Sypher, "The Meanings of Comedy" (especially
–214), in his *Comedy,* an edition of Meredith's *Essay on Comedy* and
's *Laughter* (Garden City, N.Y., 1956).

he comic poet idealises his characters by making the animal the governing
and the intellectual the mere instrument."—Coleridge, *Lectures on Shake-
.,* 1818, "Greek Drama."

---

enough to draw attention to the unanimous agreement of physiologists
of laughter on the primary ground of this monstrous phenomenon.
Nevertheless their discovery is not very profound and hardly goes very
far. Laughter, they say, comes from superiority. I should not be surprised if, on making this discovery, the physiologist had burst out
laughing himself at the thought of his own superiority. Therefore he
should have said: Laughter comes from the idea of one's *own* superiority. A Satanic idea, if ever there was one! And what pride and
delusion! For it is a notorious fact that all the madmen in the asylums
have an excessively over-developed idea of their own superiority.[9]

Physiological and psychological studies, flourishing in the later part
of the nineteenth century, described the laughing response as an
explosion of free energy or of exultation in freedom—touched off
perhaps by alternations or sudden changes of stimulus (physical, as
in tickling, or psychic, as in various surprises and releases).[10] A key to
laughter was discovered in various primitivistic analogies: the expression of the suckling infant, the laughter of children in barbarous games,
the roar of the savage in victory, the smile on the face of a tiger or
Cheshire cat.[11] Certain more generalized and softened versions of the
argument are perhaps still partly persuasive. A bit of bark in a fire-
place blazes up; people seated dreamily about the embers smile. Big
drops of rain fall unexpectedly upon the surface of a pond. Boys
sitting and gazing at the water smile. Children snicker at nothing in
a schoolroom; or spectators laugh at the slightest incident in the
tension of a courtroom. "The function of the humorous stimulus
consists in cutting the surface tension, in taking the hide off of
consciousness."[12]

All these trends may be said to attain a climax in two masterpieces
of the turn of the century—one metaphysically psychological, the
three-part book-length essay *Laughter, An Essay on the Meaning of
the Comic* (1900), by Henri Bergson; the other fully psychological,
in the subjective and clinical sense, the large volume *Wit and Its
Relation to the Unconscious,* 1905, by Sigmund Freud. Bergson,
brilliantly if not with complete persuasiveness, defines the kind of
freedom experienced or expressed in laughter as that of the triumphant
life impulse itself (the *élan vital*). By contrast, the provocative laugh-

---

[9] *On the Essence of Laughter, and, in General, on the Comic in the Plastic Arts,*
1855, in *The Mirror of Art,* trans. Jonathan Mayne (Garden City, N.Y., 1956),
pp. 135–37.

[10] See D. H. Monro, *Argument of Laughter* (Melbourne, 1951), especially pp.
214–19, 222–25, outlining theories of Greig and Menon.

[11] H. M. Kallen, *American Journal of Psychology,* XXII (April 1911), 142.

[12] Auguste Penjon, *Revue Philosophique,* 1893, quoted by L. W. Kline, "The
Psychology of Humor," *American Journal of Psychology,* XVIII (1907), 433–36.

able object (on which the emphasis of his theory falls) is the human being reduced to some form of mechanism or stereotype—in the physical automatism of stumbling, for instance, or in the mental rigidity of cliché conceptualization, absentmindedness, routine feelings, bad moral habits. Laughter, for this soberly laughing philosopher, as for Emerson and other romantics, tends to reflect and share the limitation and lowness of the laughable object, rather than that high vital spirit in contrast to which the laughable is conceived. Laughter is "a froth with a saline base. Like froth, it sparkles. It is gaiety itself. But the philosopher who gathers a handful to taste may find that the substance is scanty, and the aftertaste bitter."[13] Meanwhile the more earthy Freud was at work defining, or asserting, the degrees of psychic economy, sometimes joined with tendentious rebellion, which man the laugher contrives to achieve in several kinds of jokes, irony, and "humor." And he paralleled the covert symbol mechanisms of joking to those of dream-work and those of art and literature. He described the art form of comedy as a dreamy state where grownup people enjoy a regression to an infantile, arcadian *id* realm.

> The euphoria which we are thus striving to obtain is nothing but the state of a bygone time, in which we were wont to defray our psychic work with slight expenditure. It is the state of our childhood in which we did not know the comic, were incapable of wit and did not need humor to make us happy.[14]

Freud's speculations about the symbols and mechanisms of wit-work and dream-work were a highly suggestive service for literary criticism. And Bergson, too, in the second part of his *Essay,* laid an interesting stress upon the mechanism of jokes and verbal wit as small models of the laughable act or scene, turning, like George Meredith, to the plays of Molière for the master paradigms of his exposition.

Both Bergson and Freud, and the psychological writers who preceded them and were contemporary with Meredith, were part of a stream of ideas that had moved a long way from the classical tradition of thinking about stage comedy. The writers on the laughable from Kant and Jean Paul to Freud ushered in a new era of thinking about the laughable in literature. This laughable was differently analyzed, and in actual literature turned out to be a very different thing from the ethically critical but restrained or civil laughter of the classical stage

and its theory. The new laughter has been defined various new literary and even pictorial assertions, esp Second World War, than by any master theory ke the literature and art. Its counterparts in classical have been looked for in the cluttered and encyclope kind of satire known as Menippean[15] and in Athenia rather than in Roman "New Comedy." In the more are the Rabelaisian grotesque and its descendants— of *Melancholy,* Sterne's *Tristram Shandy,* Carlyle's Joyce's *Ulysses.* The laughter of the mid-twentieth demonic in a fully Baudelairean realization, Titan puny and whining, but always tortured (a *Guern Metamorphosis* by Kafka, a *Watt* or an *Endgame* cent, obscene, violent, "cruel," "dark," "black"— ugly, and "absurd." In the dramas of Sartre, Beck and Edward Albee the modern vein of laughter read of weariness and nullity, and at the same time a f of all determinate meaning in surrealistic symbol

"What could exceed the Absurdity of an Autho *The Comedy of Nero, with the merry Inciden Mother's Belly?"* Fielding asked the question in *Andrews* (above, p. 156). Today this question wo the level of the most advanced and spritely aca encounters nowadays the quasi-Nietzschean doctr comedy and classical tragedy belong in the cat and moral, the Gestalt-ridden and idealistic. Th a Platonic and Apollonian falsehood. It was

---

[13] *Laughter, An Essay on the Meaning of the Comic,* trans. Cloudesley Brereton and Fred Rothwell (New York, 1928), p. 200.

[14] *The Basic Writings of Sigmund Freud,* trans. A. A. Brill (New York, 1938), p. 803. I continue to use this translation because I find it readable and clear. The now standard translation by James Strachey of the book on *Wit,* or *Jokes,* appears to me in places uninterpretable.

---

[15] The third-century B.C. Cynic philosopher Menipp mixtures of prose and verse which are lost. He was Marcus Terentius Varro, whose *Saturae Menippeae* su ing to about 600 lines. Menippus figures also in the written in Attic Greek during the second century A.D. (Highet, *The Anatomy of Satire* (Princeton, 1962), pr

[16] Nathan A. Scott, Jr., "The Recent Journey in Example of Beckett and his Despair of Literature," (Spring 1962), 144–81. *Le degré zéro d'écriture* is a by the French critic Roland Barthes (p. 155). For a "The Bias of Comedy and the Narrow Escape into XLIV (Spring 1961), 9–39.

[17] Cf. Francis Fergusson, "Prometheus at Yale,' *Books,* IX, No. 2 (August 3, 1967), 30–32. " 'Zeus'. tyrant, the very 'him' or 'them' that the all-protest time needs, to take the blame for undeserved sufferi of unspecified but ubiquitous resentment would, I the work and guarantee its profundity."

modern dramatic spectacle, whether tragic or comic.[20] Something like a primitive unity of the tragic and comic in that one great bolstered mythic whole of which we spoke at our beginning (Introduction, pp. 2–3) seems today to reemerge from the swamps of time—a mammoth saurian, with a sort of brain in both head and tail.

II

Absurdity and violence, being what they are, have not made a conspicuous effort at articulate theory about themselves. Samuel Beckett's *Fin de Partie* or *Endgame* (in French at London and Paris, April 1957; in his own English at New York, January 1958; in German, *Endspiel*, at Vienna, 1958), achieved a kind of nadir of the zero trend. In a letter to his New York producer Alan Schneider, written at the moment of the play's transatlantic leap, he expresses his reluctance to cooperate with interpretation:

> ...When it comes to journalists, I feel the only line is to refuse to be involved in exegesis of any kind. And to insist on the extreme simplicity of dramatic situation and issue. If that's not enough for them, and it obviously isn't, it's plenty for us, and we have no elucidations to offer of mysteries that are all of their making. My work is a matter of fundamental sounds (no joke intended), made as fully as possible, and I accept responsibility for nothing else. If people want to have headaches among the overtones, let them. And provide their own aspirin.[21]

Another figure in the Parisian "anti-theater" or "anti-message" of the 1950s, Eugene Ionesco (*La Cantatrice Chauve, The Bald Soprano,* 1950; *Rhinocéros,* 1960),[22] has, however, been less shy about theorizing. His interviews, addresses, letters, testimonies, controversies, notes, and diaries have made up a volume, *Notes et Contre-notes* (Paris, 1962), translated[23] as *Notes and Counter Notes: Writings on the*

---

20 At the same time, he may have a queasy stomach about the archaic gusto of such scenes as that in the *Iliad* where Ulysses and Diomedes decapitate the hapless scout Dolon. Or he may notice that the "sickly laughter of the last romantics [Nietzsche, for instance, or Rimbaud] is the most confused and destructive mirth Western man has ever allowed himself" (Sypher, pp. 202, 205).

21 Samuel Beckett to Alan Schneider, December 29, 1957, "Beckett's Letters on *Endgame,*" *the village VOICE,* March 19, 1958, pp. 8, 15. (Greenwich Village, of course.)

22 His latest play, *La Soif et la Faim* (*Hunger and Thirst*) was first produced in Paris in February 1966, and had its English language premiere at the Yale University Theater in April 1967.

23 By Donald Watson.

Theatre (New York, 1964). The experience of the post-existentialist dramaturge, as professed by Ionesco, occurs in three dialectic phases, approximately as follows: (I) Disillusionment, disgust, boredom with society, establishment, convention, tradition—and in particular with the stagey unrealities and pretended illusionism of theatrical convention. (II) The thrust toward sabotage, breakage, violence— in the self-assertion of a new and liberated kind of theater (or anti-theater)—the "lucid" realization of the zero, the vacuum, the nullity, the stasis, the "embryonic farce" which our life *is* and only tries vainly, by theatrics, to transcend. (III) The conviction that the violence of this denial is a breakthrough into (what true art has always been) the experience of the absolute universal. The irrational plumbs the permanent. These three moments are well illustrated in Ionesco's forceful essay *Experience of the Theatre,* the first in his book.

In the opening pages of the essay, a certain disdain of Molière, along with many other classic and modern dramatists, is firmly stated. At the same time, one may be struck by the discussion of certain theatrical devices of broken illusion much favored by Molière. Ionesco is a noted practitioner of such tricks as framing the fiction of the play inside a second or covering fiction of actors getting themselves ready, pushing props around, pressing electric buttons, recurrently thereafter alluding to the fact that they *are* actors, acting in a play. What will these crazy actors do next? One may notice, too, certain unconscious echoes of Charles Lamb's preference for Shakespeare's tragedies unacted. In the sweep of Ionesco's distaste for and dismissal of the historic theater, it will be difficult not to ponder questions about his own epitaph.

> I. [First Phase of Ionesco's Argument.] Why could I not accept the truth of theatrical reality? Why did it seem false to me? And why did the false seem to want to pass as true and take the place of truth? Was it the fault of the actors? Of the text? Or my own fault? I think I realize now that what worried me in the theatre was the presence of characters in flesh and blood on the stage. Their physical presence destroyed the imaginative illusion.
>
> I was even bored by reading Molière. I was not interested in those stories of misers, hypocrites and cuckolds. I disliked his unmetaphysical mind. Shakespeare raised questions about the whole condition and destiny of man. In the long run Molière's little problems seemed to me of relatively minor importance, sometimes a little sad of course, dramatic even, but never tragic; for they could be resolved. The unendurable admits of no solution, and only the unendurable is profoundly tragic, profoundly comic and essentially theatrical.
>
> On the other hand, the greatness of Shakespeare's plays seemed to me diminished in performance. No Shakespearean production ever capti-

vated me as much as my reading of *Hamlet, Othello* and *Julius Caesar,* etc. As I went so rarely to the theatre, perhaps I have never seen the best productions of Shakespeare's drama. In any case, in performance I had the impression that the unendurable had been made endurable. It was anguish tamed.

So I am not really a passionate theatregoer, still less a man of the theatre. I really hated the theatre. It bored me.[24]

"Ionesco's satire," we are told by the historian of the recent French theater, "is total in that it results in the rejection" of all our supposedly reasonable norms of "behavior," our "institutions," and our "values." He wants to deprive us of all "opportunity to take ourselves seriously." "A superabundance of being" (like the rhythm or result of a "machine out of control," filling a stage with millions of eggs, with rhinoceroses, with empty chairs), intimates the "absolute impossibility of justifying the fact of being." The dialogue, "drawn out for no particular reason and filled with repetitions," ends by producing "a kind of incantation." He produces "a meaningless mirror of a meaningless world" and finds it impossible "to take the first any more seriously than the second."[25]

But the creation of a truly dramatic surface of the absurd requires, of course, more than mere absurdity. The successful dramatist of the absurd displays an engaging talent for cheating us by an exercise of ingenuity, of interest, even of wit, upon the medium of a species of absurdity. Fantasy and realism play in and out, alternately carrying each other. A sort of minimum model for absurd wit may be conceived in a kind of printed placard that can be bought at curio stores—a card on which letters and spacing have been planned so badly that the phrase has to bend and run down the side of the page. But not just any words, like NO SMOKING, or KEEP OFF THE GRASS. The card says: PLAN AHEAD. A magazine called *Mad* which circulates among teenagers will be found full of such eye-breakers raised, just a little, to the level of sex, mayhem, and disgust. The mere absurd is always lustreless and boring. As is often the supposed witty absurd. It is easy to be boring—we all do it all the time. As it enters into verbal art, boredom has been accurately described by an American rationalist

---

24 *Notes and Counter Notes: Writings on the Theatre* (New York, 1964), pp. 16–17, 19–20. This and the following excerpts from Ionesco's *Notes and Counter Notes* are reprinted by permission of Grove Press, Inc. Copyright © 1964 by Grove Press, Inc. This essay originally appeared in *Nouvelle Revue Française,* XI (February 1958), 247–70.
25 Jacques Guicharnaud and June Beckelman, *Modern French Theatre, from Giraudoux to Beckett* (New Haven, 1961), pp. 180, 182–84, 188–89. [Revised ed., 1967.] The present account owes much to this excellent book. See also especially Wallace Fowlie, *Dionysus in Paris, A Guide to French Contemporary Theater* (New York, 1959); John Gassner, *Masters of the Drama* (New York, 1954); Martin Esslin, *The Theatre of the Absurd* (Garden City, N.Y., 1961).

critic as the "fallacy of imitative form," the embodiment of the irrational in the form of the irrational. The modern school of absurd drama actually does demand of its audience certain very large concessions in favor of a staple of repetition, monotony, dirt, ugliness, boredom, and disgust. Certain directors and productions have perhaps demanded even more than the playwright counted on. Ionesco seems to shrug his shoulders and leave the text completely at the mercy of the producer.[26] But Beckett might have been bored had he witnessed a production of his *Endgame* which went on for about three hours,[27] presumptuously, before a meek and apparently masochistic New Haven audience (Yale University Theater, September 1966). The director, in a kind of seminar address from the stage, boasted of plans for a further production of twenty-four hours—with provisions for the audience to go home, and come back(?).

Ionesco is celebrated by his critics for the intensely "poetic," the "metaphysical," quality of his vision. He constructs a "metaphor of the horror of the modern world," invests his "inner fantasies with the objectivity of realism," relates the subjective and the objective "not symbolically but concomitantly." He is the creator of a *Théâtre en liberté,* a "liberated theater, the horror of the world as a nonsensical mechanism, mad in its ways, and thus giving the playwright complete freedom to indulge his fantasies."[28] Or, in his own words:

II. [Second Phase of Ionesco's Argument.] So if the essence of the theatre lay in magnifying its effects, they had to be magnified still further, underlined and stressed to the maximum. To push drama out of that intermediate zone where it is neither theatre nor literature is to restore it to its own domain, to its natural frontiers. It was not for me to conceal the devices of the theatre, but rather make them still more evident, deliberately obvious, go all-out for caricature and the grotesque, way beyond the pale irony of witty drawing-room comedies. No drawing-room comedies, but farce, the extreme exaggeration of parody. Humor, yes, but using the methods of burlesque. Comic effects that are firm, broad and outrageous. No dramatic comedies either. But

---

[26] Guicharnaud and Beckelman, p. 189. In August 1967, Jonathan Marks, a Yale undergraduate who had played in the Dramatic Society's April production of *Hunger and Thirst,* had an interview with Ionesco in Paris. "I explained to him, somewhat timorously at first, how much we had cut the scene and changed the order of lines to give it more direction. Far from being offended, he seemed pleased and interested, most of all in the gestures he saw the monks doing. . . . He wishes he had written it that way. He goes to tell his wife." ("The Gorgeous Laugh of Eugene Ionesco," in *The New Journal,* ed. Daniel Yergin, I, No. 4 (New Haven, November 12, 1967), 3–4.

[27] "A very long one act, over an hour and a half I shd think." (Beckett to Alan Schneider, October 15, 1956, *the village VOICE,* March 19, 1958, p. 8.)

[28] Guicharnaud and Beckelman, pp. 178–79, 188–90, 192.

back to the unendurable. Everything raised to paroxysm, where the source of tragedy lies. A theatre of violence: violently comic, violently dramatic.

Avoid psychology or rather give it a metaphysical dimension. Drama lies in extreme exaggeration of the feelings, an exaggeration that dislocates flat everyday reality. Dislocation, disarticulation of language too.

Moreover, if the actors embarrassed me by not seeming natural enough, perhaps it was because they also were, or tried to be, *too* natural: by trying not to be, perhaps they will still appear natural, but in a different way. They must not be afraid of not being natural.

We need to be virtually bludgeoned into detachment from our daily lives, our habits and mental laziness, which conceal from us the strangeness of the world. Without a fresh virginity of mind, without a new and healthy awareness of existential reality, there can be no theatre and no art either; the real must be in a way dislocated, before it can be reintegrated.

In my first play, *The Bald Soprano,* which started off as an attempt to parody the theatre, and hence a certain kind of human behavior, it was by plunging into banality, by draining the sense from the hollowest clichés of everyday language that I tried to render the strangeness that seems to pervade our whole existence. The tragic and the farcical, the prosaic and the poetic, the realistic and the fantastic, the strange and the ordinary, perhaps these are the contradictory principles (there is no theatre without conflict) that may serve as a basis for a new dramatic structure. In this way perhaps the unnatural can by its very violence appear natural, and the too natural will avoid the naturalistic. . . .

May I add that "primitive" drama is not elementary drama; to refuse to "round off the corners" is a way of providing a clear outline, a more powerful shape; drama that relies on simple effects is not necessarily drama simplified.

If one believes that "theatre" merely means the drama of the word, it is difficult to grant it can have an autonomous language of its own: it can then only be the servant of other forms of thought expressed in words, or philosophy and morals. Whereas, if one looks on the word as only *one* member of the shock troops the theatre can marshal, everything is changed. First of all, there is a proper way for the theatre to use words, which is as dialogue, words in action, words in conflict. If they are used by some authors merely for discussion, this is a major error. There are other means of making words more theatrical: by working them up to such a pitch that they reveal the true temper of drama, which lies in frenzy; the whole tone should be as strained as possible, the language should almost break up or explode in its fruitless effort to contain so many meanings.

Nothing is barred in the theatre: characters may be brought to life, but the unseen presence of our inner fears can also be materialized. So the author is not only allowed, but recommended to make actors of his props, to bring objects to life, to animate the scenery and give symbols concrete form.[29]

Near the start of a tradition in which Ionesco still curiously moves, Aristotelian poetics provided twin notions of an ideal or noble universal and a corresponding low comic universal or stereotype. In the neo-Platonic or Aristotelian universalism of the English Augustan age, the emphasis might fall on universal or essential poetry itself ("wit" working with "nature"—"one clear, unchanged, and universal light"); or, in at least one marked instance which we have seen, it might fall on the "biographical" realism, the "historic" truth of the *comic* character type (Fielding's lawyer "is not only alive, but hath been so these four thousand years"); or, again, it might fall on the concept of dramatic character, undifferentiated, *tragic* or *comic* (as in Samuel Johnson's Shakespeare Preface—Shakespeare gives us, not an individual, but the "species"). We have heard Meredith expound the genius of Molière for conferring upon raw local realism the redeeming stamp of the comic "idea." Bergson, in his equally classic essay *Le Rire*, was confident of a distinction between the individual *élan* of tragic characters and the stereotyped mechanism of the comic. We speak of a Tartuffe or a Harpagon, scarcely of a Hamlet.

In the closing pages of his essay, Ionesco, without claiming or confessing any kinship with the classic tradition, produces one of the most resonant professions of faith in the universal which an age and theater of absurdity, violence, and fragmentation can be imagined to inspire. His instance is drawn not from comedy but from Shakespearean tragic-history. With this passage indeed, one might ask if we have not been shot out of orbit into irrelevant tragic or nameless spaces where the idea of the comic does not follow. The same question may conceivably arise for the whole business of the drama of the absurd. It is a grimy, sad experience. The aim, we have been told, is precisely to bring the comic and the tragic closer together. Beyond comedy, no doubt. Still the clue into the area we are looking at seems to be the "absurd," which, at least ordinarily, is closer to laughter than to tears. "Tragic farce," the theater of the absurd is called by its critics— "metaphysical farce."[30] The idiom of puns and jokes, the travesty mechanisms, the movie slapstick, the clowning circus tricks, the vaudeville arrangements and "numbers," the non sequiturs, and monstrosities which prevail in this Parisian theater seem to continue to remind both authors and their critics of something less like tragedy

---

[29] *Notes and Counter Notes*, pp. 26, 28–29, 29.

[30] Guicharnaud and Beckelman, pp. 178, 189, citing Rosette C. Lamont, "The Metaphysical Farce: Beckett and Ionesco," *The French Review*, XXXII, No. 4 (February 1959).

than like comedy. Ionesco's resounding claim to a solemnly and deeply conceived human universal emerges from a context of craziness which in a special way challenges attention.

III. [Third Phase of Ionesco's Argument.] Besides contemporaneity does not conflict with timelessness and universality: on the contrary, it is subservient.

There are some states of mind, some intuitions that lie positively outside time, outside history. When, one day of grace, I awake some morning, not only from my night's sleep but also from the mental sleep of habit, and suddenly become aware of my existence and of a universal presence, when all seems strange and yet familiar, when I am possessed by the wonder of living, this is a feeling or intuition that can come to any man at any time. You can find this spirit of awareness expressed in practically the same terms by poets, mystics and philosophers, who experience it exactly as I do, and as all men have surely experienced it unless they are spiritually dead or blinded by their preoccupation with politics; you can find exactly the same spirit clearly expressed both in antiquity and the Middle Ages as well as in any of the so-called "historical" centuries. At this timeless moment in time philosopher and shoemaker, "master" and "slave," priest and layman are reconciled and indistinguishable.

Let us choose a great example in our own field: in the theatre, when the fallen Richard II is a prisoner in his cell, abandoned and alone, it is not Richard II I see there, but all the fallen kings of this world; and not only all fallen kings, but also our beliefs and values, our unsanctified, corrupt and worn-out truths, the crumbling of civilizations, the march of destiny. When Richard II dies, it is really the death of all I hold most dear that I am watching; it is *I* who die with Richard II. Richard II makes me sharply conscious of the eternal truth that we forget in all these stories, the truth we fail to think about, though it is simple and absolutely commonplace: I die, he dies, you die. So it is not history after all that Shakespeare is writing, although he makes use of history; it is not History that he shows me, but *my* story and *our* story—*my* truth, which, independent of my "times" and in the spectrum of a time that transcends Time, repeats a universal and inexorable truth. In fact, it is in the nature of a dramatic masterpiece to provide a superior pattern of instruction: it reflects my own image, it is a mirror; it is soul-searching; it is history gazing beyond history toward the deepest truth. One may find the reasons given by this or that author for wars and civil strife and struggles for power true or false, one may or may not agree with these interpretations. But one cannot deny that all those kings have faded from the scene, that they are dead; and an awareness of this reality, of this lasting evidence of the ephemeral nature of man, contrasted with his longing for eternal life, is obviously accompanied by the most profound emotion, by the most acute consciousness of tragedy, passionately felt.

All men die a lonely death, all values fall into contempt: that is what Shakespeare tells me. "Richard's cell is indeed the cell of all our solitudes."

Drama *is* this eternal and living presence: there is no doubt that it can reproduce the essential structure of tragic truth and theatrical reality. The evidence it offers has nothing to do with the uncertain truths of abstract thought or with the so-called ideological theatre: we are now concerned with the essence of the theatre, with theatrical archetypes, with theatrical idiom.[31]

III

After such knowledge, what forgiveness? Dare we return to, or even hint at, anything so unambitious as what's funny? Dare we appeal to laughter? or to entertainment? *C'est une étrange entreprise que celle de faire rire les honnêtes gens.* But have the audiences at Paris and New York nights of Beckett and Ionesco been indeed *des honnêtes gens*? Could the term be used today as a compliment? It would not have occurred to Molière or Racine, said Jacques Rivière, to claim that he wrote plays for any other reason that "to entertain cultured people." "Only with Romanticism, did the literary act begin to be thought of as a sort of attempt to reach the absolute."[32] We know a little better than that. We know that the morally didactic claim was a standard half of the Renaissance apology for poetry. We have heard Molière protest that the aim of his satire was to mock certain kinds of people out of their evil ways—*corriger les hommes en les divertissant.* Still the modern critic's statement remains largely true. We have been walking off-Broadway, looking at a very recent cleavage from the tradition. Molière was too simple a funnyman and too successful a man of the theater, with both bourgeosie and courtiers, to be countenanced by the "metaphysics" of 1960. At the same time, there is still the ordinary modern world of theater and movies, where laughter, of whatever quality, is more or less continuous, and where no large initial concession to the dirty, the monotonous, and the boring exercises any tyranny. Parts of this world too have their advanced cults—the aficionados of Charlie Chaplin, of Buster Keaton, of Laurel and Hardy. There is said to be a movie house in Paris which annually runs a two-month Laurel and Hardy festival.[33] It was Chaplin, not the theater of the absurd, which established the tramp or bum (not the bourgeois, not even the proletarian) as the modern symbol of residual, estranged humanity. "Charlot" is shadowed in *Godot*. The

---

31 *Notes and Counter Notes,* pp. 30–31, 31–32, 32, 32–33.
32 Quoted by Nathan Scott, *The Centennial Review*, VI, 144.
33 *Time,* July 14, 1967, p. 74.

bowlers worn by all four of the characters in this no-allegory testify
to their participation in the myth of the Little Man who plays at
being a man.[34]

The Broadway world, very modern in its own way, has no doubt
little more use for Molière than for Beckett, and of course no admitted
use for Aristotle, or any real use for seventeenth-century wit. Stage
revivals of New Comedy and Comedy of Manners do occur nowadays,
but it is always difficult to save these from the accent of costumery,
the atmosphere of the museum. Relentless "scientific" researches into
both the drama and the criticism of the tradition continue.[35] New
essays in criticism are written. Some of these undertake in a very
interesting way to resophisticate this drama in a contemporary psychological and ethical idiom. (See, for example, Norman N. Holland,
The First Modern Comedies, 1959, dealing comprehensively with
Etherege, Wycherley, and Congreve.[36]) Others exploit sociological com-
ponents in the genesis of drama which tell not very much about artistic
qualities. (See John Loftis's accurate charts of social and political—
merchant-aristocrat, Whig-Tory—oppositions in Augustan English
comedy.[37]) Or they may even look back with a degree of modern
sociologically enlightened scorn on all but select spots in the English
manners tradition. (See Marvin Mudrick's tart essay "The Restoration Comedy and Later," in *English Institute Essays 1954.*) Here and
there appear yet other oblique assertions of the classical spirit, shy
and jocular glances. Ionesco says: "In the long run I am all for
classicism." He means it in the transcendent sense which we have
already seen.[38] The cartoons of James Thurber twenty or thirty years
ago often enough were, in their savage way, reminiscent of the confron-
tations of man and woman in Molière, Swift, or Congreve—Alceste
and Célimène, Millamant and Mirabell, Cadenus and Vanessa, reduced
to the brutal obstupescence of a single containing line. The essay
which follows was published by Thurber in *The New York Times*
drama section in February 1960, to help mark the appearance of the
Thurber Carnival of comic sketches at the Anta Theater. In its
unabashed concern for jokes or gags (and in its equal concern, despite
certain trivial side winks, for precision and restraint in the use of
such provocatives to laughter), it illustrates one sort of flickering
survival of the antique comic spirit.

---

[34] Guicharnaud and Beckelman, p. 216.

[35] "Scientific" is a term invoked several times by even so good a writer on
Molière as W. G. Moore. See above, pp. 57–60.

[36] And see Bibliographical Aids II, D, especially the titles by Dale Underwood
and Rose A. Zimbardo.

[37] *Comedy and Society from Congreve to Fielding* (Stanford, 1959); *The
Politics of Drama in Augustan England* (Oxford, 1963).

[38] *Notes and Counter Notes,* p. 131.

The Quality of Mirth

By James Thurber

In the American theatre, or what is left of it, the quality of mirth is strained through many divergent judgments, each of them handed down with the air and tone of final authority that we Americans assume so easily.

"Who knows what's funny?" W.C. Fields used to say, meaning that all those around him were positive they knew, but intimating the real truth, that Fields was the final authority. When a producer or a director or a supervisor once came to him in Hollywood, laughing like crazy, and told him about a wonderful gagerino on a switcheroo, again he said, grimly, "Who knows what's funny?" Their idea had been that Fields would be rowing this boat—see—and suddenly the oars break in two. "The oars don't break," the great man said. "The oars bend." And in the movie they did bend, like leaden spoons, for Fields had been able to convince the multiple experts on comedy that he was right.

Surely no other American institution is so bound around and tightened up by rules, strictures, adages and superstitions as the Broadway theatre. I have been mixed up in it (and I use that verb deliberately) off and on for quite a while. Long enough, anyway to appreciate Jimmy Durante's "Everybody wants to get into the act."

There are those who are arrogant about their profound knowledge of comic effects and their long study and practice of the art of laughter, but for the most part people genuinely want to help, and are earnest in their efforts to "save the show" or "fix up that snapper at the end" or tell you what to take out or put in. Some of these specialists in humor were not even born the year I went to work for *The New Yorker,* but, at 65, I have learned that it is a good idea to listen. In the first place, at least one out of every twelve suggestions is sound and, in the second place, the suggesters have increased my knowledge of the nature of the American male and female in our time.

We all know that the theatre and every play that comes to Broadway have within themselves, like the human being, the seed of self-destruction and the certainty of death. The thing is to see how long the theatre, the play and the human being can last in spite of themselves. The biggest problem of all three is to preserve honorable laughter in a comedy. If a playwright tried to see eye to eye with everybody, he would get the worst case of strabismus since Hannibal lost an eye trying to count his nineteen elephants during a snowstorm while crossing the Alps.

Among the hundreds of adages that both help and hamper the theatre, one of the most persistent is "Only the audience knows," or "Only the audience can tell you." This is certainly true, but, in the case of a comedy, it is necessary to understand the quality of mirth in an audience.

We are a nation that has always gone in for the loud laugh, the wow, the yak, the belly laugh and the dozen other labels for the roll-'em-in-the-aisles gagerissimo. This is the kind of laugh that delights actors, directors and producers, but dismays writers of comedy because it is the laugh that often dies in the lobby. The appreciative smile, the chuckle, the soundless mirth, so important to the success of comedy, cannot be understood unless one sits among the audience and feels the warmth created by the quality of laughter that the audience takes home with it.

This failure of discrimination on the part of so many panicky and high-strung theatre people accounts, more than anything else, for the deplorable decline of stage comedy during the last decade. "Louder and funnier" should often read "louder, but less funny." There is a kind of mirth that brings forth a general audience sound a little like sighing, just as there is a kind of mirth that, in the true appreciator of it, can cause the welling up of tears.

This last phenomenon happened to me, as I once reported on this page, during the wonderful "Rain in Spain" scene in "My Fair Lady," in which comedy, song, dance, characterization and progress of plot were all beautifully conjoined.

The pre-Broadway road tour of a play is known as a "shake-down," but a better name would be "shape-up." The first term suggests shaking the holy bejudas out of it, while the second implies an effort at perfecting the "property," as lawyers always call a play. Lawyers now have a great hand in the shake-down, I have discovered, for contracts and contract clauses are waved at one as frequently as suggested gags.

Howard Dietz once said, "A day away from Tallulah is like a month in the country," which brought out of me one night, on the road with "Carnival," this thought: "Seven weeks on the road with a play is like ten years with Harold Ross."

Beginning in 1921 with the road company of an Ohio State musical comedy club called "Scarlet Mask," I have collected a vast amount of advice on how to write humor and comedy. I had written, thirty-nine years ago, the book for a musical show called "O My Omar!" and everybody then living in Cleveland, Cincinnati and Dayton told me how it should have been done.

Since then I have been told, among other things: "You can't bring a play to Broadway entitled 'The Male Animal.' " "You can't have a serious villain in a comedy" and "You've got to keep too much charm out of a comedy." The soundest critic of "The Male Animal" was Groucho Marx, who said, in Hollywood, "You got too many laughs in it. Take some of them out." He meant we should take out irrelevant gags and stick to the laughter of character and situation, and he was, of course, right.

When I tell this to the eminent authorities on comedy in our declining comic theatre, they yell, "Take laughs out of a comedy? That's crazy. Keep putting more laughs in." It means nothing to these experts that two of the biggest laughs in "The Male Animal" came on these two lines: "I felt fine" and "Yes, you are." This brings us to what I call the Fourth Strike.

The Fourth Strike grows out of the neurotic or just thoughtless conviction of many theatre people that if a line does not get a yell it isn't getting a thing. Let me give an example of the Fourth Strike. One night, on the shake-down, in a fable that has since been eliminated from the show, the line "A thing of beauty is a joy for such a little time" was inadvertently spoken this way, "A thing of joy is a beauty for such a little time." At least six friends of mine, or total strangers, shouted "Keep it in!"

I have most resented the application to what I write of such adjectives as "mild," "gentle," "pixie," and "zany." Having tried for four decades to make some social comment, it is something less than reassuring to discover that what a jittery America wants is the boppo laugh or nothing. In the section of this revue which deals with "The Pet Department," it has been assumed by practically everybody that this is sheer nonsense. What I had in mind, along with laughter, was a sharp comment on one of the worst faults of Americans of both sexes, a hasty and thoughtless lack of observation and perception, and I have tried to present this by showing, with the use of symbols, that we often cannot tell a bear from a St. Bernard, a seagull from a rabbit, or a live dog from a cast-iron lawn dog.

All through this road trip the item known as "The Owl in the Attic" has been put in and taken out and put back. I hope it will be in the play when it opens in New York, if only as a tribute to Robert Benchley, who must have been told by 10,000 people during his lifetime how to write and present comedy. He once wrote me, "I don't laugh out loud very much, any more than you do, but I did at your line, 'This is the only stuffed bird I ever saw with its eyes closed, but whoever had it stuffed probably wanted it stuffed that way.'" On stage, this does not get a belly laugh or wow; in fact, I have been told, thirty times, "It doesn't get a thing."

It got a thing for the late Robert Benchley, so, again, I hope it stays in the revue. It is, I suppose, possible, since anything in present-day America is possible, that theatre people and audiences knew more about comedy than Benchley, Perelman, De Vries, Sullivan, White and little old me, but I shall have to wait and find out. If they are right and we are wrong, I shall return to the dignity of the printed page, where it may be that I belong.

INDEX

Abington, Frances, 196n, 222 and n
Abraham, Biblical character, 146
Absurd, theater of, 293–94, 296, 298
Achilles, Homer character, 240
Acres, Bob, Sheridan character, 224n
Adams, Parson, Fielding character, 147n, 148, 159, 272 and n
Addison, Joseph, 87–88, 90–92, 94n, 111, 122, 178, 205; *Account of the Greatest English Poets*, 87; *Letter from Italy*, 87; *Campaign*, 87; *Cato*, 87, 126; *Drummer; or, The Haunted House*, 92; source of his quotation heading *Spectator* No. 249, 105n; correspondence, 106n; *Prologue* to Steele's *Tender Husband*, 110 and n; quarrel with Dennis, 126; *Whig-Examiner* No. 4, 151n (*See also Spectator; Tatler*)
Addleplot, Sir Simon, Wycherley character, 218 and n
Aegospotami, 267n
Aelianus, Claudius, 241n
Aeschylus, 3n, 4 and n, 6, 267n
Agathon, 6, 7
Agnès, Molière character, 58, 248
Aguecheek, Sir Andrew, Shakespeare character, 221n
Aimwell, Mr., Farquhar character, 241 and n
Aitken, G. A., 128n, 129n
Alarcón y Mendoya, Juan Ruiz de, *La Verdad Sospechosa*, 260n
Albee, Edward, 289
Alceste, Molière character, 57, 58, 244, 247, 248, 253–54, 254n, 255, 259, 272, 299
Alcibiades, 268n
Aldridge, A. O., 285n
Aleman, Mateo, *Guzman de Alfarache* (trans. as *The Rogue*), 53n
Alexandria, 11–12; affectations in language, 13; Library, 31n
Allen, Ralph, 165 and n
Allison, F. G., 10n
Allworthy, Squire, Fielding character, 165n
Alps, 122
Alsace, French-German area, 216n, 281 and n
Alsatia, district of London, 63n, 216 and n

Amanda, Cibber character, 109
Ameipsias, 268
Amsterdam, 102
Andrews, Joseph, Fielding character, 163n, 271n
Andronicus, Livius, 5
Angelica, Congreve character, 199 and n, 217 and n
Anta Theater, N. Y., 299
Anti-Jacobin, 268 and n
Apollodorus Carystius, 256 and n
Aquinas, Thomas, 213
Arabian Nights' Entertainments, 162 and n, 262
Arabs, 262
Arbuthnot, John, 150n
Arden of Feversham, 177n
Argan, Molière character, 58
Ariel, Shakespeare character, 237
Ariosto, Lodovico, 20, 21
Aristarchus of Samothrace, 31 and n
Aristodemus, 6
Aristophanes, 6, 10, 19, 21, 33 and n, 36, 147, 205, 233, 257 and n, 264, 265, 266, 267; eleven extant plays, 5; as character in *Symposium*, 7; *Aeolosicon*, 5n; *Archarnians*, 4n, 266n, 267n, 268 and n; *Babylonians*, 266n, 267n; *Clouds*, 36n, 257, 267n, 268 and n; *Cocalus*, 5n; *Ecclesiasuzae*, 5n, 267n; *Frogs*, 6, 240 and n, 266n, 268 and n, 278; *Knights*, 4 and n, 266n, 267n, 268 and n; *Lysistrata*, 267n; *Peace*, 267n, 268 and n; *Plutus*, 5, 267n; *Wasps*, 266n, 277 and n (*See also* E. Littré)
Aristotle, 10, 14, 22, 42, 91n, 125, 138, 147 and n, 148, 151, 156–57, 157n, 160, 163 and n, 183, 186, 194, 204, 213, 234, 235, 299; *Poetics*, 4 and n, 7, 8, 9, 11 and n, 12, 19, 33n, 35 and n, 132 and n, 137, 153 and n, 296; *Nicomachean Ethics*, 9, 234; *Rhetoric*, 10 and n, 11, 136; *Politics*, 11, 35 and n; [-ian] categories, 92; lost treatise on comedy, 168
Arnold, Matthew, 235 and n, 236 and n
Arnold, Samuel J., *Free and Easy*, 227 and n
Arnolphe, Molière character, 57, 58, 258
Arras, 16

304